A LEVEL
ECONOMICS

Ray Powell
Chief Examiner, A-level Economics

Letts
EDUCATIONAL

Every effort has been made to trace copyright holders and to obtain their permission for the use of copyright material. The author and publishers will gladly receive information enabling them to rectify any reference or credit in subsequent editions.

First published 1982
Reprinted 1985, 1986, 1987, 1993, 1994, 1995, 1997, 1998
Revised 1984, 1988, 1991, 1993, 1996

Letts Educational
Aldine House
Aldine Place
London W12 8AW
Tel: 0181 740 2266

Typeset by Jordan Publishing Design

Illustrations Barbara Linton, Tek-Art, Catherine Bourne, Nigel Jordan

Acknowledgements
I wish to express my special thanks to the staff at Letts Educational who helped me to prepare the latest edition of this book. In particular, I would like to thank my editor, Terri McCargar. I would also like to thank my wife Christine who provided valuable assistance in the preparation and proofreading of the manuscript. However, any shortcomings the book may possess are entirely my own responsibility.

Ray Powell

The author and publishers are grateful to the following examination boards for permission to reproduce questions:

Associated Examining Board, University of Cambridge Local Examinations Syndicate, University of London Examinations & Assessment Council, Northern Examinations and Assessment Board, Northern Ireland Council for the Curriculum, Examinations and Assessment, University of Oxford Delegacy of Local Examinations, Oxford and Cambridge Schools Examination Board, Scottish Examination Board, Welsh Joint Education Committee. The answers and guidance notes are the author's own and none of the examining boards can accept any responsibility for the accuracy or method of working recommended.

Figures 13.1 (p176), 13.2 (p177) and 13.4 (p186): © Crown copyright. Crown copyright is reproduced with the permission of the Controller of HMSO.

British Library Cataloguing in Publication Data
A CIP record for this book is available from the British Library

ISBN 1 85758 395 7

Note for readers: Some of the information in this book is liable to change, particularly that which is directly influenced by Government policy. Such information is correct at the time of going to press but the reader should keep in touch with current affairs to ensure an up-to-date knowledge of the subject.

Printed and bound in Great Britain by Ashford Colour Press, Gosport, Hants

Letts Educational is the trading name of BPP (Letts Educational) Ltd

CONTENTS

SECTION 1: STARTING POINTS

SECTION 2: ECONOMICS TOPICS

SECTION 3: TEST RUN

STARTING POINTS

HOW TO USE THIS BOOK

This book has been written specifically to prepare candidates for the Advanced and Advanced Supplementary Level examinations in economics set by the various GCE examining boards. It should also prove useful as a preparation for the many business studies and professional examinations in economics of a comparable standard to A-level. The book is organised in a series of chapters chosen both to represent the subject areas with which examination questions deal, and also to prepare candidates for answering questions on new subject areas as yet not well covered in existing textbooks. Thus, while the chapters are conventionally ordered, proceeding from **micro-** to **macroeconomics**, units are included on such topics as the determination of agricultural prices, market failures, privatisation and related policies, the PSBR, supply-side economics, and areas of controversy between Keynesian and monetarist economists.

Since the book does not attempt to cover every aspect of the Advanced Level syllabuses of the various examining boards, it should not be regarded as a substitute for the many excellent and detailed textbooks that are available, or for sources of up-to-date information such as the *British Economy Survey*, *The Economic Review* and *Economics Today*. It is designed for use throughout a taught economics course, and it should prove especially useful in preparing examination technique in the period immediately before an examination. Make sure that you obtain a copy of your examination syllabus. Each chapter contains two distinct but complementary parts. The first section contains two or more units, each devoted to an important syllabus topic. The last part contains a selection of representative questions chosen largely from the examination papers set in recent years by the principal examining boards.

The book's aim is to help examination candidates gain the knowledge, techniques and skills, not only to be sure of passing at A-level, but also to realise what is required to achieve the highest possible grades. At all times the book tries to explain in a clear but precise way the new developments taking place in the subject, and to show how these are reflected in recent examination questions and in the answers expected by the examiners.

THE STRUCTURE OF THIS BOOK

The key aim of this book is to guide you in the way you tackle A-level Economics. It should serve as a study guide, work book and revision aid throughout any A-level/AS-level Economics course, no matter what syllabus you are following. It is not intended to be a complete guide to the subject and should be used as a companion to your textbooks, which it is designed to complement rather than duplicate.

The book is divided into three sections. Section One, Starting Points, contains study tips and syllabus information – all the material you need to get you started on your A-level study, together with advice on planning your revision and tips on how to tackle the exam itself. Use the Syllabus Checklist to find out exactly where you can find the study units which are relevant to your particular syllabus.

Section Two, the main body of the text, contains the core of A-level Economics. It has been devised to make study as easy and enjoyable as possible, and has been divided into chapters which cover the themes you will encounter on your syllabus. The chapters are split into units, each covering a topic of study.

A list of objectives at the beginning of each chapter directs you towards the key points of the chapter you are about to read. The Chapter Roundup at the end brings the topics of the chapter into focus and links them to other themes of study. To reinforce what you have just read and learned, there are worked questions and answers at the end of each chapter. Recent examinations from all the examination boards (including Scottish Higher) provide the question practice. The tutorial notes and suggested answers to the essay question and the data response question give you practical guidance on how to answer A-level questions, and provide additional information relevant to that particular topic of study. These are followed by a Question Bank chosen as representative of the essay questions set by all the examining boards. Brief guidance notes, indicating possible pitfalls and key points accompany the question practice.

In Section Three, Test Run, we turn our attention to the examination you will face at the end of your course. First, you can assess your progress using the Test Your Knowledge Quiz and analysis chart. Then, as a final test, you should attempt the mock exam, under timed conditions. This will give you invaluable examination practice and, together with the specimen answers, will help you to judge how close you are to achieving your A-level pass.

USING YOUR SYLLABUS CHECKLIST

Whether you are using this book to work step-by-step through the syllabus or to structure your revision schedule, you will find it useful to keep a checklist of what you have covered. Keep the checklist at hand when you are doing your revision; it will remind you of the chapters you have revised, and those still to be done.

The checklist for each examination – A, AS or Higher Grade – is in two parts. First there is a list of syllabus topics covered by this book. Although some of the checklists are quite detailed, it is not possible to print entire syllabuses. You are therefore strongly recommended to obtain an official copy of the syllabus for your examination and consult it when the need arises. The examination board addresses are given after the syllabus checklists.

When you have revised a topic make a tick in the column provided and, if there are questions elsewhere in the book, try to answer them.

The second part of the checklist gives you information about the examination, providing details about the time allocated to each written paper and the weighting of the questions of each paper. The different types of questions which may be set are explained in detail later in this section under the heading The Examination.

SYLLABUS CHECKLISTS AND PAPER ANALYSIS

ASSOCIATED EXAMINING BOARD
A-level 0618

Syllabus topic	Covered in Unit No	✔
THE ECONOMIC PROBLEM	1.1, 1.2	
DEMAND, SUPPLY AND THE MARKET MECHANISM (The derivation of supply curves, but *not* demand curves is in the syllabus)	2.1, 2.2, 3.1, 3.2, 4.1, 4.2, 5.1, 5.2, 6.1, 6.2, 7.1, 7.2, 11.1, 11.2	
MARKET FAILURE AND GOVERNMENT INTERVENTION IN INDIVIDUAL MARKETS (Oligopoly but *not* monopolistic competition is in the syllabus)	7.3, 8.2, 9.1, 9.2, 9.3, 10.1, 10.2	
THE NATIONAL ECONOMY AND THE ACTIVITIES OF GOVERNMENT	12.1–20.3	

Paper analysis

For UK students, two assessment patterns are available, 0618F and 0618C. Papers 1 and 2 are common to both patterns. The final paper for 0618F is a case study. Candidates preparing for 0618C submit coursework. Overseas candidates must take Paper 3, the case study.

Paper 1   *1 hour*   40 multiple choice questions
25% of total mark

Paper 2   *3 hours*   Data response and essays
55% of total mark

Section A: Data response
2 questions set
1 to be answered
15% of total mark

Section B: Essays
8 questions set
3 to be answered
40% of total mark

Syllabus 0618F

Paper 3   *1 hour 15 minutes*   Case study on a topic announced in advance
20% of total mark

Syllabus 0618C

Coursework   Investigative study, 2500–3500 words
20% of total mark

UNIVERSITY OF CAMBRIDGE LOCAL EXAMINATIONS SYNDICATE
A-level 9070

Syllabus topic	Covered in Unit No	✓
THE CENTRAL PROBLEM OF ECONOMICS	1.1	
THEORY OF DEMAND	3.1, 3.2	
THEORY OF SUPPLY	4.1, 4.2	
PRICE AND OUTPUT DETERMINATION	2.1, 2.2, 5.1, 5.2, 6.1, 6.2, 7.1, 7.2, 7.3, 8.1, 8.2	
THEORY OF DISTRIBUTION	11.1, 11.2	
NATIONAL INCOME ACCOUNTING	14.1	
THEORY OF INCOME DETERMINATION	14.2, 14.3, 14.4	
MONEY AND THE PRICE LEVEL	12.1, 12.2	
INTERNATIONAL TRADE	18.1–20.3	
THE ECONOMIC ROLE OF GOVERNMENT	9.1, 9.2, 9.3, 10.1, 10.2 13.1, 13.2, 13.3, 15.1–17.3	
ECONOMIC DEVELOPMENT	1.2	

Paper analysis

Paper 1   *1 hour 30 minutes*   40 multiple choice questions
          30% of total mark

Paper 2   *1 hour 15 minutes*   2 data response questions
          20% of total mark

Paper 3   *3 hours*   4 essay questions to be answered from a choice of about 12
          50% of total mark

UNIVERSITY OF CAMBRIDGE LOCAL EXAMINATIONS SYNDICATE
A-level 9507 (modular),
AS-level 8556 (modular) and 8431

Syllabus topic	Covered in Unit No	✓
CORE DOUBLE MODULE 4381: MARKET SYSTEM AND MARKET FAILURE		
The economic problem	1.1	
The market system	1.2, 2.1, 2.2, 3.1, 3.2, 5.1, 5.2, 4.2, 6.1, 6.2	
Theory of the firm (Oligopoly is *not* required)	4.1, 7.1, 7.2, 7.3, 8.1	
Monopoly as a market failure	7.3	
Other market imperfections	9.1, 9.2, 9.3	
Externalities	9.2	
Government intervention in markets	9.3, 10.1, 10.2	
CORE MODULE 4382: THE NATIONAL ECONOMY		
Measurement of national income and economic performance	14.1	
The determination of output, employment and prices	14.1, 14.2, 14.3, 14.4	
Government objectives for the national economy	15.1–17.3	
Structure and essential elements of international trade	18.1–20.3	
OPTIONAL MODULES*		
4384: Economics of development	1.2	
4385: Economics of Europe	6.2	
4387: Economics of the labour market	11.1, 11.2	

*3 optional modules are studies at A-level, from a choice of 6. Modules 4383 (Industrialisation and Deindustrialisation of Britain), 4386 (Financial Economics) and 4388 (Transport Economics) are also available.

Paper analysis

Note: The Cambridge Modular Business Studies and Economics Syllabus (Syllabus 9516) is also available at A-level. This combines the core modules of the Economics syllabus with the core modules of the Business Studies syllabus.

Core Modules

4381   *3 hours*   1 compulsory case study
Plus 2 structured essays from a choice of 4
33⅓ % of total mark (66⅔% at AS-level)

4382   *1 hour 30 minutes*   Compulsory data response question
Plus 1 structured essay from choice of 2
16⅔% of total mark (33⅔% at AS-level)

Optional Modules

4383–4388   *1 hour 30 minutes (each)*   1 compulsory data response question
Plus 1 structured essay from a choice of 2
16⅔% of total mark each

UNIVERSITY OF LONDON EXAMINATIONS & ASSESSMENT COUNCIL
A-level 9120

Syllabus topic	Covered in Unit No	✓
CORE		
PART A: MICROECONOMICS I		
The economic problem and economic systems	1.1, 1.2	
Resource allocation	1.1, 2.1–5.2, 9.1–9.3	
Application of demand and supply analysis	6.1, 6.2	
PART B: MICROECONOMICS II		
Market structures	7.1–8.2	
PART C: INTERNATIONAL ECONOMICS		
International trade and exchange	18.1, 18.2	
Exchange rates	20.1–20.3	
The balance of payments	19.1, 19.2	
PART D: MACROECONOMICS		
Objectives of macroeconomic policy	17.1	
The determination of aggregate demand	14.2, 14.3, 16.2	
Aggregate supply and the natural level of output	15.1, 15.2, 16.2	
Macroeconomic policy instruments	16.1, 17.1, 17.2	
Macroeconomic policy issues	16.1, 17.3	
OPTIONS		
PART E OPTION 1: PRODUCT AND LABOUR MARKETS		
Size and growth of firms	4.1	
Analysis of price and output decisions	7.1–8.2	
Policy issues	9.1–10.2	
Demand and supply in the labour market	11.1	
The labour market in action	11.2	
Policy issues	11.2	

Note: Part F Option 2: Economic development is also available as an option.

Paper Analysis

Paper 1   *1 hour*   35 multiple choice questions on core topics
    20% of total mark

Paper 2   *3 hours*   Essay and data questions on core topics
Section A: 2 structured essay questions from a choice of 8
Section B: 1 numerically-based data response question from a choice of 2
Section C: 1 prose-based data response question from a choice of 2
    50% of total mark

Paper 3   *2 hours 15 minutes*   Option paper
Two questions from *either* option to be answered.
Section A: a compulsory stimulus question sub-divided into 2 or 3 parts
Section B: 1 from a choice of 2 data response questions (one numerical and the other prose) to be answered
    30% of total mark

UNIVERSITY OF LONDON EXAMINATIONS & ASSESSMENT COUNCIL (NUFFIELD)
A-level 9125

Syllabus topic	Covered in Unit No	✓
THE FOUR STAGES (COMPULSORY)		
1 Objectives	3.1, 7.1	
2 Efficiency	7.3	
3 Expansion	4.1, 17.1	
4 Uncertainty	8.2, 9.1	
THE OPTIONS		
1 Is inequality inevitable?		
2 Can we control the economy?	15.1, 15.2, 17.1	
3 Is there a limit to growth?	17.1	
4 Who has power in the market?	7.3–8.2	
5 How are decisions made?	3.1, 7.1, 9.3	
6 Is business accountable?		

Note: To achieve an A-level in Economics, candidates must take Options 1 and 2. Options 5 and 6 qualify for an A-level in Business Studies (9126). Any other combination of Options qualifies for an A-level in Economics and Business (9127).

An AS-level in Economics and Business Studies is also available, based on the four compulsory stages and the portfolio.

Paper Analysis

Paper 1	*2 hours 45 minutes*	Stage assessment paper 1 compulsory strategy question and 2 stimulus questions from a choice of 3 　40% of total mark
Paper 2	*3 hours*	Option assessment paper 1½ hours per selected option Section A: 1 compulsory question for each option Section B: 1 question from a choice of 2 for each option Both sections are based on stimulus material 　40% of total mark
The portfolio		6 pieces of work of an investigative and problem-solving nature to be selected from a portfolio compiled throughout the course 　20% of total mark

NORTHERN EXAMINATIONS AND ASSESSMENT BOARD
A-level

Syllabus topic	Covered in Unit No	✓
ECONOMIES AND THEIR PROBLEMS	1.1, 1.2	
THE TOOLS OF ECONOMIC ANALYSIS	2.1, 2.2	
MICROECONOMICS: THEORIES OF VALUE, MARKETS AND CHOICE	2.1–11.2	
MACROECONOMICS: THE GENERATION OF REAL INCOME AND PRODUCTION	14.1–14.4, 18.1–20.3	
MONEY AND THE PRICE LEVEL	12.1, 12.2, 15.2	
ECONOMIC POLICY AND THE ROLE OF GOVERNMENT	9.3, 10.1, 10.2, 13.1–13.3, 15.1–17.3	

Paper Analysis

Paper 1	*1 hour 30 minutes*	Part A: 50 compulsory objective test questions 30% of total mark
	1 hour	Part B: 1 question, which may include numerical and text data, designed to test comprehension 20% of total mark
Paper 2	*3 hours*	4 essay questions from a choice of 12 50% of total mark

NORTHERN EXAMINATIONS AND ASSESSMENT BOARD
AS-level

Syllabus topic	Covered in Unit No	✓
THE NATURE OF ECONOMICS AND ECONOMIC SYSTEMS		
Economies and their problems	1.1, 1.2	
The role of the government in a mixed economy	1.2	
The methods and techniques of economic analysis	2.1, 2.2	
MACROECONOMIC PROBLEMS AND POLICIES		
Unemployment	15.1	
Inflation	15.2	
Economic growth	14.1, 17.1	
International economic relations	18.1–20.3	
MICROECONOMIC PROBLEMS AND POLICIES		
Industrial issues	10.1, 10.2	
Urban and regional issues	10.2	
Social issues	13.1, 13.2	
Distribution issues	11.1, 11.2	

Paper analysis

The questions in Paper 1 will be the same as those used to test the subject core in the A-level examination, but fewer questions will be set.

Paper 1	*30 minutes*	Part A: 20 compulsory objective test questions 20% of total mark
	45 minutes	Part B: 1 question, which may include numerical and text data, designed to test comprehension 30% of total mark
Paper 2	*2 hours*	Essay paper Part A: 1 question from a choice of 4 on macroeconomic problems and policies Part B: 2 questions from a choice of 12 on microeconomic problems and policies 50% of total mark

NORTHERN IRELAND COUNCIL FOR THE CURRICULUM EXAMINATIONS AND ASSESSMENT
A-level (1997 examination)

Syllabus topic	Covered in Unit No	✔
SECTION A		
The methodology of economics	2.1, 2.2	
Basic economic problems	1.1, 1.2	
The theory of consumer behaviour	3.1, 3.2	
The theory of production	4.1, 4.2	
The operation of competitive markets	2.1, 2.2, 5.1–6.2, 7.1, 7.2	
The theory of distribution	11.1, 11.2	
The role of government in allocation and distribution	9.1–10.2	
SECTION B		
National income accounting	14.1	
The theory of income determination	14.1–14.4	
Money and banking	12.1, 12.2	
International trade	18.1–20.3	
The role of government in the management of the economy	15.1–17.3	

Paper Analysis

Paper 1   *1 hour 30 minutes*   40 multiple choice questions
30% of total mark

Paper 2   *3 hours*   4 essay questions from a choice of 10: 2 from each section
40% of total mark

Paper 3   *2 hours*   3 compulsory data response questions each using different types of real-world data
30% of total mark

1998 and after examination

Syllabus topic	Covered in Unit No	✔
SECTION A		
The market mechanism	1.2, 2.1–3.2, 5.1–6.2, 11.1, 11.2	
Production and competition	4.1, 4.2, 7.1–8.2	
Market failure and Government response	9.1–10.2, 16.1	
SECTION B		
The macroeconomic system	14.1–14.4, 16.2	
The international economy	18.1–20.3	
Macroeconomic problems and policy	12.1–13.3, 15.1, 15.2, 17.1–17.3	

Paper Analysis

Paper 1   *1 hour 30 minutes*   40 multiple choice questions
20% of total mark

Paper 2   *3 hours*   4 essay questions from a choice of 10: 2 from each section
45% of total mark

Paper 3   *2 hours 30 minutes*   3 compulsory data response questions each using different types of real-world data
35% of total mark

UNIVERSITY OF OXFORD DELEGACY OF LOCAL EXAMINATIONS
A-level 9940 and AS-level 8840 (modular or end-of-course examination)

Syllabus topic	Covered in Unit No	✓
SECTION A: FOUNDATION ECONOMICS		
Circular flow	14.1	
Demand	3.1, 3.2	
Supply	4.1, 4.2	
Price and output determination	2.1, 2.2	
Factor markets	11.1, 11.2	
Central problem of economic societies	1.1, 1.2	
Circular flow in a macroeconomic context	14.1	
Aggregate expenditure and demand	14.2–14.3, 16.2	
Aggregate supply	16.2	
Aggregate supply and demand	16.2	
International economics	18.1–20.3	
Role of government	9.3, 17.1–17.3	
SECTION B: FIRMS AND MARKETS		
Firms	7.1	
Costs and revenues	4.1, 7.2, 7.3	
Markets	1.2, 2.1, 6.1, 6.2	
Government and firms	9.3, 10.1, 10.2	
SECTION C: INDIVIDUALS AND MARKETS		
Economics of the consumer	3.1, 3.2	
Labour markets	11.1, 11.2	
Incomes and government	13.1, 13.2	
Government, individuals and markets	9.3	
SECTION D: MACROECONOMIC POLICY*		
Aggregate product markets	14.1–14.3	
Monetary and fiscal environment	12.1–13.3	
Unemployment and inflation	15.1, 15.2	
SECTION E: INTERNATIONAL ASPECTS*		
International trade	18.1–18.3	
Exchange rates and the balance of payments	19.1–20.3	
International institutions and relationships	20.3	
SECTION F: ECONOMIC POLICY* *Note*: this section partly repeats material covered in previous sections and is designed to assess understanding of the interconnections of the different syllabus elements.		
Microeconomic policy	9.3, 10.1, 10.2	
Macroeconomic policy	12.1–13.2, 16.1–17.3	

* denotes modules studied at A-level only

Paper Analysis

A-level

Module 1   *1 hour*   Foundation Economics
(compulsory)   Part A: 3 short answer questions chosen from 5
                                      Part B: 1 two-part question chosen from 3 questions
                                      15% of total mark

Module 2	*1 hour 30 minutes*	Economics of markets Part A: 1 structured question chosen from 3 Part B: 1 essay question chosen from 3 15% of total mark
Module 3	*1 hour 30 minutes*	Aggregate economics Part A: 1 structured question chosen from 3 Part B: 1 essay question chosen from 3 15% of total mark

Either

Module 4	*1 hour 15 minutes* (plus 10 minutes reading time)	Special Study A series of compulsory questions based on material issued in November before the June exam **and** some additional material. One general policy area will be named each year. 15% of total mark

or

Module 5		Individual Assignment of 2500–3000 words, externally assessed, to be based on 1 of 3 general policy areas named each year. 15% of total mark
Module 6	*45 minutes* (plus 10 minutes reading time)	Economic policy 1 data question from a choice of 2 structured data questions, each combining numbers and text. 15% of total mark
Module 7	*1 hour 20 minutes*	Objective test 40 compulsory multiple choice questions 25% of total mark

AS-level

Module 1	*1 hour*	as for A-level 30% of total mark
Module 2	*1 hour*	Objective test 30 compulsory multiple choice questions on syllabus sections A–C 30% of total mark
Module 3	*1 hour 30 minutes* (plus 10 minutes reading time)	Data/essay paper Part A: 1 data question based on numbers and text Part B: 1 essay question from a choice of 3 40% of total mark

OXFORD AND CAMBRIDGE SCHOOLS EXAMINATION BOARD
A-level 9633 and AS-level 8393

(An A-level course in Economics and Political Studies is also available.)

Syllabus topic	Covered in Unit No	✓
PAPER 1 ECONOMIC PRINCIPLES AND APPLICATIONS		
The central economic problem and resource allocation	1.1, 1.2	
The operation of the market mechanism	2.1–6.2	
The theory of the firm (formal study of oligopoly is not required)	7.1–8.1	
Market failure and government response	9.1–9.3	
International trade	18.1–20.3	
The determination of aggregate output, employment and prices	14.1–14.4, 16.2	
PAPER 2 MACROECONOMIC COMMENTARIES AND NUMERACY		
Government macroeconomic objectives	17.1	
Cyclical indicators	13.2	
Underlying principles behind the use of fiscal policy	13.2	
Underlying principles behind the use of monetary policy	12.2	
Exchange rate policy	20.1–20.3	
The effectiveness of government macroeconomic policy	17.1–17.3	
PAPER 3 ASPECTS OF ECONOMIC THEORY		
The law of variable proportions	4.1	
Imperfect competition	8.1, 8.2	
Liquidity preference theory	12.1	
Definition and measurement of income, expenditure and output	14.1	
Equilibrium level of income using Keynesian 'cross' diagram	14.1	
Inflationary and deflationary gaps	15.2	
Nature and functions of money and credit	12.1	
Demand for, and supply of, money	12.1	
Functions of the Bank of England and commercial banks	12.2	
Operation of monetary policy	12.2	

Paper Analysis

Papers 1, 2 and 3, which cover the core, are compulsory at A-level. Candidates must also take either Paper 4 or Paper 5. Papers 1 and 2 may be taken at the end of the first year of study, with the remaining two papers being taken at the end of two years; alternatively all four papers may be taken at the end of a two-year course.

At AS-level, candidates take Paper 1 and Paper 2.

Core papers

Paper 1	*2 hours 15 minutes*	3 essay questions from a choice of 10 30% of total mark (60% at AS-level)
Paper 2	*1 hour 30 minutes*	2 data response questions chosen from 4 1 question must be from each section: Section A: 2 prose-based questions Section B: 2 numerical or graph-based questions 20% of total mark (40% at AS-level)
Paper 3	*1 hour 30 minutes*	40 multiple choice questions on the topics of Paper 1, plus other aspects of Economic theory 20% of total mark

Options

Either

Paper 4   *2 hours 15 minutes*   Special Subject Paper

3 essay questions to be answered

There will be 1 question on each of 12 special subjects, for example, privatisation, welfare policy, and industry and trade unions. Consult your sullabus for a full list of these 12 subjects.

    30% of total mark

or

Paper 5   *2 hours 15 minutes*   The growth of the British economy either from 1760 to 1914 or from 1850 to the present day.

3 questions to be answered, with at least 1 chosen from each section.

Section A: 10 essay questions

Section B: 3 questions on set documents and statistical analysis

    30% of total mark

SCOTTISH EXAMINATION BOARD
Higher Grade

Syllabus topic	Covered in Unit No	✓
SCARCITY AND CHOICE	1.1, 1.2	
PRODUCTION	4.1	
CONSUMER BEHAVIOUR	3.1, 3.2, 5.2, 14.2	
SUPPLY	4.2, 5.2	
MARKETS	2.1, 2.2, 6.1, 6.2, 11.1, 11.2	
NATIONAL INCOME	14.1	
MONEY	12.1, 12.2	
MACROECONOMIC ISSUES	14.1–14.4, 15.1, 15.2	
INTERNATIONAL TRADE AND PAYMENTS	18.1–19.2	
GOVERNMENT OBJECTIVES AND POLICIES	9.3, 10.1, 10.2, 12.1–13.3, 16.1–17.3	
COMPARATIVE ECONOMIC SYSTEMS	1.2	
EXTERNAL ECONOMIC RELATIONS OF THE UNITED KINGDOM	18.3, 19.1–20.3	

Paper Analysis

Paper 1 *1 hour* 25 multiple choice questions
25% of total mark

Paper 2 *1 hour 45 minutes* 2 data response or interpretation questions, based on prose and data
30% of total mark

Paper 3 *2 hours* 3 essay questions from a choice of 9
45% of total mark

WELSH JOINT EDUCATION COMMITTEE
A-level

Syllabus topic	Covered in Unit No	✓
THE BROAD ECONOMIC FRAMEWORK	1.1, 1.2	
MARKET SUPPLY AND DEMAND	2.1, 2.2	
ELASTICITY OF DEMAND AND SUPPLY	5.1, 5.2	
AGGREGATE SUPPLY AND DEMAND	14.1–14.4, 16.2	
MARKET STRUCTURES	7.1–8.2, 11.1, 11.2	
MARKET FAILURE AND IMPERFECTIONS	9.1–9.3	
GOVERNMENT OBJECTIVES AND POLICIES	12.1–13.3, 16.1, 17.1–17.3, 19.2, 20.1–20.3	
THE MEASUREMENT AND EVALUATION OF ECONOMIC PERFORMANCE	14.1, 17.1	

Paper Analysis

Paper 1   *3 hours*   4 essay questions from choice of 9 with a mix of structured and open-ended questions
    50% of total mark

Paper 2   *2 hours*   2 data response questions from a choice of 3, containing a variety of data sources
    30% of total mark

Paper 3   *1 hour 15 minutes*   30 multiple choice questions
    20% of total mark

EXAMINATION BOARD ADDRESSES

AEB	Associated Examining Board Stag Hill House, Guildford, Surrey GU2 5XJ Tel: 01483 506506
Cambridge	University of Cambridge Local Examinations Syndicate Syndicate Buildings, 1 Hills Road, Cambridge CB1 2EU Tel: 01223 553311
ULEAC (including Nuffield)	University of London Examinations and Assessment Council Stewart House, 32 Russell Square, London WC1B 5DN Tel: 0171 331 4000
NEAB	Northern Examinations and Assessment Board 12 Harter Street, Manchester M1 6HL Tel: 0161 953 1180
NICCEA	Northern Ireland Council for the Curriculum Examinations and Assessment Beechill House, 42 Beechill Road, Belfast BT8 4RS Tel: 01232 704666
Oxford	University of Oxford Delegacy of Local Examinations Ewert House, Ewert Place, Summertown, Oxford OX2 7BZ Tel: 01865 54291

Oxford and Cambridge	Oxford and Cambridge Schools Examination Board
	(a) Purbeck House, Purbeck Road, Cambridge CB2 2PU
	    Tel: 01223 411211
	(b) Elsfield Way, Oxford OX2 8EP
	    Tel: 01865 54421

SEB	Scottish Examination Board Ironmills Road, Dalkeith, Midlothian EH22 1LE Tel: 0131 663 6601
WJEC	Welsh Joint Education Committee 245 Western Avenue, Cardiff CF5 2YX Tel: 01222 265000

STUDYING AND REVISING ECONOMICS

THE DIFFERENCE BETWEEN GCSE AND A/AS LEVEL

The majority of students who start an A-level course in economics are completely new to the subject; only a minority have studied GCSE economics. For this reason, no mention is made in the individual topic units of the difference between what is required at GCSE and A-level. There is in fact little difference in the range of subjects included in the straight economics syllabuses at GCSE and A-level, though the A-level syllabus tends to be rather wider. However, some examination boards offer combined subject syllabuses at Advanced level, such as Economics and Political Studies or Economics and Public Affairs.

The principal differences between GCSE and A-level economics lies not in the syllabus content but in the order of the skills that the examinations try to test. The GCSE examination is largely concerned with testing the lower order skills of **factual recall** and **description** together with the **understanding** and **application** of simple ideas. In contrast, at Advanced level much more emphasis is placed on the higher order skills involved in **theoretical analysis** and evaluation. Although the practice of each examining board is slightly different, students should derive useful guidance from the introductions to the syllabuses of the NEAB and the Associated Examining Board; two boards that publish in detail the aims and objectives of their economic syllabuses. By the end of the AEB course, candidates are expected to have developed:

❶ a critical understanding of the workings of a market economy and how it affects individuals and institutions operating within such a system;

❷ the ability to appraise the role of government in a market economy;

❸ an understanding of economic concepts, principles and theories in the context of current economic issues and problems;

❹ the ability to make rational and consistent judgements in matters where economic influences are at work;

❺ the skills of literacy, numeracy, data handling and the ability to communicate logically and effectively in an economic context.

Amongst other aims, the NEAB syllabus encourages the development in the candidate of:

❶ a facility for self-expression, not only in writing but also in using such additional aids as statistics and diagrams where appropriate;

❷ the habit of using works of reference as sources of data specific to economics;

❸ the habit of reading critically to gain information about the changing economy in which we live;

❹ an appreciation of the method of study used by the economist and of the most effective ways in which economic data may be analysed, correlated, discussed and presented;

❺ the ability to communicate clearly and concisely the results of investigations.

MODULAR COURSES

Some of the examining boards now offer modular courses as a flexible scheme which allows a variety of different routes to be followed in order to achieve an AS or A-level. The syllabus is divided into small units (modules), each of which is examined by an end-of-module test. These tests may be taken at appropriate times throughout the course or, if preferred, at the end of the course. The advantages of taking the tests throughout the course are that there is regular feedback on how well you are doing and there is the possibility of retaking modules in order to improve your grade. The results of modular tests may be 'banked', and then 'cashed in' at an appropriate time to obtain an AS or A-level. Some modules – including those covering the core which all economics syllabuses must cover – are compulsory. Other modules may be optional, though your teacher rather than yourself will probably choose which of the optional modules you should study.

Modular A-levels can have disadvantages however. No concession is given to the fact that you may be taking a test aged 16 and having only studied economics for a few weeks. You are likely to be less mature and less widely read than you will be at the end of a two year course. Nevertheless, a growing number of economics teachers believe that, on balance, the advantages of modular courses exceed the disadvantages. Students often work harder, and the wording of the examination questions can be more accessible and less cryptic than is often the case with the more traditional, non-modular examinations.

STUDY STRATEGIES AND TECHNIQUES

At least 80% of your time as a student will be spent on private study so it is very important for you to acquire those skills which enable you to study effectively. Many hours can be wasted reading books from which you learn very little, or drawing elaborate charts and diagrams which are soon forgotten.

Study will involve you in collecting information, analysing it, clarifying your thinking, assimilating knowledge and expressing yourself clearly. No one is born with these skills, nor are they obtained accidentally: they must be acquired by conscious effort and practice. Here are some suggestions which will help you to develop these skills and make the most of your study time.

Establish targets

Research has shown that a learning period of about 45 minutes produces the best relationship between understanding and remembering. Set yourself study tasks which can be achieved in this period of time and then take a break for 15 minutes or longer before attempting another period of work. Plan reasonable targets which you can achieve in each study session, e.g. to read twenty pages and make notes.

Focus on essentials

There are large numbers of books and articles which deal with topics in the A or AS-level syllabuses. Some of this material is inappropriate or duplicates what is written better elsewhere. Try to focus on sections of books, avoid extraneous material and select what you read intelligently.

Select key words and phrases

When you read a section of a book, select words or phrases which will help you to remember what the section is about. These words can be written down for reference and used as personal notes.

Note taking

Far too many students write notes as they write essays, in linear sequences. About 90% of what is written is wasted material and will never be remembered. It is the key words, concepts and phrases which need to be remembered and with practice you can abandon linear notes and learn more effectively by recording only the key words. This skill takes some time to acquire and can best be learned in stages by first writing down long phrases but not sentences and then, after a time, reducing your notes to just the key words and phrases. This form of note taking is suitable for notes made while reading or during a lecture. Remember to record the author and title. Sometimes the page number is also useful for future reference. A fluorescent highlighting pen is useful for identifying key words and phrases. These are not, of course, to be used on text books or journals but on notes you have made or been given.

REVISION TECHNIQUES

You can reduce the need for luck by preparing a revision programme. Plan a thorough programme and begin it several weeks before the examination, time-tabling periods of each day when you know you can work for up to two or three hours completely free of distraction. It is a good idea, however, to allow yourself a brief relaxation period every forty-five minutes or so to facilitate the absorption of the knowledge, ideas, and concepts intensively revised in the previous period. Although you must cover the whole syllabus, concentrate on key concepts and on essential economic theory rather than on detailed historical and descriptive fact.

There are various methods of revising, and not all may suit every candidate. Generally it is not a good idea to read through sheaves of notes or chapters from a textbook, and certainly it is not good practice to rote-learn pages of notes. Nevertheless, you must learn key definitions, though it is even more important to learn how and when to use them. Remember that, as a properly prepared candidate, you will only be able to use a small fraction of your total economic knowledge in a single essay or data response paper. Provided that you have revised in a reasonably structured way in the weeks before the examination, it is certainly not a good idea to work late into the night on the day preceding the examination. Answering an examination paper is a tiring task, especially if you are to display the type of skill the paper is testing; you need to arrive in the examination room as refreshed as possible and capable of thinking clearly not just for a few minutes, but for up to three hours.

If you decide to arrange your revision programme around the use of this book, we suggest that you select one or at most two topic areas for coverage at each revision session. Quickly read the relevant chapter, making a mental note of key definitions or concepts. Then try to write your own answer plans to one or both of the illustrative questions at the end of the chapter. Check your completed answer plan against the one included in the book and read through the notes on understanding the question. Go back over the chapter to make sure you understand the most important definitions and concepts, which you should now write out in a revision list. Several hours later or on the next day, write in your own words the meaning of the concepts and key definitions. Check what you have written against the explanations given in the chapter. Repeat this exercise frequently throughout your revision period until you feel confident that you thoroughly understand all the concepts and definitions. You might also attempt on later dates to write answer plans to the questions in the Question Bank.

COURSEWORK

Currently, the AEB and ULEAC (Nuffield) offer a coursework option as part of their A-level economics syllabus. (None of the boards include coursework at AS-level). You should consult your Syllabus Checklist in this book, and a copy of the board's own syllabus, for more information on coursework.

THE EXAMINATION

EXAMINATION TECHNIQUES AND QUESTION STYLES

Before reading on, check your syllabus to confirm the question styles you will meet. All AS and A-level examinations in economics include essay and data response questions. This also applies for the Scottish Higher Grade examination. However, there are variations from board to board which you are advised to check, particularly concerning the type of data response material the board includes in its examination.

Essay questions

All the boards now place strong emphasis on applied questions (questions related to current economic problems and government policy). Most boards allow a candidate the choice of selecting questions (usually four) from any part of the essay paper (or essay section of the paper). Because of the differences in both the structure of the essay paper and the house style of the questions set by each board, it is vital for a candidate to study the precise regulations of the examination for which he or she is sitting, and also to analyse a selection of recent papers or specimen papers set by the board.

Each year your teacher should get an Examiner's Report which discusses the insight into the Chief Examiner's approach and demands. Increasingly, via the publications of the Economics and Business Education Association and schools conferences, the chief examiners are becoming better known and more accessible. If the chief examiner gives a lecture in your area, go and listen! If your teacher does not know who the Chief Examiner is, get him or her to find out and study any textbook he may have written recently.

Essay technique

It is vital to arrange your time so as to answer all four questions, since all carry equal marks and no allowance is made for answering too few. Spend at least a couple of minutes at the beginning of the examination in carefully reading the paper. Carefully select four and read each through again; subconsciously you will be thinking about the other questions while working on your first answer! Choose the easiest question to answer first, but remember again to divide your time equally. When a question contains more than one section it is important to divide your time between each part, in accordance with the mark allocation indicated. NEAB essay questions are unstructured, in the sense that the mark breakdown between parts of the question is not indicated. You should assume that each part carries roughly equal marks.

If you find that you have allocated your time badly, you must take action to remedy the situation. It may be a good idea to answer one or both of the last two questions with an elongated, though carefully written, essay plan. In general, marks are awarded for relevant points made. In a properly developed essay you should have time to elaborate appropriately the points you make, but even so it is easy to spend too much time on a single argument – a variation of the law of diminishing returns applies to economics essays written under examination conditions! The marking scheme may allocate two, three, or four marks for a particularly relevant argument, and a brief mention of the argument can earn you at least half and possibly all the allocated marks if it is properly related to the question. Examiners *always* prefer short, well-structured and concise answers to long, rambling and repetitive essays.

Your essay must always be addressed to the set question. You will earn no marks at all for writing a model answer to a question not on the examination paper! It is good practice to use the first paragraph both to define precisely the terms mentioned in the question and also to state any assumptions you are making in interpreting the meaning of the question. If you think the question is open to more than one interpretation, then tell the examiner and explain why you are favouring a particular interpretation.

While diagrams, and particularly graphs are often appropriate, they should complement rather than simply repeat the information you are providing in written form. If you cannot correctly remember a particular graph or diagram, then leave it out – a wrongly drawn graph is worse than none at all. Draw your graphs large rather than small, and pay careful attention to how you label the axes and all curves.

Every essay question includes at least one key instruction, e.g. calling for a *discussion*, *evaluation*, *comparison* or *contrast*. Very few questions can be answered simply by factual description or by an uncritical historical account. Most examination questions test whether you can introduce basic economic theory in a simple but clear way in order to cast light on the specified problem.

Questions asking for comparisons or contrasts should not be answered with two separate accounts. Strictly, a comparison notes points of similarity whereas a contrast notes points of difference, though in practice examiners are unlikely to be pedantic about this distinction. However, it is important to avoid confusing questions asking for a discussion of **causes** with those concerned with the **economic effects** resulting from a particular government policy or change in the economy. When discussing causes and effects it is as well to remember the central importance in economics of the **price mechanism** and the concept of the **margin**. Most economic changes occur at the margin in response to movements in relative price or income, when an economic agent decides it is no longer worthwhile to engage in its earlier pattern of economic behaviour.

Multiple choice questions

Some examining boards set a separate multiple choice paper (or objective test paper), or include multiple choice questions in a separate section of one of their other papers.

When preparing for the multiple choice paper, candidates should check whether the paper tests the whole range of the syllabus, or just core topics. Practice varies between the boards. The structure of the multiple choice paper also varies between boards. Most of the boards only set single completion questions, but the NEAB also sets 'matching pairs' questions. Single completion questions (or simple completion questions) contain a stem (the question itself) and four or five possible answers – a single correct answer with the rest being incorrect distracters. A matching pairs question requires the candidate to select items from one list to match up with items from a second list provided in the question.

Examples of multiple choice questions have not been included in this book. By far the best way to prepare for the multiple choice paper is to work through past papers or specimen papers set by the relevant board.

Multiple choice technique

A multiple choice paper allows candidates to spend only a minute or two on each question. Some questions can usually be answered in a few seconds, but others which involve calculation or deep thought may require several minutes. It is important to avoid being delayed by such questions occurring early in the paper, preventing you reaching some easier questions in the later sections. Try to go through the paper three times in all. On the first occasion, quickly move on from any question proving difficult or involving a calculation, making sure to draw a heavy pencil line around all the questions you do not attempt and a question mark against any question you do attempt, but are not sure about. If one and a quarter hours are allowed for the paper, try to complete your first run-through in about fifty minutes. On the second run, return to the questions you have placed a mark against, and be prepared to spend several minutes on each. If time allows, scan through the paper a third time, checking whether you have correctly interpreted the wording of each question. If you have second thoughts about any of your answers, take great care to erase completely your initial mark on the answer sheet. Make sure that all your marks are in the correct positions on the answer sheet.

Finally, allow at least half a minute to guess the answers to any questions still unanswered. Your aim is to maximise your marks, so do not leave any questions unattempted. There is always at least a twenty per cent chance that your guess will turn out to be correct!

Data response questions

All the examining boards set a data response or stimulus paper, or have incorporated questions of this type into a paper which also includes essay questions.

Most boards adopt an *incline of difficulty* approach to the setting of data response questions: the question is structured into separate parts, each succeeding part becoming more difficult, in order to test the higher order skills. Thus the first part of a data response question may require the candidate to describe some aspect of the data, while later parts require an explanation of the data in terms of economic theory and an evaluation. Properly constructed questions of this type discriminate well between good and bad candidates.

Most of the examining boards only set questions on *real-world* data, extracted from a newspaper or journal article (in the case of prose or text data), or from a publication such as Economic Trends (in the case of statistical data). As an alternative to coursework, the AEB offers a case study paper which resembles an extended data response question on a topic which is announced well before the examination.

Candidates are also told that questions will be set on the topic which will test their investigative skills. Indeed all the boards now set questions somewhere in their papers which test candidates' knowledge of how professional economists undertake investigations.

It is vitally important that a candidate should be familiar with the house style of a board's data response questions. Some boards set a compulsory data response question or questions; with other boards there is a choice.

Data response technique

Many of the examination techniques relevant to essay questions are also applicable to the data response paper. It is perhaps even more important to read through the questions to make sure that you thoroughly understand both the data content and the questions. Where a choice is allowed, the rubric at the beginning of the paper will usually advise you to spend a few minutes reading through the paper; take this instruction seriously and carefully read through each question before you make your final choice.

Stimulus questions frequently start by asking for the extraction of simple facts from the data. Avoid the temptation to elaborate your answer to this part of the question since it is unlikely that more than a couple of marks will be allocated for simple description. Conversely, you must not simply describe or paraphrase the data when tackling the parts of a question that require the higher order skill of interpreting or evaluating. Sometimes a question will explicitly ask for a statement of the assumptions upon which the arguments in the data are based or upon which you are making your inferences. It may also ask for a discussion of other sources of information or data that might allow you to draw stronger inferences and conclusions.

Very often the limited amount of data included in a stimulus question is consistent with more than one interpretation, not by itself either proving or refuting a particular economic theory or hypothesis. Nevertheless, the examiner is hoping that candidates will be able to handle basic economic method by stating the assumptions being made in interpreting the data and by discussing how far the data appear consistent with at least one economic theory. You should clearly show the examiner when you are drawing conclusions based solely on the data, and when you are bringing in outside knowledge, either in the form of economic theory or descriptive fact, to help in its interpretation.

Numerical questions may be based upon various forms of data, including tabulated schedules, charts and different types of graph. Most examining boards now allow the use of electronic calculators in the data response paper (and also now in the multiple choice paper), but it is vital to show all your workings, and you should explain to the examiner what you are trying to do at each stage in the manipulation of the data. Stimulus questions try to test economic knowledge rather than arithmetical skills, though there will usually be a single correct answer to a question or part of a question involving a calculation. However, an arithmetic slip should not be heavily penalised, providing that you have clearly shown that you are using the correct economic method to answer the question.

When answering questions based on real-world data sources, it is useful to know the difference between time-series and cross-sectional data, and to be aware of the uses and limitations of data expressed in such forms as index numbers and percentages. Time-series data observe how economic variables change over time. Whereas time-series data are often highly aggregated, cross-sectional data divide up or disaggregate the data into its various components. Cross-sectional and time-series data can of course be combined together, in which case they are known as pooled data.

Time-series data measuring changes in economic variables such as national income, output and expenditure usually fluctuate both seasonally and also with the upswings and downswings of the business cycle. Seasonal fluctuations cannot of course be detected unless the data are presented in quarterly or monthly form, in which case they may be presented in either seasonally adjusted or unadjusted form. Adjusted data pick up the long-term trend from year to year whereas unadjusted data show the fluctuations occurring from season to season.

Many economic variables measured in money units are affected by inflation, which can seriously distort time-series data. Check whether data are unadjusted for inflation, in the current prices of each year, or whether the data have either been converted to the constant prices of a particular year, or been expressed in index numbers. Index numbers, which are usually based on 100, can sometimes be confused with data expressed in percentages which must, of course, add up to 100. Cross-sectional data are often expressed in percentages, sometimes in the form of a chart or pie graph. Great care must be taken in interpreting both index numbers and percentages, particularly if absolute totals are not included in the data.

Be especially wary of reading economic interpretations into the apparent steepness or flatness of curves when data are presented in graphical form. By altering the scales on the vertical and horizontal axes it is possible to show changes in an economic variable either by a steep or a flat curve (providing that the variable is rising or falling).

QUALITY OF LANGUAGE

All the examining boards are now required to award approximately 5% of the total marks for quality of language. These marks are awarded for answers to essay questions and the more extended parts of data response questions, where the answer takes the form of continuous prose. Clear expression, and to a slightly lesser extent, correct spelling are main factors determining whether the marks for quality of language are awarded. The syllabuses published by the examining boards indicate whether quality of language marks will be awarded for particular papers or types of question within papers. Candidates must check the syllabus requirements carefully. It is also a good idea to look at the marking schemes for specimen papers and for recent past papers to see how the quality of language marks are awarded.

GUIDANCE FOR SCOTTISH HIGHER STUDENTS

The Scottish Examination Board offers two certificates in Economics for the post sixteen-year-old age group:

❶ The certificate of Sixth Year Studies which is based largely on an in-depth study of one selected topic and is only open to students with previous examination success in economics;

❷ The Higher Grade which is normally a one year post-Ordinary Grade course intended for seventeen year olds, although often taken by older or Further Education candidates, for which this book is more suited. The course covers the same range of economic theory and analysis as most A-level courses, but, because of its shorter duration, the questions set may require less depth or development in order to reach a pass standard. A and B passes are required for university entrance. There are few differences between this course and a typical A-level course in the field of economic analysis covered by the syllabus. However, in Scottish Higher there is less emphasis on factual knowledge recall and on the memorising of traditional theory. More time is spent on the acquisition of numerate and interpretive skills and the application of key concepts and principles to real-world problems.

ADVANCED SUPPLEMENTARY LEVEL

Traditionally, most students in sixth forms and on equivalent courses in colleges have studied three A-level subjects, knowing that three good pass grades are usually required by universities for entry to a degree course in higher education. However, following the introduction of the Advanced Supplementary (AS) examination in 1989, pass grades in two subjects at AS-level are now regarded by universities and polytechnics as equivalent to a pass in one subject at A-level.

The objective of the AS examination is to give greater choice and flexibility, enabling you to study more of the subjects you enjoy up to A-level standard, and helping to keep your higher education and careers options open. Universities, other higher education institutions and employers recognise the value of more broadly based sixth-form studies. While it is theoretically possible to study six subjects at AS-level instead of three subjects at A-level, a more usual combination is likely to be two subjects at A-level and two at AS-level.

When AS-level was first introduced, schools and colleges were expected to offer AS-level primarily on two year courses, alongside equivalent A-level subjects. However, many schools have decided to enter students for AS-level at the end of one year, half-way through a two year course. Perhaps in recognition of this, the modular Cambridge syllabus and the Oxford and Cambridge syllabus now allow candidates to 'cash in' the results achieved in exams taken at the end of one year as an AS-level pass. Candidates can decide whether to do this, thereby ending their study of economics, or whether to proceed to a full A-level by completing the remaining parts of the course.

As AS-level requires the same standard of work as A-level, with AS-level passes being graded A to F in the same way as A-levels, it must not be regarded as easier than A-levels. In each subject, the AS syllabus has been designed to contain approximately half the syllabus content of A-level, but will be examined to test skills of exactly the same degree of difficulty. Indeed, with 'stand-alone' AS-level syllabuses it often appears that rather more than half the equivalent A-level syllabus is included in the syllabus. While the same general calibre of work is expected at AS-level as at A-level, the syllabuses aim to take account of the shorter teaching and studying time available.

Finally, it should be noted that not all the GCE examining boards offer economics as an AS-level subject. The syllabus checklists indicate which boards offer economics as an AS-level subject, either as a 'stand-alone' syllabus or as part of a flexible modular A-level syllabus.

TAKING MODULAR TESTS

Preparation for modular tests and the examination techniques you need to apply to them are largely the same as for other written examinations. However, the following points should be remembered when taking modular tests.

1 The modular examinations, even where taken after less than two terms of study, are marked to the same standard as terminal examinations. No concession is made for your relative inexperience at A-level study.

2 The modular examination usually covers a narrower range of material than other examinations. Do not be lulled into thinking that preparation can be less thorough and/or less urgent.

3 The time interval between practice (mock) test and the actual examination is likely to be short, leaving little time to compensate for deficiencies in knowledge and/or technique.

4 Terminal examinations (which are those taken after 14 February in the final year) must contribute at least 30% for the final mark/grade. These later modules often incorporate skills and understanding which have been acquired in previous modules. Do not assume all previous knowledge can be forgotten.

5 Modular tests are typically 1–1½ hours in duration, though exams for double modules may be 3 hours long. Their relative shortness makes the management of your time especially important as there is little opportunity to compensate for lost time. Answers need to be concise and to the point.

6 There is little respite from examinations, no sooner is one complete than the next appears on the horizon. Take care not to become fatigued but to build yourself up mentally for the next module.

FINAL PREPARATION

Provided you have prepared an adequate revision timetable, begun the process early and followed it through faithfully, there should be little left to do on the evening prior to your examination. If you have not revised adequately it is a mistake to imagine that a few hours of cramming can compensate for your earlier omissions.

The best advice we can give for the evening prior to an examination is to try to relax and have a good night's rest. You may find it difficult to follow this advice as it demands great confidence that your revision has been complete. If you simply cannot bring yourself to do no work, we would suggest a quick skim through your notes, textbook or this companion guide, perhaps reading headings and subheadings, to generally absorb ideas and principles. Equally, there may be a few equations or definitions which you might wish to reinforce in your memory. Avoid, however, detailed revision of topics as it is almost certainly too late for this to be of benefit and there is the very real risk of inducing panic as you struggle to come to grips with a difficult concept. This will only create confusion and undermine your confidence, making matters worse than if no work had been done at all.

Our advice is therefore to keep any revision low key, to prepare the necessary examination materials (pens, pencils, etc.) for the following day, relax, set your alarm and get a good night's sleep.

ECONOMICS TOPICS

Chapters in this section:

Each chapter features:

- *Units in this chapter:* a list of the main topic heads to follow.
- *Chapter objectives:* a brief comment on how the topics relate to what has gone before, and to the syllabus. Key ideas and skills which are covered in the chapter are introduced.
- *The main text:* is divided into numbered topic units for ease of reference.
- *Chapter roundup:* a brief summary of the chapter.
- *Illustrative questions and answers:* a typical essay and data question, with tutorial notes and our suggested answers.
- *Question bank:* a selection of essay questions, with tutorial comments on points to include and pitfalls to avoid.

THE ECONOMIC PROBLEM AND ECONOMIC SYSTEMS

Units in this chapter

1.1 *The economic problem*
1.2 *Economic systems*

Chapter objectives

This first chapter introduces you to the **economic problem** and asks you to think about the nature of the United Kingdom economy and of other types of **economic system** which are very different from the UK. It then goes on to describe a number of ways of classifying economic systems, and to explain how the main types of economic systems attempt to solve the economic problem. The chapter concludes by describing how economic systems, including the **UK mixed economy**, have been changing in recent years.

1.1 THE ECONOMIC PROBLEM

ECONOMICS AND THE ECONOMIC PROBLEM

'Economics is the science which studies human behaviour as a relationship between ends and scarce means which have alternative uses.'

Professor Lionel Robbins in an
Essay on the Nature and Significance of Economic Science, 1932.

Professor Lionel Robbin's long-established definition provides perhaps the most well-known starting point for introducing and understanding what economics is about. Economics is literally the study of economising – the study of how human beings make choices on **what to produce**, **how to produce** and **for whom** to produce, in a world in which most of the resources are limited. How can people best make decisions on the allocation of scarce resources amongst competing uses, so as to improve and maximise human happiness and welfare? This is the economic problem.

CAPITAL GOODS AND CONSUMER GOODS

Before examining the economic problem in greater detail, and how different economic systems attempt to solve the economic problem, we shall briefly introduce a number of key economic concepts. This section explains the distinction between capital goods and consumer goods. **Capital goods**, which are also known as **producers' goods**, **investment goods** and **intermediate goods**, are not bought by households for final consumption; instead they are bought by other firms as raw materials or inputs for the purposes of production. The capital goods industries, many of which are heavy industries, include the iron and steel, mechanical engineering and chemical industries. **Consumer goods** or **final goods** are bought by persons or households for the purpose of final consumption, to satisfy wants and needs. Cars, television sets, washing machines and similar goods purchased by individuals or households for ordinary consumer use are examples of **consumer durables** – consumer goods with a long average life during which they deliver a stream of consumer services. By contrast, a non-durable consumer good, such as a packet of soap powder, needs replacing after it has been used. Some consumer durable goods, especially housing, are bought for investment purposes as well as for the consumer services they deliver to the households who benefit from them.

THE ECONOMIC PROBLEM ILLUSTRATED ON A PRODUCTION POSSIBILITY DIAGRAM

The production possibility diagram drawn in Fig. 1.1 shows what can be produced with the existing quantity of labour, capital and land at a country's disposal, for a given state of 'technical progress'. Given that resources and capacity are limited, a choice has to be made on which type of good to produce.

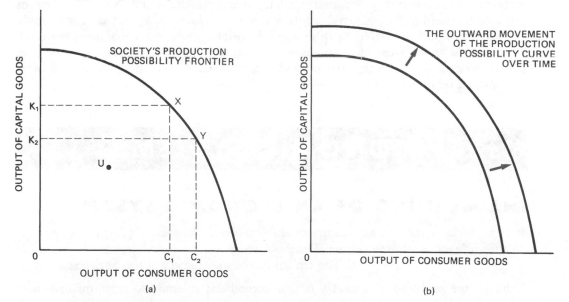

Fig 1.1 (a) The economic problem and society's production possibility curve
(b) Exonomic growth causes the frontier to move outwards over time

The production possibility frontier drawn in the left-hand panel of the diagram shows the various combinations of capital goods and consumer goods that can be produced. For example, point X on the production possibility frontier shows K_1 capital goods and C_1 consumer goods. But if the people living in the economy desire an immediate increase in their standard of living, more of society's scarce resources will have to be devoted to consumer goods and fewer to capital goods. This can be shown by the movement from point X to point Y on the production possibility frontier. Consumer good production rises to C_2, but at the expense of a fall in capital good production to K_2.

29

OPPORTUNITY COST

The movement from point X to point Y on the production possibility frontier in Fig. 1.1, illustrates a very important aspect of the economic problem, the principle of **opportunity cost**. The opportunity cost of any choice, decision or course of action is measured in terms of the alternatives that have to be given up. Hence, the opportunity cost of increasing the production of consumer goods from C_1 to C_2 is the fall in capital goods from K_1 to K_2. Indeed, we can develop the concept of opportunity cost a stage further. In economics we always assume that **economic agents** (for example, individuals, households or firms) behave rationally in the sense that they try to make decisions which are in their self–interest and which maximise their private benefit. When a choice has to be made, the best alternative will always be chosen, which means that the 'second best' or 'next best' alternative has to be rejected! Hence, the opportunity cost of any decision or choice can be defined as the next best alternative sacrificed or foregone.

ECONOMIC GROWTH

A decision to choose more consumer goods and fewer capital goods means that people are choosing higher living standards now rather than in the future. Suppose that people made the opposite choice, deciding to sacrifice current consumption in favour of a higher level of future consumption. More of society's scarce resources would go into **investment** or the production of capital goods, enabling the country's capital stock to grow larger. Over time, the production possibility frontier would shift outwards, as shown in the right-hand panel of Fig. 1.1, showing economic growth to be taking place. Economic growth can be defined as an outward movement of the economy's production possibility frontier, or an increase in its production potential.

FULL EMPLOYMENT AND UNEMPLOYMENT

All points on an economy's production possibility frontier (such as points X and Y) represent **full employment** of the economy's available resources. However, a point such as U inside the frontier is associated with **unemployment**. Here it is no longer true that the opportunity cost of increasing the output of consumer goods is the sacrifice of some production of capital goods – production of both capital goods and consumer goods can be stepped up by utilising unemployed resources.

1.2 ECONOMIC SYSTEMS

THE MEANING OF AN ECONOMIC SYSTEM

> '*An economic system is a set of institutional arrangements whose function is to employ most efficiently scarce resources to meet the ends of society.*'
>
> The United Nations Dictionary of the Social Science.

Although the **problem of scarcity** is fundamental and common to all forms of human society, from humble tribal groupings of hunters or gatherers in the Amazonian forest, to rich national states such as the United States of America, different societies have produced different institutional frameworks and methods for allocating scarce resources among competing uses. The set of institutions within which a community decides what, how and for whom to produce is called an **economic system**.

MARKET ECONOMIES AND COMMAND ECONOMIES

Perhaps the most widely used method of defining and classifying economic systems is according to the **allocative mechanism** by which scarce resources reach the people who eventually consume or use them. Although there are a variety of ways in which wealth and purchasing power can be allocated amongst individuals – including inheritance and other types of gift, theft, luck or chance, such as winning a fortune on the National Lottery – the two allocative mechanisms by which economic systems are defined are the **market mechanism** (or **price mechanism**) and the **command mechanism** (or **planning mechanism**). An economic system in which goods and services are purchased through the price mechanism in a system of markets is called a **market economy**, whereas one in which government officials or planners allocate economic resources to firms and other productive enterprises is called a **command economy** (or **planned economy**).

MARKET ECONOMIES

In a pure market economy, it would be the **market mechanism** (the **price mechanism**, the **price system** or simply **market forces**) that performs the central economic task of allocating scarce resources amongst competing uses. A market economy comprises a large number of markets varying in the degree to which they are separated and interrelated. A **market** is a meeting of buyers and sellers in which goods or services are exchanged for other goods or services. Occasionally, the exchange is direct and is known as **barter**. Normally, however, the exchange is indirect through the **medium of money**. One good or service, such as labour, is exchanged for money which is then traded a second time for other goods or services, sometimes immediately, but usually some time later after a delay. The exchange must be voluntary; if one party forces a transaction upon the other, it is not a market transaction. While some markets exist in a particular geographical location, e.g. a street market or a car boot sale, many markets do not, and transport costs and lack of information may create barriers which separate or break up markets. In past centuries, such barriers often prevented markets from operating outside the relatively small geographical areas of a single country or even a small region within a country. In recent years, developments in modern communications have allowed goods to be transported more easily and at lower cost, and for market information to be transmitted via telephone, telex and fax. These developments have enabled many markets, especially commodity and raw material markets and markets in financial services, to become truly global or international markets functioning on a world-wide basis.

The conditions needed for a market to function efficiently

Markets are **decentralised** and **unorganised** in the sense that there is no government or central authority to decide how much is going to be traded and how much each buyer or seller in the market must trade. The three principal conditions necessary for a market to operate are:

1. the individual buyers and sellers decide what, how, how much, where and when to trade or exchange;

2. they do so with reference to their self-interest and to the alternatives or opportunities open to them;

3. prices convey to the market participants information about self-interest and opportunities.

For a market to allocate resources between different types of activity and to co-ordinate the activities of the separate but interdependent units that make up an economy, **prices must respond to the forces of supply and demand**.

How the price mechanism allocates scarce resources

In a market economy, prices perform three main functions:

1. **The signalling function.** Prices signal what is available, conveying the information which allows all the traders in the market to plan and co-ordinate their economic activities. Markets will function inefficiently, sometimes breaking down completely or leading to **market failure**, if prices signal wrong or misleading information.

2 The incentive function. Prices create incentives for **economic agents** (for example households and firms) to behave and make decisions in ways consistent with pursuing and achieving the fulfilment of their self-interest.

3 The rationing or allocative function. For markets to operate in an orderly and efficient manner the buyers and sellers in the market must respond to the incentives provided by the price mechanism. Suppose that in a particular market demand rises relative to supply, causing the market price to rise. An immediate result is that the rising price serves to limit to some extent the increase in the demand for the good or service which has now become more expensive compared to other goods, thereby creating an incentive for consumers to economise in its use. But simultaneously, the possibility of higher profits creates an incentive for firms to shift resources into producing the goods and services whose relative price has risen and to demand more resources such as labour and capital in order to increase production. In turn this may bid up wages and the price of capital, causing households and the owners of capital to switch the supply of labour and capital into industries where the prices of inputs or factors of production are rising. In this way, the changing prices of goods and services relative to each other **allocate** and **ration** the economy's scarce resources to the consumers and firms who are willing and able to pay most for them in the pursuit of what they perceive to be their self-interest.

COMMAND ECONOMIES

A complete **command economy** would be an economy in which all decisions about what, how, how much, where and for whom to produce would be taken by a **central planning authority** issuing commands or directives to all the households and producers in the society. Such a system could only exist within a very rigid and probably totalitarian political framework because of the restrictions on individual decision-making that are obviously implied. In fact, in much the same way that a pure market economy (in which the price mechanism alone allocates resources) is a theoretical abstraction, so no economy in the real world can properly be described as a complete or pure command economy.

Resource allocation in a command economy

Until the late 1980s and the early 1990s, the Soviet Union (or USSR) and other communist-ruled countries in eastern Europe relied primarily on the command mechanism rather than the market mechanism to allocate scarce resources amongst competing uses. But none of these economies were complete command economies. It has been calculated that in a large economy the size of the old USSR, a central authority would have to issue over 200 billion orders in respect of just a single commodity if the authority were to decide exactly how much each household must consume as well as the quantity each enterprise must produce.

Quite clearly, it would be completely impossible for an economy to be organised in this way. The command economies which until recently existed in the communist countries of central and eastern Europe could be better described as 'planned economies with some household choice'. The command or planning system made the production decisions of what, how and how much to produce, allocating resources to particular industries and productive units. Households and individual consumers were free to choose the final goods (or consumer goods) they wished to buy, subject to availability. In these economies, a central plan was used to allocate resources to industries and productive units which were then required to meet the output targets of the master plan. The central planners sometimes set the prices of essential consumer goods such as meat and bread, but they usually allowed factory managers to set prices of less essential goods. The prices that were set by the central planners to ration those goods and services which were scarce in relation to an overwhelming unfilled consumer demand are examples of **shadow prices**. By seeking to ration demand in relation to supply, the prices set by the central planners resembled or 'shadowed' market prices. However, in a market economy, prices provide incentives for producers to enter or leave industries, as well as incentives for households to modify their consumption behaviour. The first of these incentives is lacking in a command economy, unless planners and factory managers are able to respond to the signals of scarcity by diverting more resources into the particular industry.

For several decades before the 1980s, several successes could be claimed for the complex and highly centralised system of central planning with existed in the command economies of the Soviet Union (USSR) and its 'client states' in central and eastern Europe. Central planning and state ownership had delivered sustained economic growth which had been generally free of the fluctuations in economic activity brought about by the business cycle in western market and mixed economies. Successful industrialisation had occurred – though heavy industry rather than the production of consumer goods dominated manufacturing industry – and populations had generally enjoyed a modest increase in living standards. Unemployment and inflation were officially non-existent.

OWNERSHIP AND ECONOMIC SYSTEMS

So far economic systems have been defined in terms of the mechanism (the market mechanism or the planning mechanism) which is used to solve the economic problem of allocating scarce resources amongst competing uses. Economic systems can also be defined in terms of who owns the means of production: private individuals or the state. **Capitalism** is a system in which the means of production are privately owned by individuals (or capitalists) who employ labour to combine with the capital they own in order to produce an output for sale at a profit. By contrast, in a **socialist** economic system the means of production is owned by the state.

MIXED ECONOMIES

Many economies, particularly those of the developed countries of Western Europe, such as the United Kingdom, are called mixed economies. A **mixed economy** is a mixture of different types of economic system. Fig. 1.2 illustrates two ways of defining a mixed economy: in terms of the mechanism for allocating resources, and in terms of ownership. The upper panel of Fig. 1.2 shows a mixed economy as being intermediate between a market economy and a command economy, containing large **market** and **non-market sectors**, while the lower panel defines a mixed economy in terms of the large **public and private sectors** it contains.

a) The Spectrum of Economic Systems defined in terms of allocative mechanism

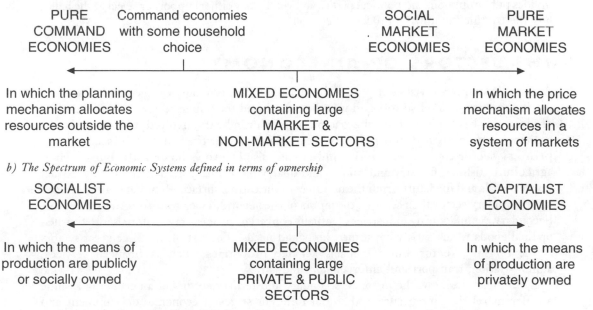

b) The Spectrum of Economic Systems defined in terms of ownership

Fig. 1.2 Alternative ways of looking at the mixed economy

The United Kingdom economy as a mixed economy

The modern British mixed economy dates from the 1940s when a number of important industries such as coal, rail and steel were taken into public ownership by **nationalisation**, and the provision of public sector services outside the market economy was greatly extended by the 1944 Education Act and by the creation of the National Health Service.

For about thirty years after the end of the Second World War, from the 1940s to the 1970s, a large measure of agreement or consensus existed in the United Kingdom about the virtues of the mixed economy. Many economists and the major political parties believed that certain types of economic activity, particularly the production and distribution of most consumer goods and services, were best suited to private enterprise and the market economy. There was also general agreement also that some industries which are 'natural' monopolies or utility industries ought to be nationalised, and that important services such as education, health care and roads should be provided by government 'outside the market' and financed through the tax system. In short, a consensus existed around the belief that the mixed economy was 'about right' for Great Britain.

Recent changes in the UK mixed economy

From the 1960s onward, a growing minority of economists and politicians began to blame the mixed economy for Britain's deteriorating economic performance relative to that of its main competitors in Western Europe and Japan. They argued that the public and non-market sectors of the economy, which they regarded as 'wealth consuming' and inefficient, had become too big and that a concerted effort should be made to change fundamentally the nature of the British economy in the direction of greater private ownership and market production.

Indeed, during the 1980s and early 1990s, Conservative Governments implemented policies which succeeded in changing the nature of the mix in favour of private ownership and market forces, at the expense of public ownership and state planning. The UK economy is now much closer to being a pure market and private enterprise economy than it was twenty years ago. The three main policies used to change the nature of the British economy have been **privatisation** (the selling off of state-owned assets, such as nationalised industries, to private ownership); **marketisation** or **commercialisation** (charging a market price for goods and services that the state previously provided 'free') and **deregulation** (the removal of government red tape, bureaucracy and barriers to entry from the operation of markets). These policies are covered in more detail in Chapter 10. It is currently too early to say whether the process of dismantling the mixed economy and creating a fully-fledged social market economy will be completed. By its very nature, the liberalisation of the British economy deeply divides public opinion, and political parties and voters may either support or reject at the ballot box the continuation of the process of change.

THE SECTORS OF AN ECONOMY

A sector is simply a division or part of the economy. The economy can be divided into the market and non-market sectors and into the private and the public sectors. A third method of division is based on the type of economic activity or industry involved. On this basis, the economy can be divided into **primary**, **secondary** and **tertiary** industrial sectors. The **primary sector** contains **extractive industries**, also known as **basic industries** such as agriculture, fishing, forestry and mining and quarrying. Primary industries literally extract raw materials and foodstuffs from the resources of the earth's surface. Raw materials produced by the primary sector then serve as the inputs of the **secondary** or **manufacturing sector**. Secondary manufacturing industries eventually convert or **process** raw materials into finished or final goods which satisfy consumer wants and needs. The last of the three great sectors is the **tertiary sector** which contains **service industries**, such as financial services, administration, transport and entertainment industries.

Fig. 1.3 illustrates how, the primary, secondary and tertiary sectors of an economy assume a different relative importance and size at different stages of economic development and growth. In **preindustrial** or **traditional societies**, agriculture and related activities form the largest part of the economy, which is therefore dominated by primary activity with very small secondary and tertiary sectors. Indeed, in true traditional societies, the secondary sector is restricted largely to village crafts such as shoe repairing and weaving, because the factory or 'industrialised' production typical of the manufacturing sector in more advanced economies have not yet been developed. In the process of **industrialisation**, the secondary or manufacturing sector grows to become the largest and dominant sector of the economy.

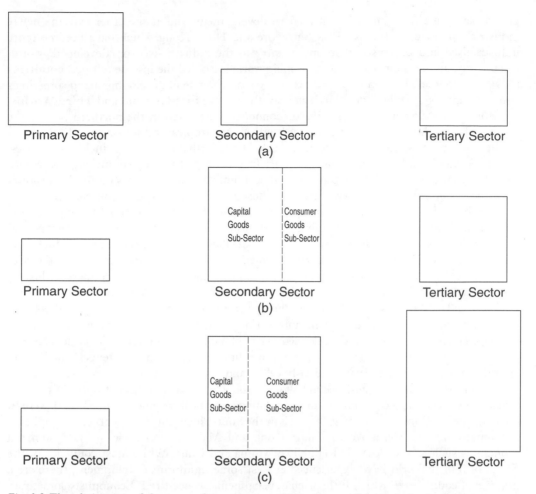

Fig. 1.3 The relative sizes of the sectors of an economy at different stages of economic development.
(a) Pre-industrial societies; (b) Industrialising societies; (c) Mature industrial societies

During the earlier stages of industrialisation, capital goods (heavy industry) are usually more important than the production of consumer goods. As the economy matures and develops a wider range of manufacturing industries, consumer goods gradually become more important. Eventually the tertiary sector grows even faster than the secondary sector, becoming the largest sector in the economy. Indeed, mature industrialised economies in North America and Western Europe, including the United Kingdom, are often said to have entered a new **post-industrial** phase of development in which the secondary or manufacturing sector of the economy declines. Personal incomes remain high, but the demand for consumer goods is now met by imports from countries such as South Korea, Malaysia and Singapore which, together with other **newly-industrialising countries (NICs)** on the Pacific Rim and elsewhere, are now some of the main manufacturing countries in the world economy.

In post-industrial economies such as the United Kingdom, the decline of traditional manufacturing industries, known these days as the **de-industrialisation process**, has been rapid and great. The growth of employment in the service sector and new manufacturing industries benefiting from new technologies has failed to replace the declining employment in older industries. Total manufacturing output has stagnated or grown at a very slow rate. Persistently high unemployment, concentrated especially in the regions of manufacturing decline, has been perhaps the main manifestation of the de-industrialisation process and of post-industrial society.

DEVELOPED AND DEVELOPING ECONOMIES

Economies in the United States, Japan and much of Western Europe, which contain large manufacturing sectors but even larger service sectors, are often referred to simply as **developed economies**. Other countries then comprise the **developing world**, a rather unsatisfactory and 'catch-all' label, since it includes at one extreme countries of very great poverty lacking almost any form of modern development, and at the other extreme newly industrial countries (NICs) such as Singapore and Hong Kong which have become more industrialised and urbanised than any country in the industrialised or 'developed' world. Collectively, all the countries of the developing world are called the **less developed countries (LDCs)**. Other labels often used to describe a country's state of development and sometimes also its political system include, **North** and **South**, and the **First, Second** and **Third Worlds**.

Most of the developed industrialised economies are located in the northern part of the northern hemisphere. The countries of the South are the tropical and sub-tropical LDCs lying on the whole to the south of the developed world. The North does of course include countries, such as Australia and New Zealand, which are further south than any countries of the South proper, because most of their population and economic development has occurred in similar non-tropical or temperate climatic zones to those of other countries in the North.

The First and Second worlds are part of the North: the **First World** comprises the developed Western market or capitalist economies of North America, Western Europe and Japan. Before their recent disintegration, the socialist and command economies of the Soviet Union and other Eastern Block countries formed the **Second world**, a group of countries which were described – only semi-jokingly – as combining a First World military-industrial complex with a Third World economic infrastructure and living standards for their inhabitants. Living standards were generally lower, the agricultural population was larger, there was greater reliance on heavy secondary manufacturing industry, and service industries were less developed than in the First World market economies of the West. As described in the next section, these and other factors led to the collapse of the political and economic systems in the Second World countries in the late 1980s and early 1990s, and to the beginning of a process of change.

In contrast to the First and Second Worlds, the Third World does not reflect a political division between non-communist and communist political regimes. The **Third World** contains the developing economies of LDCs or the South, including both market and capitalist economies such as South Korea, Hong Kong and Malaysia and socialist and command economies such as the People's Republic of China and Cuba. While most countries of the South or Third World have experienced at least some significant development, there are a number of countries in which little or no development has occurred. Economists sometimes identify a **Fourth World** comprising the most under-developed and poverty-stricken countries of the South, for the most part located in Sub-Saharan Africa.

THE BREAKUP OF THE COMMAND ECONOMIES OF EASTERN EUROPE

With the breakdown of communist rule, the command mechanism has now largely disintegrated in eastern and central Europe, which are currently in the process of transformation into market or mixed economies. While a few command economies still remain in other parts of the world – like the People's Republic of China, North Korea, Vietnam and Cuba – the role of markets and the price mechanism has been increased in significant areas of some of these economies.

These changes result from the fact that during the 1980s, it became increasingly apparent that the disadvantages of the central planning were far exceeding the benefits. First and foremost, the successes listed earlier in this chapter had only been achieved at the expense of severe political repression and loss of personal freedom. Strictly economic disadvantages of central planning included:

- poor investment decisions and slow growth of output per worker (or labour productivity);
- persistent shortages and poor quality of consumer goods and many foodstuffs;
- unfavourable economic performance in comparison to both the mature market and mixed economies in Western Europe and such anti-communist Asian NICs as South Korea and Taiwan;
- the failure of partial reforms to improve the central planning system.

As a result of these disadvantages, in the late 1980s the countries of eastern and central Europe, such as Poland, began to break away from Soviet influence and the central planning system.

The Soviet Union also began to break up as constituent republics sought to secede. To speed this process several republics banned the export of key industrial materials and products to other Soviet republics. The central planning system degenerated into chaos. Factory managers began to ignore directives from the central planners in Moscow, relying instead on bilateral trading agreements between individual Soviet republics and direct bartering between factory managers to keep production going.

With a growing inability to produce the consumer goods that people wanted, a deteriorating infrastructure (particularly for distributing agricultural goods to the cities), worsening shortages and the growth of black markets, and a widening gap in economic performance and standards of living between the USSR and the western market economies, the Soviet government realised that fundamental change was inevitable. The Soviet people would no longer accept the political and economic systems imposed upon them. When the Soviet Communist Party lost power and the USSR finally broke up in 1992, the central planning system was abandoned. As recent experience has shown, Russia and the other newly-independent ex-Soviet countries now face formidable difficulties in trying to make the simultaneous transition to western-style political democracy and to a market economy and capitalism. As yet, it is by no means guaranteed that the abandoning of central planning and the adoption of capitalism and a market economy will transform all the ex-communist countries into 'leading light' examples of the advantages of the market system. Some may simply end up added to the list of the less successful market economies, with various forms of **market failure** replacing the **government failure** which characterised the central planning system in these countries.

For successful transformation into a market economy, inflation and government finances must be stabilised and the price mechanism set free to co-ordinate supply and demand, and production and consumption decisions. The most vital requirement for the successful growth of a market economy is arguably the formation of an **enterprise culture** or **entrepreneurial climate** which encourages risk taking, 'deal making', hard work and effort, and the ability to accumulate and direct savings into productive channels. Alongside this 'entrepreneurial culture', there must also be appropriate governmental, legal, financial and educational institutions. Amongst the problems facing ex-Soviet and some of the eastern European countries, is the fact that at the time of the breakup of the command economy, much of both the required institutional and infrastructural framework was missing, as was the entrepreneurial culture, which had been deliberately suppressed during the communist era. Neither could be implanted overnight; it may take years for both to be properly established. In the transformation process, one of the government's first tasks has been to establish private property rights, i.e. who owns what. This has involved privatisation, but in a country in which the state previously owned almost everything, privatisation has been by no means as simple a task to undertake as in countries like the UK. One of the dangers is that during the intervening period when the government attempts to transform the economy, the emerging market economy performs extremely inefficiently. Legitimate market institutions may be subverted by a criminalised black market economy, or *gangster capitalism*, typified by racketeering, speculation and the seizure of property and effective power by Mafia-style gangs more reminiscent of Chicago in the 1920s or the drug economy of Colombia today, than that of a progressive, successful and politically liberal Western European or North American market economy.

Chapter roundup

The chapters which follow examine in greater detail the nature and problems of resource allocation and economic performance in market and mixed economies. Since the problems of command economies will not be examined again in this book, a significant section of this chapter has been devoted to surveying the process of economic change currently taking place in the ex-command economies of eastern Europe. Chapters 2 to 5 describe how the price mechanism operates in a market economy. Chapters 7 to 9 then go on to examine how a market economy may often function less than perfectly, while Chapter 10 investigates in greater detail some of the policies, such as privatisation, which have been used in recent years to change the nature of the UK mixed economy.

Illustrative questions and answers

1 Essay Question

'Most economic systems consist of a mixture of market forces and government intervention.'

(a) Explain what is meant by an "economic system". (5)

(b) Discuss why some planned economies have recently tried to place greater emphasis on the use of market forces. (10)

(c) Explain why governments intervene in an economy and give examples of such intervention. (10) *SEB*

Tutorial note

(a) Explain that an economic system is an institutional framework in society for organising production, distribution and exchange and for addressing the fundamental economic problem of scarcity. It is within the framework of an economic system that a community decides such questions as what, how and for whom to produce. Briefly explain that economic systems can be classified on the basis of ownership (capitalism and socialism), in terms of how scarce resources are allocated between competing uses (command economies, market economies and mixed economies), or in terms of the stage of development that an economy has reached.

(b) Although the question does not mention explicitly the process of economic transformation in the former command economies of eastern Europe, this is obviously what the question is about. It would be a good idea to bring the experience of Russia and some of the former communist countries of eastern Europe, such as Poland, into your answer. You might begin your answer by outlining any benefits of planned economies, such the delivery of sustained economic growth and modest increases in living standards without the fluctuations in economic activity brought about by the business cycle in western market and mixed economies. Then go on to explain how, especially during the 1980s, it became apparent that the disadvantages of the central planning were far exceeding these benefits. Outline the disadvantages, such as political repression and the failure to produce consumer goods and services in sufficient quantity and quality to improve the economic welfare of the bulk of the population. A feature of the central planning system had been the concentration of national production of a particular product in a single factory within the Soviet Union or eastern Europe in order to achieve the maximum possible economies of scale. Thus three-quarters of the most common 6000 industrial products were produced in just one factory. As a result, factories depended on the centralised planning process to ensure the delivery of key components produced in a single factory which might be located thousands of miles away in another Soviet republic or country in eastern Europe.

Explain why the market system was introduced and how it was hoped that the price mechanism would create incentives for a much more efficient utilisation of economic resources, correcting the severe economic failures of the command system, without introducing significant problems of market failure to take their place.

(c) There is no need to tie your answer to this part of the question to the process of economic change in eastern Europe. You might begin your answer by explaining that governments may intervene in an economy for a number of political reasons which include the desire to create conditions in which their policy objectives might be achieved. Objectives may include the wish to change the nature of society, and to maintain the political control of the party in power. But devote most of your answer to explaining how governments intervene to correct or reduce the market failures that occur in an unregulated market economy. Make sure you give at least two or three examples. Market failure occurs whenever markets perform unsatisfactorily. There are two main types of market failure, related respectively to inefficient and inequitable functioning of markets. In the former case, governments intervene to deal with problems caused by monopoly, to provide public goods, and to try to ensure the socially optimal level of production of merit and demerit goods, and of externalities. Left to itself to pursue the objective of private profit maximisation, a monopoly tends to produce too low an output at too high a price. Producer sovereignty may replace consumer sovereignty, meaning that the monopoly decides what to produce, restricting consumer choice. Likewise, unregulated markets tend to produce too little of a merit good such as health care and of a positive externality such as a beautiful view. The opposite happens with demerit goods (such as tobacco products) and negative externalities (such as pollution). In both these cases, unregulated markets result in overproduction, above the socially-optimal level (where marginal social benefit equals marginal social cost). In all these cases, governments may intervene through the use of regulation and/or taxes or subsidies to try to correct the market failure. Public goods present a rather different case. Markets may fail completely to provide any quantity at all of a public good such as defence; an alternative system of provision is therefore required, for example government provision of the public good which is financed through the tax system.

Many people believe that an unregulated market economy produces an unacceptably unfair and unequal distribution of income and wealth, providing an example of market failure occurring on the ground of inequity. Governments can use progressive taxation and transfers of income to lower income groups to try to reduce inequalities and correct this market failure. On a global scale, the massive inequalities between the rich First World countries of the North and the poorest Third World countries of the South provide an example of a particularly intractable market failure. Finally, it is worth noting that governments often intervene within the domestic economy to try to eliminate or reduce such market failures as unemployment and regional inequalities, which may be deemed both an inefficient use of the economy's resources and inequitable. You should see Chapter 9 for further detail and explanation of market failure.

2 Data Question

The following data relate to the output of the UK economy.

Main sectors of economic activity	Value added £ billion 1988	Employees '000 Dec 1989	Volume change in output % per annum	% share of GDP at current factor cost 1988
Agriculture, forestry and fishing	5.8	279	2.6	1.5
Energy and water supply	21.9	459	3.6	5.5
Manufacturing	95.8	5,165	0.7	24.3
Construction	27.9	1,030	2.2	7.1
Distribution, hotels and catering	56.4	4,609	2.8	14.3
Transport and communications	28.7	1,339	3.0	7.3
Financial services	76.9	2,596	7.5	19.5
Ownership of dwellings	21.4	143	1.1	5.4
Education and health	35.2	3,233	1.6	8.9
Public administration	27.0	2,010	0.1	6.8
Other services	25.8	1,696	3.9	6.5
Adjustment and residual	−28.0			
GDP at factor cost	394.8	22,559	2.2	100

(Source: *An Economic Profile of Britain, 1989*, Lloyds Bank Plc.)

(a) Using examples from the table, distinguish between the primary, secondary and tertiary sectors of the economy. (3)

(b) Explain what is meant by the terms:
  (i) value added;
  (ii) volume change in output. (4)

(c) The largest sector, manufacturing, had one of the lowest percentage increases in output between 1979 and 1988 while financial and other service sectors had amongst the largest increases in output over the same period.

   (i) Examine the factors which may have contributed to these trends. (6)

   (ii) Examine the implications of these trends for:

   (a) the level of employment;

   (b) the structure of the balance of payments. (4)

(d) To what extent would you expect the rate of change in output in the main sectors of economic activity to be typical of other advanced industrial countries? (3)   *ULEAC*

Tutorial Note

(a) To earn all three marks you must give examples, but remember that an example on its own is not a definition. Define the primary sector as comprising those industries or economic activities which extract resources from the earth's crust, the secondary sector as the manufacturing and processing sector, and the tertiary sector as the service sector. Give an example of an industry in each sector, e.g. agriculture (primary sector); construction (secondary sector) and public administration (tertiary sector). You might note that many of the outputs of the primary sector become inputs (raw materials and sources of energy) for the secondary sector.

(b) (i) Value added is the difference between the price or value of inputs, and the price at which a business sells its output – ignoring any complications resulting from taxes or subsidies. Suppose a manufacturer in the breakfast cereal industry (in the secondary sector) purchases bags of grain for £1000 from farmers (in the primary sector), which after processing into cornflakes, are sold for £1500 to supermarket groups (in the tertiary sector). The value added by the breakfast cereal manufacturer in this example is £500.

   (ii) If the breakfast cereal manufacturer in the above example increased production of cornflakes from 1000 tons in 1995 to 1040 tons in 1996, the volume change in output would be 40 tons, or 4%. Such a *volume* change in output must not be confused with a change in the *value* of output, which would be measured in monetary units.

(c) (i) Be careful not to overwrite your answer to this part of the question – this could easily be an essay question! Make sure that for each economic activity specified (manufacturing and financial services), you describe and briefly discuss at least two factors that might have influenced the sector's rate of growth over the period 1979–88. However, take care not to stray into discussing the implications of the trends – this is the subject of part (ii) of the question. It is worth noting that for much of the period, manufacturing was severely hit by the recession which the UK economy suffered from 1979 to 1981. There was an absolute decline in manufacturing output during these years, marked by the closure of many factories and whole industries. Contributory factors were the collapse of aggregate demand, and the effects of high interest rates (in the tight 'monetarist' monetary policy being pursued at the time despite the fact that the economy was in deep recession) and an overvalued exchange rate induced by the high interest rates. Recovery from recession began in 1981, but by 1988 (towards the end of a long period of economic recovery nicknamed the 'Lawson boom'), manufacturing output was only just above the level achieved in 1979 just before the onset of recession. As well as discussing the short-run factors we have just outlined, you could also discuss longer-term factors affecting the competitiveness of UK manufacturing, such as a failure to undertake sufficient investment, loss of comparative advantage (discussed in Chapter 18), and the shift of manufacturing investment (often by UK manufacturing companies) to the NICs in the Far East. By contrast with much manufacturing, the UK may possess a comparative advantage in the financial services industry, so develop this point. Other relevant factors promoting the growth of financial services such as banking and insurance could include the effects of high interest rates (which so damaged manufacturing) in raising banks' profitability and attracting 'hot money' flows into the UK financial system (discussed in Chapter 19).

(ii) (a and b) Fewer marks are available for this part of the question, so once again take care not to overdevelop your answer. Obviously, if one important sector of the economy grows much faster than another – but with both growing – we would expect the overall level of employment to increase and for the composition of employment to change in favour of the faster growing sector. However, the overall level of employment in the manufacturing sector fell over the period despite the growth in output. This is because traditional labour-intensive methods of manufacturing declined, with a consequent laying-off of workers, while growth took place in manufacturing sectors which employ automated production lines. Factors contributing to occupational and geographical immobility of labour were also significant in explaining why workers were unable to shift between the two sectors. Many of the workers who lost their jobs in the manufacturing sector could not find employment in the financial services industry, because they lived in the wrong parts of the country and lacked appropriate skills and aptitudes. With regard to the balance of payments, the main implication is that the balance of visible trade (or trade in goods) would deteriorate, while the balance of invisible trade (or trade in services) would improve. Whether the overall balance of payments on current account (the sum of the visible and invisible trade balances) improved or deteriorated, would depend on whether or not the extra overseas earnings of the financial services industry was sufficient to offset the growing import penetration of manufactured goods and the possible loss of export markets for manufactured goods.

(d) As already noted, an important explanation for the failure of the UK manufacturing sector to grow by more than 0.7 per cent over the period, lies in the shift of manufacturing industry to NICs. Almost all advanced industrialised countries have suffered from this trend, though in some, particularly Japan and Germany, manufacturing was both more important and more competitive and resilient than it was in the UK over the period covered by the data. Nevertheless, manufacturing has fallen as a *proportion* of national output or GDP in *all* advanced industrial countries, even in those countries such as Japan where manufacturing has grown significantly in absolute terms. This is because as countries grow wealthier, their inhabitants choose to spend a growing proportion of their incomes on services and a smaller proportion on food and manufactured goods. Hence the growing importance of the service sector in all advanced industrial countries. The primary sector has generally fallen in relative importance (though not usually in absolute output) in all these countries, and will continue to do so. However, each country's experience has depended on factors such as climate and availability of land (for agriculture) and events such as the discovery and exploitation of oil, gas and other mineral resources.

Question bank

1 (a) Compare the ways in which resources are allocated in market and command economies. (12)

  (b) What criteria might be used to decide whether the allocation of resources in an economy is 'efficient'? (13)   *WJEC*

2 'Most countries have a mixed economy; the only debate is about the strength of the mixture.'   (Sir A. Cairncross)

  (a) What is meant by a mixed economy? (30)

  (b) Examine the above statement with respect to the problem of determining what should be the 'strength of the mixture'. (70)   *ULEAC*

3 (a) Explain what is meant by a market economy and consider the extent to which it is an accurate description of your country's economy. (12)

   (b) Discuss the economic problems that are likely to occur as a country moves from central planning towards a market economy. (13) *Cambridge*

Pitfalls

When answering questions such as Question 1, all too often candidates rewrite the question as 'Write all you know firstly about market economies and then about command economies'. Similarly, when asked to describe the main features of a mixed economy, candidates write two separate accounts of market and mixed economies and complete their answers with the statement that 'a mixed economy is half way between the two'. At best, such answers will only secure a low pass mark. 1(a) asks for a comparison, so you must avoid the temptation to write two separate accounts. The key concepts in 1(b) are resource allocation and efficiency; you must relate your answer to allocative efficiency (which is explained in Chapter 7), taking care not to drift into a general account of all the various ways in which economists use the word efficiency. Questions 2 and 3 ask you to apply the concepts of mixed and market economies to the analysis of real world economies. You must show some awareness of how economies change over time and of the problems that change brings about. Your answer to Question 2 should show awareness of how the nature of the mix of the UK mixed economy has changed over the years. With 3(b), you must not restrict your answer to an explanation of the standard market failures which occur in a market economy (see Chapter 9); you must go a stage further and relate these to the processs of change in the former command economies of eastern Europe.

Key points

All three questions centre on the way resources are allocated (or misallocated) in an economic system, so this theme must run through all three of your answers. Explaining how the price mechanism allocates scarce resources amongst competing uses must figure strongly in your answers to Questions 1 and 3. Go on to explain (in your answer to the second part of Question 1) the criterion for efficient resource allocation, namely that the price charged to consumers must equal the marginal cost of production (P = MC) in all markets. With Question 2, you could debate the view that the mix of private and public sector production and market and non-market provision deemed efficient a generation ago, might have become inefficient. If so, this would provide justification for the shift of the mix away from public sector and non-market provision towards greater reliance on markets and private enterprise. However, greater reliance on market forces is not without problems. Your answer to 3(b) could discuss the problems now being experienced in the east European ex-command economies – the problems of establishing the culture, legal framework and institutions necessary for a successful market economy, as well as the problems relating to the standard market failures explained in Chapters 7, 8 and 9.

PRICE DETERMINATION

Units in this chapter

Chapter objectives

In Chapter 1 a market economy was defined as an economic system in which the price mechanism allocates scarce resources amongst competing uses. In this chapter, the functioning of the price mechanism in a single market within a market economy is examined. Two very important concepts which recur in later chapters, namely **equilibrium** and **disequilibrium**, are introduced and the chapter outlines how, when there is disequilibrium in a market evidenced by excess demand or excess supply, the price adjusts to restore market equilibrium. The chapter concludes by explaining how an equilibrium may be disturbed by a shift of a supply or demand curve, and how in this situation, a new equilibrium will be established at a different price and with a different quantity bought and sold.

2.1 MARKETS, SUPPLY AND DEMAND

MARKETS AND PRICES

In Chapter 1 we defined a market as a voluntary meeting of buyers and sellers for the purpose of trading or exchanging a good or service. We also explained that within a market, prices serve the important functions of:

- **signalling** the information which allows all the traders in the market to plan and co-ordinate their economic activities;
- **creating incentives** for buyers and sellers to behave in a manner which allows the market to operate in an orderly and efficient manner; and
- **rationing and allocating** scarce resources between competing uses.

THE GOODS MARKET AND THE FACTOR MARKET

You will have noticed from the preceding section that both households and firms are simultaneously operating within two sets of markets. On the one hand, consuming households face business enterprises in the retail or goods market, where households are the source of demand. For this demand to be an **effective demand** (demand backed up by money), the households must sell their labour services in the labour market, where it is now the firms who exercise demand. Although a market economy will usually be made up of a vast number of different and often specialised markets, for many purposes we can generalise and consider just a **goods market** and a **factor market** (one where households sell the services of the labour and capital they own) – the two markets being linked together through the decisions of both households and firms.

DEMAND AND SUPPLY CURVES

For the rest of the chapter we shall ignore the factor market and restrict ourselves to exploring in greater detail the process of price determination within a single market in the goods market. Fig. 2.1 illustrates the essential features of such a market.

A **demand curve** D_1 represents household or consumer behaviour in the market, while the **supply curve** S_1 maps out the supply decisions of firms. You will notice that the downward-sloping demand curve shows that consumers demand more of a good at low prices than at high prices. Be very careful of how you interpret this. It is insufficient to say that a demand curve slopes downwards because more is demanded at low prices than at high prices; we need to go further than this and to 'get behind' the demand curve by developing a theory of consumer behaviour to explain demand. This is done in Chapter 3. In a similar way, Chapter 4 develops a theory of the behaviour of firms to get behind the supply curve and explain supply. For the time being, however, we shall accept that for the most part, demand curves slope downwards and supply curves slope upwards.

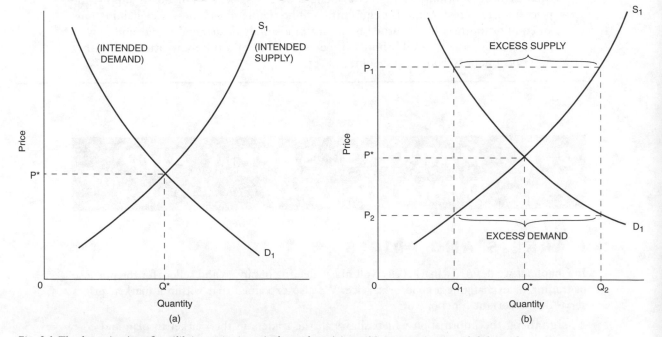

Fig. 2.1 The determination of equilibrium price in a single market: (a) equilibrium requires intended demand to equal intended supply; (b) the price mechanism ensures convergence towards equilibrium

MARKET PLANS AND MARKET ACTION

The distinction between **market plans** and **market action** is of crucial importance to a proper understanding of the way a market works, yet it is a distinction which appears unknown to a significant proportion of candidates at A Level. A demand curve, such as D_1 in Fig. 2.1, shows how much of a good all the consumers in the market intend to demand at the various possible prices. **Intended demand** is also known as **planned demand** or **ex ante demand**. Similarly, the supply curve S_1 shows intended supply (planned supply or ex ante supply). It is easy to show that, at almost all prices, it is impossible for both the firms and the consumers to fulfil their plans simultaneously. Suppose that for some reason the price in the market is P_1, as represented in Fig. 2.1b. Firms would like to supply quantity Q_2 at this price, but households are only willing to purchase Q_1: intended supply is greater than intended demand and **excess supply** results.

You should now ask yourself what will be the quantity actually traded if the price remains at P_1. The answer is quantity Q_1. The amount bought is Q_1, and the amount sold is Q_1; the two are the same, as indeed they must be. Now the amount bought is just another name for **realised demand** (actual demand or ex post demand), and the amount sold is another name for **realised supply** (**actual supply** or **ex post supply**). It follows that realised demand will always equal realised supply whatever the price. This represents an **identity**.

THE CONCEPT OF EQUILIBRIUM

The concept of equilibrium is of the utmost importance in economic theory and analysis. Equilibrium is a **state of rest**, when there is no reason for anything to change unless disturbed by an outside shock. Households and firms will be in equilibrium if they can both fulfil their market plans. In Fig. 2.1b, the price P_1 is not an equilibrium price because the firms are unable to fulfil their plans at this price. Realised demand, of course, equals realised supply at Q_1, but this is largely irrelevant: the crucial point is that intended supply is greater than intended demand at this price.

We now introduce a very important assumption about economic behaviour, which will recur throughout the book: if any economic agent (such as a household or firm) is unable to fulfil its market plans, a reason exists for it to change its market behaviour. At the price of P_1 in Fig. 2.1b, the firms are unable to fulfil their market plans. If firms react to their unsold stocks (or excess supply) by reducing the price that they are prepared to accept, then the market will **converge** towards the equilibrium price.

Similarly, if the initial price is P_2 in Fig.2.1b, it may be supposed that the households, who are unable to fulfil their market plans at this price, will bid up the price to eliminate the excess demand in the market.

The equilibrium price, P^*, is the only price which is consistent with the market plans of both households and firms, who consequently have no reason to change their plans. At the equilibrium price, intended demand = intended supply. This is often known as the **equilibrium condition** to clear the market; it must not be confused with the identity: realised demand $\equiv$ realised supply.

To summarise the main conclusions of this very important section of the chapter:

① if intended supply > intended demand, price will fall (disequilibrium condition);

② if intended supply < intended demand, price will rise (disequilibrium condition);

③ if intended supply = intended demand, price stays the same (equilibrium condition);

④ realised supply $\equiv$ realised demand, at all prices (identity).

SHIFTS IN DEMAND AND SUPPLY

When we draw a demand curve to show how much of a product households intend to demand at the various possible prices, it is assumed that all the other variables which may also influence intended demand are held unchanged or constant. This is known as the *ceteris paribus* assumption. (In economic shorthand we write: $Q=f(P)$, ceteris paribus.) In a similar way, all the other variables which may influence supply are held constant when a supply curve is drawn. Common sense suggests that household income and fashion will influence demand, and costs of production will affect supply decisions, but you should refer to Chapters 3 and 4 for a more detailed explanation. In this section, we shall restrict the analysis to a brief investigation of a change in the **conditions of demand**, when one of the variables which influences demand is assumed to change. The reader should have little difficulty in extending the analysis to a change in the conditions of supply.

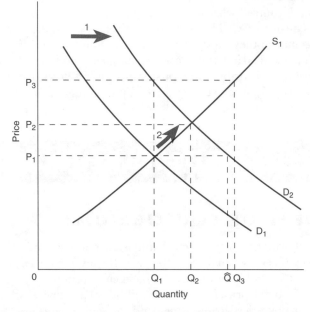

Fig. 2.2 The effect of a shift in the demand curve within a single market

In Fig. 2.2, the demand curve D_1 and the supply curve S_1 are drawn to show the initial condition of supply and demand. The equilibrium price which clears the market is at P_1, where quantity Q_1 is traded. A successful advertising campaign persuades households to demand more at all prices and the demand curve shifts upwards (or rightwards) to D_2 (arrow 1). At the existing price of P_1, households now demand $\hat{Q}$. But because conditions of supply have not changed, firms still only intend to supply Q_1 at this price, which is therefore no longer an equilibrium price. Excess demand exists in the market.

It is worthwhile at this point to take a closer look at how the price mechanism eliminates excess demand. If the firms are unable to increase supply immediately, the supply curve will be temporarily vertical and the price will be bid up to P_3. (Chapter 4 explains how supply is completely **inelastic** in the momentary time period.) In the short run, however, firms will respond to the incentive provided by P_3 and increase supply as soon as they can. An adjustment in supply, in response to price, takes place along the supply curve (arrow 2). If the price remained at P_3, the firms would be prepared to supply Q_3. If this amount is released onto the market the price will fall, as the consumers will only take Q_1 at this price. The price falls to the new market–clearing equilibrium at P_2.

Chapter roundup

The next seven chapters develop important aspects of the basic single-market supply and demand model which has been described in this chapter. In particular, Chapters 3 and 4 explain demand and supply curves, and Chapter 5 introduces the concept of elasticity. The other chapters investigate how markets may function when different assumptions are made about market circumstances – time-lags in the supply of agricultural products, producer power, barriers to entry, perfect and imperfect information, etc. Finally, Chapter 9 investigates various circumstances, known as 'market failure', in which the price mechanism fails to perform satisfactorily, resulting in resource misallocation.

Illustrative questions and answers

1 Essay Question

(a) Explain why, in principle, the price mechanism performs both a 'rationing' and a 'signalling' function. (10)

(b) Explain why each of the following phenomena may be explained by the absence of, or restrictions on, the operation of the price mechanism:
    (i)   Waiting lists for certain operations in the National Health Service. (5)
    (ii) Surplus stocks of farm commodities subject to the EC Common Agricultural Policy. (5)
    (iii) Traffic congestion at peak times on city centre roads. (5)   *WJEC*

Tutorial note

(a) Draw a supply and demand diagram to show a market in disequilibrium, with the price set below the equilibrium or market-clearing price. Explain the resulting excess demand at this price, and how in a free market situation the price will rise to eliminate the excess demand and restore equilibrium. This illustrates the rationing function of the price mechanism. The signalling function of the price mechanism is best explained by introducing more than one market into your analysis. You could assume, for example, that a successful advertising campaign or a change in fashion has recently made a good – say training shoes – more popular, thus shifting the demand curve rightwards. The price would then rise, signalling to firms in other markets and industries that high profits might be made by producing trainers. In response to this incentive signalled by the high price, firms would shift resources into the production of training shoes. This would cause the supply curve also to shift rightwards, which in turn would bring down the price of trainers. At this point you could return to the rationing function of the price mechanism, since the process you have described illustrates how the price mechanism allocates and rations society's scarce resources between different types of production, and ultimately consumption.

(b) (i) As explained in Chapter 9, the government may decide to provide certain types of goods, known as **merit goods**, free for the consumer. Health care is an example. By providing many health care services at zero price, the government has decided to by-pass the price mechanism as a method of allocating resources, but it has not abolished scarcity. **Quantity rationing** (e.g. via queues, waiting lists and assessment of degree of need) have replaced prices as the mechanism for rationing scarce resources between competing uses.

(ii) European Union butter and grain mountains and wine lakes, etc. illustrate one of the problems facing governments when they try to stabilise agricultural prices. The EU offers a guaranteed price for certain agricultural products, which is sufficient to earn the farmer **supernormal profits** (see Chapter 7). Guaranteed prices and supernormal profits create signals and incentives for farmers to increase production, knowing that the EU will buy all they produce. As a result the rationing function of the price mechanism does not perform properly; continuing overproduction results, which must be destroyed, stored, or converted to an alternative use, e.g. famine relief. See Chapter 6 for further details.

(iii) Traffic congestion at peak times on city roads represents another case of a **market failure** which are explained in Chapter 9. Congestion is an example of what economists call a **negative externality** or **external cost**. In the absence of a system of road pricing such as tolls, motorists who cause congestion fail to pay a price for motoring which reflects the true cost of their use of the road. While they pay for petrol and for the wear and tear of their own vehicles, they do not pay a price for the congestion they cause other road users to suffer. As a result, motoring in congested areas is underpriced; the price of motoring is sending out the wrong signals, encouraging too many cars to use the roads, thus causing congestion.

'Overconsumption' by motorists also means that the rationing function of the price mechanism is not working properly; too many scarce resources are being used by motorists at the expense of their use in other markets and industries.

2   Data Question

ANOTHER PLUNGE IN THE PRICE OF COCOA

We are eating more chocolate every year, but the price of cocoa plunges ever lower. On the London market yesterday, beans could be bought for May delivery at £6.13 per tonne, the lowest market price in real terms for more than 14 years. World consumption, about 2.2 million tonnes a year, keeps hitting new records; yet production is growing even faster. The result has been surpluses for the past six seasons. Oversupply of cocoa is good news for big chocolate eaters such as the British and the Swiss. Countries in Eastern Europe and the Soviet Union have a per capita cocoa consumption which is a third of Britain's and there is the possibility of expanding markets outside the chocolate industry, for instance in pharmaceuticals and cosmetics. Chocolate prices generally have not been cut and are unlikely to be, say industry sources. This is because cocoa accounts for perhaps no more than 10 per cent of the cost of a bar of chocolate, the rest being sugar, powdered milk, labour and other costs. Years of glut have helped chocolate makers to keep their prices remarkably stable worldwide, so boosting purchases. However, the impact of low cocoa prices has been devastating for the economies of the big producers such as the heavily indebted Ivory Coast and Ghana, which rely on bean exports as the main source of revenue.

(Source: *The Guardian*, February 1990)

1   What does the writer mean by the phrase 'the lowest market price in real terms'? (line 3)   (2)

2   Explain and illustrate, using demand and supply analysis, why the market price of cocoa has been falling.   (4)

3   Discuss the factors which are likely to influence the price manufacturers of chocolate charge for their products.   (8)

4   What actions could the major cocoa producers take to protect their economies from the situation described in the passage?   (6)   AEB

Tutorial note

1   Economists distinguish between **nominal prices** and **real prices**. Nominal prices (which are also known as **money prices**) are simply the prices you pay for a good, for example in a shop. By contrast, a real price is measured by taking inflation into account. Suppose, for example, that the UK market price of cocoa (which is a nominal price) rose by 3% between 1990 and 1991, but that inflation was 7%. Then in real terms the price would have fallen by 4%!

2   The information in the passage certainly indicates that the world supply curve of cocoa has shifted rightwards. The demand curve (exercised by chocolate manufacturers) has probably also shifted rightwards, but not to the same extent. The net effect is thus for the market price to fall.

3   Discuss both cost factors and the market power (on the demand side) of the chocolate manufacturers. The passage indicates that chocolate prices have remained stable (which given the rate of inflation, means that in real terms chocolate prices have

fallen, but not by as much as cocoa prices). Falling cocoa prices, amounting to about 10% of total production costs, may have been balanced by increases in other costs of production, e.g. labour. Another possibility is that the chocolate manufacturers have sufficient market power to maintain the price of chocolate, thereby benefiting from bigger profit margins as a result of reduced raw material costs. Finally, you could bring in the concept of **price elasticity of demand** (see Chapter 5). Consumers may not be very sensitive to the price of chocolate (i.e. demand may be inelastic), and particularly for luxury brands, they may sometimes regard a high price as a sign of quality and exclusivity.

4   Cocoa growers might form a worldwide producers' organisation which would attempt to restrict output, for example by assigning a quota or production limit to each country. Governments rather than individual farmers would have to organise the scheme. The success of such a producers' 'cartel' would be aided by the fact that there is no substitute for cocoa (as, for example, synthetic rubber is a substitute for natural rubber), but there might be great difficulty in getting the participation (without cheating) of all the cocoa producers in the world. The cocoa-producing countries might also try to diversify their economies in order to become less dependent on cocoa exports (see also Chapter 6).

Question bank

1   (a) In a market economy prices:
   (i)   give signals to participants in the economy;
   (ii) act as a rationing device;
   (iii) provide incentives.
   Explain **each** of these functions. (12)

   (b) Evaluate the economic arguments **for** and **against** introducing a system where schools charge their own fees and the government gives parents a voucher for each child which is used to contribute towards school fees. (13)   *AEB*

Pitfalls

(a) is straightforward in that the three functions of prices are clearly stated. However, each must be explained and illustrated at some length, and care must be taken to balance the answer. With (b), you must obey the instruction to 'evaluate'; a simple list of advantages and disadvantages is not enough. There is a danger of writing all you know about every aspect of supply and demand, so make sure you adapt your knowledge to the particular needs of the question. You must avoid the temptation to write an overtly political essay, though you might reasonably make the point that the introduction of educational vouchers is a politically controversial issue.

Key points

Explain how, by providing information about what is available at what price, prices create incentives for people to behave in particular ways. Households and firms respectively alter their demand and supply decisions in response to price changes, and through this process scarce resources are allocated amongst competing uses – the allocative or rationing function of prices. Start your answer to (b) by explaining how vouchers create an internal market within the educational system. Relate this to the three functions of prices explained in your answer to (a). Go on to outline at least two advantages and disadvantages of educational vouchers. Advantages relate to consumer choice and increased parental ability to shop around amongst schools, and the incentive for schools to improve in order to attract customers and voucher income. Disadvantages include the fact that vouchers favour schools in good catchment areas which already find it easy to attract pupils. Schools in deprived areas might lose voucher income and enter a spiral of decline, exacerbating the social and economic problems of the neighbourhood and widening inequalities. Finally, indicate whether, in your opinion, the advantages of a voucher system exceed the disadvantages.

2 'Government intervention into the free working of the price mechanism causes disruption and can lead to shortages and gluts.'

(a) Explain how the price of a good in a free market will settle at the equilibrium level. (10)

(b) (i) Explain how the granting of a government subsidy on a good will affect the equilibrium price and quantity of that good. (8)

(ii) Explain how the imposition of a maximum price can disrupt the market for a good. (8)

(iii) Give **one** reason why governments might grant a subsidy and **one** reason why they might impose a maximum price. (4)

[Diagrams may be useful in answering this question] *SEB*

Pitfalls

You must include at least one relevant diagram in each of your answers to (a), (b) (i) and (ii) of the question. A failure to use diagrams in your answer will lead to lower marks, but remember that diagrams should complement and not simply repeat your written answers. When answering (b) (iii), you could give the same reason for granting a subsidy *and* imposing a maximum price (to reduce the price of the good); however, it is better to think of two different reasons, for example the boosting of producers' incomes in the case of a subsidy.

Key points

Explain (and illustrate) the concept of market equilibrium, but make sure you devote most of your answer to (a) to explaining the process through which equilibrium is achieved (the elimination of excess demand or excess supply in the market). In your answer to (b), explain how, by shifting the supply curve rightwards, the granting of a subsidy disturbs a previously achieved equilibrium and triggers a fall in price and establishment of a new equilibrium. By contrast, the imposition of a maximum price prevents the price rising to eliminate excess demand, providing the maximum price is set below the market-clearing or equilibrium price.

3 (a) How can the changes in house prices which have occurred in recent years be explained? (15)

(b) Discuss the effects of these changes upon the United Kingdom economy. (10)

AEB

Pitfalls

The question does not tell you how house prices have changed in recent years, so it would not be sensible to answer this question if you are completely ignorant of property prices and how they have fluctuated. It is probably best to interpret 'recent years' as referring to the last ten years or so. You must avoid relying solely on a common sense approach; at least some economic theory, albeit combined with sensible application, is needed to secure a good pass mark. (a) is about causes, while (b) is about effects; make sure you don't confuse the two.

Key points

Identify the fact that in the UK, house prices rose at a much faster rate than inflation in general in the late 1980s, before stagnating and falling in the early and mid 1990s. Make the point that prices can change as a result of the demand curve shifting, the supply curve shifting, or both curves shifting. Shifts of demand (up and down a relatively steep and inelastic supply curve) provide the main explanation of recent house price changes. Make sure you explain the roles of the availability of credit (in the form of mortgage finance), investment and speculation in determining the demand for housing.

DEMAND

Units in this chapter

Chapter objectives

In this chapter we 'go behind' the market demand curve in order to demonstrate how its shape and essential characteristics are derived from basic economic principles, and from a set of initial assumptions about how consumers behave. Different assumptions about consumer behaviour lead to differently shaped demand curves, so that although conventional downward-sloping demand curves are normally to be expected, it is best to avoid describing this characteristic as a 'law' of demand (which suggests a misleading inevitability about the existence of downward-sloping demand curves).

3.1   EXPLAINING THE SHAPE OF THE DEMAND CURVE

MARKET DEMAND AND INDIVIDUAL DEMAND

Students often confuse the **market** (or industry) demand curve, which shows how much of a commodity all the consumers in the market intend to buy at all possible prices, and the **individual demand** curve of a single consumer or household in the market. The relationship between the two is very simple: the market demand curve is obtained by adding up all the individual demand curves for every consumer in the market. Henceforth in this chapter, 'demand' will mean individual demand rather than market demand. It will also mean **effective demand** – a demand backed by purchasing power or money.

THE UTILITY APPROACH AND THE INDIFFERENCE CURVE APPROACH

Two different methods can be used to derive demand curves from a set of initial assumptions – the **utility approach** and the **indifference curve approach**. While both approaches lead to the same conclusions, the indifference curve method is preferred at a university level because it is more rigorous and the technique can be extended to other aspects of advanced economic theory. However, at the school or college level, our experience is that students are far better advised to learn simple theories well rather than risk fouling up a more complicated, if academically respectable, theory. For this reason, only the utility approach is explained in this chapter. You should also check whether the derivation of demand curves is required by your examination board; for example, the AEB and Cambridge modular syllabuses no longer require candidates to derive demand curves, though knowledge of related concepts such as utility and consumer surplus is still required.

UTILITY MAXIMISATION

The assumption which underlies demand theory is that consumers always seek in the market place to maximise the total **utility** they obtain from the set of goods they buy. Utility cannot be seen, touched, or even properly measured. It is sometimes defined as the pleasure which a consumer obtains from using a good or service. However, it really means rather more than this. Some goods, such as medicine for example, are consumed because they **fulfil a need** rather than because they give the consumer direct pleasure. The assumption of **utility maximisation** also implies that consumers act **rationally**, which in the sense used here means that people act in their own self-interest.

THE EXISTENCE OF CONSTRAINTS

If consumers had unlimited income, or if all goods were free, a consumer would maximise utility by obtaining those goods which gave utility up to the point of **satiation**. However, all but a few lucky and very wealthy consumers face a number of constraints which limit their freedom of action in the market place. The principal constraints are:

- **Limited income**. Consumers do not possess unlimited means with which to purchase all the goods which would give them utility. The **opportunity cost** to a consumer of choosing one good is the lost opportunity to choose the next best alternative. (Note that the assumption of rationality implies that the 'best' alternative will always be chosen.) A limited income constrains a consumer's freedom of choice, and so, together with the given set of prices the consumer faces, it imposes a **budget constraint** on his market action.

- **The consumer faces a given set of prices**. A single consumer is unable to influence the market prices of any of the goods he might wish to buy: he is a **price-taker** rather than a **price-maker**.

- **Tastes and preferences are fixed**. A consumer who prefers Good A to Good B today will also prefer Good A tomorrow: the consumer is said to behave *consistently* if his preferences are stable over time.

MAXIMISING V MINIMISING BEHAVIOUR

Demand theory is thus concerned with the way in which a consumer with a limited income and fixed tastes behaves in the face of changing prices. The consumer attempts to maximise a desired objective (utility), subject to a set of constraints. The assumption of maximising or minimising behaviour (on the part of consumers, firms, workers and even perhaps the government) is central to orthodox microeconomic theory. You should note that a **maximising objective** can always be rewritten in minimising terms. We can rewrite the consumer's assumed objective 'to maximise the utility obtained from a purchased bundle of goods' as: 'to minimise the outlay, expenditure or cost of obtaining the same set of goods'. They are different sides of the same coin.

Whether we set up an assumed objective in maximising or minimising terms depends upon our convenience; we can do either. The reader will find further examples of maximising and minimising behaviour in later chapters, for example in Chapters 7, 8 and 11.

DIMINISHING MARGINAL UTILITY

The principle of diminishing marginal utility states that although the total utility derived from a good increases with the amount consumed, it does so at a decreasing rate. It is quite possible that a person may experience increasing marginal utility when more of a good is consumed, at least for the first few units of that good. This is why we refer to diminishing marginal utility as a **principle** rather than as a **law**. The principle is illustrated in Fig. 3.1. The upward (or positive) slope of the total utility curve in Fig. 3.1a indicates that **total utility** rises with consumption. The last unit purchased is always the **marginal unit**, so the utility derived from it is the **marginal utility**. (Formally, the marginal utility derived from the n'th unit = the total utility of n units minus the total utility of (n–1) units. If 20 units are consumed, n = 20.) You will notice that the principle of diminishing marginal utility is shown by the **diminishing rate of increase** of the slope of the total utility curve in Fig. 3.1a. The marginal utility derived from each unit of consumption is plotted separately in Fig. 3.1b. The principle of diminishing marginal utility is represented by the negative or downward slope of the curve in this diagram.

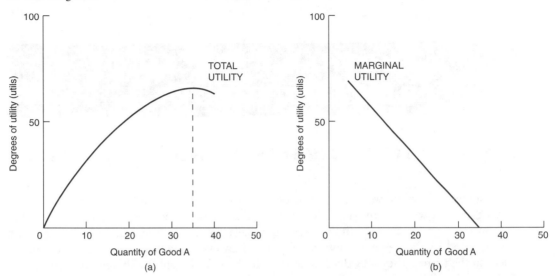

Fig. 3.1 Utility curves (a) total utility rises at a diminishing rate as an individual's consumption of Good A increases (b) this can also be shown by a marginal utility curve – note that at the peak of the total utility curve, marginal utility drops to zero

CONSUMER EQUILIBRIUM AND THE DERIVATION OF THE DEMAND CURVE

A consumer, constrained by limited income, fixed tastes and the prices which he faces in the market place, will continue to buy units of a commodity until the marginal utility which he gains is the same as that he could have obtained by spending a similar amount of money on another commodity. To put it another way, he should purchase or demand a good up to the point at which the marginal utility derived from the last unit of the good consumed equals the good's price, i.e. until MU = P. With respect to any good such as chocolate, a newspaper or a soft drink, to maximise utility, a consumer must demand a good up to the point at which MU = P. This is known as an equilibrium condition. It is an easy matter to extend the analysis to the case where a consumer buys many commodities. Successive units will be bought of each commodity to the point where its marginal utility equals its price. This can be rearranged as a multi-commodity equilibrium condition:

$$\frac{\text{Marginal Utility of Good A}}{\text{Price of A}} = \frac{\text{Marginal Utility of Good B}}{\text{Price of B}} = \frac{\text{Marginal Utility of any Good}}{\text{Price of any Good}}$$

Suppose that a consumer can only choose between Good A and Good B and he starts off from a position of consumer equilibrium. At existing prices he is satisfied with the combination of Goods A and B that he buys. The price of Good A now falls, and the situation can now be represented by:

$$\frac{\text{M.U. of Good A}}{\text{Price of A}} > \frac{\text{M.U. of Good B}}{\text{Price of B}}$$

The consumer is no longer in equilibrium: he would be better off substituting more of the good whose relative price has fallen for a good whose relative price is now higher. He is not now maximising utility, and so he has a motive for changing his market behaviour.

When he consumes more of Good A, and less of Good B, he moves down the marginal utility curve for Good A, and back up the marginal utility curve for Good B. As he substitutes more of Good A for less of Good B, the marginal utilities adjust until he is once again in equilibrium, when no alternative reallocation will increase his total utility. The equilibrium is achieved at a point of equi-marginal utility, where the marginal utility derived from each good as a ratio of its price is the same for all goods. The essential point is that more is demanded of the good whose relative price has fallen. The **substitution** effect, whereby consumers substitute more of a good whose relative price has fallen for goods whose relative price has risen, helps to explain the downward-sloping demand curve.

3.2 FURTHER ASPECTS OF DEMAND THEORY

THE SUBSTITUTION EFFECT AND THE INCOME EFFECT

If consumer behaviour was determined only by the substitution effect of a price change, demand curves would only slope downwards. This is provided that customers are utility maximisers who experience diminishing marginal utility, and assuming also that they are uninfluenced by future uncertainty or by status. However, if consumers expect even higher prices in the future, they may demand more at high prices for speculative reasons. Similarly, if a high price indicates status, 'status maximisers' may be expected to demand more of a good at higher prices.

When we introduce the **income effect** of a price change, matters become rather more complicated. If the price of one good falls, a consumer's **real income** rises. The nature of this income effect depends upon whether the good is a **normal good** or an **inferior good**. If expenditure on a good rises when a consumer's real income rises, then the good is a normal one. Conversely, if expenditure on the good falls when income rises, then that good is classed as inferior. It is important to stress that the same good can, for a particular individual, switch from being normal to inferior as his income rises. Suppose that the Income-Expenditure graph in Fig. 3.2a represents an individual's expenditure on bus travel at different levels of real income. When the person is poor, his expenditure on bus travel rises as his income rises: bus travel is a normal good. But beyond the level of income Y_1, bus travel becomes an inferior good, presumably because the person can now afford to travel by car.

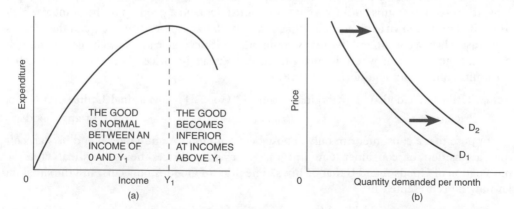

Fig. 3.2 The effects of income on demand (a) an income expenditure curve for a good which is inferior at high levels of income (b) a shift in the price demand curve for a normal good following an increase in income

For normal goods, the substitution effect of a price change is reinforced by the income effect, and the two effects together explain the downward-sloping demand curve. But in the case of inferior goods, the income effect works in the opposite direction to the substitution effect. The income effect is, however, likely to be much smaller than the substitution effect, because expenditure on a single good is probably only a tiny proportion of a consumer's total spending; real income hardly alters at all if the price of a single good changes. Nevertheless, a theoretical possibility exists that the income effect of a price change will not only be in the opposite direction to the substitution effect but that it will also be stronger. This is the special case of an inferior good known as a **Giffen good** – less of a Giffen good is demanded as the price falls, hence the demand curve slopes upward.

SHIFTS OF DEMAND

In the previous section, the analysis explains how a change in real income, resulting from a change in the price of a good, influences the shape of the demand curve. It is important to separate this effect from the effects of a change in real income which is independent of a change in the good's own price. If a person's real disposable income rises as a result of a wage increase or a cut in income tax, then the demand curve of each of the goods that the person buys may shift. If the good is a normal one, the demand curve will shift to the right (or upwards) and more will be demanded at every price. This is illustrated in Fig. 3.2b. In the case of an inferior good, however, a rise in real income causes the demand curve to shift to the left (or downwards).

A change in real disposable income is only one of the possible causes of a shift in the demand curve. In general, a change in any of the constraints facing the consumer (sometimes known as the **conditions of demand**) will shift the demand curve. The good's own price is not listed as one of the conditions of demand because the demand curve is itself a 'map' showing how demand responds to price changes. However, changes in the price of a **complementary** or **substitute good** will normally shift a demand curve. Most people in Britain regard bread and butter as complementary goods. If the price of bread rises, the demand curve for butter will probably shift to the left and less butter will be demanded at all prices. Conversely, a rise in the price of a substitute for butter, such as margarine, will normally cause the demand curve for butter to shift rightwards.

The time-period under consideration will also influence demand. Strictly speaking, the horizontal axis of a demand graph should specify the time-period for which demand is being measured. If the time-period is changed, for example from monthly to yearly demand, the ability of consumers to respond to a change in price will also alter. This aspect of demand theory will be investigated in Chapter 5.

CONSUMER SURPLUS

The concept of consumer surplus is illustrated in Fig. 3.3, which shows the market demand curve of all the consumers in the market.

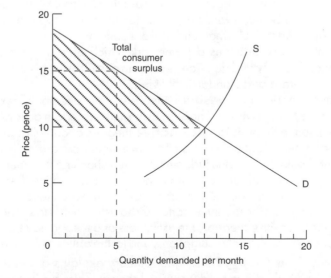

Fig. 3.3 Consumer surplus: the shaded area shows total consumer surplus when the market price is 10 pence

In Fig. 3.3, the equilibrium price of 10 pence is the price which every consumer in the market pays for the good in question. It is also the price which the marginal consumer is only just prepared to pay in order to obtain the good. If the price rose above 10 pence, the marginal consumer would either drop out of the market or reduce his demand. However, some consumers, who value the good more highly, would be prepared to pay 15 pence for it. They gain a consumer surplus (or surplus utility) equal to the difference between what they would be prepared to pay and what they actually need to pay. The total consumer surplus, the utility which consumers enjoy but do not pay for, is shown by the shaded area of the graph.

Chapter roundup

Although the determination of the shape of the demand curve has been the central theme of this chapter, we have largely ignored a very important aspect of the shape·and slope of demand curves: the concept of elasticity of demand. Chapter 5 should be regarded as a very useful follow-up to this chapter.

In this chapter we have dealt only with the microeconomic theory of consumer behaviour – how consumers choose between alternative goods and services. The macroeconomic theory of consumption (covered in Chapter 14) explains how consumers divide their limited income between aggregate consumption on all goods and saving. Although economists agree that a sound macroeconomic theory should be based firmly on microeconomic foundations, students are often confused by the parallel existence of micro- and macro-consumption theory. Think carefully about the context of the question, when you decide how to structure and plan your answer to a question on consumer behaviour.

Illustrative questions and answers

1   Essay Question

What is the purpose of economic theory? Is it necessary for consumers, firms and governments to have an economic theory in order to make rational decisions? (25)

NEAB

Tutorial note

Economic theory has two main purposes. Firstly, it provides a 'tool kit' enabling economists to explain the working of both the whole economy (at the macro-level), and of the markets, industries, firms and individuals that undertake economic activity at the micro-level. Secondly, economic theory provides a framework which aids governments, firms and individuals in economic policy and decision making, in pursuit of the objectives of improving people's economic welfare and standards of living.

Most economic theories are **positive** theories: they attempt to explain how the economy works and to predict what will happen in the future if certain actions are taken now. However some economic theories are **normative** theories about what ought to happen: a theory of optimal government policy is a normative theory because it is concerned with how a government should make value judgements when choosing between different policy options. The theory of demand (or consumer behaviour) is a positive theory: the problem or puzzle to be explained is how consumers make decisions when faced with the choice of how to spend their incomes. (The theory does not say how they *ought* to spend their incomes.) Restricting ourselves to positive theories, the usefulness of a theory may be judged by three criteria: (a) relevance; (b) realism of assumptions; and (c) the ability to survive empirical tests.

(a) **How relevant is a theory?** If a 'good' theory explains a trivial problem of no interest to anybody, then it is hardly a useful theory. This, for instance, is the basic Marxist criticism of orthodox economics. Marxists argue that orthodox economics is dominated by the study of the 'uninteresting' problem of individual behaviour in a 'timeless' economy, thereby sidestepping the interesting problems (to a Marxist) of how a capitalist economy comes into existence and changes over time, and the economic relations between *classes* (as distinct from relations between *individuals*).

(b) **How realistic are the theory's assumptions?** All economic theories involve a set of *simplifying assumptions* about economic relationships or how people behave. Thus, in demand theory, economists assume that consumers have the single aim of utility maximisation. This is obviously a simplifying assumption as sometimes people will have other aims, but it may still be a useful way of simplifying.

(c) **Can a theory survive empirical tests?** The *predictions* (or *implications*) of a theory follow logically from its initial assumptions. Thus demand theory predicts a downward-sloping demand curve, but if the initial assumption in the construction of the theory had been that people are status maximisers and that status is indicated by a high price, then the theory would predict an upward-sloping demand curve, showing people demanding more of a good as the price rises. Such a theory would be unlikely to survive an empirical test, except perhaps as a special case. *Empirical testing* means that the predictions of a theory are tested against observed behaviour in the real world. Useful theories survive the process of empirical testing, whereas theories whose predictions are plainly at odds with observed behaviour are discarded.

As we have seen in this chapter, to succeed in maximising utility, a household must consume a good up to the point at which MU = P. However, a consumer does not need direct knowledge of this 'marginalist rule', or to have studied an economics course for the theory and the assumption to have relevance. The theory provides an explanation of how people behave, but it not a blueprint that the people themselves must possess to guide rational decision making. However, possession of at least some theoretical understanding can often aid rational decision making. Suppose, for example, that snow and ice are forecast for the next month. A consumer who realises that adverse weather is likely to reduce the supply of fresh vegetables and cause their prices to rise, may well decide to stock up now when vegetables are readily available and prices are low. Consumers who do not understand this basic relationship between supply, demand and prices will fare less well.

Suggested answer

- Explain the purpose of economic theory which we have described.
- Illustrate with a selection of economic theories. Indicate that not all theories are necessarily correct or useful. An incorrect theory may do more harm than good if used as a guide for decision making.
- Explain that economic agents can act rationally, i.e. in pursuit of self-interest, without explicit knowledge of economic theory. Nevertheless some theoretical knowledge might improve the decision-making process. Give examples.

2 Data Question

Study the tables below and, using your knowledge of economics, answer the questions which follow.

Passenger Transport

Table 1 Use and prices

	1981	1986	1988	1989
Use: billion passenger kilometres travelled by;				
Rail	34	37	41	41
Road: Buses and coaches	42	41	41	40
Cars, taxis, and two-wheeled motor vehicles	409	470	526	563
TOTAL	485	548	608	644

Retail price indices (Jan 1987 = 100)				
Bus and coach fares	69	98	111	119
Rail fares	69	96	108	117
Motoring expenditure	82	98	108	114
Retail prices (all items)	75	98	107	115

Table 2 *Transport, expenditure and income*

	1981	1984	1986	1989
Consumer expenditure per head on: (£ per week at 1985 prices)				
Net purchase of motor vehicles, spares and accessories	2.86	3.34	3.82	4.83
Maintenance and running costs of motor vehicles	4.36	4.81	5.24	6.26
Railway fares	0.46	0.49	0.52	0.55
Bus and coach fares	0.69	0.65	0.62	0.61
Expenditure on transport and vehicles as a *percentage* of total consumers' expenditure	14.6	15.1	15.3	16.2
Real household disposable income per head: (Index numbers 1985 = 100)	92	96	106	123

Source: Adapted from *Social Trends 21*, 1991;
reproduced with the permission of the Controller of HMSO and the
Office for National Statistics

Using the data in Table 1:

(a) (i) Compare the changes in the use of public transport* with the changes in the use of private transport**.

    (ii) Describe the changes in public tranport use as a percentage of total transport use.

    (3)

(b) (i) Use the data for 1981 and 1989 in Table 1 to compare the changes in the prices of public transport, motoring expenditure and the retail price index. (2)

    (ii) What would happen to the quantity demanded of a product if its price relative to that of other goods changes? (2)

    (iii) To what extent do the data in Table 1 support the theoretical predictions you gave as an answer to (b) (ii) above? Comment on your findings. (5)

(c) (i) What is meant by the term 'real household disposable income per head'? (2)

    (ii) Using the data in Table 2, how does expenditure on public and private transport appear to vary with changes in real household disposable income per head? What does this suggest about he economic nature of these two 'goods'? (5)

(d) Suggest policy options to deal with the threat of increased road congestion. Where possible use the information given in Tables 1 and 2 to support your argument. (6)

*   defined as rail, bus and coach services
** defined as cars, taxis and two-wheeled vehicles

Oxford

Tutorial note

(a) (i) Only 3 marks are available for both parts of this question, so you must avoid the temptation to write too much. For part (i), simply identify the fact that starting from a much higher initial usage of 409 billion passenger kilometres in 1981, private transport grew by about 37% over the period shown by the data, whereas public transport only grew by about 6.5%.

    (ii) Since your answer to part (i) has shown that private transport usage rose faster than public transport usage, the use of public transport must have fallen as a proportion of the total. For both parts of this question, simply make use of the data for the first and last years in the data series; you can safely ignore the intermediate years. In 1981, public transport accounted for nearly 16% of total transport use, declining to less than 13% in 1989.

(b) (i) The wording of this question explicitly instructs you to use the data for 1981 and 1989 only. It is a good idea to start with the data for the Retail Price Index, which shows the price level rising by 53% over the period. For public transport, bus and coach fares rose by 72% while rail fares increased by 69% – both rising faster than the RPI. By contrast, the cost of private motoring rose by only 39%, which was less than the rate of inflation. The overall conclusion is that the prices of all forms of transport rose in nominal terms; the price of public transport rose in real as well as in nominal terms; but the real price of private transport fell.

(ii) Only 2 marks are available here, so once again do not overwrite your answer. Simply note that for most goods, more will be demanded when the relative price of the good falls. Consumers substitute the good for the other goods whose relative price has risen. For normal goods, the income effect of the relative price change reinforces this effect.

(iii) According to the 'law' of demand outlined in (b) (ii), the demand for public transport should have fallen, while the demand for private motor transport should have risen. This is because the price of public transport rose and the price or private motoring fell in real terms over the period shown by the data. The data shows that the demand for private motor transport and public road transport were both consistent with this prediction. However, demand for rail transport rose slightly over the period despite the increase in its real price. The price of rail travel fell relative to the price of its close substitute, bus travel, so there was a marginal switching of demand from bus to rail travel.

(c) (i) Real household disposable income per head can be defined in the following way. Total disposable household income measures all the income from various sources such as wages and dividends, received by all the households in the economy, after the deduction of income tax and national insurance contributions, and after receipt of state welfare benefits. By dividing this total figure by the number of household members in the economy, household income per head is calculated. Finally, by presenting the data in index number form, the distorting effects of inflation are removed from the data, i.e. the data is in *real* rather than *nominal* form.

(ii) The years 1981 to 1989 were a period of almost continuous growth in the UK economy, as the economy recovered from a severe recession at the beginning of the 1980s. The period culminated in the 'Lawson boom' in the late 1980s – the nickname given to the years of extremely rapid growth at the end of the upswing in the business cycle. The data does not show the effects of a second severe recession at the end of the 1980s and the beginning of the 1990s. Over the period shown by the data, real household income per head rose by nearly 34%. Over the same years, total real expenditure on motoring rose by 53%; on rail transport it rose by nearly 20%, while real expenditure on bus travel fell by 11.5%. This might suggest that private motor travel and rail travel are both normal goods and that bus travel is an inferior good. Indeed we could go a stage further and argue that private motor travel is a superior good while rail travel is a basic good. This is because expenditure on motor travel rose at a faster rate than real income, while total expenditure on rail travel also increased, but at a slower rate than real income. However, we must be cautious about reaching these conclusions. The data shows changes in expenditure rather than demand, and significant relative price changes also affected demand for, and total expenditure upon, the various forms of transport over the period 1981 to 1989.

(d) The main policy options are: regulation; taxation; road pricing; building more roads; and subsiding public transport, especially rail transport. You must describe in some detail how at least two of these might reduce road congestion, or describe three or more of the policy options in less detail. To earn all 6 marks you must also make some use of the data. For example, you might assess whether the data indicates that demand for each type of transport is price elastic, and also whether there might be significant cross-price elasticities of demand between the various forms of transport. This information would assist in deciding whether the policies of taxing and pricing private road transport and subsiding public transport would be effective in reducing congestion.

Question bank

1 (a) How do the forces of demand and supply determine price in a free market? (7)

(b) Explain why the demand for a product tends to rise as its price falls. (6)

(c) Identify the factors, other than price, which affect the demand for a product. Use appropriate examples and discuss how important these 'non-price' factors are in determining the demand for a product. (12)   *SEB*

2 (a) Explain how, according to economic analysis, a rational consumer determines his or her pattern of consumption. (10)

(b) Consider how far this analysis can explain what might happen in the market for housing if there were:
   (i) a rise in mortgage rates,
   (ii) a rise in incomes. (15)   *Cambridge*

3 Using any economic theory with which you are familiar, explain how consumers allocate expenditure over different products. Discuss how persuasive advertising and marketing of products affect, if at all, the value of this theory. (25)   *NEAB*

Pitfalls

In all three questions, you must avoid restricting your answer to the part of the question requiring an explanation of the shape of the demand curve, to statements like: 'because it is cheaper and more attractive' or 'because more is demanded as a good's price falls'. As explained in the chapter, you must *get behind* the demand curve and use marginal utility theory to explain this basic 'law' of demand. Make sure you use appropriate examples to illustrate the theoretical points you make, especially in your answer to 1(c).

Key points

In your answers to all three questions, use the principle of diminishing marginal utility, the the condition of equi-marginal utility, and the substitution and income effects resulting from a price decrease, to explain why demand increases for a good as the good's price falls. With Questions 2 and 3, make sure you relate this to a consumer's overall pattern of expenditure. The final parts of all the questions are concerned with factors which shift demand curves, though persuasive advertising and marketing (in Question 3) may also serve to increase and firm's monopoly power and make the demand curve steeper and more inelastic – see Chapter 5.

CHAPTER 4

COST AND SUPPLY

Units in this chapter

Chapter objectives

In much the same way that the characteristics of demand curves depend upon the typical behaviour of consumers, so the properties of supply curves depend upon the behaviour of producers or firms. The market supply curve, which shows how much all the firms in an industry intend to supply at various possible prices, is obtained by adding up the separate supply curves for individual firms. For the rest of this chapter, we shall assume that there are a large number of firms within a well-defined industry and that each firm is a passive price-taker, unable to influence the market price by its own decisions on how much to supply. We are really constructing the theory of supply within a perfectly competitive industry, though a more comprehensive treatment of perfect competition is delayed until Chapter 7.

4.1 PRODUCTION AND COST THEORY

THE FIRM

A firm is a **productive unit** or business enterprise which sells its output at a price, within the market economy. In the **private sector** of the economy, firms may range from a one-man window-cleaning business (a **sole trader** or **individual proprietor**) to huge multinational **public joint-stock companies**, such as ICI, with branches and plants in many countries. **Public corporations** or **nationalised industries** in the public sector of the economy are also considered as firms because they sell their output within the market economy. It is not usual, however, to regard **public services**, such as the National Health Service, as firms or business enterprises. Although the NHS is a major customer or market for firms which supply it from within the market economy, most of its own activities take place outside the market economy. However, in the UK at least, the distinction between businesses and public sector services has blurred in recent years. Via the privatisation programme, the Government has transferred services such as dentistry and eye tests into the market sector, and it has instructed managers who still run those services that remain within the public sector to adopt the best private sector business practices.

PROFIT-MAXIMISING BEHAVIOUR

In constructing a theory of supply we are not especially interested in the organisational complexities of firms, such as the different forms of ownership and control and the existence of multi-product and multi-plant enterprises. In this chapter we abstract from the internal organisation of firms and concentrate instead upon the **external** behaviour of firms when they make decisions on the production and sale of a good or goods within the market. In the context of this chapter, it does not matter who makes the decisions within the firm, as long as the decisions are consistent with a desired goal or objective which is assumed to exist for all firms. In the traditional theory of the firm it is assumed that all firms, whatever their internal structure and whatever the form of market in which they exist, share the common goal of **profit maximisation**.

FACTORS OF PRODUCTION

Economists conventionally divide all the inputs necessary for production to take place into four categories, or **factors of production**. These are land, labour, capital and enterprise (or the entrepreneurial factor). For the rest of this chapter we shall simplify and assume that just two inputs, labour and capital, are all that is needed for production to take place.

THE SHORT RUN AND THE LONG RUN

In economic theory the **short run** is defined as a period of time in which at least one factor of production is fixed. In the short run a firm can only increase output or supply by adding more of a variable factor, in this case labour, and combining it with the fixed input, capital. In the **long run** it is assumed that all factors of production are variable. The **scale** of the fixed factors can only be altered in the economic long run. From a firm's point of view, the short run is thus a time-period in which its ability to increase supply is constrained by the size of its fixed capital. We must distinguish between a firm's **short-run** or **constrained supply curve**, and its **long-run supply curve**, which is unconstrained except by factors such as the available technology and the prices it must pay to obtain the services of labour and capital.

THE PRINCIPLE OF DIMINISHING RETURNS

If a firm attempts to increase output or supply in the economic short run by adding a variable input, such as labour, to a given amount of fixed capital, then eventually **diminishing marginal returns** to labour will set in: an extra worker will add less to total output than the previous worker. (Diminishing marginal output and diminishing marginal product are alternative expressions of the same principle.) You should note that the principle of diminishing marginal returns refers to the physical productivity of labour and not to either the money cost of employing labour (the wage) or to the money value of the output which labour produces. The principle of diminishing returns is sometimes known as a law, but it must be stressed that when the first units of labour are added to fixed capital increasing marginal returns are likely to be experienced. This is because the employment of an extra worker allows greater **specialisation** and **division of labour** to take place, with the result that total output increases more than proportionately as workers are added to the labour force.

There are two useful ways of illustrating the principle of diminishing returns in a diagram. In Fig. 4.1, a production possibility curve has been drawn to show how many cars or bicycles a labour force of 100 men can produce if combined with fixed amounts of capital in either the car or the bicycle industry. If all the men are employed in the bicycle industry, the maximum output is 6000 bicycles and no cars. Similarly, 70 cars and no bicycles can be produced if all the men are switched to the car industry. The production possibility curve, drawn between these two extremes, represents all the combinations of bicycles and cars which are possible if some of the men are employed in one industry and some in the other. The point Z on the production possibility curve shows that the total possible output is 5000 bicycles and 45 cars if 50 men are employed in each industry.

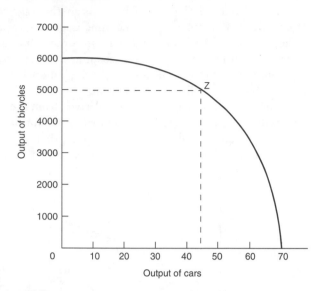

Fig. 4.1 A production possibility curve

Now ask yourself what will happen if workers move out of the car industry into the bicycle industry (or vice versa). Whereas the first 50 workers in the bicycle industry produce a total of 5000 bicycles, the addition of a second 50 workers only increases output by an extra 1000 bicycles. The slope of the production possibility curve, which is concave to origin, is evidence of **diminishing marginal returns** in both industries.

Fig. 4.2a again illustrates the principle of diminishing returns to labour, but in this example within a single industry. You will notice that the diagram distinguishes between **diminishing marginal returns** to labour and **diminishing average returns** – a source of confusion to many students. The concept of marginal returns refers to the addition to output attributable to the last worker added to the labour force. (Formally, the marginal returns of the n'th worker = total returns of n workers minus total returns of (n–1) workers.) The average return per worker is simply the total output divided by the number of workers employed (total returns/n). The mathematical relationship between any marginal variable and the average to which it is related is:

● if the marginal > the average, the average will rise;

● if the marginal < the average, the average will fall;

● if the marginal = the average, the average will neither rise nor fall.

This is a universal mathematical relationship with a host of economic applications. It is essential for students to understand what it means and to avoid the very common error of misrepresenting the relationship. It does *not* state that an average will rise when a marginal is rising, or that an average will fall when the marginal is falling. Fig. 4.2a clearly shows that the marginal returns curve begins to fall as soon as the point of diminishing marginal returns is reached. The average returns curve continues to rise as long as the marginal output of an extra worker is greater than the existing average output, thereby pulling up the average curve. The point of diminishing average returns is reached only when the output of an extra worker falls below the existing average.

SHORT-RUN COST CURVES

The total cost of producing a particular output is made up of the cost of employing both the variable and the fixed factors of production. This can be expressed as the identity:

$$TC \equiv TVC + TFC$$

Average total cost can be written as:

$$ATC \equiv AVC + AFC$$

In Fig. 4.2b, the average variable cost (AVC) curve is illustrated alongside (in Fig. 4.2a) the average returns curve from which it is derived. Variable costs are the wage costs of employing the variable factor, labour. If all workers are paid the same wage, total wage costs will rise proportionately with the number of workers employed. However, while increasing average returns are being experienced, workers on average are becoming more efficient. It follows that average variable costs per unit of output will fall as output rises, but once diminishing average returns set in, average variable costs will rise with output.

In a very similar way, the marginal cost (MC) curve is derived from the nature of marginal returns to the variable inputs. If an extra worker adds more to total output than the previous worker, yet the wage cost of employing him remains the same, then the MC of producing an extra unit of output must fall. When diminishing marginal returns set in, however, the MC curve will rise.

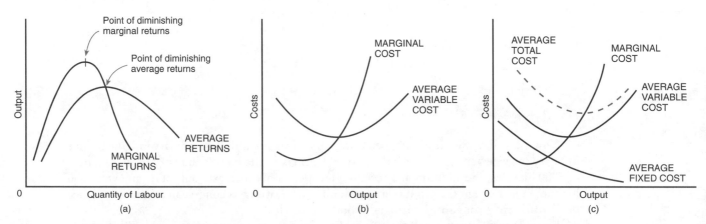

Fig. 4.2 The derivation of the firm's short-run cost curves (a) diminishing marginal returns and diminishing average returns to labour set in (b) these can be translated into money costs as the marginal cost curve and the average variable cost curve (c) the average total cost curve is obtained by including average fixed costs in the diagram

While the nature of average and marginal returns to the variable factors of production determines the shapes of the AVC and MC curves, a separate, but very simple, explanation is needed for the average fixed cost (AFC) curve. Because total fixed costs do not vary with output in the economic short run, AFC per unit of output will fall as the fixed costs or overheads are spread over larger and larger outputs. A falling AFC curve is drawn in Fig. 4.2c, which also includes the average total cost curve obtained by adding up the AVC and AFC curves. The short-run ATC curve is typically U-shaped, showing that average total costs first fall and later rise as output is increased. You should note that the MC curve cuts both the AVC and the ATC curves at their lowest points. Check back to the preceding section to make quite sure that you know why this must be so. However, the point where the MC curve cuts the AFC curve is of no significance because the MC curve is derived only from variable costs and not from fixed costs.

4.2 SUPPLY CURVES

THE FIRM'S SHORT-RUN SUPPLY CURVE

We are now in a position to show how the short-run supply curve of a firm in a perfectly competitive industry is derived from its marginal cost curve. (The characteristics of perfect competition as a market form are examined in Chapter 7.) A perfectly competitive firm, being a price-taker, will sell its output at the same market-determined price or average revenue, whatever the output it decides to supply to the market. This means that **total revenue** will always rise by the amount of price or **average revenue** when the firm decides to release an extra unit of output on the market. Now, **marginal revenue** is defined as the addition to total revenue resulting from the sale of an extra unit of output. It follows that marginal revenue equals average revenue for a perfectly competitive firm and is represented by a horizontal price-line such as P_1 in Fig. 4.3.

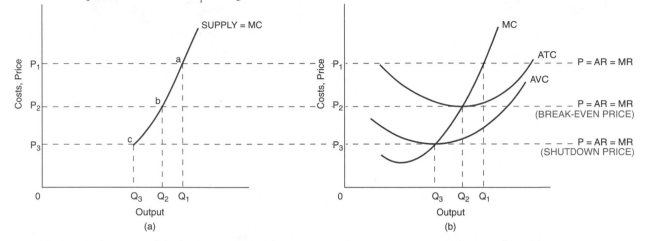

Fig. 4.3 (a) The derivation of the firm's short-run supply curve from its MC curve (b) only the part of the MC curve above AVC is the firm's supply curve

It can easily be shown that any profit-maximising firm, whatever the market form or structure, will produce the output where $MR = MC$. (We are now using MR as the economic shorthand for marginal revenue and not marginal returns!)

- If $MR > MC$, the firm is sacrificing the profit it could make from an extra unit of output. Therefore, it should increase output.

- If $MR < MC$, the firm is making a loss on at least the final unit of output produced. Therefore, it should decrease output.

- If $MR = MC$, there is no incentive to increase or decrease output. This is the equilibrium condition for a profit-maximising firm.

Returning to Fig. 4.3, let us suppose that the market-determined price is P_1. Using the equilibrium condition, the firm will choose to supply Q_1 onto the market, but if the price falls to P_2, supply will be reduced to Q_2. This is the **break-even price**, since the firm will start to make a loss if the price falls below the ATC curve. Nevertheless, if the price falls below P_2 it may still be consistent with profit-maximising behaviour for the firm to continue to supply an output, in the short run at least, even though it is making a loss. As long as the price covers AVC, the size of the loss will be less than the fixed costs the firm will incur if it produced zero output. The **short-run shut down price** is P_3, at which the firm just covers its variable costs. However, if the price failed to cover to at least break-even price, P_2, the firm would be better off closing down and leaving the market. P_2 is **long-run shut down price**.

Our conclusion is that the firm's MC curve, above AVC, is its short-run supply curve. The curve maps out how much the firm is prepared to supply to the market at each price. We have shown that the MC curve slopes upwards because of diminishing marginal returns to the variable factors of production. It is extremely useful to remember that the slope of the supply curve is derived from the principle of diminishing marginal returns and the assumption of profit-maximising behaviour by firms. You should note the parallel between this analysis and the derivation, in Chapter 3, of the demand curve from the principle of diminishing marginal utility and the assumption of utility-maximising behaviour by households.

SHIFTS IN SUPPLY

In the preceding analysis, the productivity of labour reflected in the principle of diminishing returns, and the wage or money costs of hiring labour determined the position of the firm's

MC curve or short-run supply curve. A change in any of the **conditions of supply** will shift the supply curve. If labour becomes more productive, if wage costs fall, or if taxes on the firm are cut, then the supply curve will shift rightwards (or downwards), showing that the firm is prepared to supply more at existing prices.

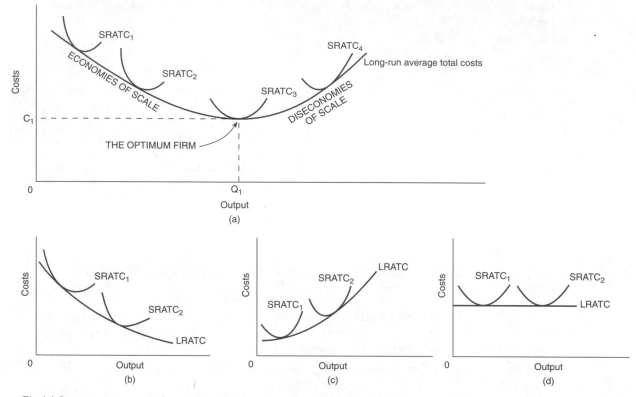

Fig 4.4 Long-run average total cost curves (a) economics of scale followed by diseconomies of scale (b) an industry with economies of large scale production (c) an industry with diseconomies of large scale production (d) an industry without economies or diseconomies of scale

LONG-RUN COSTS AND SUPPLY

In the long run, a firm can change the **scale** of the fixed factors of production and move to a new size of productive unit (or a new short-run situation). The long-run average cost curve, which is illustrated in Fig. 4.4, is a mathematical line drawn as a tangent to a 'family' or set of short-run cost curves, each representing a feasible size of productive unit. A firm can thus move in the long run from one short-run supply curve to another, which is associated with a different scale of fixed capacity. (It is useful to remember that firms can also enter or leave the industry in the long run. This means that the **industry short-run supply curve**, obtained by adding the individual supply curves of each firm, can shift its position in the long run when firms enter or leave the industry.)

The shape of the long-run ATC curve depends upon whether **economies** or **diseconomies of scale** are experienced. Long-run average costs may be falling, rising, or constant. If an increase in all the inputs or factors of production results in falling long-run average total cost, economies of scale exist. Eventually diseconomies of scale may set in when the long-run ATC curve begins to rise. The textbook example of a U-shaped long-run ATC curve is drawn in Fig. 4.4a. There is no reason, however, why the curve must be U-shaped. An industry, such as the automobile industry, with **economies of large-scale production** is represented in Fig. 4.4b, while Fig. 4.4c illustrates **the economies of small-scale production** which might be more typical of agriculture. Statistical studies have suggested an absence of significant economies and diseconomies of scale in many industries, in which case the correct long-run ATC curve would be the horizontal line in Fig. 4.4d. If the firm's long-run marginal cost curve is also its long-run supply curve, this would imply a horizontal (or perfectly elastic) long-run supply curve in industries with constant long-run average costs. Firms of many different sizes could coexist without significant differences in costs.

RETURNS TO SCALE

Many textbooks confuse **economies of scale** with the closely related concept of **increasing returns to scale**. Economies of scale refer to long-run money costs of production, whereas long-run returns to scale relate only to the physical output of the factors of production or inputs. If physical output increases more than proportionately as the scale of all the inputs is changed, increasing returns to scale occur. (Decreasing returns to scale and constant returns to scale are other possibilities.) Increasing returns to scale contribute to economies of scale (in the form of technical economies), but some economies of scale are not explained by increasing returns to scale – for example, bulk-buying economies, when a firm uses its market power to buy inputs at low prices.

While it is useful to understand the difference between economies of scale and increasing returns to scale, it is much more important for the student at A level to be absolutely clear about the difference between short-run returns, explained earlier in the chapter, and the long-run returns to scale described in this section. It is the impact of diminishing marginal returns on the costs and profits of a firm in the economic short run that encourages the firm to change the scale of its operations in the long run.

Chapter roundup

In this chapter it has been assumed that a firm exists within a perfectly competitive industry. Further aspects of the supply and output decisions of firms in conditions of perfect competition and monopoly are developed in Chapter 7, while Chapter 8 extends the analysis to imperfect competition. Elasticity of supply is explained in Chapter 5, which is followed in Chapter 6 by a survey of the special problems of agricultural supply.

Illustrative questions and answers

1   Essay Question
'In the short run, average costs eventually must rise. What happens to average costs in the long run is uncertain.' Discuss. (25)   *Oxford*

Tutorial note

This is a relatively straightforward question testing your understanding of the most significant difference between short-run and long-run costs. Because of the way we define the short run – at least one factor of production being held fixed – the law of diminishing returns affects the way output increases in the short run, causing first marginal costs and then average costs to rise. But in the long run, all factors of production are variable and the law of diminishing returns is no longer relevant. Instead, returns to scale operate in the long run with three possibilities: increasing, constant, or decreasing returns to scale. Increasing returns to scale cause long-run average costs to fall (assuming constant factor prices, i.e. wage rates and the prices of capital goods), whereas long-run average costs are constant with constant returns to scale, and rising with decreasing returns to scale. Hence, whether long-run average costs fall, remain constant or rise is indeed uncertain, since the outcome depends on the nature of the returns to scale experienced by the firm as it expands the scale of its productive capacity.

Suggested answer

- Distinguish between the short run and the long run.
- Explain the law of diminishing returns and how the operation of the law causes short-run average costs to rise. Illustrate on diagrams.

- Explain increasing, constant, and decreasing returns to scale, and how each affects long-run average costs. Illustrate each on a diagram.
- Conclude by agreeing with the assertion in the question.

2 Data Question

'Prices of primary aluminium are at their lowest level in real terms. Analysts estimate that at least 60 per cent of production capacity outside the former eastern bloc countries is operating at a loss. They suggest that producers should have cut back production some time ago to have prevented stocks rising and given prices a chance to stabilise.

Mr David Morton, chairman of Alcan Aluminium, second biggest of the western producers, says: "The industry in general – and I don't exclude Alcan – will have to look seriously at its operating rate." Shutting down capacity temporarily in the aluminium industry is not a short-term or cheap process. It is expensive to start up aluminium pot lines once they have cooled. Mr Morton says Alcan has not turned off capacity. "As a low-cost producer, we are still better off producing than closing down," he says.

The dividend has been cut and capital expenditure drastically reduced – by 30 per cent. The company has a flexible capital programme. This enabled the company to speed up spending as it benefited from windfall profits in 1988 when aluminium prices soared and net income was nearly $1bn. Alcan is feeling the effect of this recession more heavily than its competitors because in several countries Alcan operations are geared towards the domestic economies. "This is the first time that our geographical spread has worked against us," Mr Morton says. In future Alcan hopes to minimise the effect of the cycles by choosing its products and markets which are not so badly affected during down-turns.'

(Source: K. Gooding, 'Alcan faces production crunch as prices hit nadir',
The Financial Times, 2 October, 1991)

(a) Using economic analysis, at what price would an economist suggest that an aluminium producer is likely to cease production? (3)

(b) What does the passage suggest is the relationship between fixed costs and total costs in the aluminium industry? (3)

(c) Discuss **three** factors which could prompt some aluminium producers to carry on in production despite currently falling prices. (6)

(d) Why have firms such as Alcan established production bases in more than one country? (4)

(e) How can an aluminium firm try to minimise the fluctuation in demand for its products?
(4)
ULEAC

Tutorial note

(a) This question is testing your understanding of the difference between break-even price (or long-run shut down price) and short-run shut down price. Economic theory suggests that when the price of aluminium falls below average total cost, while remaining above average variable cost, producers should continue to produce and sell aluminium – at least in the short run, or providing they expect the resulting losses to be temporary. This is because in the short run, the loss incurred from continuing production turns out to be less than the loss made at zero output. In the latter case, the firm's loss equals its fixed costs of production. By continuing to produce, the firm earns sufficient revenue to more than cover its variable costs. In this situation, *part* but not all of fixed costs are covered, so the loss incurred turns out to be less than the size of fixed costs. The firm is better off continuing to produce, in the hope that the price will recover, rather than ceasing production. However, if the firm believed that the price would never recover sufficiently to cover average total costs, it should make a long-run decision to close down completely, transferring its capacity to alternative use or selling off its fixed capacity. The price which just equals the lowest average total cost of production is therefore the long-run shut down price.

(b) The key sentence in the passage relating to this part of the question is: 'It is expensive to start up aluminium pot lines once they have cooled.' This, together with the statement that Alcan is a low-cost producer, means that once the pot lines have been heated and are operating, the variable costs of producing aluminium are low. The implication is that fixed costs are high relative to variable costs. The costs incurred when initially investing in fixed capacity are high, and if production were closed down, the costs of maintaining the fixed capacity would rise.

(c) We have already drawn attention to two factors that could prompt aluminium companies to continue producing despite falling prices: the possibility that prices continue to remain above average variable cost; and the high start-up costs incurred once plant has been shut down. Other factors *not* mentioned in the passage are: the granting of government subsidies to aluminium producers; predatory pricing, whereby an aluminium company deliberately sets the price below cost in order to drive competitors out of business; and deliberate stockpiling for sale at a later date once prices have recovered. Discuss any three of these factors, remembering that when answering this type of question, it is a good idea to indicate clearly when you are making a point contained within the data, and when you are bringing in your outside knowledge.

(d) Economists generally assume that firms aim to maximise profits. The underlying reason for locating production plant (and possibly subsidiary companies) in different countries is a firm's belief that this will lead to larger sales and profits. Also, the government of a country in which a company wishes to sell may give preferential treatment to the company if it locates some of its production within the country instead of importing everything from outside. Risks can be spread and reduced, partly because not all countries are likely to suffer the recessionary phase of the business cycle at the same time. For companies such as Alcan, it is also worth noting that aluminium production involves bulky inputs and outputs, and a significant energy input into the smelting process. The industry is highly dependent on low-cost access to its raw material (bauxite) and cheap energy supplies. There is a strong economic advantage in locating production capacity near to suitable sources of energy, and also when possible, near to local markets.

(e) As mentioned in relation to part (d), because market conditions vary between countries, an aluminium firm such as Alcan can minimise the fluctuation in the demand for its product by selling in a number of different countries around the world. A company might also operate a buffer stock policy, though for this to be successful, co-operation with other aluminium companies and possibly with governments may be necessary. You should outline briefly how a buffer stock (or support buying) operates – see Chapter 6 for details.

Question bank

1 (a) Outline and explain the 'law of variable proportions' (or 'diminishing returns'). (15)

(b) How does the behaviour of marginal physical product determine the shape of the marginal cost curve? (10)   *Oxford & Cambridge*

Pitfalls

There are two principal pitfalls awaiting the unwary with this question. Firstly, in (a) you must avoid confusing the short-run law of diminishing returns with the long-run concepts of returns to scale and economies of scale. Secondly, in (b) you might not realise that marginal physical product is simply alternative terminology for marginal returns.

Key points

Start your answer by explaining the law of diminishing returns, making sure that you illustrate the law with a numerical example and a graph. Then go on to explain and illustrate how, when the marginal output of an extra worker begins to fall, the cost of producing an extra unit of output starts to rise. Diminishing marginal returns result in increasing marginal costs of production.

2 (a) Explain the terms total, average and marginal cost. (10)

   (b) Show how these relate to total, average and marginal revenue for a profit maximising firm in perfect competition. (10)   *Oxford & Cambridge*

Pitfalls

The wording of the question seems to imply that the shape of a firm's revenue curves is affected or determined by its cost curves. This is untrue. The factors affecting cost curves are not the same as those determining revenue curves, though both cost and revenue curves reflect the same mathematical principles.

Key points

Start your answer by precisely defining total, average and marginal cost, and then briefly explain the relationship between the three, particularly in the economic short run. Then explain (briefly) the meaning of a perfectly competitive market and the shape of a perfectly competitive firm's revenue curves. Make the point that total, average and marginal revenue curves follow the same mathematical rules as the corresponding cost curves. Finally, note that a firm's profit-maximising level of output occurs where marginal revenue = marginal cost and where total revenue exceeds total cost by the greatest amount.

3 (a) Explain the economic principles which can be illustrated by a production possibility curve. (15)

   (b) How and why might a production possibility curve shift outwards. (10)   *WJEC*

Pitfalls

Assuming that you understand the meaning of a production possibility curve, the main pitfall lies in restricting your answer to just one economic principle which can be illustrated by such a curve. In this chapter we have explained how a production possibility curve illustrates opportunity cost and the returns to the factors of production which a firm employs. However, production possibility curves can also illustrate terms and concepts explained later in this book, such as economic growth and comparative advantage. In your answer to (b), make sure you address both instructions: how and why.

Key points

Make sure you accurately draw a production possibility curve, taking care to label the axes correctly. Explain how the shape of the curve depends on the nature of the returns or productivity of factors of production as they are switched between industries, and how the curve illustrates the principles of opportunity cost and comparative advantage. Go on to explain how, if used in a macroeconomic context (for example with capital goods and consumer goods on the axes of the diagram), a production possibility curve can illustrate economic growth taking place, with the curve shifting outwards. This leads into the second part of the answer: the availability of more factors of production or inputs and technical progress are the main factors causing a production possibility curve to shift outwards.

ELASTICITY

Units in this chapter

Chapter objectives

Chapters 3 and 4 explained why for most goods, a demand curve usually slopes downward from left to right and a supply curve normally slopes upward. However, the slope of a demand or supply curve is not always an accurate indicator of the extent to which households or firms respond to price change. In this chapter the concept of **price elasticity** as a measure of the responsiveness of households or firms to a change in a good's price is introduced and explained. We then show how elasticities of demand or supply can be measured with respect to changes in any of the conditions of demand or supply, for example, **income elasticity of demand** and **cross-elasticity of demand**.

5.1 INTRODUCTION TO ELASTICITY

THE MEANING OF ELASTICITY

Consider the demand curves which are drawn in Fig. 5.1 and which show the demand for a product such as electronic calculators in two separated markets, the London area market and a market for the rest of the United Kingdom. Demand curve D_2 is quite clearly flatter than D_1. Students are often tempted to use the flatness or steepness of a demand or supply curve to describe its elasticity – the responsiveness of demand or supply to a change in price. However, a careful inspection of Fig. 5.1 reveals that the slope of the curves is misleading and that flatness or steepness is not a proper indicator of elasticity. In each market a 20% reduction in price from £20 to £16 results in a doubling of the quantity which households intend to buy: despite their different slopes, the demand curves display identical elasticities whenever the price changes. In this example we could calculate the **average elasticity** when the price changes from £20 to £16. Strictly, however, elasticity is a measure of the response of demand to a price change at a **specific point** on a curve, and the concept should not be used to describe quite large changes in price.

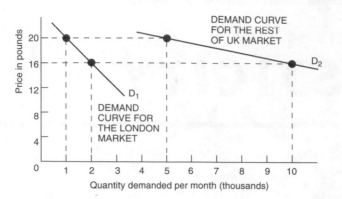

Fig. 5.1 Demand curves with the same elasticities but different slopes

Whenever one variable responds to another variable, an elasticity can be estimated. Elasticity is an especially useful descriptive statistic of the relationship between any two variables because it is independent of the units, such as quantity and price units, in which the variables are measured. A knowledge of supply and demand elasticities is particularly useful to decision makers both in firms and in government. If we are told, for example, that the demand elasticity of Scotch whisky is 2, then this single statistic contains the information that a 1% price-rise causes a 2% fall in quantity demanded. (Strictly, the elasticity is −2 as the price-rise causes a fall in quantity demanded, but the minus sign is frequently omitted.) The size of the elasticity will indicate the extent to which sales may drop when a tax is imposed upon Scotch whisky: the more elastic the demand (and supply) curves, the greater will be the fall in sales. Since the government's tax-revenue equals the amount of the tax multiplied by the after-tax quantity of sales, the government will experience the least loss in tax-revenue when it imposes a tax on goods with low demand and supply elasticities.

THE ESTIMATION OF ELASTICITY

Suppose a businessman wishes to estimate how his customers will respond when the price of his product is increased. If he possesses perfect market information, as in perfect competition, there will be no problem: he simply reads off, from a chart or graph displayed on his office wall, the quantities that would be demanded at all possible prices. Unfortunately, many students at A level seem to think that all business decisions are made in this way! Businessmen, however, seldom, if ever, possess perfect information and this means that they cannot be sure how their customers will react to price changes. One method of estimating the elasticity of demand for a good is to collect data on the quantities actually bought at different prices in previous years – but the elasticity statistic which is obtained from such an exercise must be treated with caution. It will have been calculated on **ex post** rather than **ex ante** data: the amount actually bought may not have been the same as the quantity that households had planned or intended to buy. Also, conditions of demand and the general price-level may have changed over the years. To overcome these problems, a businessman could hire a market research team to go into the street with questionnaires, to ask people how much they would buy at various prices.

ELASTICITY FORMULAE

When an examination question requires you to discuss the measurement and interpretation of elasticity statistics, you must bear in mind the data-collecting problems described in the preceding section: measurement of elasticity involves more than just a textbook formula. Nevertheless, once the information on the planned demand of households or the supply intentions of firms has been collected, a simple formula is used to estimate the elasticity:

- Price elasticity of demand $= \dfrac{\text{Proportionate change in quantity demand}}{\text{Proportionate change in price}}$

- Price elasticity of supply $= \dfrac{\text{Proportionate change in quantity supplied}}{\text{Proportionate change in price}}$

- Income elasticity of demand $= \dfrac{\text{Proportionate change in quantity demanded}}{\text{Proportionate change in income}}$

- Cross-elasticity of demand for Good A with respect to Good B $= \dfrac{\text{Proportionate change in quantity of A demanded}}{\text{Proportionate change in price of B}}$

For example, if the price rises by a third and consumers respond by reducing the quantity demanded by two-thirds, the price elasticity of demand is 2 (strictly –2).

5.2 ELASTICITIES OF DEMAND AND SUPPLY

PRICE ELASTICITY OF DEMAND

If a price change results in a more than proportionate change in demand, demand is said to be **elastic**. The elasticity statistic, calculated from the formula, will be greater than 1. Similarly, if the change in demand is less than proportionate, demand is **inelastic**, and the elasticity statistic will be less than 1. It is usually misleading, however, to refer to the whole of a demand curve as elastic or inelastic since the elasticity will generally vary from point to point along the curve.

Before we show how the elasticity varies along the curve, it is useful to introduce an alternative way of describing demand elasticity in terms of price changes:

- If total consumer expenditure **increases** in response to a **price fall**, demand is relatively **elastic**.

- If total consumer expenditure **decreases** in response to a **price fall**, demand is relatively **inelastic**.

- If total consumer expenditure remains **constant** in response to a **price fall** elasticity of demand = unity.

Fig. 5.2a illustrates some possible changes in consumer expenditure which might follow a reduction in price. When the price falls from P_1 to P_2 in Fig. 5.2a, total consumer expenditure increases by the shaded area k, but decreases by the area h. The area k, which represents the proportionate increase in the quantity demanded, is clearly larger than area h, which represents the proportionate change in price. Demand is thus elastic at all points on the demand curve between a and b on curve D_1. However, if the price falls from P_3 to P_4 on the same demand curve, the shaded area k' is smaller than the area h'. Total consumer expenditure falls, and demand is inelastic at all points between c and d on the demand curve.

We are now in a position to explain the misleading generalisation that a flat demand curve is elastic and a steep curve is inelastic. Moving along all linear (straight-line) demand curves that slope down from left to right, elasticity of demand falls from point to point along the curve. The 'flat' demand curve illustrated in Fig. 5.2b is really only the upper part of a curve which, if extended far enough rightwards or downwards, would eventually become inelastic in its lower reaches. Similarly, the 'steep' inelastic demand curve in Fig. 5.2c is the lower part of a curve which would become elastic in its upper reaches if these could be included in the diagram.

Intuition suggests that if elasticity varies from point to point along a downward-sloping **linear** curve, then we require a **non-linear** curve to show a constant elasticity at all points. The **rectangular hyperbola** illustrated in Fig. 5.2d is the special case of a non-linear demand curve which shows a **unit elasticity** at all points on the curve.

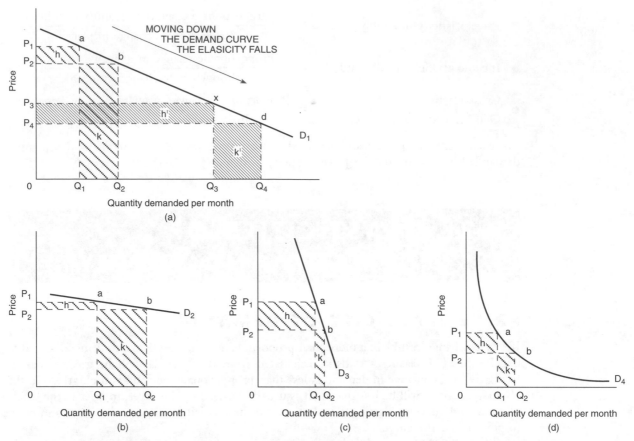

Fig. 5.2 Price elasticity of demand (a) elasticity varies from point to point along a linear downward-sloping curve (b) demand is elastic along this stretch of a 'flat' demand curve (c) demand is inelastic along this stretch of a steep demand curve (d) a rectangular hyperbola shows unit elasticity at all points on the curve

INFINITE ELASTICITY AND ZERO ELASTICITY

Infinitely elastic (or perfectly elastic) demand or supply can be represented by a horizontal curve, such as those drawn in Fig. 5.3a. The diagram illustrates a trap awaiting the unwary student. In the case of the perfectly elastic demand curve, consumers demand an infinite amount at a price of P_2 or below; if the price rises above P_2, demand falls to zero as consumers switch to the perfect substitutes which are assumed to be available. In the case of the perfectly elastic supply curve, however, firms are prepared to supply an infinite amount at a price of P_1 or above. If the price falls below P_1, the firms refuse to supply any output onto the market!

Fig. 5.3b illustrates a completely inelastic supply curve: whatever the price, the same amount is supplied onto the market. Similarly, completely inelastic demand would be shown by a vertical demand curve.

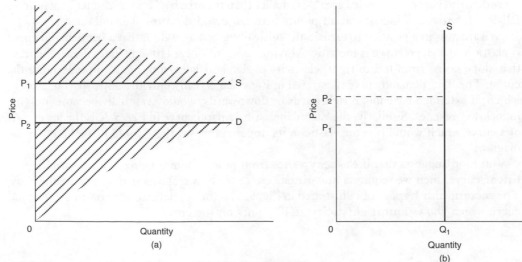

Fig. 5.3 (a) Infinitely elastic supply and demand (b) zero elasticity of supply

THE DETERMINANTS OF DEMAND ELASTICITY

- **Substitutability**. When a perfect substitute for a product exists, consumers can respond to a price rise by switching their expenditure to the substitute product. Commodities – for example, British cars – which have close substitutes available tend to be in more elastic demand than those that do not.

- **Percentage of income**. Items on which many people spend a large proportion of their income, such as summer holidays, tend to be in more elastic demand than goods such as matches, on which only a fraction of income is spent.

- **Necessities v luxuries**. Necessities tend to be in inelastic demand, luxuries in elastic demand. Salt is often cited as a commodity with a very inelastic demand: it is a necessity, with no close substitutes, and expenditure on it is only a small part of most households' total spending.

- **The width of the definition**. The wider the definition of a commodity, the lower the elasticity. Thus, the demand for a particular brand of a commodity will be more elastic than the demand for the commodity as a whole. In a similar way, the elasticity of demand for bread will be greater than that for food as a whole.

- **Time**. The longer the time-period involved, the greater the elasticity of demand is likely to be. This is because it takes time to adjust to a change in price. If the price of gas rises, people may be unable to switch immediately to alternative household heating systems because they are 'locked in' to their existing investments in gas-fired appliances. However, the opposite may be true in certain circumstances: some consumers might react to a sudden increase in the price of cigarettes by giving up smoking altogether, and then gradually drift back to their old habits.

PRICE ELASTICITY OF SUPPLY

Supply curves normally slope upwards from left to right, and the mathematical properties of upward-sloping (or positive) curves are different from those of downward-sloping (or negative) curves. The key points to note are:

❶ **Any straight-line (linear) supply curve** drawn from the origin (point O) will display **unit elasticity of supply** at all points along the curve. This is illustrated in Fig. 5.4a, where a doubling of the price causes an exact doubling of the quantity supplied.

❷ The **'flat' supply curve** drawn in Fig. 5.4b is **elastic** at all points along the curve, since any price-change would result in a more than proportionate change in supply. But the elasticity falls towards unity, moving from point to point up the curve to the right.

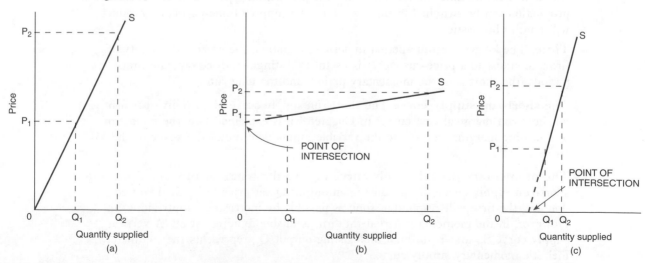

Fig. 5.4 Price elasticity of supply (a) unit elasticity of supply (b) elastic supply (c) inelastic supply

❸ Similarly, the 'steep' curve in Fig. 5.4c is **inelastic** at all points, since any price-change results in a less than proportionate change in supply. But in this case the elasticity rises towards unity, moving from point to point up the curve.

❹ However, as in the case of demand curves, the flatness or steepness of a supply curve is a misleading guide to its elasticity. The key point is not the flatness or steepness of the curve, but **whether the supply curve intersects the price axis or the quantity axis**.

The rule is:

● If a linear supply curve intersects the **price axis**, the curve is **elastic** at all points.

● If a linear supply curve intersects the **quantity axis**, the curve is **inelastic** at all points.

● If a linear supply curve intersects the **origin**, the elasticity is **unity** at all points along the curve.

In the case of non-linear supply curves, it is possible to use the rule to check the elasticity at a particular point on the supply curve by drawing a **tangent** to the point, and by noting the axis which the tangent intersects. We leave it as an exercise for the reader to do this, and also to draw a steep supply curve intersecting the price axis. You will find that the curve is elastic at all points, showing that a 'steep' curve can be elastic!

THE DETERMINANTS OF SUPPLY ELASTICITY

Suppose the demand for a good such as a car component suddenly doubles at all prices. The factors which may determine whether supply is able to respond include:

● **The number of firms in the industry**. Generally, the greater the number of firms in an industry, the more elastic is the industry supply.

● **The length of the production period**. If production converts inputs into outputs in the space of a few hours, supply will be more elastic than when several months are involved, as in agriculture.

● **The existence of spare capacity**. If spare capacity exists and if variable inputs such as labour and raw materials are available, it should be possible to increase production quickly in the short run.

● **The ease of accumulating stocks**. If it is easy to store unsold stocks at low cost, firms are able to meet a sudden increase in demand by running down stocks. They can respond to a sudden fall in demand and price by taking supply off the market and diverting production into stock-accumulation.

● **The ease of factor substitution**. Many firms produce a range of products and are able to switch machines and labour from one production type to another. If factors of production can be switched in this way, then the supply of one particular product will tend to be elastic.

● **Time**. The longer the time-period under consideration, the greater the ability of firms to adjust to a price-change. It is useful to distinguish three separate time-periods, the short run, the momentary period, and the long run.

❶ **The short-run supply curve** The short-run supply curve of an individual firm is its short-run marginal cost curve. In Chapter 4 it is explained how the impact of diminishing marginal returns to the variable inputs determines the shape of the MC curve.

❷ **The momentary period supply curve** Fig. 5.5 illustrates the case of a firm on its short-run supply curve, S_2, producing an output Q_1 at price of P_1. If the price doubles, the firm will respond as soon as possible by increasing supply along S_2. However, in the momentary period the firm is unable to adjust at all. A vertical supply curve S_1, drawn through the existing output Q_1, represents the completely inelastic momentary supply curve.

❸ **The long-run supply curve** The perfectly elastic long-run supply curve, S_3, drawn in Fig. 5.5 represents the special case of a firm in an industry with constant long-run average costs. In the special circumstances of Fig. 5.5, a firm can increase output beyond Q_1 either by moving in the short run up S_2, or by moving in the long run along S_3 to a new size or scale of fixed capacity. The precise shape of the long-run supply curve will depend upon whether economies or diseconomies of scale are experienced, but in general we may expect long-run supply to be more elastic than short-run supply.

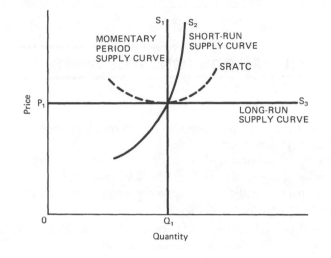

Fig. 5.5 The elasticity of the supply curve varies with the time period

INCOME ELASTICITY OF DEMAND

The income elasticity of demand – which measures how demand responds to a change in income – is always **positive** for a **normal good** and **negative** for an **inferior good**. The quantity demanded of an inferior good falls as income rises. Normal goods are sometimes further subdivided into luxuries or superior goods, for which the income elasticity of demand is greater than unity, and essential or basic goods with an elasticity of less than one. Although the quantity demanded of normal goods always rises as income rises, it rises more than proportionately with income for superior goods (such as dishwashers). Conversely, demand for a basic good such as soap rises at a slower rate than income.

CROSS-ELASTICITY OF DEMAND

This is a statistic which describes the **complementary** or **substitute relationship** between two commodities. A cross-elasticity of demand of −0.1 for bread with respect to the price of butter indicates that a 10% rise in the price of butter is associated with a 1% fall in the demand for bread. In contrast, a cross-elasticity of +0.8 for margarine with respect to the price of butter shows that a 10% rise in the price of butter will result in an 8% increase in the demand for margarine. Whereas the **mathematical sign of a cross-elasticity statistic** depends on the nature of the relationship between the two commodities, the **absolute size of the statistic** indicates the strength of the relationship. Cross-elasticities are negative for complementary goods, and positive for substitutes. A cross-elasticity statistic very close to zero is likely when there is no complementary or close substitute relationship between two goods.

Chapter roundup

There are three important applications of the elasticity concept in public finance, exchange-rate policy, and agriculture. The possible effects of the elasticity of supply and demand on government tax revenue are explained in Chapter 13. Elasticity of demand for exports and imports has an important effect upon exchange-rate policy, which is the subject of Chapter 20. Meanwhile, Chapter 6 develops the theme of how the inelastic supply and demand for agricultural products results in very unstable prices and incomes for primary producers.

Illustrative questions and answers

1   Essay Question

A bus operator understands that the elasticities of demand for coach travel are as follows:
- (i)   income elasticity of demand is –0.4;
- (ii) price elasticity of demand is –1.2;
- (iii) cross elasticity of demand in respect of rail fares is +2.1

The bus operator is unsure whether to continue running a particular service between two towns because it is not currently profitable.

(a) Discuss how the above information might be expected to influence the bus operator in determining whether to continue with the service. (70)

(b) What other factors might also be relevant to this decision? (30)   *ULEAC*

Tutorial note

(a) The demand for coach travel is price elastic. This means that the coach operator can increase sales revenue – and possibly move into profit – by reducing prices and attracting more customers. By contrast, sales revenue would fall if prices were raised. The minus sign of the income elasticity tells us that coach travel is an inferior good. This means that if real incomes are rising and people are becoming better-off, demand for bus travel will fall. In these circumstances the coach service is likely to become even less profitable. But if real incomes fall – as in a recession – then demand for coach travel will increase, with the possibility that the service between the two towns can become profitable. Finally the plus sign of the cross-elasticity of demand for coach travel with respect to the price of rail fares indicates that the two methods of travel are substitutes (higher rail fares lead to an increase in the demand for coach travel as people switch to the cheaper method of travel). A cross-elasticity of +2.1 is in fact quite high: it implies that a 10% rise in rail fares relative to coach fares will lead to a 21% increase in coach passengers, i.e. passengers are highly responsive to changes in the relative prices of the different forms of transport. In these circumstances, the coach operator would clearly need to form a view on how rail fares are likely to change relative to the prices he can charge, because this is likely to have a substantial effect on demand, sales revenue and profitability.

(b) There are a large number of possibly relevant factors that you could bring into your answer to this part of the question. You should try to avoid writing a lengthy 'shopping list' of, say, ten or twelve points, without any elaboration or substantiation of any of the factors you list. It is better to introduce just two or three factors and then devote a paragraph to each – bearing in mind that less than a third of the total marks are available for this part of the question. One obvious point to make concerns operating costs. We have already noted that (with demand elastic) sales revenue will rise if the bus operator reduces prices, but will total costs rise faster than revenue? This will have a crucial bearing on profitability. If in the initial situation, the coach always runs two-thirds empty between the two towns, a reduction in fares would probably lead to revenue rising faster than costs as the vacant seats are filled up, at least until the coach is full. But if the service is unprofitable even when the coach is full, fare-cutting is not going to provide a solution. Another factor you could introduce into your answer is the topical issue of regulation and deregulation of bus services. Under the regulated system which existed in the UK until the late 1980s and which still exists in London, bus operators were granted a monopoly. There was no competition and rival companies could not operate the same routes. But in return for protection from competition, bus and coach operators were required to provide loss-making services on routes with relatively few passengers, using revenues from their profitable routes to 'cross-subsidise' the loss-making routes. With bus deregulation, however, there is no obligation for an operator to continue to provide an unprofitable service. Nevertheless under some circumstances it might be considered worthwhile. It could be a 'feeder' route for the already profitable routes the bus company operates, or the bus company might be trying to force rival operators out of business, hoping the route will become profitable after the competitors have been defeated and forced to withdraw.

2 Data Question

1993 was a difficult year for the hotel business. The English Tourist Board reported that 'occupancy rates'* were down, price cutting was prevalent, profit levels were being squeezed and many businesses, large as well as small, were either in liquidation or close to it.

This national experience is typified by the case of the Bootham Hotel, York, a 70 bedroom private hotel in one of the UK's most important tourist centres. Its bed occupancy rates in 1993 are shown in the table below:

Table 1 *Bootham Hotel: Bed Occupancy Rates* in 1993 (percentages)*

January	26	July	61
February	34	August	62
March	36	September	60
April	40	October	51
May	45	November	40
June	53	December	32
Annual Average 45%			

*An occupancy rate is a measure of the extent to which the accommodation which is available is actually sold to hotel guests. It can be calculated in terms of room or, as in this case, bed occupancy.

The basic problem in the hotel business is that the product is perishable, i.e. if a hotel room or all beds in that room are not occupied by guests, that represents a loss of revenue to the business. Unlike goods produced by a manufacturing firm facing similar problems of seasonal demand, the product cannot be stored. A hotelier's problems are compounded by the nature of the cost structure, as shown in the table below:

Table 2 *Bootham Hotel: Cost Structure*

	% of total cost incurred in 1993 (excluding profit)
food and drink costs	12
staff costs	33
other customer-related costs	13
marketing costs	5
administrative costs	6
routine maintenance costs	4
rent and property taxes	9
interest and depreciation	18
	100%

The outcome of the problems of seasonal demand and cost structure is that many hotels choose to close for certain parts of the year. To date, the Bootham Hotel has opened all year round but the closure option is being considered by its owner.

Market research carried out by consultants has estimated that the hotel's price elasticity of demand is −1.8 and that the income elasticity of demand is 1.3. The hotel currently charges £40 per night per person and keeps its prices at this level throughout the year. Its prices have been unchanged since 1991.

(a) (i) Briefly explain the difference between fixed costs and variable costs.   (2)

   (ii) Which of the items in Table 2 might represent fixed costs? Explain your answer.   (4)

   (iii) Sketch and explain the likely shape of the hotel's short-run average cost curve. (4)

(b) The hotel's owner is considering whether to close the hotel during December and January. On what basis should the decision be taken? Identify any additional information which would be required to make this decision. (12)

(c) (i) In what sort of market structure do you believe this hotel operates? Explain your answer. (4)

   (ii) How would you expect it to compete with other hotels? (4)

(d) Explain the meaning of the two elasticity estimates referred to in the last paragraph and their significance to the hotel's owner. (10)

(e) Discuss how these elasticity estimates might have been obtained by the market research company and assess their reliability. (10)   *Cambridge*

Tutorial note

(a) For part (i) of this question simply state that fixed costs are overhead costs which stay the same in the short run, whether or not a business produces any output. Variable costs vary with the level of output, being zero when no output is produced and rising as output increases. In part (ii), go on to identify which of the costs in Table 2 are fixed and which are variable, making sure you provide a *brief* explanation of the basis for your decision. Food and drink, staff and other customer-related costs are variable, while the remaining costs in the table are variable. However, you might argue that the costs of staff on annual salaries should be treated as fixed whereas those incurred from employing hourly-paid and casual labour are variable. For part (iii), you must draw a steeply falling downward-sloping average cost curve, explaining its shape in terms of the spreading of fixed costs.

(b) You should start your answer by arguing that in the short run, for the hotel to remain open, the hotel must cover its variable costs and possibly earn sufficient revenue towards fixed costs. Go on to suggest at least two or three sources of additional information which would aid the decision on whether to stay open or close down in the winter. Since the Bootham Hotel currently charges the same price per night per person throughout the year, it would be useful to research the likely effects upon demand and revenue of 'special deal' pricing, e.g. low weekend rates, special family rates, conference rates, and special promotions, such as at Christmas. Further information about the breakdown of costs would also be useful, together with information about competitors' pricing, marketing and expansion strategies.

(c) Like most businesses, hotels operate in imperfectly competitive markets. Since York is a major British tourist centre containing a large number of hotels, you might argue that the market most closely resembles monopolistic competition. (See Chapter 8 for an explanation of monopolistic competition.) For example, there are a large number of slightly differentiated products, each hotel faces a downward-sloping demand for its product, and new hotels can enter the market in the long run. For part (ii), mention that the Bootham Hotel could undertake price competition, but since this may lead to a self-defeating price war, make sure you explain a number of forms of non-price competition such as offering special attractions (e.g. a gastronomic weekend) and an improved quality of service.

(d) Briefly explain the meaning of the two elasticities mentioned in the passage, but devote most of your answer to discussing their significance for the hotel's owner. Demand is price elastic, indicating that a 10% price reduction from £40 per person to £36 would increase bed occupancy by 18%. The income elasticity statistic of +1.3 indicates that a hotel is a normal good, or perhaps a superior good or luxury, since demand rises at a faster rate than income. The data in Table 1 shows that there were unoccupied beds throughout the year in 1993, so price cutting might be a sensible business strategy, providing variable costs are covered. With regard to the income elasticity of demand, you might note that the UK economy was coming out of recession in 1993 and that the economy was expected to continue to recover in 1994 and 1995. Providing the hotel owner expected real disposable incomes also to rise in the period of national economic recovery, demand and occupancy rates should increase by 1.3% for every 1% increase in household spending power. In the absence of price cuts, a policy of relying on demand to recover as the economic climate improved would probably not be enough to increase significantly the hotel's bed occupancy rate.

(e) The examination syllabuses and methods of assessment of all the A Level examining boards now require candidates to have some knowledge of the investigative methods used by economists to research economic data. One method of calculating elasticities is to collect nationally published data on prices and incomes, and on demand for hotel beds. Government publications such as the Family Expenditure Survey and the National Income 'Blue Book' may provide relevant information, together with the publications of tourist bodies and hotel trade associations and the company reports of large hotel groups. If a particular hotel such as the Bootham Hotel wishes to estimate the price and income elasticities of demand for its product, it might commission a customer survey and questionnaire, possibly asking all customers to answer a questionnaire on the completion of their stay in the hotel. Of course, the data gathered by both such methods of research may not be reliable. Elasticities estimated from national statistics are much too highly generalised to act as accurate pointers to likely changes in demand if the Bootham Hotel were to change its pricing strategy. When people respond to market research surveys, their statements about how they will behave in the future are often fanciful because of the hypothetical nature of the questions they are answering.

Question bank

1 Estimates of Demand Elasticities in the UK economy

Product	Price Elasticity	Income Elasticity
Housing	−0.23	+0.54
Tobacco	−0.26	+0.77

(a) Explain the meaning of these price and income elasticities of demand for housing and tobacco. (10)

(b) In the light of these elasticities, discuss the appropriate government policies for achieving **reduced** tobacco consumption and **increased** demand for housing. (15)
AEB

2 A company which owns a chain of shops hiring out pre-recorded films on video has estimated that the elasticities of demand for the product are as follows:
   (i)   price elasticity of demand is –**0.8**;
   (ii) income elasticity of demand is +**2.0**;
   (iii) the cross elasticity of demand with respect to the price of tickets to the cinema is +**1.5**.

(a) Explain carefully what is meant by **each** of these figures. (12)

(b) Assuming the elasticities are correct, discuss the implications for company policy. (13)

AEB

3 (a) Distinguish between 'elastic supply' and 'inelastic supply'. (20)

(b) Explain why the short-run supply of fresh flowers is likely to be less elastic than the supply of video recorders. (40)

(c) Contrast the effect on price of sudden increase in demand for both of these of these products. (40)

ULEAC

Pitfalls

There are a number of pitfalls you must avoid when answering questions on elasticity. Firstly, make sure you don't confuse the different elasticities: in exam conditions candidates frequently write about elasticity of supply as if it were a demand elasticity. The wording of 3(c) invites you to fall into this trap: the question is about elasticity of supply, *not* demand. Secondly, you must state the various formulae accurately. Make sure you refer to *proportionate* changes in demand, supply, price, income etc, and not to *absolute* changes. Another common mistake is to state the formulae upside down. Finally, when numerical examples are provided for you (as with Questions 1 and 2), make sure you take note of the plus and minus signs and carefully interpret what they mean.

Key points

These three questions are typical of many questions on elasticity. In each case, the first part of the question asks you to explain the meaning and/or the significance of some key elasticity concepts, illustrated with figures in the case of Questions 1 and 2. With Questions 1 and 3 you must also explain or suggest factors responsible for particular elasticities. In your answers to 1(b) and 2(b), you must consider the impact of the elasticities detailed in the question on government policy (in Question 1) and the behaviour of firms (in Question 2).

AGRICULTURAL PRICES

Units in this chapter

6.1 *Causes of price instability for agricultural products*

6.2 *Government policies and agriculture*

Chapter objectives

Agriculture is an industry in which there are thousands of producers, few of whom can influence the market price by individual decisions to supply or not to supply. At the same time many agricultural products, for example soft wheat, are relatively uniform or **homogeneous** commodities for which the world price is a ruling market price. In other words, it would seem that agriculture approximates to the economist's abstraction of **perfect competition** as a market form. Yet, if we look more closely, we also see that agriculture is the industry in which governments of a variety of political persuasions have consistently intervened in order to support farm prices and agricultural incomes. In this chapter we examine the causes of fluctuating prices and incomes, and compare some of the ways in which governments can intervene to create greater stability.

6.1 CAUSES OF PRICE INSTABILITY FOR AGRICULTURAL PRODUCTS

Throughout history, agriculture has experienced two closely related problems.

❶ There has been a **long-run downward trend** in agricultural prices relative to the prices of manufactures and services.

❷ Agricultural prices and incomes have been **unstable from year to year**.

The long-run trend is largely explained by shifts in agricultural supply and demand curves through time, while the short-run instability results from the inelastic nature of agricultural supply and demand, and the effects of good and bad harvests on the position of the short-run supply curve from one year to another.

THE LONG-RUN DOWNWARD TREND IN RELATIVE PRICES

In Fig. 6.1, the equilibrium price and output of food in an earlier historical period is shown at point E_1. Over time, both the supply and the demand for foodstuffs have increased, but the supply curve has shifted further to the right. Thus the new long-run equilibrium at E_2 represents a larger output at a lower price. The shift in the demand curve for food is explained mainly by an increase in the population and higher incomes. However, food is a necessity with a low income elasticity demand: when real income doubles, food consumption also increases, but by a smaller proportionate amount. Meanwhile, improvements in agricultural technology, such as the introduction of machinery and fertilisers, have rapidly increased farm yields, thereby causing the much greater long-run shift in supply.

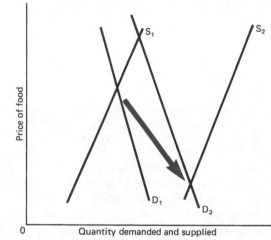

Fig. 6.1 The long-run fall in agricultural prices

SHORT-RUN CAUSES OF PRICE INSTABILITY

The year-to-year instability in farm prices is caused by **low short-run elasticities of supply and demand** combined with **random fluctuations** in the harvest. Because of the length of the production period between planting and harvesting a crop, it is often appropriate to depict the short-run supply curve as a vertical or completely inelastic line. We are assuming that once the crop is harvested, it will be sold for whatever it will bring. The supply curve S_1, drawn in Fig. 6.2a, represents supply in a 'normal' year. However, weather conditions and other factors outside the farmers' control will shift the position of the supply curve from year to year. The size of the resulting price fluctuations will depend upon the price elasticity of demand. Demand for foodstuffs in general is inelastic because food is a necessity, so significant fluctuations in price occur as the vertical supply curve shifts up or down the relatively inelastic demand curve.

FLUCTUATIONS IN AGRICULTURAL INCOMES

From a farmer's point of view, fluctuations in his income are more serious than fluctuations in price. If demand is elastic, a fall in price causes a rise in farm income, but when demand is inelastic the opposite is true: income falls when price falls. Following a bad harvest, the supply curve in Fig. 6.2a shifts to S_3 and agricultural incomes are represented by the rectangle OP_2BQ_2. In the event of a good harvest, the diagram shows that farm incomes decline to the area OP_1AQ_1. Paradoxically, therefore, a farmer may benefit more from a bad harvest than from a good one, when demand is inelastic.

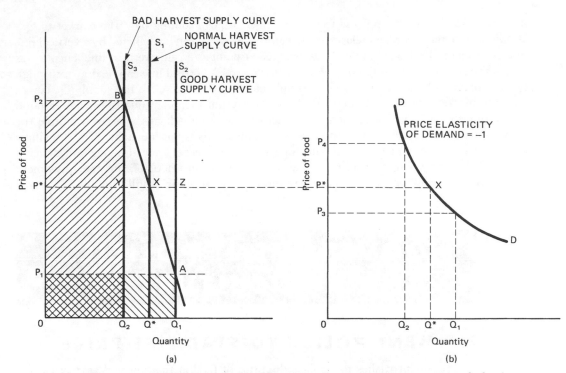

Fig. 6.2 Short-run price instability of agricultural products (a) without government intervention, both prices and farm incomes fluctuate (b) target prices to stabilise farm incomes

DYNAMIC CAUSES OF PRICE INSTABILITY

Because of the length of the production period, there may be a supply lag between the decision to produce and the actual supply coming onto the market. We can assume that this year's price has no effect on this year's supply but instead determines next year's supply. Year-long supply lags can be typical of crops such as wheat, though the original cobweb model – described below – was based on the market for hogs in the USA.

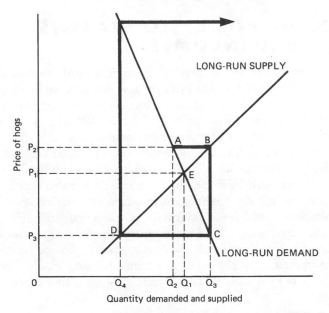

Fig. 6.3 Dynamic causes of price instability: the cobweb theory

Fig. 6.3 illustrates how the adjustment mechanism from one year to the next may be unstable, being associated with ever-increasing fluctuations in price and output. Suppose that equilibrium is at E where long-run supply and demand intersect. An outbreak of pig disease

85

now disturbs the system and reduces the number of hogs coming onto the market to Q_2. Within the current year, an inelastic short-run supply curve can be depicted by a vertical line drawn through Q_2. A new price P_2, determined at point A on this vertical line, encourages farmers to supply Q_3 onto the market in the next year. A vertical line can be drawn through Q_3 to represent the inelastic short-run supply curve next year. When the supply Q_3 comes onto the market, the price drops to P_3. Price and output then continue to oscillate around the equilibrium in a series of increasing fluctuations. Although in the above example the cobweb model is associated with increasing instability, this is not inevitable. Try drawing a cobweb diagram in which the long-run supply curve is steeper than the long-run demand curve. Following a disturbance, price and output will again fluctuate, but the adjustment mechanism will now be stable, converging towards the long-run equilibrium at E.

6.2 GOVERNMENT POLICIES AND AGRICULTURE

GOVERNMENT POLICY TO STABILISE PRICE

Suppose a government wishes to stabilise the price of food at the 'normal' year price, P*. Following a good harvest, the government buys up the amount Q_1–Q^* to prevent the market price falling below P* to P_1. If in the next year a bad harvest occurs, the government will supplement supply by releasing food onto the market from its stocks; this will prevent the price from rising above P* to P_2. Provided that agricultural products can be stored, that the government is prepared to meet the cost of storage, and that good and bad harvests are roughly evenly divided, then the price can be stabilised at P*. If the government wished to make the policy self-financing, it could buy at a lower price and sell at a higher price. Price would now be stabilised within a range, and the costs of storage could be met from the difference between the two **intervention** or **stabilisation** prices, as in the Common Agricultural Policy of the European Union or EU.

GOVERNMENT POLICY TO STABILISE AGRICULTURAL INCOMES

The policy described in the previous section is an example of a **buffer stock policy**. Although such a policy may successfully stabilise price, it does not necessarily stabilise agricultural incomes. In the event of a good harvest, farmers' income will be the rectangle OP^*ZQ_1 if the price is stabilised at P*. Incomes will decline to the area OP^*YQ_2 following a bad harvest. Farm incomes thus vary directly with the size of production, the exact opposite of the situation in which prices are left free to fluctuate in conditions of inelastic demand.

How then can a government use a buffer stock policy to stabilise incomes rather than prices? The answer is provided by Fig. 6.2b. The curve DD, with a unit elasticity, is drawn through X, the point which determines farm incomes in a normal year. DD shows the complete range of prices at which the government must operate its buffer stock policy if it is to stabilise incomes. Following a good harvest in which output Q_1 comes onto the market, the government must buy at the price P_3: farm incomes will then be exactly the same as in the normal year. Symmetrically, the government must release part of its buffer stocks onto the market at the price of P_4 in order to stabilise incomes when output falls to Q_2 in a bad year.

AGRICULTURAL SUPPORT POLICIES IN THE UNITED KINGDOM

A fundamental change in British agricultural policy took place when, in the early 1970s, the United Kingdom joined the European Community or EC, as the European Union was then called. British farmers are relatively high-cost producers when compared with their counterparts in areas such as the American Midwest, although they are efficient within the constraints imposed by farm size and the British climate. In most agricultural sectors, British farmers are relatively low-cost producers when compared with European farmers.

In Fig. 6.4, the high British costs of production are represented by the long-run domestic supply curve S_1. On the same diagram, the world price of food is shown by a perfectly elastic supply curve drawn at a lower level of costs P_1; this perfectly elastic supply curve represents an infinite supply of imports at the ruling world price. The diagram implies (rather unrealistically) that, without some system of protection or support, British farmers would produce no food: the supply curve S_1 cuts the price axis at a price higher than P_1.

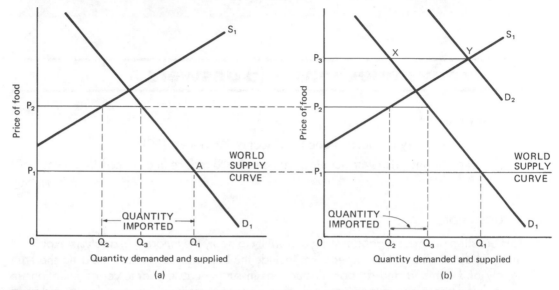

Fig. 6.4 Farm price support systems (a) a deficiency payment system (b) A buffer stock system plus an external tariff

Before the United Kingdom joined the EC, **deficiency payments** or **producer subsidies** were the main form of agricultural support. Essentially, the policy was a **cheap food policy**, financed out of general taxation: the price of food in Britain was determined by the world price and subsidies were paid to British farmers to keep them in business. This is illustrated in Fig. 6.4a. British farmers were guaranteed a price of P_2 at which they supplied Q_2. Nevertheless, domestic production was sold to the consumer at the world price P_1, the difference in the two prices being the deficiency payment to the farmers provided by the government. Under this system, the total demand Q_1 was determined at A. Quantity Q_2 was domestically produced and the remainder was imported.

In contrast, the Common Agricultural Policy (CAP) of the EU deals with the problem of cheap imports by imposing an **external tariff or levy** which brings the price of imports up to the level of cost, plus normal profits, of European farmers. Suppose the tariff is fixed at P_2 in Fig. 6.4b. The total amount demanded will be reduced to Q_3 as compared to Q_1 in the deficiency payment scheme. Quantity Q_2 will still be domestically produced and the rest imported.

The external tariff on food imports is only one part of the CAP. As earlier indicated, the EU also operates a buffer stock policy with upper and lower stabilisation prices. The problem has been that for many products the lower of these two intervention prices has been set too high, at a level such as P_3 in Fig. 6.4b. An excess supply of XY is encouraged and the price can only be sustained if the EU continuously intervenes to purchase the overproduction. This is represented by the shift in the demand curve to D_2. The effects of bad harvests in causing temporary leftward shifts in the short-run supply curve have been insufficient to reverse the accumulation of the butter 'mountains' and wine 'lakes' which have resulted from the policy.

Recently, the EU has tried to reduce excess production by lowering the prices guaranteed to EU farmers and by paying farmers to take land out of production in a **set-aside scheme**. For obvious reasons, set-aside policies are much more popular with farmers than lower guaranteed prices; indeed, the strength of the farmers' pressure group has made it extremely difficult for the EU to agree on price reductions.

Chapter roundup

In recent years it has become fashionable to talk of 'supply–side economics', which covers government microeconomic policy. This aims to improve the structure of the economy and the performance of industry. Government policy to support agricultural incomes and prices can be considered as a part of this wider microeconomic policy, other aspects of which are developed in Chapter 10 and Chapter 16. Subsidies to the agricultural sector form part of public spending (Chapter 13), whilst external tariffs influence trade (Chapter 18) and the Balance of Payments (Chapter 19).

Illustrative questions and answers

1 Essay Question

(a) Why are primary products prone to fluctuations in price? (50)

(b) What problems arise with schemes that attempt to reduce fluctuations in prices? (50)

ULEAC

Tutorial note

This question provides a good test of your ability to apply the theoretical analysis explained in this chapter. You will be expected to include the key analysis on how inelastic short-run supply and demand and random fluctuations in supply cause year-to-year fluctuations in agricultural prices and output. You could then go on to explain the long-run downward trend in agricultural prices and, if you have the time, the cobweb theory.

Suggested answer

● Agriculture is dominated by a large number of small producers who are price-takers. In contrast, industrial firms are more likely to be monopolists or price-makers, with the market power to stabilise prices if they wish.

● The agricultural production period is usually longer and individual farmers may be unable to accumulate stocks. Explain how an inelastic short-run supply curve results. Conversely, as manufacturers produce more durable goods, their supply curve tends to be more elastic.

● Analyse year-to-year price instability in conditions of inelastic supply and demand.

● Explain the long-run downward trend in agricultural prices relative to the price of manufactured goods. Manufactured goods are more income-elastic and producers may have the ability to create demand.

● Supply lags in agriculture, illustrated by the cobweb theory, may also cause fluctuating prices.

● Briefly explain how, in principle, a buffer stock scheme reduces price fluctuations.

● Outline the problems of financing the scheme, etc.

2 Data Question

A SLIMMER SACRED COW

Brussels has signalled that it is sizing up the most sacred of all European Community (EC) cows, the Common Agricultural Policy (CAP) farm subsidies regime, not to slaughter it, certainly, but to slim it down substantially.

Mr Ray MacSharry, the EC's Agriculture Commissioner, is calling for severe cuts in Community subsidies to farmers and smaller production quotas to stop them producing far more than the EC consumes.

He foresaw EC farm spending rising this year by about 7 billion European Currency Units (ECUs), or 25%, to over 32 billion ECUs, nearly 60% of the Community budget. In 1992 it would rise further by 12.5%. By the end of this month, EC–held beef stocks will have increased to 930 000 tonnes, comfortably over 1987's high of 800 000 tonnes: butter, skimmed milk and cereals are on the same mountain path.

It is the growing cost of a system which concentrates upon price support and rewards ever-greater output whatever the market demands, which is at the root of the reform drive.

The intervention price for cereals would drop from ECU 169 to ECU 90 a tonne, a 47% cut. The subsidised price for beef would fall by 15 per cent and for milk by 10%, with the milk quota for the EC as a whole being cut by 5%.

The CAP, beyond its post-war aim of food self-sufficiency – long since achieved – was always part of social policy to help smaller farmers stay in business. It merely operated in an anti-social way: 60% of cereals output is produced by 6% of cereals farmers, who take 60% of the subsidy even though they are highly competitive. In milk and beef the same sort of ratios occur.

(Source: *Financial Times*, January 24 1991 (adapted))

Answer **each** of the following questions, explaining your reasoning in **each** case.

(a) Explain the basic purposes of the Common Agricultural Policy (CAP).   (6)

(b) Explain why the Common Agricultural Policy (CAP) led to the EC holding ever-larger stocks of beef, butter and other agricultural products.   (6)

(c) Why might Common Agricultural Policy (CAP) subsidies be regarded as an inefficient use of European Community (EC) revenues?   (6)

(d) What are the likely effects of reducing the intervention prices and production quotas? (7)   WJEC

Tutorial note

(a) As we have explained in this chapter, agricultural prices are much more unstable from year to year than the prices of most manufactured goods, unless they are supported by some form of administration or regulation. The Common Agricultural Policy (CAP) came into being as a result of the decision to include agriculture in the common market established under the 1957 Treaty of Rome which created the European Community, now called the European Union. The CAP's aims are to modernise agriculture, to ensure supplies to the consumer and to give an adequate return to the farmer.

(b) Beef, butter and grain 'mountains' and wine 'lakes' have accumulated because the guaranteed prices offered to farmers for supported products under the CAP were set too high. In effect, high CAP prices guaranteed farmers risk-free super-normal profits. Under these circumstances, as Chapter 7 explains, the super-normal profits created an incentive for farmers who were already producing the supported crops and meats to increase output, and for other farmers to switch their land into agricultural activities supported by the CAP guaranteed pricing system. And once the CAP prices were set, the political power of EU farmers has usually been sufficient to prevent any significant reduction in their levels.

(c) An economic policy can be regarded as efficient if it achieves its desired objective with minimum undesired side-effects or distortions. But as the passage indicates, the CAP's aims of self-sufficiency and an adequate return for farmers could be achieved with a lower level of subsidy. This in turn means that the EU funds wasted on unnecessary farm subsidies could be better spent elsewhere. Large farmers or 'agribusiness' interests enjoy most of the subsidies, even though they were intended to help the small farmers. Finally, butter and grain 'mountains' that become unfit for human consumption and have to be destroyed, themselves represent a grossly inefficient use of resources in a world in which most of the planet's population is underfed.

(d) EU revenues might be put to alternative (and possibly better) use; contributions to the EU budget from member states might be reduced; farmers might be forced in a more competitive environment to adapt, diversify and reduce costs; rural living standards would probably fall; 'marginal' farmers would be likely to go out of business; land would be diverted into non-agricultural uses, e.g. leisure activities such as golf courses; overproduction would be reduced or eliminated; food prices might fall for the consumer. Three or four of these points explained in a little depth would be sufficient to earn the 7 available marks.

Question bank

1 (a) Analyse the problems facing farmers when the prices of agricultural products are determined solely by market forces. (50)

(b) To what extent does government intervention in the determination of the prices of agricultural products solve these problems? (50) *ULEAC*

Pitfalls

A Level economics students often seem to believe that once a government has identified an economic problem, any attempt to use economic policy to correct the problem will inevitably be 100% successful. A few moments reflection on the track record of the Common Agricultural Policy of the European Union, should quickly dispel such fantasies! When answering part (b) you must not simply describe government intervention or assume that it will necessarily succeed in achieving its objective(s); rather you must assess the extent to which government intervention has been successful, using real world examples of intervention, such as the CAP.

Key points

You must identify and then analyse at least two problems, taking care to deal with problems facing producers rather than those affecting consumers. You might explain how farmers' incomes may collapse in the event of a rightward shift of the supply curve and a falling market price, or a leftward shift of supply in the event of a bad harvest which decimates production. Alternatively, you might deal with the effect of a collapse of demand upon farmers' incomes, for example relating your answer to recent health scares concerning the effects of consuming beef. Make sure you devote at least half your answer to explaining how governments have intervened to alleviate the problems you have described, and to evaluating the success of such intervention.

2 Agricultural support policies presented the greatest difficulties for a successful conclusion of the GATT negotiations in the early 1990s.

(a) Explain why governments in developed countries adopted agricultural support policies. (50)

(b) Discuss the likely effects on the markets for agricultural products of abandoning such policies. (50) *ULEAC*

Pitfalls

Although the scenario to this question mentions the international negotiations to reduce tariffs which took place in the early 1990s, the question is not actually about GATT (the General Agreement on Tariffs and Trade). Take care not to drift into irrelevance, though by all means mention the fact that governments have often used agricultural support policies as a method of protecting their farmers, and that the liberalising of international trade in agricultural products might require the abandoning of such support policies. Note also that part (a) is about *why* but not *how*.

Key points

Briefly explain the meaning of an agricultural support policy and suggest at least two reasons why governments have introduced such policies. For example, governments may wish to support farmers' incomes, or stabilise prices for consumers, or ensure an element of self-sufficiency. The obvious point to make in your answer to part (b) is that the abandoning of support policies will simply lead to the recurrence of the problem the policy was designed to prevent. Assess the extent to which you think this is likely, and note also that support policies produced their own problems such as overproduction and inefficient feather-bedded farmers. Abandoning support policies might reduce such problems and also, by opening up the markets of developed economies, aid farmers in Third World countries.

3 (a) Discuss the extent to which agricultural markets resemble the model of perfect competition. (12)

(b) Explain why and how governments intervene in agricultural markets to influence prices and levels of output. (13)   *AEB*

Pitfalls

There is a danger here of writing all you know about perfect competition and of assuming that agricultural markets are indeed perfectly competitive. In this question, part (b) is concerned with both *why* and *how*, so make sure you address both.

Key points

Define perfect competition, and discuss the extent to which agricultural markets conform or fail to conform to the six or so conditions of perfect competition. Explain at least two reasons why governments intervene in agricultural markets and at least two methods of intervention, e.g. support buying or buffer stock intervention, set-aside policies, and subsidies granted to farmers. Try to note real world examples, but the question does not require you to discuss the problems resulting from the policies you explain.

PERFECT COMPETITION AND MONOPOLY

Units in this chapter

7.1 *Market structure and the theory of the firm*
7.2 *Perfect competition*
7.3 *Monopoly*

Chapter objectives

In Chapter 4 the cost and supply conditions of a firm were examined, without at that stage considering in detail the **market structure** in which the firm sells its output. It was assumed simply that the firm exists in a competitive market, able to sell as much or as little as it pleases at a ruling market price determined in the market as a whole. In fact, it was assumed that the firm produces and sells its output within a **perfectly competitive market structure**. This chapter takes a more detailed look at perfect competition, before examining a second type of market structure, **monopoly**. The chapter concludes by comparing the desirable and less-desirable properties of **profit-maximising** or **equilibrium firms** in perfect competition and monopoly.

7.1 MARKET STRUCTURE AND THE THEORY OF THE FIRM

MARKET STRUCTURE

Perfect competition and **monopoly** are examples of **market structures** or **market forms**. They are opposite or polar extremes which separate a spectrum of market structures known as **imperfect competition**. Fig. 7.2 illustrates the main types of market structure, including **monopolistic competition** and **oligopoly** which we shall examine in Chapter 8. Monopoly itself can be considered to be the most extreme form of imperfect competition, since there is no competition at all within an industry if a single firm produces the whole of an industry output. Nevertheless, monopoly is usually a relative rather than an absolute concept. This is because a firm will almost always experience some competition from substitute products produced by firms in other industries, even when it has an absolute monopoly in the production of a particular good or service.

Although the analysis in this chapter is restricted to perfect competition and pure monopoly, you must avoid the temptation to consider either of these two market structures as typical or representative of the real world. **Pure monopoly** is exceedingly rare. The **public monopolies** or **nationalised industries**, such as the Post Office, provide perhaps the best examples, though following privatisation, there are few nationalised industries now left in the UK. Perfect competition is actually non-existent – it is a **theoretical abstraction** or **model**, defined by the conditions which are listed in Fig. 7.1. Some economists argue that the emphasis given to perfect competition encourages students to adopt a false perspective in the belief that a perfect market is an attainable ideal.

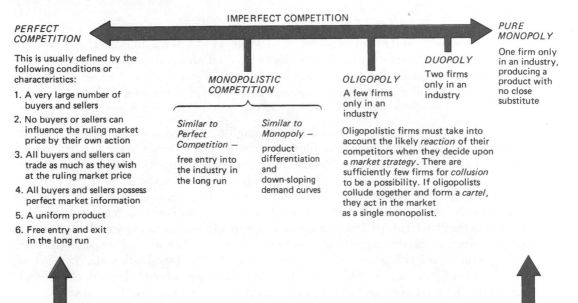

Fig. 7.1 Different market structures

THE TRADITIONAL THEORY OF THE FIRM

For many years the theory of the firm was principally concerned with the nature of perfectly competitive markets. The development of this theory owes much to the great nineteenth-century British economist, Alfred Marshall. During Marshall's lifetime the British economy was still dominated by a large number of small firms, for many of which a single owner/decision-maker, or entrepreneur, could be identified. Thus, perfect competition may have been a reasonable approximation to what the economy was like in the late nineteenth century.

ALTERNATIVE THEORIES OF THE FIRM

During the first half of the twentieth century, many economists became dissatisfied with perfect competition as *the* theory of the firm. Their dissatisfaction was a response to the growth in the size of firms and the increasing domination of markets by a small number of large business enterprises. Theoretical models of monopoly and imperfect competition were developed by Edward Chamberlin and Joan Robinson in an attempt to give a greater realism to the theory of the firm. More recently, some economists have attacked the **profit-maximising** assumption that is fundamental to the traditional theories of monopoly, imperfect competition and perfect competition. The new theories of the firm are called **managerial theories** and **organisational (or behavioural) theories**: both claim to be more realistic and hence better at explaining actual behaviour than the traditional profit-maximising theories of the firm. Managerial theories, popularised by J K Galbraith in his book *The New Industrial State* (1967), take as their starting point the split between shareholders as owners and managers as decision-makers in large modern business corporations. It is argued that managers aim to **maximise managerial objectives**, such as sales, growth, and managerial career prospects, rather than shareholders' profits. In contrast, organisationalists such as Professor Herbert Simon, a winner of the Nobel Prize for Economics, see the firm as an organisation or **coalition of different groups**, such as managers, production workers, research scientists, etc. The firm is a '**satisficer**' rather than a **maximiser**, attempting to satisfy the aspirations of the groups which make up the coalition.

PROFIT-MAXIMISING BEHAVIOUR

This assumption is fundamental to the traditional theory of the firm. Profit can be represented by a simple identity:

$$\text{Total Profits} \equiv \text{Total Revenue} - \text{Total Cost}.$$

The firm aims to produce the level of output at which TR-TC is maximised. This is one way of stating the **equilibrium condition of the firm**, for if profits are being maximised, there is no reason or incentive for the firm to change its level of output. Nevertheless, it is usually more convenient for analytical purposes to state the equilibrium condition in alternative form:

$$MC = MR$$

This means that profits are maximised when the addition to total costs that results from the production of the last unit of output (**marginal cost**) is exactly equal to the addition to total revenue resulting from the sale of the last unit (**marginal revenue**). Imagine, for example, a horticulturalist who is unable to influence the price of lettuces in the local market, in which case average revenue equals marginal revenue. Suppose the price of lettuces is 30p each, and that when the horticulturalist markets 98 lettuces each day, the cost to him of producing and marketing the 98th lettuce is 29p. If he decides not to market the lettuce he will clearly sacrifice lp of profits. Let us now suppose that his total costs rise by 30p and 31p respectively when a 99th lettuce and 100th lettuce are marketed. The marketing of the 100th lettuce causes total profits to fall by lp, but the 99th lettuce neither adds to nor subtracts from total profits: it represents the level of output at which profits are exactly maximised. To sum up:

❶ If MC < MR, it pays to increase output (disequilibrium condition)

❷ If MC > MR, it pays to decrease output (disequilibrium condition)

❸ If MC = MR, it pays to keep output unchanged (equilibrium condition) provided that the MC curve cuts the MR curve from below.

THE CONCEPT OF NORMAL PROFIT

The concepts of **normal** and **abnormal** (or **supernormal**) profit are completely abstract concepts, which have nothing to do with how an accountant will measure a company's profits. **Normal profit** is defined as the minimum level of profit required to keep existing firms in production, yet being insufficient to attract new firms into the industry. As such, normal profit is regarded as a necessary cost of production, which is included in the average cost curve. **Abnormal profit** is defined as any extra profit over and above normal profit. We shall now examine what happens to abnormal profits in conditions of perfect competition and monopoly.

7.2 PERFECT COMPETITION

SHORT-RUN EQUILIBRIUM IN CONDITIONS OF PERFECT COMPETITION

Perfect competition can be defined in terms of the conditions of perfect competition, which are listed in Fig. 7.1. While you must learn the conditions of perfect competition, it is seldom relevant to an examination question merely to repeat the list. Instead, you must learn to use the conditions to analyse the essential properties of a perfectly competitive firm and industry in equilibrium, compared with those of a monopoly in equilibrium. For example, the assumptions that a perfectly competitive firm can sell as much as it wishes at the ruling market price, and that it cannot influence the ruling market price by its own actions, allow us to say that the firm is a **price-taker**. The perfectly competitive firm faces an infinitely elastic demand curve, determined by the ruling market price in the industry as a whole. This **horizontal demand curve** or **price line** is also the perfectly competitive firm's **average revenue** and **marginal revenue curve**.

To show the equilibrium output of a perfectly competitive firm in the short run, we superimpose this horizontal average and marginal revenue curve upon the average and marginal cost curves which were derived in Chapter 4. Using the equilibrium condition $MC = MR$, the resulting equilibrium output is illustrated at Q_1 in Fig. 7.2a. Total abnormal profits at this output are represented by the shaded area obtained by subtracting the total cost area (OC_1xQ_1) from the total revenue area (OP_1yQ_1).

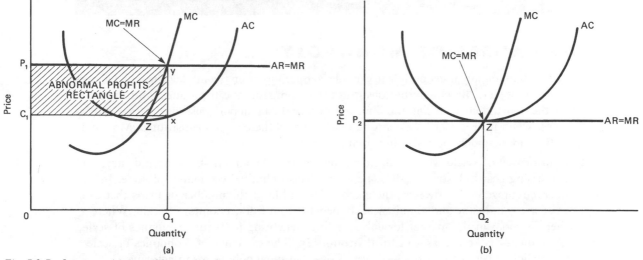

Fig. 7.2 Perfect competition equilibrium (a) short-run equilibrium (b) long-run equilibrium

LONG-RUN EQUILIBRIUM IN CONDITIONS OF PERFECT COMPETITION

In order to distinguish between **short-run** and **long-run equilibrium** in perfect competition, we assume complete freedom of entry and exit by firms in and out of the industry in the economic long run. The market price signals to firms whether abnormal profits, normal

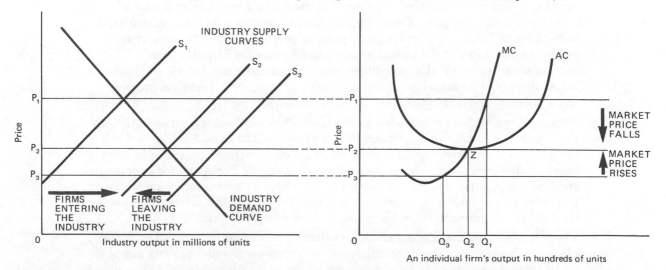

Fig. 7.3 Perfect competition long-run equilibrium: the entry and exit of firms produces a long-run equilibrium for an individual firm output Q_2 and price P_2

profits or losses can be made. The existence of abnormal profits will provide the incentive for new firms to enter the industry, and, in a similar way, existing losses will create the incentive for firms to leave. As illustrated in Fig. 7.3, the entry of new firms causes the industry supply curve to shift rightwards and the ruling market price falls. Symmetrically, the departure of firms causes the industry supply curve to shift leftwards and the price line rises. Long-run equilibrium will occur when there is no incentive for firms to enter or leave the industry: this is represented by the output Q_2 at the price of P_2 in Fig. 7.2 and 7.3b. The total revenue area now equals the total cost area, illustrating the fact that abnormal profits have been competed away. It must be stressed at all times that it is **impersonal market forces** and **individual self-interest**, operating in conditions of freedom of entry and exit, which bring about this long-run equilibrium outcome.

7.3 MONOPOLY

THE CAUSES OF MONOPOLY

An effective monopoly must be able to exclude competitors from the market through barriers to entry. However, the closer the substitutes that competitors can produce, and the more elastic the demand curve facing the firm, the weaker the monopoly position. A monopoly is strongest when it produces an essential good for which there are no substitutes. Monopoly is likely to exist under the following circumstances:

● **Economies of scale** Many industries, for example the aircraft-building industry, are decreasing cost industries with scope for perhaps unlimited economies of scale. In most circumstances, however, the market size will limit the number of firms that can exist in an industry and simultaneously benefit from full economies of scale. Where there is room in the market for only one firm benefiting from full economies of scale, the industry is known as a **natural monopoly**. The existence of economies of scale is a major cause of the growth of large firms and monopoly in manufacturing industry. It may also explain how a large supermarket can monopolise the grocery trade in the limited market of a small town or suburb as a result of driving small grocery stores out of the business.

● **Public utility industries are a special type of natural monopoly** Utility industries such as the electricity, gas, water and telephone industries experience a particular marketing problem. They produce a service which is delivered through a distribution grid or network of pipes or cables into millions of separate homes and businesses. Competition can often be wasteful since it requires the duplication of expensive distribution grids. Given the likelihood of monopoly in these industries, a public policy choice exists between the option of **private monopoly subject to public regulation** and the **public ownership of monopoly**, usually as a **nationalised industry**. (Chapter 10 explains why some, though not all, the utility industries should no longer be regarded as natural monopolies. Technical progress and regulatory agencies have opened them up to competition.)

● **Other government-created monopolies** Not all nationalised industries have been either utility industries or monopolies. Nevertheless, industries such as the coal and rail industries were nationalised in order to create state-owned monopolies. In other instances, the government may deliberately create a private monopoly, for example by granting a **franchise** to a TV company which operates without competition within a particular geographical area. As another example, the **patent law** creates an exclusive right for an inventor to exploit his invention for a number of years.

● **Control of raw materials and market outlets** Firms may try to establish exclusive control over the source of raw materials for their products in order to deny access to competitors. In a rather similar way, British breweries have been known to buy up public houses in order to establish exclusive market outlets for the beer they produce.

● **Advertising as a barrier to entry** It is sometimes argued that small firms are prevented from entering an industry because they cannot afford the minimum level of advertising which is necessary to persuade retailers to stock the goods they produce. Their products are crowded out of the market by the mass advertising, brand-imaging, and other marketing strategies of much larger established firms.

MONOPOLY EQUILIBRIUM

Despite the likelihood of economies of scale in conditions of monopoly, for the time being we shall assume that we are investigating an industry with no economies or diseconomies of scale. It follows from this assumption that the lowest long-run average costs which a firm can achieve will be the same in conditions of perfect competition and monopoly. Nevertheless, the revenue curves will be different in the two market forms. Since the monopoly is the industry, the **monopolist's demand curve** and the **industry demand curve** are identical. There are two ways of looking at this. If we regard the monopolist as a price-maker, then when he sets the price he must be a **quantity-taker**. Alternatively, if the monopolist acts as a quantity-setter, the demand curve determines the maximum price the monopolist can charge in order successfully to sell the chosen quantity. This is an example of a **trade-off**, an important economic concept which is closely related to opportunity cost. A problem of choice exists because the monopolist does not possess the freedom to set both price and quantity: if he acts as a price-maker, the demand curve determines the maximum output he can sell and vice versa.

Since the **demand curve** shows the price the monopolist charges for each level of output, it is also the monopolist's **average revenue curve**. The demand curve is not the marginal revenue curve, which must be below the average revenue curve. We can use Fig. 7.4 to explore the relationship between the AR and MR curves in conditions of monopoly. If the monopolist decides to produce output Q_1 in Fig 7.4a, the area OQ_1AP_1 will represent total revenue. When output is increased by one unit to Q_2, total revenue changes to the area OQ_2BP_2. Two shaded areas are drawn on the diagram. The area marked as the gain in revenue represents the extra unit sold multiplied by the new price – or the average revenue per unit at the new level of output. The other shaded area shows the 'loss in revenue' which results from the fact that all the units of output comprising the previous level of output Q_1, must now be sold at the price of P_2 rather than P_1. The marginal revenue associated with Q_2 is obtained by subtracting the loss in revenue from the gain in revenue (or average revenue). The resulting MR curve which is drawn in Fig. 7.4b is twice as steep as the AR curve. This will always be the case provided that the monopolist's demand or AR curve is linear (a straight line), though this mathematical property will not apply if the AR curve is non-linear.

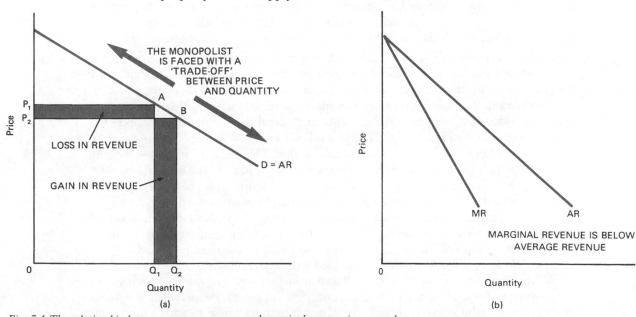

Fig. 7.4 The relationship between average revenue and marginal revenue in monopoly.
(a) MR equals the gain in revenue minus the loss in revenue (b) the MR curve is always below the AR curve

The equilibrium output in conditions of monopoly is illustrated in Fig. 7.5. Equilibrium is determined at point A, where MC = MR. It is worth repeating that the equilibrium condition MC = MR applies to any firm, whatever the market structure, as long as the firm is a profit-maximiser. You must avoid the temptation to read off the equilibrium price at point A: point B on the AR curve locates the monopolist's equilibrium price.

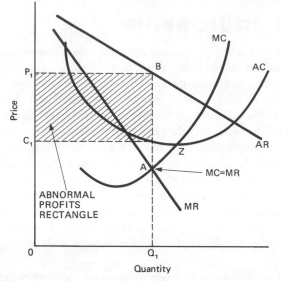

Fig. 7.5 Monopoly equilibrium

As in the case of short-run equilibrium under perfect competition, the monopolist makes abnormal profits, represented by the shaded area of Fig. 7.5. However, the existence of barriers to entry allows the abnormal profits to persist into the long run, whereas in perfect competition abnormal profits are essentially temporary.

THE MEANING OF ECONOMIC EFFICIENCY

Before we attempt a comparison of the desirable or undesirable properties of perfect competition and monopoly, it is necessary to explain some of the meanings which economists attach to the word **efficiency**:

- **Productive efficiency** This is often called technical efficiency, although in fact the two concepts are slightly different. Production is technically efficient when output is maximised from a given set of inputs (or when the inputs needed to produce a given level of output are minimised). To achieve productive efficiency, or cost efficiency, a firm must use the techniques which are available at the lowest possible cost. Productive efficiency is measured by the lowest point on a firm's average cost curve.

- **Allocative efficiency** This rather abstract concept is of crucial importance to the understanding of economic efficiency. Allocative efficiency occurs when marginal cost is equated to price in all the industries in the economy. If all industries are perfectly competitive and if equilibrium prices prevail, allocative efficiency will automatically occur (provided that we ignore the existence of externalities discussed in Chapter 9). If you check back to Figs. 7.2 and 7.3, you will see that P = MC in conditions of perfect competition. Let us look more closely at this. The price, P, indicates the value in consumption placed by buyers on an extra unit of output. At the same time, MC measures the value in production of the resources needed to produce the extra unit of output. Suppose P > MC, as is the case in monopoly: households will pay for an extra unit an amount greater than the cost of producing it. At this price the good will be **underconsumed**. If in contrast P < MC, the value (P) placed on the last unit of the good by consumers will be less than the cost (MC) of the resources used to produce the extra unit. At this price the good will be **overconsumed**.

Whenever P > MC or P < MC, allocative inefficiency will occur. For any given employment of resources, total consumer utility or welfare can be increased if resources are shifted out of industries where P < MC and into those where P > MC, until a state of allocative efficiency (P = MC) exists in all industries.

● **X-efficiency** In the 1960s the American economist Liebenstein argued that due to 'organisational slack' resulting from the absence of competitive pressures, at any level of output monopolies and many other imperfectly competitive firms are always likely to incur unnecessary costs of production. He coined the term **X-inefficiency** to explain this. A firm can incur unnecessary costs in two ways. Firstly, it may combine its inputs in a technically inefficient way. Overmanning, and the purchase of business equipment which remains unused, are two common examples. Secondly, X-inefficiency can be caused by the firm paying its workers or managers unnecessarily high wages and salaries, or buying its raw materials or capital at unnecessarily high prices. A recent example centres on the allegedly excessive salaries and perks paid to the directors of privatised utilities such as British Gas and water companies, who worked for much less in the same organisations when they were in the public sector. If we define a firm's total and average cost curves as showing the lowest possible costs of producing various levels of output (either in the short run or in the long run), then X-inefficiency results in a firm producing 'off' and above its total and average cost curves. All points on these curves are X-efficient, all points above are X-inefficient.

EVALUATING PERFECT COMPETITION AND MONOPOLY

If you refer back to Figs. 7.2b and 7.3, you will see that a perfectly competitive firm achieves both **productive** and **allocative efficiency** in long-run equilibrium. (The productively efficient output is the lowest cost output, shown at point Z in Figs. 7.4 and 7.5 – it is often called the **optimum output** of the firm.) Strictly speaking, however, the firm will be allocatively efficient only if all other industries are perfectly competitive and if there are no externalities present. In contrast, in conditions of monopoly, average cost is above the minimum possible level, and price is not equated to marginal cost. In Fig. 7.6, the analysis is extended to compare monopoly with the whole of a perfectly competitive industry, rather than with a single firm within the industry. The curve S_1 represents the supply curve of a perfectly competitive industry or the MC curve of a monopoly if all the firms aggregate together to form a monopoly. In conditions of perfect competition, industry price P_1 and output Q_1 are located at point A. In contrast, monopoly price P_2 and output Q_2 are determined at point B where MC = MR. The diagram neatly illustrates the standard case against monopoly: that it restricts output and raises the price. Furthermore, this restriction of output is at a point above minimum average cost, resulting in productive inefficiency.

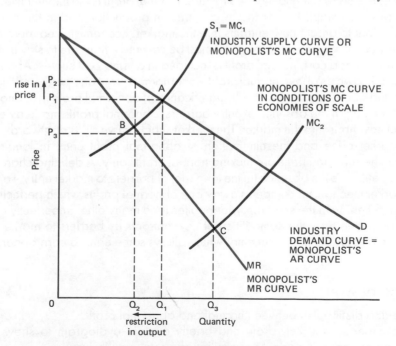

Fig. 7.6 The effects of economies of scale on price and output in monopoly

Consider, however, the possibility that a monopoly, but not a perfectly competitive firm, can benefit from **economies of scale**. The curve MC_1 is no longer relevant to the analysis of monopoly price and output, which is now determined at point C. The monopoly price P_3 is now lower and output Q_3 is higher than those achieved in perfect competition. It is possible that the benefits which result from economies of scale may exceed the productive and allocative efficiency losses which occur in monopoly. In these circumstances, monopoly may be viewed as being preferable to perfect competition.

Chapter roundup

Various other aspects of the behaviour or conduct of monopolies, such as price discrimination towards different groups of customers, are examined in Chapter 8. Because the market price conveys misleading information in conditions of monopoly, the existence of monopoly provides a very important form of market failure, the subject of Chapter 9. Finally, Chapter 10 examines government policy towards nationalised and privatised monopolies.

Illustrative questions and answers

1 Essay question

(a) What is meant by the terms 'normal profit' and 'abnormal profit'? (5)

(b) Why, in a perfect market, are firms unable to earn abnormal profits in the long run? (12)

(c) Explain why, in the UK today, some firms are able to earn abnormal profits indefinitely. (8) *SEB*

Tutorial note

This is a straightforward question testing your knowledge and understanding of some key theoretical concepts relating to market structure. Normal profit is the minimum level of profit necessary to keep established or incumbent firms in production and in the market, while being insufficient to attract new entrants into the market. Economists treat normal profit as a cost of production which, in the long run, must be covered if firms are to stay in the market. Since it is treated as a cost, normal profit is included in a firm's cost curves. Abnormal profit (which is also known as above-normal profit, supernormal profit and pure profit) is any extra profit over and above normal profit. The significance of abnormal profit in economic theory lies in the fact that, in the absence of entry barriers, abnormal profits made by established firms attract new firms into the market. The market supply curve shifts rightwards, triggering a fall in market price and the elimination of abnormal profit until, in long-run market equilibrium, the surviving firms are making normal profits only. A defining characteristic of perfect competition is the absence (in the long run) of barriers to market entry, so in the long run, the market mechanism competes away any abnormal profits which perfectly competitive firms might enjoy in the short run. Monopolies (and many other imperfectly competitive firms) are protected from the competition of new entrants by barriers to market entry. It is the existence of barriers to market entry which allows some firms to earn abnormal profits indefinitely.

Suggested answer

● Define and distinguish between normal and abnormal profit.
● Define a perfect market; draw and briefly explain a diagram to show abnormal profits being made in perfect competition short-run equilibrium.

- Explain how, in the absence of barriers to entry, these abnormal profits attract new market entrants, causing the market price to fall.
- Draw and explain a diagram to show perfect competition long-run equilibrium, with surviving firms making normal profits only.
- Explain that no real world markets in the UK are perfectly competitive; most are imperfectly competitive and a few are monopolies.
- Draw a diagram to show abnormal profits in monopoly equilibrium, explain that barriers to entry protect the monopolist's abnormal profits.

2 Data Question

Study the passage below and answer **all** the questions which follow.

THE FLYING MONOPOLISTS

Should Boeing and Airbus be forbidden to team up to build a super-jumbo?

In some businesses, the high cost of developing new products raises a barrier to would-be competitors. That day has already arrived in civil aerospace. America's *Boeing* and the partners of Europe's *Airbus Industrie* are the only companies capable of building a range of commercial jets. Once arch-rivals, they are now thinking of building an 800-seat super-jumbo together.

The idea poses a dilemma for governments. Without collaboration, and perhaps without public money as well, the super-jumbo may never be built – which would be a pity. But suppose the partnership goes ahead. If it succeeds, and the super-jumbo is much in demand, the partners will have a partial monopoly – one which they may seek to extend. This could hurt airlines and their customers, the travelling public. If the partners fail, and the super-jumbo loses money, any public investment in it will have been wasted.

This trade-off between innovation and competition will become increasingly troublesome. Many of the industries governments care most about – high-tech, high-wage industries with a claim to be 'strategic' – are suited to international, and anti-competitive, collaboration. The plans for the super-jumbo are a test case. How should governments respond?

Just good friends?

Entirely new commercial airliners are already too costly for any one producer to develop on its own. To bring a super-jumbo to market could cost $15 billion. A partnership, as Boeing and Airbus point out, would spread the risk. The aircraft makers also say that the super-jumbo serves a public interest: it would help to relieve overcrowded airports. That, they say, is why they should be allowed to collaborate, and perhaps be given some public money, too.

The case for a public subsidy is weak. Some argue that financial markets are short-termist and therefore mistakenly discriminate against big projects of this kind. But the record of governments in judging the viability of such undertakings is abysmal – witness Concorde. Financial markets may be imperfect, but in matters of this sort, they are a lot better than governments. Once governments become involved in highly publicised schemes involving the 'national interest', politics takes over and wishful thinking overrides economic reality.

A public subsidy for the super-jumbo venture should therefore be ruled out. A harder question is whether to forbid the collaboration altogether. The crucial issue is whether the new super-jumbo would have a monopoly, or whether competition could be left to regulate its price. If the partners tried to exploit any monopoly power by charging too high a price for the new aeroplane, you might think, airlines could use smaller aircraft. The trouble is, these smaller aircraft are also produced by the partners. They would be tempted to set the prices of their existing aircraft to make their super-jumbo viable. In short, collaboration on the super-jumbo would be both the reason and the means to build an aircraft-pricing cartel.

Boeing may be trying to protect the monopoly-of-sorts it already enjoys with the 747. Airbus had considered making its own, slightly smaller, super-jumbo. This would have stolen sales from the 747. The defection of one or two Airbus partners to the Boeing camp could break up the European consortium.

All this suggests that a partnership should be forbidden on competition grounds. In that event, the super-jumbo may never be built – but that may not be such a bad thing. Airbus and Boeing would continue to build bigger jets.

In aerospace, as in other industries, competition remains the most reliable spur to innovation. In this case, and in the many others that are sure to arise, governments should be guided by a simple rule: do not be drawn into supporting partnerships that are chiefly attempts to corner a market.

Source: Adapted from *The Economist* ©, June 1993

(a) What is meant by a monopolist? (2)

(b) The passage states that 'the high cost of developing new products raises a barrier to would-be competitors' (lines 1–2).

   (i) Why does the 'high cost of developing new products' (line 1) act as a barrier to entry? (4)

   (ii) Briefly explain one other barrier to entry which could occur in the aircraft manufacturing industry. (3)

(c) Evaluate the arguments put forward to support the creation of this monopoly. (6)

(d) The passage suggests that neither companies nor governments are very good at assessing the desirability of investments. Discuss **two** different ways by which economists would try to determine whether an investment, such as building this new aeroplane, should take place. (10)
         AEB

Tutorial note

(a) Define a pure monopoly as one firm only in a market (i.e. a firm producing 100% of the market output) but also state briefly that the term is often used more loosely to describe any market in which there is just one dominant firm.

(b) For part (i) make the point that any new entrant into the market would have to invest extremely heavily in both fixed capacity and in product development. For part (ii), you can argue that it would probably be several years before a new entrant into the aircraft construction industry would receive any revenue from selling aircraft to airlines; as a result, persistent losses expected for several years would deter market entry.

(c) Avoid the temptation to write about monopoly in general, taking care to focus your answer on *this* monopoly, i.e. possible monopoly in the aircraft industry. The main argument put forward in the passage to support the creation of a monopoly is the contention that no firm, however big, can on its own afford to develop the next generation of large passenger-carrying aircraft. Without co-operation between the world's two major aircraft companies (the American company, Boeing, and the European Airbus consortium), a 'super-jumbo jet' will not be built, and passengers or consumers will suffer. This leads to a secondary argument, that the whole community will benefit (presumably from lower levels of noise pollution and congestion at airports) when and if super-jumbos replace the current generation of smaller aircraft. You must now use economic theory to evaluate the strength of these arguments. Introduce the concepts of economies of scale and dynamic efficiency in support of the case for monopoly, while making the point that the monopoly might exploit its position by charging excessive prices. The author of the passage clearly believes that the forces of competition are likely to create incentives for larger aircraft to be built, and that on balance, competition is preferable to monopoly in the aircraft industry. You should conclude by stating whether you agree or disagree.

(d) Two methods by which economists assess the desirability of investments are known as the **payback** method of investment appraisal and the **discounted cash flow (DCF)** method of investment appraisal. (A third method, known as **cost-benefit analysis** or **CBA** is explained in detail in the tutorial note to the essay question in

Chapter 9.) The payback method is quite simple. For example, if a firm subjects all possible investment decisions to a three year payback rule, the firm will go ahead with all investment projects which pay for themselves within 3 years. This means the firm will invest in a project whose earnings over the first three years of operation exceed the initial cost of the investment.

The DCF method of investment appraisal is based on estimating the value to the firm now, of revenues that an investment is expected to make over whole of the expected future economic life of the project. This process, which is called **discounting the future**, is based on the fact the money expected in the future is worth less to a firm than the same amount of money in hand now. Using the DCF method of investment appraisal, a firm calculates the value now (known as a **present value** or **PV**) of the income an investment project is expected to yield in the future. If for example, the present value to the firm of the income the project is expected to yield, is less than the initial cost of the investment, the project has failed the DCF test and should be rejected. Conversely, the firm should invest in the project if the present value of the expected future income yielded by the project exceeds its initial cost.

Question bank

1　(a)　What are the main features of equilibrium for a product in a competitive market? (10)

(b)　Given a cost-reducing innovation, trace the stages of adjustment to a long-run equilibrium. (15)　　　　　　　　　　　　　　*Oxford & Cambridge*

Pitfalls

The question is about perfect competition long-run equilibrium, though because of the vagueness of the wording, some credit would probably also be awarded if you interpret the question to be about monopolistic competition. In either case, make sure you don't waste time in part (a) by describing in great detail the process by which equilibrium is brought about. In part (b) you must devote your answer strictly to the adjustment process which establishes a new equilibrium once a previously established equilibrium has been disturbed.

Key points

Begin by drawing a diagram to illustrate perfect competition long-run equilibrium. Note its key characteristics: normal profits only, productive, allocative and X efficiency. Then go on to explain how, by shifting a firm's cost curves downwards, a cost-cutting innovation enables the innovative firm to make abnormal profits. Abnormal profits attract new entrants into the market, causing the market price to fall until a new equilibrium is established at a lower market price where firms make normal profits only.

2　'No point is better accepted than that the monopoly price is higher and the output smaller than is socially ideal. The public is the victim.' (J K Galbraith, *Economics and the Public Purpose*, 1974)

(a)　Use economic analysis to explain Galbraith's statement that 'monopoly price is higher and the output smaller than is socially ideal'. (15)

(b)　Do you consider that when monopoly exists the public is always the 'victim'? (10)　　　　　　　　　　　　　　　　　　　　　　　　*Cambridge*

3　(a)　Carefully explain the meaning of economic efficiency. (13)

(b)　Can monopolies ever be economically efficient? (12)　　　　　　*AEB*

Pitfalls

Both these questions are concerned with the costs and benefits of monopoly. Pitfalls lie in writing a generalised account of monopoly without addressing the costs and benefits, rewriting the question as one requiring a comparison of perfect competition and monopoly, and failing to use to concept of economic efficiency to analyse the properties of monopoly.

Key points

With 2(a), you must relate the words 'social ideal' to the concept of economic efficiency, the concept which of course is explicit in Question 3 and which must form the core of the answer to part (a) of this question. With both questions, you should include in your answer an explanation of the fact that, left to itself, a monopoly is likely to produce an output and to charge a price which is productively, allocatively and possibly X inefficient, leading to an outcome which is not socially ideal. You must then go on to explain the counter arguments, namely that by attaining economies of scale, a monopoly can improve productive efficiency, and that there may also be gains in terms of dynamic efficiency.

Dynamic efficiency refers to efficiency gains occurring through time, for example when successful innovation and research and development result in completely new products, better quality products, and improved methods of producing existing products.

IMPERFECT COMPETITION

Units in this chapter

Chapter objectives

Imperfect competition is the label attached to the wide variety of market structures between the extremes of perfect competition and pure monopoly. A great many theoretical models of imperfect competition have been devised, each model pertaining to a precisely defined market structure and a set of assumptions about how the member firms behave. In this chapter just three of the possible market structures will be examined:

❶ **monopolistic competition**, in which it is assumed that firms act independently of each other.

❷ **competitive oligopoly**, an example of a market structure in which interdependent firms must take account of the reactions of one another when forming a market strategy.

❸ **collusive oligopoly**, which occurs when firms attempt to overcome the uncertainty associated with guessing how competitors will react by colluding together and forming a cartel.

8.1 MONOPOLISTIC COMPETITION

A FURTHER LOOK AT PROFIT-MAXIMISATION

As in the theories of perfect competition and monopoly, the **profit-maximising assumption** is fundamental to the models of imperfect competition considered in this chapter. If you refer back to the introduction to Chapter 7, you will see how **managerial** and **behavioural theories of the firm** attack the assumption of profit-maximizing behaviour as being an unrealistic objective for large modern business corporations.

Even if imperfectly competitive and monopolistic firms aim to maximise profits, they may simply not possess the accurate information about their market situation needed to equate marginal cost and marginal revenue. For this reason, imperfectly competitive firms are often modelled as **price-searchers**, seeking by trial and error the price which will maximise profits. In some circumstances, firms may produce a wide variety of differentiated products and services, for which the marginal cost of producing each particular good or service is different. In these conditions, imperfectly competitive firms commonly resort to **rule of thumb** pricing, without ever consciously setting MC equal to MR. Businessmen may ask their accountants to estimate the cost of one unit of output when producing at near to full capacity. This estimate is called a **standard cost** and is used for price setting. On the basis of this standard cost, firms may adopt **cost-plus** or **mark-up pricing**, by adding a profit margin to the standard cost. The choice of the profit margin may itself be based on rule of thumb, or historical experience, or what a firm thinks it can charge without falling foul of a government monopoly investigation.

Nevertheless, many economists argue that the gap between the MC=MR rule and actual business pricing behaviour can be bridged. When cost-plus pricing gets businessmen too far out of line with what they would achieve with profit-maximising pricing, they will modify their pricing. Firms which stray too far from the profit-maximising path will experience low profits and falling share prices. While such firms are unlikely to be competed out of business in a highly imperfect market, they may become vulnerable to discipline by the capital market. This means that firms which perform badly are vulnerable to takeover by managers who believe that they can manage the firms' assets more successfully.

THE THEORY OF MONOPOLISTIC COMPETITION

The theory of monopolistic competition was introduced by Edward Chamberlin in 1933 as an early attempt to model the characteristics of imperfect competition. As the name implies, monopolistic competition resembles both perfect competition and monopoly in some respects. Each firm's product is assumed to be a little different from those of its competitors; if it raises its price slightly, it will not lose all its customers. Thus a firm faces a downward-sloping demand curve, rather than the horizontal or infinitely elastic demand curve of perfect competition. Nevertheless, the absence of barriers to entry allows market forces, through the entry of new firms, to shift the demand curve and to compete away abnormal profits in the long run.

The **short-run equilibrium** in monopolistic competition is little different from the monopoly equilibrium illustrated in Fig. 7.4, except that the demand or average revenue curve is likely to be rather more elastic. Fig. 8.1 shows the long-run equilibrium, achieved after the entry of new firms has eliminated abnormal profits. As in the case of monopoly, monopolistic competition involves both **productive inefficiency** (the lowest-cost output is not produced) and **allocative inefficiency** (P > MC). However, the consumer is presented with a considerable choice between differentiated goods. There may be circumstances in which consumers prefer a wider choice at the expense of an improvement in productive efficiency.

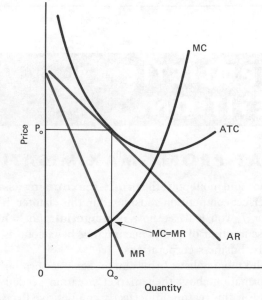

Fig. 8.1 Long-run equilibrium of a firm in monopolistic competition

Nevertheless, it is also possible that firms are using advertising and brand-imaging to present the consumer with a false choice between essentially similar goods, in which case advertising is an unnecessary cost and a waste of resources. Advertising may manipulate consumer wants by persuading people to buy products through the association of the product with other desirable properties such as social success. Many economists distinguish between **informative advertising**, which helps the consumer to make a more rational choice between products, and **persuasive advertising**, which distorts the choice.

8.2 OLIGOPOLY

COMPETITIVE OLIGOPOLY

Monopolistic competition shares with perfect competition and monopoly the characteristic that member-firms choose their market strategy in a way which is completely independent of the likely reactions of other firms. However, this may not be very realistic, particularly when there are only a few large firms competing within an industry. An **oligopoly** is sometimes defined in terms of an industrial concentration ratio: for example, a four-firm concentration ratio of 70% means that the four largest firms account for 70% of sales. Alternatively, an oligopoly can be defined in relation to the behaviour or market strategy of the member-firms. **Oligopolists are mutually interdependent** since each firm is concerned about the reactions of its competitors. There are a great many separate theories of oligopoly, each modelling a different set of assumptions about how the rivals react. Many of these theories are examples of **game theory**, in which each oligopolist is regarded as a player in a game, choosing a best strategy subject to retaliations.

REASONS FOR THE EXISTENCE OF OLIGOPOLY

In many industries there are **economies of large-scale production**, but **diseconomies of scale** begin to set in while output is still well below the total market size. The result is a **natural oligopoly** in which a few firms can produce the total industry output and simultaneously benefit from full economies of scale. In other circumstances, countervailing power may explain the existence of an oligopoly: large **duopolists** such as Unilever and Proctor & Gamble may each possess sufficient market power in the detergent industry to prevent the other emerging as a sole monopolist. Government monopoly legislation may also deter the creation of an outright monopoly.

PRICE STABILITY AND THE KINKED DEMAND CURVE

Although oligopolistic markets are characterised by competitive behaviour, the competition often takes the form of **non-price competition** such as:

❶ advertising competition, packaging, brand-imaging and product differentiation;

❷ marketing competition, including the attempt to obtain 'exclusive outlets' through which to sell the product;

❸ quality competition, including the provision of after-sales servicing.

Fig. 8.2 illustrates the **theory of the kinked demand curve**, a theory originally proposed in 1939 by Paul Sweezy as an explanation of supposed price rigidity and the absence of price wars in conditions of oligopoly. Suppose that an oligopolist, for whatever reason, produces an output Q_0 at a price P_0, determined at point X on the diagram. He perceives that **demand will be relatively elastic in response to an increase in price**, because he expects his rivals to react to the price rise by keeping their prices stable, thereby gaining customers at his expense. Conversely, he expects his rivals to react to a decrease in price by cutting their prices by an equivalent amount; he therefore expects **demand to be relatively inelastic in response to a price fall**, since he cannot hope to lure many customers away from his rivals. In other words, the oligopolist's initial position is at the junction of two demand curves of different relative elasticity, each reflecting a different assumption about how the rivals are expected to react to a change in price. Indeed, if demand is inelastic (and marginal revenue negative) when the oligopolist reduces his price, the best policy may be to leave the price unchanged.

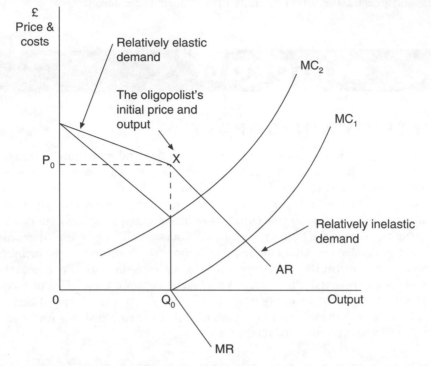

Fig. 8.2 The 'kinked' demand theory of oligopoly

A second explanation of price rigidity is also suggested by Fig. 8.2. In mathematical terms, a discontinuity exists along a vertical line above output Q_0, between the marginal revenue curves associated with the relatively elastic and inelastic demand (or average revenue) curves. Costs can rise or fall within a certain range without causing a profit-maximising oligopolist to change either price or output. At output Q_0 and price P_0, MC = MR as long as the MC curve is between an upper limit of MC_2 and a lower limit of MC_1. Although the kinked demand curve theory provides a neat and apparently plausible explanation of price rigidity, it has been subject to many attacks. It is an **incomplete theory** because it does not explain how and why an oligopolist chooses to be at point X in the first place. Empirical evidence casts great doubt on whether oligopolists respond to price changes in the manner assumed. Oligopolistic markets often display evidence of **price leadership**, which provides an alternative explanation of orderly price behaviour. Firms come to the conclusion that price-cutting is self-defeating and decide that it may be advantageous to follow the firm which takes the first step in raising the price. If all firms follow, the price rise will be sustained to the benefit of all the firms.

Collusive oligopoly

The theory of the kinked demand curve illustrates an important characteristic of competitive oligopoly: the existence of uncertainty. An oligopolist can never be sure how his rivals will respond, yet he must take their expected reactions into account when determining his own market strategy. An incentive may exist for oligopolists to collude together in order to reduce uncertainty. Also, by acting collectively the firms may achieve an outcome which is better for all of them than if they had remained a competitive oligopoly. This can be shown by the **principle of joint profit maximisation**, which is illustrated in Fig. 8.3. We shall assume that there are three firms with similar cost curves in an industry. The cost curves of one of the firms are drawn in the left-hand panel of Fig. 8.3. Suppose the firms now decide to get together and act as a single monopolist, yet at the same time maintaining their separate indentities. The monopoly MC curve, which is illustrated in the right-hand part of the diagram, is obtained by adding up the identical MC curves of the three separate firms. Monopoly output of 750 units is determined where MC = MR, and each firm charges a price of £10. You should notice that the monopoly output is well below 1000 units, which would be the output if the industry was perfectly competitive. The shaded area in the right-hand panel represents the efficiency loss which is caused by the cartel raising the price to £10 and restricting the industry output to 750 units.

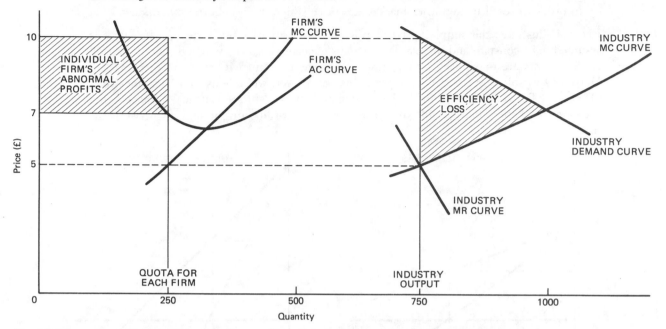

Fig. 8.3 *Joint profit maximisation by a three-firm cartel in which the market is shared equally by the three firms*

If the firms decide to split the output of 750 units equally between themselves, each firm will be allocated a quota of 250 units to produce. In this situation, the shaded area in the left-hand part of the diagram shows the abnormal profits made by an individual firm. Other forms of market-sharing, based for example on geography or historical tradition, are of course possible.

It is important to stress that the formation of a cartel does not completely eliminate uncertainty. Each member of the cartel has an **incentive to cheat** on the other members: this is because the marginal cost of producing the 250th unit is only £5, yet the marginal revenue received, which equals the price, is £10. A firm can increase its total profit at the expense of the other members of the cartel by secretly selling an output over and above its quota at a price which is less than £10 but greater than the marginal cost incurred. This is an example of a **divergency between collective and individual interest**. The firms' collective interest is to maintain the cartel so as to keep sales down and the price up. Nevertheless, an individual firm can benefit if, while the other members maintain the cartel, it secretly undercuts the agreement by selling more than its allotted market share.

The possibility of price discrimination

Monopolies, and other firms in highly imperfect markets, regularly charge a number of different prices to different groups of customers. Sometimes more than one product is involved, as in the case of first- and second-class rail travel; in other instances the prices may reflect the different transport and handling costs which are incurred in delivering the good or service to the customer. You must not confuse these examples of differentiated prices with the concept of monopoly or oligopoly price discrimination. **Price discrimination** occurs when a firm is able to charge **different prices** for an **identical product,** with the same costs of production and supply. Price discrimination will benefit a firm if it increases the firm's total profits. The necessary conditions for successful price discrimination are:

❶ It must be possible to **identify different groups of customers** or markets for the product.

❷ There must be a **different elasticity of demand** at each price in each market.

❸ Total profits will be increased by **selling at a higher price in the market where demand at each price is less elastic.** (Demand will never be inelastic, since this would imply that marginal revenue is negative.) The markets must be separated to prevent **seepage**, which occurs when customers buy at the lower price in one market in order to resell in the other market at a price which undercuts the monopolist.

Fig. 8.4 illustrates the simplest case of price discrimination, when a firm's MC curve is assumed to be constant and there are two groups of customers, each with a different demand curve. Profits are maximised by equating MR to the constant MC curve in each market. Output Q_1 is sold at a price of P_1 in the industrial market, while household customers buy Q_2 at price P_2. Marginal revenue is the same in each market at these outputs. If this was not the case, the firm would be able to increase profits by reallocating its output between the markets.

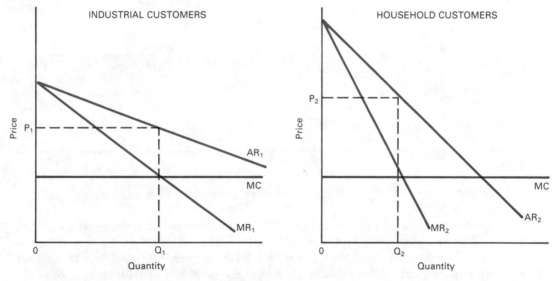

Fig. 8.4 Price discrimination

Although price discrimination can benefit the producer in terms of higher profits, there may be circumstances in which it is also in the interest of consumers. The classic case concerns the demand for the services of a doctor in an isolated small town. If all the townspeople are charged the same price for health care, the town's doctor is unable to make a sufficient income to cover his opportunity cost: it is in his interest to move to a larger city, thus leaving the townspeople without any medical care. If, however, the doctor is permitted to charge a higher price to the few rich citizens who can afford to pay, he may be able to earn sufficient income to make it worth his while to treat the poorer people at a lower price. Everybody ends up by getting some benefit from the introduction of price discrimination – though, as the next chapter explains, collective provision of a **merit good** such as health care outside the market may be judged more desirable than private provision through the market.

Chapter roundup

This chapter has followed on from Chapter 7 in extending the coverage of market structures to include the main forms of imperfect competition. Certain aspects of the behaviour or conduct of large firms which have been examined in some depth in this chapter are equally applicable to the case of pure monopoly. Chapter 10, on privatisation and related policies, describes and analyses government policies towards the behaviour of firms in imperfectly competitive markets.

Illustrative questions and answers

1 Essay Question

(a) Why may firms wish to reduce competition by colluding with each other: for example, by forming a cartel? (12)

(b) Is such a collusion in the public interest and what might be the economic effects of prohibiting collusion? (13) *AEB*

Tutorial note

(a) Begin by arguing that the desire to collude is most likely to occur in a competitive oligopoly. Firms wish to collude to reduce the uncertainty resulting from their interdependence. You can also argue, perhaps with the aid of the theory of joint profit maximisation, that collusion can result in a better outcome for all the firms in terms of increased profits. However, avoid circular statements such as that firms wish to collude to avoid competition, since this information is already contained in the wording of the question. Also, avoid confusing collusion with merger activity, a common mistake.

(b) Define the public interest. Explain that collusive activity which reduces output, raises the price and generally exploits the consumer through manipulation and the promotion of producer sovereignty, is likely to be against the public interest. But some forms of collusion may be more benign, even though they reduce competition. Examples might include joint product development, industry-wide labour training initiatives and the sharing of distribution grids by competitive utility companies.

When dealing with the last part of the question, an obvious point to make is that competition will be promoted! Output may rise and price fall. Covert collusive activity could also replace overt cartel agreements.

2 Data Question

In the typical industrial market – that of a few firms or oligopoly – prices in the neoclassical model are held to be set so as to reflect the maximum return to producers as a group. This, subject to some imperfection in the tacit communication between oligopolists, is the same price that would be charged

5 by a monopolist. No point is better accepted by the neoclassical model than that the monopoly price is higher and the output smaller than is socially ideal. The public is the victim. Because of such exploitation, oligopoly is wicked.

Yet exploitation by modern oligopoly leads to no serious public outcry that production is too small or prices too high. The automobile industry,

10 rubber industry, oil industry, soap industry, processed food industry, tobacco industry and intoxicants industry all fit precisely the pattern of oligopoly. All are held by neoclassical theory to maximise profits as would a monopoly. In all (these industries), comparative overdevelopment – as compared, for example, with housing, health care, urban transit – is regularly cited in

15 complaint and the effects of their growth on air, water, countryside and health are held against them. Never – literally – is it suggested that their output is too small. Nor are their prices a major object of complaint.

We now see the reason – and we begin to see one of the major dividends from a clear view of economic reality. The firms in these industries control

20 prices in response to protective need – in response to heavy capital investment, long-time horizons, extensive specialisation and organisation and, in consequence, the high proportion of overhead costs.

The same technology and organisation allows for increasing productivity and falling costs. Of these the public approves. These firms set prices with

25 a view to expanding sales – to growth. Of this, the antithesis of monopoly pricing, the public also approves.

(Source: J K Galbraith, *Economics and The Public Purpose* (1974); reproduced with the permission of Andre Deutsch Ltd.)

(a) Explain briefly the statement that 'the monopoly price is higher and the output smaller than is socially ideal' (line 6). (6)

(b) Why might it, in practice, be difficult for oligopolists to set prices 'so as to reflect the maximum return to the producers as a group' (lines 2–3)? (8)

(c) Why does Galbraith say that firms in oligopoly 'control prices in response to protective need' (lines 19–20)? (6)

(d) How would you expect 'the high proportion of overhead costs' (line 22) to affect the elasticity of supply of the firms discussed? (5)   *Oxford*

Tutorial note

(a) With the aid of diagrams similar to those in Chapter 7, compare monopoly and perfect competition equilibrium – in the latter case for a whole market rather than for just one firm within the market. Explain that compared to perfect competition, monopoly produces a smaller output at a higher price. Assuming economies of scale are not possible, and externalities are not produced (see next chapter), the 'social ideal' is the perfectly competitive price and output.

(b) Galbraith is assuming that the oligopolists behave according to the theory of 'joint profit maximisation' which we have explained in this chapter. But this requires collusion by the oligopolists. Even if the government permits the necessary collusion, individual oligopolists may be tempted to cheat on the agreement in order to win more sales and larger profits at the expense of their rivals.

(c) Galbraith might be implying that oligopolists use prices as a barrier to entry, so as to protect their market shares. This may involve setting prices deliberately low in order to deter new entrants to the market. At first sight, such a pricing policy seems to imply that the oligopolists are deliberately sacrificing profits and therefore not behaving as 'profit maximisers'. Behaving in this way, the oligopolists would certainly be sacrificing *short-term profits*, but by successfully protecting the market, it can be argued that they would be maximising *long-term profits*. Such a pricing policy is often called **limit pricing** (i.e. using deliberately low prices to limit entry to the market) or **predatory pricing**, if prices are reduced below costs and force competitors out of business.

(d) The answer to this question depends on whether we are considering short-run or long-run supply. In the short run, supply might be quite elastic – provided that initially the firms have plenty of spare capacity and assuming that the spare capacity can easily be brought into production. Supply would become inelastic as full capacity was approached. Once full capacity was reached, the firms could only step up supply by investing in extra capacity, and since they have 'a high proportion of overhead costs', this implies that a large investment would be required. This could take months, if not years, so in these circumstances long-run supply would be inelastic.

Question bank

1 (a) With reference to the characteristics of market structure, explain why a video rental shop is an appropriate example of monopolistic competition and the car manufacturing industry an appropriate example of oligopoly. (12)

(b) Discuss how these businesses might compete in their respective market structures.
(13)
Cambridge

Pitfalls

There is a danger here of misinterpreting monopolistic competition as pure monopoly. However, you don't have to agree with the assertion in the question. You might argue that a video rental shop in an isolated village is indeed a monopoly, or that based on your own personal experience, many video rental shops behave interdependently, as if they were oligopolists.

Key points

Make sure you define (but don't over-elaborate) the key features of monopolistic competition and oligopoly, before describing how video rental shops and car manufacturers typify (or fail to typify) the respective market structures. Go on to explain the various forms of price competition and non-price competition that video rental shops and car manufacturers may undertake, relating competitive strategies to business objectives, such as profit maximisation and market share maximisation.

2 (a) Why might an oligopolist believe his demand curve is kinked at the existing price? (10)

(b) Comment on the significance of the kink for the behaviour of an oligopolistic market over time. (15) *Oxford & Cambridge*

Pitfalls

A key word in part (a) is *believe*. Real world firms seldom, if ever, know the precise shape and position of the demand curve for their product or products. There is actually little evidence to support the theory of the kinked demand curve, but many if not most A Level students continue to answer questions on oligopoly as if the kinked demand curve is a self-evident truth.

Key points

Having outlined the meaning of oligopoly, briefly describe what a kinked demand curve shows. Go on to explain that an oligopolist may believe the demand curve to be kinked, either on the basis of evidence of how how rival firms have behaved in the past, or because of expectations of how rival firms might behave in the future. In your answer to the second part of the question, you should relate the kinked demand curve to possible price stability in oligopolistic markets, and to collusion and non-price competition in markets dominated by just a few firms.

3 (a) Distinguish between the behaviour of firms in competitive and collusive oligopoly. (12)

(b) Discuss the view that provided firms are free to enter or leave oligopolistic markets there is no need for the government to intervene to protect the interest of consumers. (13) *AEB*

Pitfalls

Part (b) is a disguised question on the application of the theory of contestable markets (explained in Chapter 10); there is an obvious likelihood that you will fail to appreciate this fact. You must resist the temptation to write a general historical account of government policy towards monopoly and oligopolistic industries.

Key points

Define an oligopoly as a market in which there sufficiently few firms for each firm to be mutually or strategically interdependent. Explain how, in a competitive market, each oligopolist must take into account the possible or likely reactions of its rivals when choosing its price and level of output. Go on to explain how, in a competitive situation, an oligopolist cannot be certain of rivals' reactions, and relate this to the incentive to collude. Describe different forms of collusion such as cartel agreements and joint product development. In your answer to part (b), you should explain and debate the argument that, providing the market is contestable (there are no significant barriers to market entry), there is no need for a government to interfere with the market structure or with the behaviour or conduct of the established firms in the market. The government can restrict its intervention to ensuring that the market remains contestable.

MARKET FAILURES

Units in this chapter

Chapter objectives

Chapter 7 explained how market forces operating in perfect markets can, in principle, achieve a long-run equilibrium which is **economically efficient**. This chapter introduces the term **market failure** to describe all the circumstances in which market forces fail to achieve an economically efficient equilibrium. The main examples of market failure examined are **public goods**, **merit goods** and **demerit goods**, and **externalities**.

9.1 INTRODUCTION TO MARKET FAILURE

THE MEANING OF MARKET FAILURE

In previous chapters we have assumed that the price mechanism generally works efficiently to improve economic welfare and human happiness, provided only that markets are sufficiently competitive. In this chapter we introduce the term **market failure** to describe all the circumstances in which market forces fail to achieve an economically efficient equilibrium. The main examples of market failure we shall identify are:

● **Failure associated with market structure** Monopolistic and imperfectly competitive market structures provide the best-known examples of market failure. The 'wrong' quantity is produced and sold at the 'wrong' price. In comparison with perfect competition, too little is produced at too high a price, and the market outcome is neither allocatively efficient nor productively efficient. Nevertheless, the market can still function in conditions of imperfect competition, producing at least some of the good or service.

● **Failure associated with the market mechanism** Even when most of the conditions of perfect competition are met, informational problems may prevent the market mechanism from working properly. A certain minimum level of organisation of a market is required to allow information about market prices to be transmitted to all the participants. A lack of sufficient information about prices in other parts of the market may cause a market to degenerate into bilateral bargaining, where a buyer and seller enter into an exchange in a state of ignorance about prices in other parts of the market.

In other instances, the adjustment process towards equilibrium may be too slow or unstable, and equilibrium may never be reached. As a result, trading may always take place at disequilibrium prices.

MARKET FAILURE v MARKET INADEQUACY

A market fails completely when there is no incentive for firms to produce a good or service, even though utility would be gained from its consumption. We shall show why markets fail to provide **pure public goods** such as national defence, which by its nature has to be consumed collectively rather than individually. Markets also fail to regulate the production and consumption of **externalities**, with the result that too much of an external 'bad' such as pollution and too little of an external good such as a beautiful landscape may be produced.

In other circumstances, markets will provide some of the good or service, but an inadequate quantity: monopoly and imperfect competition have already been mentioned in this respect. The market mechanism may provide too little of a **merit good**, such as education or health care, and too much of a 'good' such as narcotic drug or alcoholic drink – goods which are sometimes classed as **demerit goods**.

THE PROBLEM OF SELF-INTEREST

Merit goods, demerit goods, and externalities all illustrate the existence of **divergencies, and possible conflicts, between private and social costs and benefits**. A central proposition of economic theory is that an economic agent in a market situation only considers the private costs and benefits to the agent itself of its market actions, i.e. it always seeks to maximise its self-interest. However, if in maximising its private benefit or interest, it imposes costs on other economic agents or the wider community, private benefit maximisation will not coincide with social benefit maximisation. In an unregulated market, the 'wrong' quantity of the good will be produced and consumed – the 'correct' quantity being that which maximises the social benefit rather than merely the private benefit of individuals.

9.2 SOME EXAMPLES OF MARKET FAILURE

PURE PUBLIC GOODS AND QUASI-PUBLIC GOODS

A pure public good such as national defence is defined by the properties of **non-exclusion and non-diminishability**. A person can benefit from national defence without having to pay for it. Furthermore, if an extra person benefits from defence, this in no way diminishes the benefits available to others. Most public goods, for example roads, street lighting and broadcasting, are **quasi-public goods** or **non-pure public goods**. Markets could, in principle provide the goods, but for various reasons they do not. Instead, the goods or services are usually collectively provided by the state, often at zero price, and financed out of general taxation.

The essential properties of a public good can be explained with the use of the well-known example of a lighthouse. This is illustrated in Fig. 9.1. The lighthouse provides a service (a beam of light) for which there is a need; if the service is not provided more ships will be

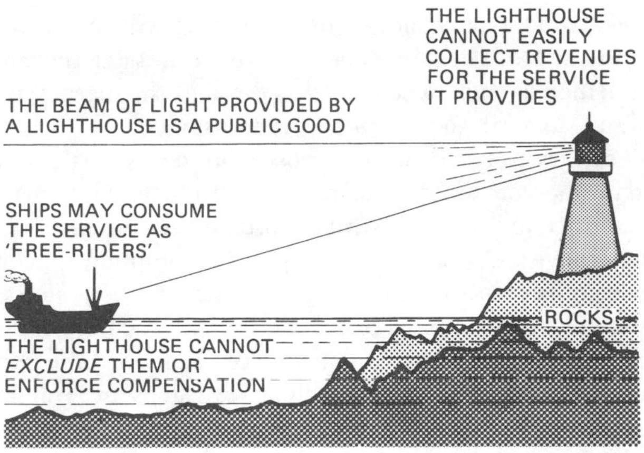

Fig. 9.1 The essential features of a public good

wrecked and transport costs will rise. Lighthouses could be provided through the market if entrepreneurs were able successfully to charge a price to passing ships. Now, most goods are called **private goods** because an entrepreneur who provides them can **enforce private property rights** and exclude people who do not wish to pay for consuming the goods. In the case of quasi-public goods, it is theoretically possible to exercise private property rights and to exclude **free riders** – people who consume without paying. A motor toll-road provides an example. However, in many cases the difficulty and cost of collecting revenue may prove prohibitive. A lighthouse company might try moral persuasion in order to collect revenue from passing ships, relying on the fact that it is in the interest of all ship-owners for the service to be provided; an incentive nevertheless exists for any individual ship-owner to become a free-rider, providing that the other ship-owners still pay up. In these circumstances, most ship-owners may be expected to become free-riders, thereby destroying the incentive for the private provision of the lighthouse. While **non-excludability** explains how private provisioning of a public good through a market may break down, the property of **non-diminishability** (or **non-rivalry**) suggests why the good should be provided at zero price or free. Whenever an extra person consumes a public good such as defence or a lighthouse beam, no additional resources are used up. Thus the consumption can be met without transferring resources out of other industries. The marginal cost of meeting the extra consumption is zero. Consumer welfare will be maximised if the greatest possible consumption is achieved – and this will only happen if the price is zero.

Public goods and government goods

A public good is sometimes defined as any good or service provided by the public sector. This is not a very satisfactory definition. The provision of postal services by a nationalised industry should be regarded as a private good provided through the market. Other goods and services such as education and health care are merit goods rather than public goods, though they share with public goods the characteristic of being collectively provided at zero price, and being financed out of taxation. It is useful to note that public collective provision is not inevitable in the case of public goods: in some instances, private collective provision is possible. A co-operative of ship-owners could provide lighthouses, though it might be necessary to make membership legally compulsory. Modified market provision is another alternative. For example, the difficulty of charging a price to consumers of commercial TV and radio programmes is circumvented by charging advertisers for access to the public good!

MERIT AND DEMERIT GOODS

A merit good such as health care or education is a good or service from which the **social benefits** of consumption to the community as a whole **exceed the private benefits** to the consumer. In the case of a demerit good such as tobacco or alcohol, the **social costs** of consumption **exceed the private costs**. If merit and demerit goods are provided through markets at prices unadjusted by any subsidy or tax, people will choose to consume too little of a merit good and too much of a demerit good. It is worth stressing that an incentive certainly exists for merit and demerit goods to be provided through the market, but merit goods will be underconsumed and demerit goods will be overconsumed.

The government can try to encourage the consumption of merit goods and to discourage and sometimes outlaw the consumption of harmful products or demerit goods. **Demerit goods must not be confused with nuisance goods or economic 'bads'.** Most products and services are economic goods that yield utility in consumption – people are prepared to pay a price in order to obtain them, unless of course they can consume the goods as public goods without paying. The consumption of a demerit good, such as a narcotic drug, may not be in the consumer's best interest but it certainly gives pleasure to the person who consumes it, as it fulfils a need. In contrast a product such as garbage is an economic 'bad' because it yields only unpleasantness or disutility: people are prepared to pay a price in order to have an economic bad taken away.

Merit goods and the informational problem

Uncertainty of information may partially explain why people choose to consume too little of a merit good such as health care if it is privately provided at market prices. For example, a person does not know in advance when, if ever, he is going to need the services of a specialist surgeon: sudden illness may lead to a situation in which he is unable to afford the surgeon's services. One market-orientated solution is for a **private insurance market** to come into being, in which case health care would be collectively provided through the market. However, this may still fail to provide a service for the chronically ill or the very poor. **Public collective provision** through a compulsory state insurance scheme is therefore another solution. It is interesting to note that both private and public collective schemes are a response to the fact that the demand or need for medical care is much more predictable for a large group of people than for an individual – an application of the law of large numbers.

EXTERNALITIES

An externality is a **special type of public good or 'bad'**, its crucial characteristic being that it is generated and received outside the market. This can be demonstrated by considering the well-known example of pollution as an external cost. Fig. 9.2 illustrates the generation of pollution by a brickworks. The nearby laundry is an unwilling free rider receiving the pollution as a nuisance good or economic 'bad'.

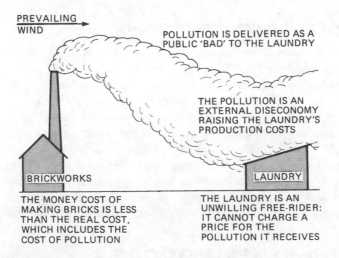

Fig. 9.2 Case study of an externality: Pollution

External costs such as pollution, which increase the production costs of the firms that receive them, are examples of **external diseconomies**. Symmetrically, a firm may generate **external benefits** which are **external economies** if they lower the production costs of other firms. The laundry is unable to charge a price through the market to the brickworks for the pollution it unwillingly consumes. In a similar way, a power station discharging warm water into a lake cannot charge a price to fishermen for the external benefit they receive in the form of larger catches of fish. The **market thus fails to provide an incentive** for the brickworks to generate less pollution and for the power station to discharge more warm water. Without such an incentive, too much of an external cost and too little of an external benefit are likely to be generated. Thus governments may become involved in adjusting markets via taxes and subsidies in order to discourage economic bads and to encourage external benefits.

Externalities are essentially **spin-offs** which are generated by one economic agent in the pursuit of its private self-interest and received outside the market by other agents or third parties. Divergencies are likely to arise between the private cost and benefit of the generator of the externality and the social cost and benefit to all who receive them. An external cost such as pollution can be regarded as part of the production cost of bricks which is evaded by the brickworks by being dumped on others. The **real cost** of bricks is greater than the **money cost** at market prices because the real cost includes the cost of pollution; bricks are therefore underpriced at market prices, price being less than the true marginal cost. Too many bricks are produced, causing a misallocation of resources (allocative inefficiency).

In this example, pollution is an externality which is both generated and received in production, thereby increasing the production cost of the firms receiving the pollution. Externalities may also be generated and received in consumption. This, and the other possibilities, are summarised in the table below.

The different types of externality

	External costs	External benefits
Generated in production and received in production	Pollution discharged by a brickworks and received by a nearby laundry. (External diseconomies)	Warm water discharged by a power station and received in the form of bigger fish catches by nearby commercial fishermen. (External economies)
Generated in production and received in consumption	Pollution discharged by a brickworks and received by nearby households	Warm water discharged by a power station and received in the form of bigger fish catches by private anglers
Generated in consumption and received in production	Congestion caused by private motorists increasing production costs for firms. (This is another type of external production diseconomy)	Commercial bee-keepers benefiting from the private gardens of nearby households. (This is another type of external production economy)
Generated in consumption and received in consumption	Congestion caused by private motorists causing a utility loss to other private motorists, pedestrians and households	Passers-by enjoying the view of nearby private gardens

9.3 THE GOVERNMENT AND MARKET FAILURE

PUBLIC POLICY AND MARKET FAILURE

Public goods are usually provided 'free' by the state since otherwise they would not be provided at all. This is an example of **public provision** replacing the market. In the case of merit and demerit goods, the government can either **replace** or **modify** the market. A demerit good such as heroin may be judged so harmful that its consumption and sale are made illegal. A **complete ban** on a good is the ultimate **quantity control** which a government can use to regulate sale or consumption. Nevertheless a market may still exist in the form of an illegal black market. Black markets emerge when free markets are severely regulated or suppressed. In other circumstances, a government may decide that less severe quantity controls are more appropriate, such as the creation of no-smoking areas and restrictions on the sale of tobacco and alcohol. The symmetrical equivalent to a complete ban on heroin is to make the consumption of a merit good such as education or vaccination compulsory.

At the same time, **price controls** provide another form of regulation which can be used to modify the market. Minimum price legislation can discourage the consumption of demerit goods, whereas maximum price legislation increases the demand for merit goods – though problems of excess supply and demand are likely to result. For this reason governments may prefer to influence demand by taxing demerit goods and by subsidising merit goods. If a 100% subsidy is given to the private producers of a merit good, it becomes effectively 'free', in the sense that it is available at zero price. An example occurs when free places in private schools are financed by the state. Alternatively, the state can provide the merit good itself at zero or token price, similarly financed out of general taxation.

The problem of externalities can be tackled in a rather similar way with a combination of quantity controls or regulations, and taxes and subsidies to influence price. Discharge of pollution may be made illegal or restricted to certain times of the day or year. Maximum emission limits can be imposed. Since the central problem is the failure of the market to provide incentives to generate fewer external costs and more external benefits, taxes and subsidies can be used to provide the desired incentives. The government could, in principle, calculate the money cost of pollution and impose this as a pollution tax upon the polluter. The imposition of such a tax internalises the externality! More controversially, subsidies can be paid to encourage external benefits, for example those which result from the planting of trees.

In recent years, a more market-oriented solution has been introduced in the United States: the creation of a market in pollution permits. The government grants licences or pollution permits to firms. Those firms which succeed in reducing the pollution they emit can then sell their spare pollution permits to other firms. The firms buying the permits are those that find it more difficult to comply with the **maximum limits** or **ceilings** on pollution which are imposed at the same time as the pollution permits are granted.

MARKET FAILURE VERSUS GOVERNMENT FAILURE

As the previous section implies, it is often assumed that market failure can be either reduced or completely eliminated, once it has been identified, through appropriate government intervention, for example by imposing taxes, controls and regulation. This rather benign view of the role of government in the economy – centring on the use of public policy to correct market failure wherever it is found to exist – illustrates what may be called the **public interest theory of government behaviour**. Broadly, the public interest theory argues that governments intervene in a benevolent fashion in the economy in order to eliminate waste and to achieve an efficient and socially desirable resource allocation. However, there is another, competing, theory of government behaviour, known as **public choice theory**, that takes a very different and potentially critical view of the role of government intervention in the economy. According to public choice theory, not only can market failure arise in situations such as those we have described in this chapter; there is also the possibility – perhaps even the likelihood – of **government failure** occurring whenever the state attempts to improve on the working of the market.

Government failure can result from the fact that, in democracies such as the United Kingdom and the USA, politicians face re-election every four or five years in the electoral voting cycle. Failure can also result from the role of bureaucracy in the machinery of government. Public choice theory assumes that both politicians and bureaucrats (the officials or civil servants employed in government departments) behave so as to maximise their self-interest – vote maximisation and being re-elected in the case of politicians, and for bureaucrats, the maximisation of their departments' budgets and spending plans. For politicians, the electoral pressure to find favour with voters can lead to very short-time horizons in the government decision making process, causing government ministers to favour public spending programmes with an immediate payoff, while rejecting those with an initially high investment cost but whose benefits lie several years ahead. Governments may be tempted to duck expenditure on research, training, conservation and environmental protection, in favour of a spending programme which boosts voters' short-term consumption prospects, particularly in the run-up to important political elections.

To some extent, the role of bureaucrats in the implementation of public policy works in the opposite direction, causing governments to do too much for too long. In the model of bureaucracy behaviour developed by William Niskanen in 1971, it is assumed that government officials aim to maximise the budget of the department in which they work. The bigger the budget, the greater the department's prestige and the opportunities for promotion for departmental officials. Since the civil servants employed within a particular department have a vested interest in increasing the department's budget and spending plans, they think up arguments to justify extra spending. If all government departments behave in this way, the net effect is to exert upward pressure on government spending. When allied to the fact, that unlike in private business, many government spending programmes do not face the discipline of a profit and loss statement by which their economic value can be calculated, this leads to a tendency for the government to over-expand its activities and for spending projects to develop their own momentum and to be difficult to stop or rein back, once they have been started.

Chapter roundup

In this chapter we have investigated in some depth the circumstances in which the signalling and incentive functions of prices (described in Chapter 2) may break down, resulting in the failure of markets to function smoothly. In some situations, markets may fail to function at all. The relative merits of the market economy and the planning mechanism (covered in Chapter 1) link directly to the question whether individual markets function smoothly or badly. If a case exists for the public provision of public goods and some merit goods, then this will influence the level and pattern of both government spending and government revenue. These examples of market failure are reintroduced in Chapter 13 on taxation and public spending.

Illustrative questions and answers

1 Essay Question

(a) What are the main features of cost-benefit analysis? (12)

(b) Discuss the difficulties which are likely to be encountered when cost-benefit analysis is used to assess whether or not to construct a new nuclear power station. (13)   *AEB*

Tutorial note

Cost benefit analysis (CBA) is a technique for evaluating all the costs and benefits of any economic action or decision, i.e. the social costs and benefits to the whole community and not just the private costs and benefits accruing to the economic agent undertaking the action. In the past, CBA has most often been used by governments to help decide whether to invest in a major public project such as a motorway, an airport, or a major investment by a nationalised industry. However, there is no reason in principle why a private sector investment such as the Channel Tunnel, or indeed any action by a private economic agent or by the government (e.g. a tax change), cannot be examined by CBA. It is worth noting that in the 1980s and early 1990s, British Conservative governments largely abandoned CBA, believing it to be a waste of public money and that all investment projects, including those undertaken by the state, should be assessed solely on commercial or private profit criteria.

CBA is really an extension of the method by which many private sector businesses assess whether an investment in a major capital project, such as a new factory, is likely to be profitable and worthwhile. (This is the **discounted cash flow** method of investment appraisal. You should see the tutorial note for the data question in Chapter 7 for further details.) Private sector firms attempt to calculate all the private costs and benefits occurring in the future as a result of an investment or decision undertaken now. The central problem is guessing and putting money values to an unknown and uncertain future. However, when assessing whether an investment project is likely to be profitable, a private sector firm considers only the likely future private costs and benefits, ignoring any external costs and benefits resulting from its private action. CBA attempts to attach monetary values to *all* the current and future costs and benefits resulting an action undertaken now. When submitting an investment project such as a nuclear power station to cost-benefit analysis, monetary values must be placed on the positive and negative externalities resulting from the construction and operation of the power station, and not just on the private costs incurred and revenues received by the power station operator. Externalities are, however, notoriously difficult to quantify. How does one put a monetary value to the saving of a human life resulting from fewer accidents on a proposed motorway? What is the social cost of the destruction of a beautiful view? It is extremely difficult to decide on all the likely costs and benefits, to draw the line on which to include and exclude, to put monetary values to all the chosen costs and benefits accruing immediately with those which will only be received in the distant future.

Critics of CBA argue that it is 'pseudo-scientific' – value judgments and arbitrary decisions disguised as objectivity. As we have noted, CBA is also criticised as being a costly waste of time and money and as a method whereby politicians distance themselves from and delay unpopular decisions, deflecting the wrath of local communities away from themselves and onto the impartial experts undertaking the CBA. Nevertheless, supporters of CBA argue that for all its defects it remains the best method of appraising public investment decisions because all the likely costs and benefits are exposed to public discussion.

Suggested answer

- Explain that CBA is a technique of appraising whether a decision to be undertaken now is likely to be in the public interest (or the social interest), by assessing all the costs and benefits involved.

- Contrast CBA with private decision making which takes account solely of current and expected future private costs and benefits. Emphasise that CBA attempts to place monetary values on external costs and benefits as well as private costs and benefits.

- Explain that CBA is applicable, in principle, to public sector investment projects because, in pursuit of social welfare maximisation, all the costs and benefits generated by the project should be assessed, and not just the private costs.

- Outline the difficulties of undertaking CBA: difficulties of quantifying and placing monetary values on externalities, and of drawing the line on which externalities to include and how far to extend the analysis into the future.

- Apply these points to the particular case of a nuclear power station, emphasising that any external costs, stemming for example from a radioactivity leakage, may affect future generations and people living in quite distant countries.

2 Data Question

SINGAPORE'S TRAFFIC PROBLEMS

Singapore is a small, densely populated island of 2.6 million people. In 1987 there were almost half a million motor vehicles competing for space on a limited congested road network.

In order to combat this problem, the government introduced policies to control the use of motor vehicles through differential taxation and a system of road pricing. This involves the payment of a City Area Licence charge for vehicles travelling into central Singapore with fewer than four passengers from 7.30 a.m. to 10.15 a.m., Monday to Friday.

(Source: Singapore: Annual Vehicle Licensing Costs and Purchase Price 1987)

Cost to motorist ($)	Type of vehicle			
	Replacement family car 1600 cc	Additional company car 1600 cc	Goods vehicle	
			2.5 tonnes	1.5 tonnes
Approx purchase price of a new vehicle	40 000	40 000	30 000	60 000
First registration fee (tax)	35 000	70 000	1500	3000
Annual registration fee (tax)	1000	5000	7000	15
City area licence annual charge	1200	2400	–	–
Road tax	1200	2400	1000	2600

(a) (i) How does the total 'on the road' payment for an additional company car differ from that for a replacement family car? (2)

    (ii) Suggest two economic reasons why companies purchase cars for certain employees. (2)

(b) The annual City Area Licence charge is payable as a tax.

    (i) Explain the likely purpose of such a tax. (2)

    (ii) Suggest why goods vehicles are excluded. (2)

(c) (i) What do economists mean by the term 'externalities'? (4)

    (ii) What evidence is there in the table to suggest that the Government of Singapore wishes to reduce negative externalities? (4)

    (iii) If this policy is successful, what are its implications for economic welfare? (4)

Cambridge

Tutorial note

(a) (i) This part of the question is testing simple arithmetic: just add up the data in the first two columns and compare the totals! You might note that the annual City Area Licence Charge could be optional for a motorist who did not wish to use his vehicle in central Singapore during office hours with less than four passengers.

    (ii) Businesses allow employees the use of company cars because: a car may be necessary for the worker to do his job; to give the employee status; as a hidden pay rise and method of tax avoidance; and to achieve greater employee loyalty.

(b) (i) The City Area Licence charge aims to relieve the negative externality of congestion by discouraging marginal road users from driving in central Singapore at the most congested times, and by encouraging efficient use of vehicles through car sharing.

    (ii) Many goods vehicles have to load and deliver during office hours. Presumably the Singapore authorities took the view that the financial costs incurred by the island's economy would exceed any benefits in the form of reduced congestion.

(c) (i) Give a concise definition of an externality as an economic 'good' or 'bad' produced and received 'outside the market'. Clearly make the distinction between negative and positive externalities (external costs and benefits), and give an example of each.

    (ii) The data shows that the effective tax rate on family cars is nearly 100% and on additional company cars nearly 200%. While these tax rates could be viewed simply as 'revenue raisers', it is much more likely, particularly given the fact that Singapore is a small completely urbanised island, that the high levels of taxation are designed to reduce the negative externalities of congestion, and also vehicle pollution.

    (iii) Economic welfare will have increased, provided the reduction in external costs (the costs of the negative externalities) exceeds the increase in private motoring costs incurred by vehicle owners and users.

Question bank

1 Explain what is meant by market failure. Discuss, with examples, how environmental pollution may be viewed as an example of market failure. (25) *NEAB*

2 (a) Distinguish between public goods and merit goods. (20)

(b) Discuss the economic arguments for and against public provision of *either* health care *or* education. (80) *ULEAC*

3 (a) Explain what is meant by an externality. (30)

(b) Examine the impact if introducing any **two** of the following:
  (i) pollution taxes;
  (ii) legal maximum controls on pollution emissions;
  (iii) tradeable pollution licence permits. (70) *ULEAC*

Pitfalls

Sometimes, when asked to define or explain the meaning of a concept, exam candidates fall into the trap of believing that all they need do is list a number of examples. This is particularly the case with questions on market failure. With Question 1, you must go beyond the statement that imperfectly competitive markets, public goods, merit goods and externalities are examples of market failure. You must explain why markets may fail completely to provide some goods, such as public goods, while providing the wrong quantity of other goods such as merit goods and demerit goods. With Question 2, an answer which defined public goods and merit goods respectively in terms of defence, police and roads, and education and health care, would not meet the requirements of the question.

With Questions 1 and 3 on externalities, you must avoid the temptation to drift into a 'greenish-tinged' account of how environmental pollution destroys animal life and corrodes buildings. Instead you should stick to the economics of inefficently functioning markets and inequitable market outcomes. When answering Question 2, make sure you don't confuse public goods and merit goods, or define them as goods which are provided by the government.

Key points

Economic efficiency (and in particular, allocative efficiency) is the key concept to introduce into your answers to all three questions. You must clearly explain how allocative efficiency requires that the price charged to consumers must equal the marginal cost of production ($P = MC$), or strictly the marginal social cost of production ($P = MSC$). When, in the course of production, negative externalities are discharged and received by third parties (Questions 1 and 3), markets result in too much of the good being produced. In a competitive market, the good's price will equal the marginal private cost of production ($P = MPC$). However, when negative externalities such as pollution are discharged, the price turns out to be less than the marginal social cost of production ($P < MSC$). The price is too low, encouraging overconsumption and overproduction of the good and of the externality. In Question 3 you must go on to explain and evaluate the effectiveness of two of the policies stated in the question, for correcting the overproduction and overconsumption.

The wording of Question 2 clearly indicates that merit goods can be provided through public spending rather than by markets. You must explain the reason for this: to correct the failure of underprovision that occurs when merit goods are provided solely by markets. You must then go on to consider the possible disadvantages of public sector provision. These include: overprovision of the merit good; consumers undervaluing services they receive free; and distortions and inefficiencies created elsewhere in the economy, for example through the higher taxes needed to finance public provision of the merit goods. You should then finish your answer with a statement as to whether, in your view, the advantages of public sector provision exceed the disadvantages.

Finally with public goods (Question 2), the allocatively efficient level of consumption occurs at zero price, but even when markets provide public goods, they will tend to be underprovided. The price would have to be greater than zero to create the incentive for entrepreneurs and markets to provide public goods commercially.

CHAPTER 10

PRIVATISATION AND RELATED POLICIES

Units in this chapter

Chapter objectives

This chapter examines some of the most significant of the micro-economic policies implemented by UK governments in recent years, which are the policies relating to the relative sizes and roles of the private and public sectors in the UK mixed economy. We begin by investigating the policy of **privatisation** through which previously state-owned or **nationalised industries** have been transferred to the private sector. The second part of the chapter surveys related policies of **economic liberalisation**, such as **regulation** and **deregulation**, which have been used along with privatisation to increase competition and to promote the efficient working of the market economy.

10.1 PRIVATISATION POLICIES

THE BACKGROUND TO PRIVATISATION

From the end of the Second World War until the late 1970s, the economic policies pursued by successive British governments were generally **interventionist**, extending the size of the public sector and the extent to which the government interfered with prices and markets. At this time the prevailing view was that economic problems result from a *failure of market forces*, and that the problems can be cured (or at least reduced) by appropriate government intervention. By contrast, the industrial policy pursued by UK governments from 1979 to the mid-1990s has been **anti-interventionist** and based on the belief that the correct role of government is not to reduce the role of market forces, but to create the conditions in which *market forces can work effectively and efficiently*.

THE MEANING OF PRIVATISATION

Privatisation means the transfer of state-owned assets to private ownership. For the most part this has involved the sale by the British government of nationalised industries to the general public, but council houses and land owned by local authorities have also been privatised. While in the public sector, most of the nationalised industries were organised as **public corporations**, responsible to central government. Shortly before actual privatisation, the legal status of these industries was usually changed from public corporation to **public limited company (Plc)**, with the state initially owning 100% of the share capital. Privatisation then occurred when 51% or more of a state-owned company's shares was sold to the general public. This could involve the sale of shares to private individuals, to financial institutions such as insurance companies and pension funds, to industrial companies already in the private sector, to overseas companies, or to the business's managers in a management buyout.

Since 1979 over twenty nationalised firms and industries been privatised in the UK. The main privatisations of nationalised industries, and the year in which they took place, are shown in the following table.

Table 10.1 *The main privatisations in the UK*

British Aerospace	1981	British Airways	1987
National Freight Corporation	1982	British Steel	1989
British Leyland (Rover)	1984	Water authorities	1989
British Telecom (BT)	1984	Electricity distribution (area boards)	1990
British Shipbuilders	1985	Electricity generation (Power Gen and National Power)	1991
National Bus Company	1985	British Coal	1994/5
British Gas	1986	Rail Track (ex British Rail)	1996
British Airports Authority	1987		

NATIONALISATION

Prior to the modern era of privatisation, the previous decades had witnessed the opposite process of **nationalisation**, or the taking of industries and companies into state ownership. The history of nationalisation in the UK extends back to the middle of the 19th century, when the Post Office was established as a civil service department. The first **public corporation** was the Port of London Authority, created in 1908. Other early public corporations were the Central Electricity Board, London Passenger Transport Board and the BBC, which were set up by Acts of Parliament in the 1920s.

Industries were nationalised in the UK for two main reasons: as an **instrument of socialist planning** and control of the economy; and as **a method of regulating the problem of monopoly** – in particular the problem of natural monopoly in the utility industries.

Socialist planning

The main period of nationalisation and extension of public ownership were in the late 1940s when a Labour Government was in office. Back in 1929 the British Labour Party had adopted the commitment to common ownership of the means of production, distribution and exchange. For many decades, the Labour Party argued that increased public ownership was necessary to give the government proper control of the key industries (or commanding heights of the economy), deemed vital for the socialist planning of the economy. The Labour Party also believed that nationalisation leads to improved industrial relations, and to a more equitable or fair distribution of income and wealth amongst the population.

Control of monopoly

Many of the British nationalised industries were **utility industries**. Utility industries such as gas, water and electricity supply, sewage disposal, telecommunications and postal services, are usually cited as the most obvious examples of natural monopoly. They have a particular production and marketing problem; they must deliver their service into millions of separate homes and places of work, usually through distribution grid of cables or pipelines. High fixed costs of investment in these distribution networks, together with ongoing maintenance costs, can mean that there is a case for only one gas pipeline or electricity cable per street, so as to avoid unnecessary duplication. In the past, the strength of this argument led to general agreement that utility industries should be organised as monopolies. Economists argued that, for utility industries and other natural monopolies, the main policy choice should not be between **competition and monopoly**, but between two different systems of ownership: public versus private monopoly. The key question was: *Should natural monopolies be organised as nationalised industries, or should they be left in private hands, but subject to strong and effective public regulation?*

Most of the early public corporations created before the Second World War – by Conservative as well as Labour governments – represent what has been called **gas and water socialism** – the regulation through public ownership of an essential utility or service regarded as too important to be left to the vagaries of private ownership and market forces. At this time, British governments of all political parties generally favoured public ownership of the utility industries – partly because they accepted the argument that public ownership facilitated the provision of a properly planned and organised system of distribution and a national standard of service for the whole population.

Other possible reasons for nationalisation

These might be: to regulate the production of merit demerit goods and to improve public health; to use monopoly profit as a source of state revenue; to provide defence and national security; to promote and protect 'national champion' industries and national prestige, and to protect industries from international competition and from being bought up by foreign competitors.

Table 10.2 *Privatisation and related industrial policies*

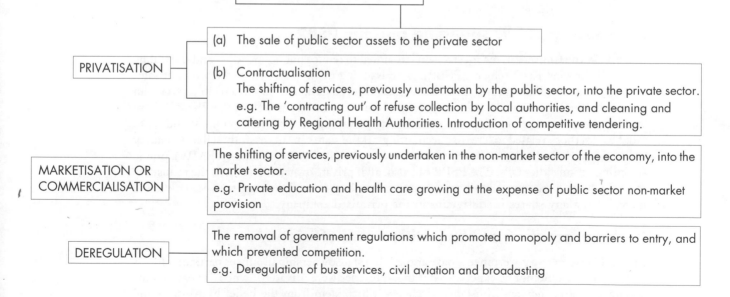

(i) Complete nationalised industries (public corporations), which are first transferred into public companies, followed by the sale of at least 51% of their share capital.
e.g. British Aerospace (1981) British Airways (1987)
British Telecom (1983) British Steel (1988)
British Gas (1986) the Water Authorities (1989)
Regional Electricity Distribution Boards (1990)

(ii) The sale of governernment-owned shares in existing public companies.
e.g. British Petroleum (BP)

(iii) The sales of other assets.
e.g. Council houses and land

PRIVATISATION

(a) The sale of public sector assets to the private sector

(b) Contractualisation
The shifting of services, previously undertaken by the public sector, into the private sector.
e.g. The 'contracting out' of refuse collection by local authorities, and cleaning and catering by Regional Health Authorities. Introduction of competitive tendering.

MARKETISATION OR COMMERCIALISATION

The shifting of services, previously undertaken in the non-market sector of the economy, into the market sector.
e.g. Private education and health care growing at the expense of public sector non-market provision

DEREGULATION

The removal of government regulations which promoted monopoly and barriers to entry, and which prevented competition.
e.g. Deregulation of bus services, civil aviation and broadasting

THE ADVENT OF PRIVATISATION

Following the major nationalisations of the 1940s, the next thirty years witnessed relatively little additional nationalisation. Many of the Acts of Nationalisation undertaken by Labour governments merely reorganised assets already in the public sector. Equally, there was relatively little denationalisation or privatisation when Conservative governments were in office. The 1950s to the 1970s were the decades of the mixed economy, when the major political parties agreed that the mix of public and private enterprise worked and was right for Britain. However, with the election of a radical free-market orientated administration under Margaret Thatcher in 1979, this consensus broke down. The Conservative governments of the 1980s and early 1990s set about the task of breaking up the mixed economy and moving the UK economy closer towards a pure market economy.

This has involved an industrial policy based on the inter-related processes of **privatisation**, **contractualisation**, **marketisation** (or **commercialisation**) and **deregulation** which are illustrated and defined in Table 10.2.

THE CASE FOR PRIVATISATION

The general case for privatisation can only be properly understood when seen as part of the revolution (or counter-revolution) in economic thinking which occurred in the 1970s and 1980s. This is the **neo-classical revival**. Other descriptive labels which have been attached to the free-market approach of the neo-classical revival – or to particular elements of the revival – include **monetarism**, **New Classical economics**, the **New Right**, the **radical right** and **supply-side economics**.

In the past, socialists often seemed to regard nationalisation as an end in itself, apparently believing that by taking an industry into public ownership, efficiency and equity would automatically improve and the public interest be served. In much the same way, many **economic liberals** at the opposite end of the political and economic spectrum, seem to believe that private ownership and capitalism are always superior to public ownership, whatever the circumstances, and that the privatisation of state-run industries must inevitably improve economic performance. Rather more specific arguments that have been used to justify the privatisation programme include the following.

1 Revenue raising

Privatisation, or the sale of state-owned assets, provides the government with a short-term source of revenue, which in some years has reached £3–4 billion. Obviously an asset cannot be sold twice, so eventually privatisation must slow down when there are no more assets left to sell.

2 Reducing public spending and the PSBR

Since 1979 the Conservative Government has aimed to reduce public spending and the Public Sector Borrowing Requirement (PSBR). By classifying the monies received from asset sales as *negative expenditure* rather than as *revenue*, the government has been able, from an accounting point of view, to reduce the level of public spending as well as the PSBR. There are, of course, rather more concrete reasons why privatisation may cause public spending to fall, besides those related to 'creative accounting'. If the state can successfully sell loss-making industries such as the Rover Group (now owned by the German car company, BMW), public spending on subsidies falls. The PSBR can also fall if private ownership returns the industries to profitability, since corporation tax revenue will be boosted and the state may earn dividend income from any shares it still retains in the privatised company.

3 The promotion of competition and efficiency

Recent Conservative governments have argued that state ownership produces particular forms of abuse that would not be experienced if the industries were privately owned. These include a general inefficiency and resistance to change which stem from the belief by workers and management in the state-run monopolies that they will always be baled out by government in the event of a loss. According to the Conservative view, monopoly abuse occurs in nationalised industries, not from the pursuit of private profit, but because the industries are run in the interest of a 'feather-bedded' workforce which is protected from any form of market discipline. The Conservatives believe the privatisation of state-owned monopoly should improve efficiency and commercial performance because privatisation exposes the industry to the threat of takeover and the discipline of the capital market.

4 Popular capitalism

Undoubtedly an important reason for the privatisation programme in the UK has been the **motive of promoting an enterprise culture** through extending share ownership to individuals and employees, who previously did not own shares, so as to widen the stake of the electorate in supporting a private enterprise economy. Privatisation has proved generally popular with voters, and the Conservative Government has seen no point at all in changing a winning programme.

THE CASE AGAINST PRIVATISATION

1 Monopoly abuse

Opponents of privatisation argue that far from promoting competition and efficiency, privatisation increases monopoly abuse by transferring socially-owned and accountable public monopolies into weakly-regulated and less-accountable private monopolies. Evidence of consumer dissatisfaction with the services provided since privatisation particularly with regard to the water companies and British Gas, has been used to support this argument. (Defenders of the privatisation programme counter by arguing that agencies such as OFTEL and OFGAS set up at the time of privatisation to regulate the utility industries once they were in the private sector, have been much more effective in preventing monopoly abuse than the government departments to whom the industries were previously answerable.)

As we have seen, at the time of their privatisation many of the nationalised industries were natural monopolies which are difficult to break up into competitive smaller companies without a significant loss of economies of scale and productive efficiency. There has also been a practical conflict between the aims of promoting competition and raising revenue. To maximise revenue from the sale of a nationalised industry such as BT or British Gas, the government chose to sell the industry whole, without breaking up the monopoly. Critics argue that privatisation has tended merely to switch industries from public to private monopoly, with little evidence that either competition or efficiency has been promoted, despite the introduction of some market discipline via the capital market. They reject the argument that privatisation has injected entrepreneurial flair into these industries, citing that in many cases the privatised companies are still run by the same people who managed them while in the public sector, albeit on greatly inflated salaries.

2 Selling the family silver

Opponents of privatisation argue that if a private sector business were to sell its capital assets simply to raise revenue to pay for current expenditure, it would rightly incur the wrath of its shareholders. The same should be true of the government and the sale of state-owned assets: taxpayers ought not to sanction the sale of capital assets, owned on their behalf by the UK government, to raise revenue to finance current spending on items such as wages and salaries. In reply, supporters of the privatisation programme argue that, far from *selling the family silver*, privatisation merely *returns the family's assets to the family*, i.e. from the custody of the state to direct ownership by private individuals.

3 The free lunch argument

Opponents of privatisation also claim that state-owned assets have been sold too cheaply, and in some cases almost given away, encouraging the belief amongst first-time buyers that there is such a thing as a free lunch. This is because the offer-price of shares in newly-privatised industries has normally been pitched at a level which has guaranteed a risk-free capital gain or 'one-way bet' at the taxpayer's expense for people buying the government's sell-offs, thereby encouraging the very opposite of an enterprise economy or risk-taking venture capitalism.

10.2 OTHER POLICIES OF ECONOMIC LIBERALISATION

Privatisation has been just one of a number of policies pursued by recent UK governments (and increasingly by governments throughout the world) to promote the roles of markets and private enterprise, while simultaneously reducing the role of the state in the economy. Related policies have been **contractualisation**, **competitive tendering**, the creation of **internal markets**, **marketisation** and **deregulation**.

CONTRACTUALISATION

Contractualisation or **contracting-out,** which is sometimes included in the definition of privatisation, takes place when services such as road cleaning and refuse collection are put out to private sector tender, though the tax payer still ultimately pays for the service. In the 1980s, the government ordered local government and health authorities within the NHS to contract out many low-level services, such as catering in hospitals and schools, and refuse collection. More recently this has been extended to higher-level services such as the contracting-out of much civil service, police and defence work to outside agencies and private enterprise firms, and the placing of contracts to provide surgical services for the NHS with private sector hospitals.

COMPETITIVE TENDERING

Competitive tendering is a variant of contracting out, though it can involve *contracting in* as well. In a fully developed system of competitive tendering, outside suppliers submit bids to supply all of a public sector organisation's business functions which could conceivably be undertaken by an external private sector firm. However, relevant departments within the public sector organisation may also be allowed to tender for the contracts. If an internal bid offers better value than those of the external suppliers, the business function can continue to being performed 'in house' by public sector workers, though now under contract as if they were outside suppliers. Supporters of the policy believe that regular competitive tendering improves the efficiency of civil service departments and public sector organisations such as NHS hospitals, and provides better value for taxpayers.

INTERNAL MARKETS

Most markets are *external* in the sense that trade and exchange take place between independent buyers and sellers. In an *internal* market, different parts of a larger organisation trade with each other, subject to ground rules or regulations laid down by a higher authority within the overall organisation. Actual money need not be involved; special units of account, such as budgetary units or vouchers created by the organisation, may be used to finance the working of the internal market. Sometimes the higher authority sets the **transfer prices** at which the various subsidiary parts of the organisation trade with each other.

In the early 1980s, the Conservative Government decided to base reform of the National Health Service on the creation of an internal market. In an important sense, the internal market has been a *substitute* for privatisation, since the Health Service has remained within the public sector. The government argued that through the signalling, incentive and allocative functions of prices, the internal market would improve the efficiency of the health service, while maintaining the principle of free medical care available to all at point of need, and collective finance through the tax system. Budgets are allocated by the state to local doctors or general practitioners (GPs). The GPs (the *purchasers* in the internal market) then shop around, buying surgical services for their patients from those hospitals (the *providers*) which in the doctor's opinion offer the best overall value.

A second internal market based on **education vouchers** has been proposed for the state education system, and is currently being introduced for nursery education. Free-marketeers argue that the existing system of financing state education system is producer-driven and does not respond sufficiently to the needs of parents and schoolchildren. This is because the money needed to finance state education is paid by central government directly to the providers, i.e. local education authorities and grant-maintained schools. By contrast, an internal market would be consumer-driven. Under such a system, the state would give education vouchers to parents to spend in the schools of their choice. Schools would be financed by voucher income rather than by state grants, and would expand or contract according to whether they could attract voucher income. Supporters argue that an internal market based on vouchers would have two significant advantages over the current system of state education. Firstly, consumer choice would increase, and secondly, there would be an incentive for schools to improve and offer a better product, so as to attract voucher income. Critics argue that an internal market would give an unfair advantage to already privileged schools in middle-class neighbourhoods, which would grow at the expense of less-favoured schools serving poorer communities. Arguably, social and economic divisions separating rich and poor would be exacerbated. Critics also fear an extension of the voucher system to cover private as well as state education, with parents able to use their vouchers to cover part of the cost of private education. Although this would increase consumer choice for those parents who would not otherwise be able to afford private education, by draining funds away from public sector schools, the voucher system would contribute to the erosion and creeping privatisation of the state educational system.

MARKETISATION

Although marketisation or **commercialisation** is a closely related policy, it must not be confused with either contractualisation or privatisation. Whereas privatisation involves transferring assets from the public sector to the private sector, marketisation simply shifts the provision of services from the non-market sector into the market sector by charging a price for a service which consumers previously enjoyed free of charge. There are many examples of marketisation, of which one of the oldest is the prescription charge for medicines provided through the National Health Service.

DEREGULATION

Deregulation means the removal of any previously imposed regulations and restrictions which have previously restricted or constrained the freedom of individuals and firms to undertake the activities of their choice. **Regulations** can be imposed by governments for all sorts of reasons, many of them virtuous, for example to protect consumers' rights, and Health and Safety at Work regulations to protect workers from rogue employers. The government has justified the opposite policy of deregulation for two main reasons. These are:

1 to remove unnecessary red-tape and bureaucracy which, by imposing extra costs on British firms, makes them less efficient and uncompetitive in world markets;

2 in the past regulations have often been imposed which create monopoly power by erecting artificial barriers that prevent or inhibit the entry of new competitors into a market. An obvious way to promote free markets and reduce monopoly power is to remove any artificial barriers created by previously imposed regulations which restrict market entry.

REGULATORY CAPTURE

A possibly unforeseen result of the spread of regulation is that the big business corporations, which regulations are designed to control, may succeed in capturing and manipulating the regulatory system to their own advantage. This is known as **regulatory capture**. The beneficiaries of regulation may be the regulated firms themselves, rather than consumers or outside firms trying to enter the market. Possible regulatory capture was disclosed in 1995 when the government-appointed regulator of the National Lottery was found to have accepted the gift of free air travel from one of the member firms of Camelot, the National Lottery organisation.

THE THEORY OF CONTESTABLE MARKETS

Whether or not regulatory capture has actually occurred, there is little doubt that the spread of government intervention before 1979 greatly extended the role of regulation and the regulators. In particular, the role of regulation increased in the field of **competition policy**, which covers government policy towards monopolies and the concentrated ownership of industry, mergers, and trading restrictive practices. A number of government agencies and courts were set up – the **Monopolies and Mergers Commission (MMC)**, the **Office of Fair Trading (OFT)** and the **Restrictive Practices Court (RPC)** – to administer competition policy. The general approach by government to the problems posed by monopoly and industrial concentration was to increase the level of regulation and intervention.

However, in recent years a new theory, called the **theory of contestable markets**, has begun to exert a growing influence in the opposite direction, providing much of the theoretical justification for the policies of liberalisation and deregulation that have been pursued. Before the advent of the contestable market theory, economists normally measured monopoly power by the number of firms in the market and by the share of the leading firms. By contrast, in the theory of contestable markets, monopoly power is defined, not by the number of firms in the market or by market shares, but simply by the potential ease or difficulty with which new firms may enter the market. According to the theory, monopoly is not regarded as a problem – even if there is only one established firm in the market – providing that the absence of barriers to entry and exit creates the potential for new firms to enter and contest the market. Actual competition in a market may not be necessary; instead the threat of entry by new firms may be quite sufficient to ensure efficient and non-exploitative behaviour by existing firms in the market.

The theory of contestable markets is important because it implies that, provided there is adequate potential for competition, an interventionist regulatory policy is unnecessary. Instead of increasing the amount of intervention and interference in the economy, the government should restrict its policy to discovering which markets and industries are potentially contestable, and then, through a process of deregulation and the removal of entry barriers, it should develop conditions which ensure that contestability is possible.

THE REREGULATION OF THE PRIVATISED UTILITIES

In the context of the privatised utility industries, deregulation has created a rather strange paradox and source of possible conflict. On the one hand, by setting markets free, deregulation reduces the role of the state, but on the other hand new watchdog bodies have been created which have extended the regulatory role of government and its agencies. Industry-specific regulatory agencies such as the Office of Telecommunication Regulation (OFTEL) and the Office of Gas Regulation (OFGAS) have been established for each of the privatised utility industries, together with OFRAIL for the railway industry and OFLOT for the National Lottery. The establishment of these new regulatory bodies represents what can be called the reregulation of the utility industries. However, these watchdog bodies created by the reregulatory process, are themselves actively involved in deregulating the industries they oversee, for example by enforcing the removal of barriers which prevent the entry of new firms. Supporters of the programme of economic liberalisation hope that the new watchdog agencies will prove so successful in liberating and promoting entry into markets previously regarded as natural monopolies, that eventually the agencies can wither away when there is no further need for their regulatory activities

Although new firms are beginning to compete in the markets previously completely dominated by state-owned utilities, the market power and natural monopoly position of the established utility companies means that for the foreseeable future, the regulators must continue to act as a surrogate for competition. Indeed, critics have argued that far from withering away, the new regulatory agencies seem to be gradually extending their powers and functions.

THE ROLE OF THE REGULATORY AGENCIES

The regulation of all the privatised utilities has displayed the following main features:

1 Each privatised utility has been created by Act of Parliament or statute, which has also established the general regulatory framework.

2 The privatisation statute lists the duties and responsibilities of the regulatory agency. Formally all the new regulatory bodies are non-ministerial government departments headed by a Director General appointed by Government. Along with the OFT and the MMC, the regulatory agencies such as OFTEL and OFGAS are examples of **QUAGOS (quasi-autonomous governmental organisations)**. The regulatory agencies are sometimes called QUANGOS but this is a slightly inaccurate label because the regulators and their staff are civil servants who are employed by the government.

3 The real power of a regulator lies in the fact that the privatisation statute requires that a utility must meet the terms of its operating licence. The details of each industry's licence were initially laid down by the government at the time of privatisation, but after privatisation it is the regulator who reviews and renews or changes the terms of the utility's licence.

4 The licence sets out the duties of both the privatised utility and the regulator. In all the utility industries, the regulators have a duty to promote effective competition by liberalising entry to the market. This means that they must ensure a level playing field, to enable both established firms and new entrants to compete fairly. Nevertheless, there is some diversity in the regulators' responsibilities. The regulators must also protect customers and ensure that the social aspects of a utility's operations are maintained, for example by providing a universal service to all parts of the United Kingdom.

5 The most significant feature of the licensing system has been the **pricing formula** set out in each industry's licence, which limits the privatised utility's freedom to choose its own prices. It is this pricing formula, (known as RPI minus X) and the regulator's power to change the formula, which lies at the heart of the current system of regulation of the utility industries in the UK. The prices charged by a privatised utility are effectively capped because the utility must limit average price increases to X percentage points below the rate of inflation as measured by the Retail Price Index. For example, a price cap of RPI minus 5, set when the rate of inflation is 4%, would mean that the industry must actually reduce average prices by 1%.

6 The newly-created regulators act in conjunction with older established agencies such as the Office of Fair Trading and the Monopolies and Mergers Commission. The OFT systematically scans all of British industry for evidence of monopoly abuse. If the Office discovers evidence of anti-competitive behaviour by one of the privatised industries, it may decide to investigate the industry in more depth. The OFT can also refer the industry to the Monopolies and Mergers Commission for further investigation, and any restrictive agreements could be referred to the Restrictive Practices Court.

7 The Monopolies and Mergers Commission also has a role in the review of the licence terms and pricing formulas, which are the joint responsibility of the Director Generals of the regulatory agencies and the MMC. Formally, the MMC acts as an appeal court for licence revision and the price formulas if industry and regulator fail to agree. In practice, however, the MMC is seldom directly involved because all the negotiation and bargaining is undertaken by the regulatory agencies. The threat of possible referral to the Commission is usually sufficient to ensure that the utility agrees to its regulator's demands.

A CLOSER LOOK AT THE RPI MINUS X PRICING FORMULA

The key feature of this pricing formula is that for a pre-specified period of four to five years, a utility company can make any changes it wishes to prices, provided that the average price of a specified basket of its goods and services does not increase faster than RPI minus X, where X is initially set by the Government. At the end of the period, the level of X is reset by the regulator, and the process is repeated. The X factor reflects the improvements in productive efficiency which the regulator believes that the utility can make and share with its consumers each year. It is designed to put pressure on the utility to improve productivity and to cut costs. With X set in the price cap formula for a known period of five years, the utility has the incentive to reduce costs by more than X per cent and to pocket the difference as increased profits.

There are a number of problems with the RPI minus X pricing formula. The incentive for the utilities to improve efficiency and reduce costs disappears if the regulators then claw back the utility's share of the productivity gain by increasing the X factor the next time the utility's licence is renewed. On most occasions, the regulators have raised X when the factor has come up for renewal. The incentive for a utility to improve efficiency is further reduced if the regulators succumb to the temptation to reset X before the five year review is due, on the grounds that the utility is making excess profits. In such a situation, critics argue that the RPI minus X pricing formula degenerates into a form of punishment which destroys the incentive for the privatised utility companies to improve efficiency.

RPI minus X can work if the regulator has a good idea of how efficient the privatised utility is, and of how efficient it might become. In order to set the X factor for a period of five years ahead, the regulators must possess considerable technical information about the industries they oversee. If a regulator fails to foresee the direction that technical progress takes over the next five years, X may have to be reset before the five years is up, thus triggering the disadvantages just outlined. A regulator is most likely to set X accurately when the technology in the industry is fairly mature and not subject to sudden change. In these circumstances the rate at which the regulator can learn about the industry is faster than the rate at which technology changes.

THE BREAKDOWN OF NATURAL MONOPOLY

The greatest problems of regulation and implementing the RPI minus X pricing formula have occurred in the telecommunications industry where rapid technical progress has been taking place. Recent technical developments are changing many of the so-called natural monopolies into less natural and even unnatural or artificial monopolies. In the telecommunications industry, satellite technology and the falling real cost of laying carbon fibre land lines allow Mercury to compete effectively with BT, and it is becoming increasingly possible for other new firms to enter the market. In the electricity, gas and water industries as well as in telecommunications, sophisticated computerised metering and payments systems can allow new firms to enter the market by renting the services of the existing distribution network or grid, thus bypassing the need to invest in their own distribution system. The development of these new electronic information and recording systems might shortly allow customers living, say in Manchester, to buy electricity from a distribution company located in another region. In theory, developments such as these will make it possible for customers to shop around and find the regional distributor which offers the most attractive price. But technical developments such as these will only stand a chance of breaking the monopoly power of the gas, electricity and water companies if the regulatory agencies force the established utilities to open their distribution systems to the new market entrants.

Left to itself, an established utility company is likely, of course, to try to preserve its monopoly position. It might do this by charging prohibitively high prices to new entrants who rent the services of the established firm's distribution system. This is especially likely when the established utility is a vertically-integrated monopoly, such as BT or British Gas, with complete control over all aspects of production, distribution and retailing. In this situation, there is a strong case for active intervention by the regulator to try to ensure that the established utility company does not prevent the entry of new firms by setting artificially high prices for the use of its distribution network. Indeed, the regulatory process may be taken one stage further by vertically disintegrating the established utility into separate production, distribution and retailing companies. Such vertical disintegration is outside the remit of regulatory bodies such as OFGAS, but the Office of Fair Trading is currently forcing British Gas to open the gas industry to competition by separating gas distribution from gas production.

Chapter roundup

The economic policies we have examined in this chapter have emerged as some of the main free market orientated supply-side policies in the economic programme of recent British Conservative governments. It should be noted also, that although originally hostile, a Labour government is unlikely to reverse the changes brought about by privatisation and reregulation, though such a government would be unlikely to extend these policies much further. We shall touch upon these policies further in Chapters 13, 16, and 17, which respectively cover fiscal policy, supply-side economics, and Keynesianism and monetarism.

Illustrative questions and answers

1   Essay Question

'In recent years, governments have aimed to improve efficiency and growth through policies of privatisation and deregulation.'
(a) Explain what you understand by
   (i) privatisation; and
   (ii) deregulation. (8)
(b) Explain how privatisation and deregulation may lead to improved efficiency and growth in product markets. (9)
(c) Discuss the implications for consumers of such policies. (8)   *SEB*

Tutorial note

(a) With a question like this students often seem to succumb to the temptation to answer a question which has not actually been set, namely to write all they know on the history of privatisation and/or the advantages and disadvantages of privatisation. You must resist this temptation! Define privatisation as the sale or transfer of public sector assets (such as nationalised industries and council flats) to the private sector, perhaps also including 'contractualisation' in your definition, i.e. putting services such as waste disposal previously provided completely by the public sector, out to private sector tender or contract. Deregulation is literally the removal of previously imposed government regulation, particularly those regulations that have promoted barriers to market entry, and restricted competition. Give examples such as the deregulation of the TV and bus industries.

(b) You might not agree that privatisation and deregulation have actually succeeded in promoting efficiency and growth, but you will lose marks heavily if you fail to discuss how they may have these results. Privatisation introduces the profit motive and important sources of 'market discipline' to inefficient firms, via the possibility of bankruptcy or takeover if they continue to perform badly. However, in itself, privatisation may merely transform public monopoly into private monopoly, so deregulation is necessary to supplement privatisation by removing barriers to entry and promoting efficiency through effective competition.

(c) In principle, privatisation and successful deregulation can improve consumer sovereignty by reducing costs, profits and prices and by promoting better services, product development and choice. But it is worth noting that consumer complaints have increased dramatically since privatisation, though this may simply reflect the fact that consumers now believe that the agencies set up to regulate the privatised industries 'possess teeth' and that complaining about the standards of service will now produce results. With this point in mind, you might also note that by setting up external regulatory bodies such as OFTEL, OFGAS, OFWAT, and OFFER, the Conservative government has found it necessary to increase rather than reduce the regulation of the privatised 'utility' industries, telecommunications, gas, water and electricity. This has been called the 'reregulation of the privatised utilities'.

2   Data Question

REGULATION OF PRIVATISED INDUSTRIES

Nobody thought regulating privatised monopolies would be easy. The inherent conflict between the interests of shareholders and consumers in privatised utilities makes it inevitable that there will be continual debate about regulation. While shareholders and consumers have both done well since privatisation, it is the
5   shareholders who have had the better deal. The government was insufficiently ambitious, early on, in introducing competition into hitherto monopolistic industries; pricing formulas did not take into account the full extent of the efficiency gains. Now that the pricing arrangements have been tightened and increased evidence brought to bear, both management and investors feel
10   uncomfortable. There is certainly a danger that an initially lax regulatory framework can turn into one in which regulation overtly favours the consumer.
   The primary duty of the regulator is to promote competition. The UK places a fundamental emphasis on putting the creation of competitive markets ahead of the restraint of monopoly. Simple faith in such tools as the price-capping formula
15   is not adequate. Much more work needs to be done on the impact that the regulators are having on the investment, efficiency and quality of service of the industries. As a general proposition, regulation should be run down as competition becomes a force.

(Adapted from an article in *The Sunday Times,* April 1994
© Times Newspapers Limited, 1994)

(a) Why is there an 'inherent conflict between the interest of shareholders and consumers' (lines 1–2)? (3)

(b) Explain the role of pricing formulas. Why have these 'pricing arrangements been tightened' (line 8)? (4)

(c) What evidence is there so far to suggest that 'regulation overtly favours the consumer' (line 11)? (4)

(d) Assess the effect of regulation on 'the investment, efficiency and quality of service' (line 16) in any **one** of the privatised utilities. (6)

(e) What attempts have been made to introduce greater competition into privatised industries? Should 'regulation be run down as competition becomes a force' (lines 17–18)? (8)

Oxford & Cambridge

Tutorial note

(a) The main point to make is that consumers benefit from low prices whereas high prices may boost company profitability and allow higher dividends to be paid to shareholders.

(b) Privatised utility companies possess considerable monopoly power. Economic theory suggests that left to itself, a utility company may set a high price which exploits consumers and results in an allocatively inefficient level of production and consumption. The price is likely to be above the marginal cost of production (P > MC).

At the same time, the nature of the utility industries tends to rule out the policy option of creating competition by breaking up established utility companies into a number of smaller firms. The benefits of economies of scale would be lost and unnecessary duplication of distribution networks and other sources of fixed costs would result. In the UK, the chosen policy solution has therefore been to allow utility companies to survive largely intact, but to create external regulators with the remit to prevent the utilities from exploiting their market power. This is the main function of the RPI minus X pricing formula imposed by UK regulators such as OFTEL and OFGAS. In addition, the pricing formula enables both companies and customers to benefit from any improvement in production efficiency achieved by the utility companies. By allowing the companies to keep some of the gain as increased profits, while passing on the rest of the gain to consumers in the form of lower prices, the pricing formulas encourage the utility companies to innovate and reduce costs. However, the passage indicates that originally the level at which the regulators set Factor X favoured the companies at the expense of their consumers. The pricing arrangements were tightened to tilt the balance away from the utility companies and towards the consumers.

(c) The passage implies that when the regulators reset Factor X, the balance swung too far away from the utility companies and their shareholders, and too much in favour of consumers, but there is no actual evidence in the passage to support this view, apart from the statement that with 'increased evidence brought to bear, both management and investors feel uncomfortable'. A good answer might draw on information picked up from recent stories in the newspapers about utility company chairmen and financial analysts complaining about the pricing formulas.

Over the years since they were first established, the regulatory agencies – particularly OTFEL and OFGAS – have gradually taken on more powers. It is sometimes claimed that this is at odds with an original intention of privatisation, that a **regulatory bargain** should be struck between government and the managers and shareholders in the newly floated utilities. In this regulatory bargain, the regulatory system would follow agreed rules which would hold for several years. These rules could be reviewed and possibly changed every few years, but between reviews the utilities would be left free to get on with their normal commercial activities. Providing that the utility companies continued to obey the price formulas and other guidelines implicit in the regulatory bargain, there would be no sudden and unpredictable discretionary intervention by the new regulatory authorities. Critics of the regulatory system argue that even if the authorities ever intended to hold to such a regulatory bargain, the promise certainly has not been kept. On several occasions the regulators have intervened and altered the pricing rules they had recently set, in order to protect consumers and maintain quality of service.

(d) When answering this question, you must avoid the temptation to slip into a one-sided political diatribe either against or in favour of privatisation, with little or no proper use of the evidence. You might, however, make the point that since the passage argues that much more work needs to be done on the impact of regulation on the performance of the privatised industries, it may well be impossible for a mere student to answer the question properly! It would be sensible to select an industry such as telecommunications, where there is plenty of evidence of improved investment, efficiency, and quality of service. However, the telecommunications industry has been benefiting from extremely rapid technological progress and expanding markets; it is debatable how much of the improvement is down to privatisation and the role of the regulators in preventing monopoly abuse and opening up the market to new entrants. By contrast, you might the choose a utility such as the water industry where there has been much less scope for technological progress. You might argue that at least some of the water companies have exploited their monopoly position and neglected to invest sufficiently and improve the quality of service. Make sure you provide evidence (such as high leakage rates from old water pipes, leading to a failure to meet demand), before possibly concluding that regulation has not been successful in improving performance.

(e) We have noted in the main body of the chapter how the regulators have attempted to introduce competition by removing or lowering market barriers, so that new firms can enter the market. Partly through the incentives created by the RPI minus X pricing formulas, the regulators have also encouraged **technology-driven competition**. This occurs when firms try to gain cost and competitive advantages over their rivals through successful research and development, innovation and improvements in dynamic efficiency.

The regulator's task in promoting technology-driven competition is made considerably easier when technology is developing in such a way that it breaks down entry barriers and attracts new competitors into the market. In the telecommunications industry, the regulator can challenge BT with the prospect of entrants coming into the market with new technologies such as cable television and mobile telephones. At the other end of the spectrum in the water industry, there are fewer prospects for technology-driven competition. This has led the water regulator to adopt **yardstick competition**. After comparing the performance and costs of all the water companies, OFWAT sets prices so that all the water companies have to match the standards achieved by the best in the industry. As the other utility regulators run up against the realistic limits to competition in their industries, they too may have to turn to yardstick competition to assess the efficiency of the companies they oversee.

As the passage implies, free-market economists hope that the regulatory agencies will prove so successful in liberating and promoting entry into markets previously regarded as natural monopolies, that eventually the agencies can *wither away* when there is no further need for their regulatory activities. You might argue that although new firms are beginning to compete in the markets previously completely dominated by state-owned utilities, the market power and natural monopoly position of the established utility companies means that, for the foreseeable future, the regulators must continue to act as a *surrogate* for competition. Indeed, some free-market economists believe there is a danger that, far from withering away, the new regulatory agencies may gradually try to extend their powers and functions.

Question bank

1 (a) Explain what is meant by privatisation. (8)

   (b) Do you support the trend towards privatisation found in many economies? (17)

   Cambridge

2 (a) Explain the benefits which supporters of the government's privatisation programme expect to result from the privatisation of industries such as gas, water and telecommunications. (12)

   (b) To what extent, if any, has the creation of regulatory agencies such as OFGAS, OFWAT and OFTEL minimised the disadvantages of privatisation? (13)   *AEB*

3 Explain how, in theory, price competition affects the economic efficiency of organisations. What basis is there for the view that government policies on internal markets and privatisation are likely to be effective in promoting greater economic efficiency in areas such as education, health and rail transport? (25)   *NEAB*

Pitfalls

With a topic such as privatisation there is a danger of writing a standard answer to the type of question which used to be set a few years ago, without realising that over the years examiners subtly change the wording of the questions they set to test different knowledge and skills. When the topic of privatisation first began to appear in A Level examination papers in the mid-1980s, the questions usually asked for an explanation of the meaning of the term, and for a discussion of the advantages and disadvantages of privatisation. This sort of question has now rather fallen out of fashion with examiners, though Question 1 is a recent example of a question of this type. As Question 2 shows, these days examiners are much more likely to set a question which is based to some extent on assessing the track record of the industries since they have been privatised, and/or of the regulators. Have the industries performed well or badly, and what criteria should be used to judge performance? Question 3 illustrates another type of question which has become quite common in recent years. To answer this question properly you must assess the performance of another of the policies of economic liberalisation (besides privatisation) which we have surveyed in this chapter. If you rewrite these questions as 'write all you know about privatisation', you won't do very well.

Key Points

Privatisation is, of course, the key concept in Questions 1 and 2, but with both these questions you must discuss privatisation as a means to an end, rather than as an end in itself. (For free-marketeers, privatisation is a policy *instrument*, rather than a policy *objective*.). With both questions, you must discuss how privatisation may improve economic efficiency and performance, and benefit consumers and taxpayers. Both questions also ask for a discussion of possible adverse effects resulting from privatisation, and you must finally provide some overall assessment or evaluation of whether the beneficial effects of privatisation are likely to exceed the adverse effects.

With Question 3, your approach should be rather different. You must explain briefly how the price mechanism operating in competitive markets, may achieve economic efficiency. Go on to state that in less-competitive markets, including those in which nationalised industries used to operate, the price mechanism fails to eliminate productive, allocative and X inefficiency. Describe how privatisation and the creation of internal markets may improve efficiency. Make the point that privatisation simply shifts industries from the public sector to the private sector, without in itself increasing competition. Supplementary policies such as the removal of barriers to entry, may be needed to increase competition. You can also make the point that in an important sense, internal markets are a substitute for privatisation, since they are used by the government to promote competition in services (e.g. health care and possibly education) which continue to be provided by the public sector, free to consumers and financed through the tax system. Conclude your answer to Question 3 by assessing whether the two policies will actually succeed in improving economic efficiency.

CHAPTER 11

THE LABOUR MARKET

Units in this chapter

Chapter objectives

Earlier chapters examined the behaviour of firms and how prices are determined when firms sell their output in the goods market or product market. It is generally assumed that the prices of the inputs necessary for production, or the **prices of factor services**, were given. We now reverse the assumption, and examine how the prices of factors of production are determined in the factor market, assuming that conditions and prices in the product market are generally given. The chapter concentrates on the **labour market** and the **determination of wages**, applying analysis where necessary to the other factors of production and their prices.

The first unit of this chapter explains how wage rates and levels of employment are determined in **perfectly** competitive labour markets. The second unit examines **imperfectly** competitive labour markets and the effects of trade union activity upon wages and employment.

11.1 PERFECTLY COMPETITIVE LABOUR MARKETS

DISTRIBUTION THEORY

This theory is concerned with how the incomes generated by production are distributed between the various factors of production whose services contribute to the output which firms produce. Distribution theory introduces no new methods of analysis and only a few new theoretical concepts. It is merely the price theory of the earlier chapters, but viewed from the other side. As we shall see, it can be subjected to the same criticisms as other aspects of conventional price theory. In earlier chapters we examined the interaction of households and firms in the goods market, where households are the source of demand for goods and services supplied by firms. We now view households as the source of supply of factor services, which are demanded by firms in the pursuit of profit.

You should note:

❶ **Wages and other factor prices are assumed to be determined by supply and demand.**

❷ **The assumption of maximising behaviour.** The assumptions of profit-maximising behaviour on the part of firms and utility maximisation by households are as crucial to distribution theory as they are to the rest of price theory. Firms will only demand the services of factors of production if profits can be increased by their employment. Similarly, households will only supply more labour, or hire out the capital or land they may own, if it maximises their net advantage. The concept of **net advantage** covers all the rewards, monetary and non-monetary, which a household gains from the sale of its factor services. For example, if a person enjoys his work, the net advantage obtained from employment will include the pleasure gained from the work itself, as well as the utility of the wage – or more strictly, the utilities obtained from the goods and services bought with the money wage.

❸ **The demand for factor services is a derived demand.** The essential difference between consumer demand in the goods market, and a firm's demand for factor services, is that the latter is a derived demand: the services of labour or land are demanded only because they are necessary in the production of goods and services to sell for profit.

❹ **Entrepreneurial profit, and indeed the entrepreneurial function, is regarded as different from those of the other factors of production.** The entrepreneurial function of risk-taking and the bearing of uncertainty is undertaken by the owners of a business, who bear the financial risks. However, the existence of such a separate entrepreneurial function in modern companies can be questioned. Very often all the important decisions are made by management, who are a part of the labour force. In so far as entrepreneurial profit exists, it is essentially a residual, the difference between the total revenue obtained from the sale of output in the product market, and the other factor rewards which constitute the firm's costs of production.

❺ **Transfer earnings and economic rent.** So far, we have used the term 'rent' in its everyday meaning as the price which must be paid to hire the services of land. To the economist, however, rent or economic rent has a rather different meaning. It is a more general meaning which applies to all the factors of production, yet it is more specific since it refers to only a part of the earnings of each factor. Fig. 11.1 illustrates the demand and supply for a particular type of labour. L_1 represents a worker who is just prepared to supply labour if the wage is W_1, but who would withdraw from this particular labour market if the wage fell below W_1. We now assume that the firm pays the same wage to all the workers it employs. This is the equilibrium wage W_2, determined where the demand and supply curves intersect at A. Worker L_1 receives the wage of W_2 even though he would be prepared to work for the lower wage of W_1. The part of his wage above the supply curve at point B is economic rent, while the part below is transfer earnings. **Transfer earnings** represent the **factor's opportunity cost**, while economic rent is the difference between what the factor is actually paid and its opportunity cost. If the wage falls below W_1, worker L_1 will transfer out of this particular labour market, or at least decide to supply less labour. Taking all the workers together, their economic rent is shown by the shaded area above the supply curve, while their transfer earnings are shown by the area below. Worker L_2 is the **marginal worker**, who is only just prepared to supply labour at the wage of W_2. All his wage is transfer earnings. The concept of economic rent is sometimes applied to entrepreneurial profit, as well as to the earnings of the other factors of production. In this case, **normal profit** is regarded as a transfer earning, since the entrepreneur will leave the industry if normal profit is not earned. **Abnormal profit** which is earned over and above normal profit becomes the 'economic rent of enterprise'.

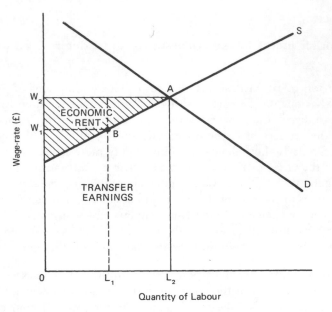

Fig. 11.1 Economic rent and transfer earnings

THE SUPPLY OF LABOUR

The **aggregate supply of labour** in the economy is ultimately constrained by the size of the total population. Nevertheless, for a given total population size, the aggregate supply can increase or decrease if, for example, married women decide to enter or leave the working population, which is determined by demographic factors and migration. However, for the purpose of this chapter we are more interested in examining the supply of labour within a single labour market than with investigating the factors which cause the aggregate supply of labour to change.

The **market supply curve of labour** is the sum of the supply curves of each worker in the labour market. A **worker's supply curve of labour** can either **slope upwards**, showing that more labour is supplied as the wage rises; or it can **bend backwards**, a case where wage rises cause less labour to be supplied. In both cases, the labour supply reflects the fact that at the margin, a worker must choose between supplying an extra hour of labour and enjoying an extra hour of leisure time. Now both the money wage and leisure time yield utility, but both also respond to the law of diminishing marginal utility. When more labour is supplied at a particular wage rate, the extra income yields less and less extra utility. At the same time, each extra hour of leisure sacrificed results in an increasing utility loss. To maximise utility, labour must be supplied up to the point at which the **MU of the wage = the MU of leisure**; at which point the worker has no incentive to supply more labour at the existing wage rate. A higher wage would be needed to encourage a worker to supply more labour beyond this point; hence the upward-sloping supply curve of labour.

This explanation relates to the **substitution effect** of a wage increase. For example, an hourly wage rate increase from £10 to £12 raises the price of an hour of leisure from £10 to £12. Because leisure has become more expensive, workers decide to supply labour and earn the wage instead.

However, an **income effect** also operates which can result in less labour being supplied. The wage increase raises both the worker's real income and his demand for normal goods. For most people, leisure time is a normal good. Hence, the income effect of the wage increase suggests that less labour will be supplied, since more leisure is being demanded.

The slope of a worker's supply curve of labour will thus depend on the **relative strengths of the substitution and income effects**. If the substitution effect is stronger than the income effect, an upward-sloping supply curve results: but, if the income effect is the more powerful, the supply curve is backward-bending or regressive.

An alternative approach to the backward-bending supply curve is to assume that workers aim to achieve a **target real income**, measured in terms of bought goods and services. A wage increase allows the target to be reached with a lower input of labour, allowing the worker to enjoy more leisure time rather than extra material goods. This is a plausible behavioural assumption when the work itself is unpleasant, (e.g. coal mining).

A backward-bending supply curve has an important implication for tax policy. If the supply curve is upward-sloping, an increase in income tax results in less labour being supplied, because the tax is equivalent to a cut in wages. If, however, the supply curve is backward-bending, the rise in income tax causes people to work longer hours in order to maintain their target incomes.

THE DEMAND CURVE FOR LABOUR

We have already indicated that the demand curve for a factor of production is a derived demand. We assume that a firm will only voluntarily employ an extra worker if this increases total profit. To find out whether profits will indeed increase, a firm must know (a) how much the worker adds to total output, and (b) the money value of the extra output when it is sold in the product market. The amount which is added to a firm's revenue by employing one more worker is called the **marginal revenue product (MRP) of labour**. The two elements which comprise the MRP of labour are represented by the identity:

$$\text{Marginal Revenue Product} \equiv \text{Marginal Physical Product} \times \text{Marginal Revenue}$$
$$\text{(MRP)} \qquad\qquad \text{(MPP)} \qquad\qquad \text{(MR)}$$

In Chapter 4 we explained the law or principle of **diminishing marginal returns**, which states that a variable factor such as labour will eventually add less and less to total output as labour itself is added to other factors which are held fixed. In the context of distribution theory it is usual, if rather confusing, to refer to the **marginal physical product (MPP)** of labour. This is exactly the same as the marginal returns of labour. The falling MPP curve which is drawn in Fig. 11.2a is explained by the principle of diminishing returns!

To find the money value of the MPP of labour, we multiply the MPP by the addition to total revenue resulting from the sale of the physical output in the goods market. In other words, we must multiply MPP by marginal revenue. In Fig.11.2 it is assumed that conditions of perfect competition exist in the goods market. In a perfectly competitive market, MR is identical to the good's price. Thus the MRP curve is derived by multiplying MPP by a constant price at each level of output. In these conditions, the slope and elasticity of the MRP curve are determined by MPP alone, though a change in the good's price will shift the position of the MRP curve. If the goods market is a monopoly or imperfectly competitive, MR will decrease with output. This causes the MRP curve to be steeper than when the goods market is perfectly competitive.

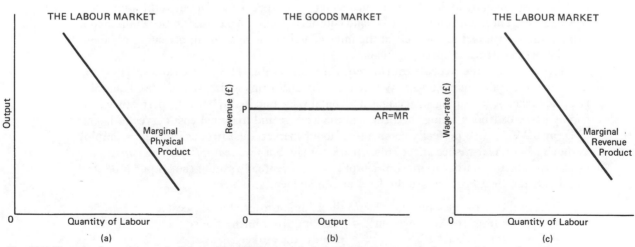

Fig. 11.2 How the demand curve for labour (the MRP curve) is derived, assuming a perfectly competitive goods market

THE EQUILIBRIUM WAGE IN A PERFECTLY COMPETITIVE LABOUR MARKET

In a competitive labour market, the MRP curve of labour is the **employer's demand curve for labour**. An employer demands labour up to the point where MRP = the marginal cost of employing an extra worker. If the employer goes beyond this point and hires a worker who adds more to total costs than to total revenue, profits must fall. Conversely, if the firm decides to limit the size of the workforce at a point where the MRP of the last worker is greater than the marginal cost incurred by employing him, the firm is sacrificing potential profits.

Figure 11.3 illustrates the determination of the **equilibrium wage rate** and **level of employment** in a perfectly competitive labour market, both in the **whole market** (a), and for just **one of the firms** in the market (b), and the demand for labour at the level of a single firm within the market.

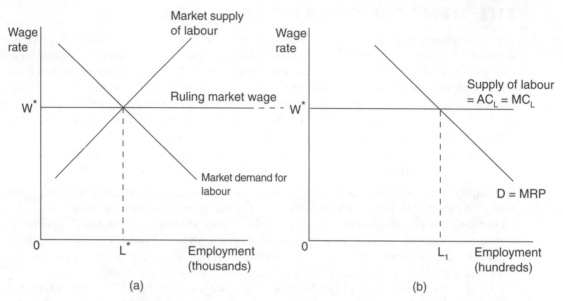

Fig. 11.3 Wage and employment determination in a perfectly competitive labour market (a) the whole market (b) one firm within the market

The equilibrium wage and equilibrium employment for the whole labour market are shown in Fig. 11.3(a), at the intersection of the market demand curve for labour and the market supply curve of labour. We have already explained that the market supply curve of labour is obtained by adding up the individual supply curves of all the workers in the market at different possible wages. In a similar way, we add up the demand curves for labour of all the firms in the market to obtain the market demand curve for labour. Since each firm's demand for labour is shown by its MRP curve, the market demand curve for labour is the sum of the MRP curves. The equilibrium wage W* and equilibrium employment L* in the whole labour market are determined in Fig 11.3 at the intersection of the market supply curve of labour and the market demand curve for labour.

Having derived the **overall market equilibrium** in Fig. 11.3(a), we can use 11.3(b) to show how the ruling market wage W* affects individual firms within the market. Each firm is a price-taker at the ruling wage. This horizontal wage line is also both the perfectly elastic supply curve of labour facing the firm, and the average and marginal cost curves of labour (AC_L and MC_L). In a perfectly competitive labour market, each firm can therefore employ as much labour as it wishes at the ruling market wage, but it *cannot influence the ruling wage by its own actions*. In order to maximise profits when eventually selling the output produced by labour, the firm *must* choose the level of employment at which:

the addition to sales revenue resulting from the employment of an extra worker	=	the addition to production costs resulting from hiring the services of an extra worker

or: $$MRP = MC_L$$

This is the equilibrium equation, determining each firm's optimal or profit-maximising level of employment in the labour market. In a perfectly competitive labour market, since the marginal cost of labour equals the wage rate, the equilibrium equation can also be written as:

$$MRP = W$$

In Fig 11.3(b), the firm's equilibrium level of employment is L_1, where MRP = W. You should note that while the equilibrium equation MRP = W determines each firm's level of employment (or demand for labour), it does not determine the wage. As already explained, the wage is determined in Fig. 11.3(a) where the demand for labour of *all* the firms in the labour market equals the market supply of labour. As we are dealing with a perfectly competitive labour market, individual firms within the market passively accept and are unable to influence the ruling market wage.

Wage equalisation in a perfectly competitive market economy

If all labour markets in the economy were perfectly competitive, there would be no artificial barriers preventing the movement of workers from one labour market to another. In this situation, competitive market forces would tend to reduce differences in wages between different occupations, though it must be stressed that because of natural barriers such as different skill requirements, wage differences would not be completely eliminated. Higher wages in one occupation would attract workers from other labour markets, causing the supply curve of labour to shift rightwards in the high-wage labour market and leftwards in the low-wage market. At the same time, the wage-differentials would create incentives for firms in the high-wage market to reduce their demand for labour by substituting capital for labour, and for firms in the low-wage labour markets to adopt more labour-intensive methods of production. Demand and supply curves and wages would adjust until no further incentive existed for firms to change their method of production or for workers to shift between labour markets. By this equalising market process, wage differentials would be reduced throughout all labour markets.

Explanations of different wage levels

The most obvious explanation of different wage levels, despite the **equalising market process** described above, lies in the fact that the labour demand and supply curves are in different positions in different labour markets, reflecting such factors as different labour productivities, abilities and required skills. Also, as explained in 11.2, real life labour markets are imperfectly competitive, characterised by imperfect market information and by barriers and sources of friction which prevent or restrict movement between markets. However, even within the rarefied and abstract assumptions of perfect competition, we might expect certain wage differentials to exist at any point of time. This is for two main reasons:

❶ **Different jobs have different non-monetary characteristics** We have already explained how the net advantage of any type of work includes job satisfaction or dissatisfaction as well as the utility of the wage. Other things being equal, a worker must be paid a higher wage to compensate for any relative unpleasantness in the job. We can define an **equalising wage differential** as the payment which must be made to compensate a worker for the different non-monetary characteristics of jobs, so that following the payment, the worker has no incentive to switch between jobs or labour markets.

❷ **Disequilibrium trading** It is reasonable to assume that an economy is subject to constant change, involving the development both of new goods and services and of improved methods of production or technical progress, and subject also to changing patterns of demand. In response to such ongoing change, markets, including factor markets, are characterised by disequilibrium rather than by equilibrium. This means that although market forces tend to equalise wages and other factor prices across competitive markets, at any point of time disparities exist which reflect the disequilibrium conditions existent at that time.

Differences in the elasticities of supply and demand

The elasticities of both the supply of and demand for labour are likely to differ between separated labour markets. If the demand for labour is relatively elastic, a rightward shift of the supply curve will have a greater effect on employment than on the wage level. In a similar way, the effect of a shift in demand will depend on the elasticity of the supply curve. A shift in either curve will have the greatest effect on the wage in a particular market when both the supply and demand curves are relatively inelastic. The time period in question is an important influence on both elasticities, with elasticities being higher in the long run than in the short run. It follows that a sudden change in the conditions of either supply or demand in a particular labour market will cause a larger change in the equilibrium wage in the short run than in the long run. In the long run, market forces serve to reduce wage differentials through the impact of labour mobility and factor substitution.

The supply of unskilled labour is generally more elastic than the supply of a particular type of skilled labour, since the training period of unskilled labour is usually very short. The existence of unemployed labour will also influence the elasticity of supply.

In general, the demand for labour will be relatively inelastic if:

- wages costs are only a small part of total production costs – this is sometimes known as the 'importance of being unimportant';
- the demand for the good produced by the firm is inelastic;
- it is difficult to substitute other factors of production for labour, or other types of labour for the particular type in question.

CRITICISMS OF DISTRIBUTION THEORY

1 The most important propositions of conventional distribution theory are that:

- in competitive markets, the equilibrium wage will equal the value of the marginal product of labour in each market;
- the condition that the wage equals the marginal product of labour in each market is a necessary condition to achieve allocative and productive efficiency throughout the economy;
- the actual combination of labour and other factors of production employed will depend upon their relative prices. In competitive markets, where the price of each factor equals its marginal cost, a firm will employ factors until the

$$\frac{\text{MRP of labour}}{\text{wage}} = \frac{\text{MRP of land}}{\text{rent}} = \frac{\text{MRP of land}}{\text{rate of interest}}$$

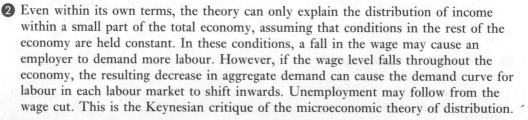

The most fundamental criticism of distribution theory is that it does not really explain anything at all. The **theory is circular**. The demand or MRP of a factor depends upon the value of what is produced; this in turn depends upon the effective demand of consumers exercised in the goods market; finally, the consumers' effective demand depends upon the distribution of income. Hence, the distribution of income is dependent upon the distribution of income! To give the theory some sense, an initial distribution of income must be assumed, and this initial distribution cannot of course be explained by the theory.

2 Even within its own terms, the theory can only explain the distribution of income within a small part of the total economy, assuming that conditions in the rest of the economy are held constant. In these conditions, a fall in the wage may cause an employer to demand more labour. However, if the wage level falls throughout the economy, the resulting decrease in aggregate demand can cause the demand curve for labour in each labour market to shift inwards. Unemployment may follow from the wage cut. This is the Keynesian critique of the microeconomic theory of distribution.

3 The theory assumes that the marginal productivity of labour can be separated from the marginal productivity of capital. However, in many technical processes capital and labour are complementary rather than substitutes. Output can only be raised by increasing both capital and labour in some fixed ratio. In these circumstances the marginal productivity of labour is impossible to isolate and identify.

4 The MRP theory of wage determination can only be used to explain the wages of workers employed in the market economy. It is impossible to place a market value on the labour productivity of those members of the British labour force employed in the public services provided by central and local government. The determination of public sector pay provides one example of the importance of differentials, comparability and relativity in wage bargaining. It is by no means always clear, however, whether public sector pay is determined by comparability with the 'rate for the job' for similar employment in the private sector, or vice versa.

5 Distribution theory is sometimes criticised for unrealistically ignoring the role of collective bargaining and other methods of pay determination in the British economy. In one sense the lack of realism is not very important. The theory states that a firm can only maximise profits if it employs labour up to the point where the MRP of labour equals the MC of labour. If this equality does not hold, the firm cannot be maximising profits! In a perfectly competitive world it would be the forces of competition rather than the deliberate decisions of firms that would bring about the situation where $MRP = MC_L$. Firms which strayed away from profit-maximisation would either be competed out of existence, or they would have to mend their ways. However, in a world in which firms may not be profit-maximisers, and in which markets are imperfectly competitive, there is no reason why the predictions of distribution theory should come true.

Nevertheless, distribution theory does tend to encourage the attitude that perfectly competitive markets are normal, that workers are paid what they deserve in terms of the value of what they produce, and that real-world bargaining patterns and institutions such as trade unions are distortions in otherwise perfect markets. While the markets for capital and land may be closer to the conditions of perfect competition, labour markets would probably be highly imperfect even without the existence of trade unions. Indeed, the principal argument used to justify trade unions is that, in their absence, market power would lie in the hands of employers. It is doubtful if labour markets ever existed in which all employers and all workers act as passive price-takers. More typically, market power would lie in the hands of the employers in a labour market in which a small number of employers bargained individually with a large number of workers unrepresented by a trade union. By bargaining collectively through a trade union, workers are seeking to create a market power to equal or exceed that possessed by the employer.

11.2 IMPERFECTLY COMPETITIVE LABOUR MARKETS

IMPERFECT COMPETITION IN THE LABOUR MARKET

As already noted, wage differences between workers are likely to be greater in imperfectly competitive labour markets than in conditions of perfect competition because of factors such as barriers separating labour market, imperfect market information, and the market power of particular employers and groups of workers. In this unit we cover three departures from the model of a perfectly competitive labour market which we examined in 11.1. These are:

1 a **monopsony** labour market;

2 the effect of introducing a **trade union** as a **monopoly supplier of labour** into an otherwise perfectly competitive labour market; and

3 the effect of introducing a **trade union** as a **monopoly supplier of labour** into a monopsony labour market.

Monopsony labour markets

Monopsony means a **single buyer**, just as monopoly means a single seller. In a monopsony labour market, workers find that they cannot choose between alternative employers, since there is only one firm or employer hiring their services. In this situation the firm's employees might quite naturally react by trying to form a trade union to act as a monopoly supplier of labour, to counter the market power of their employer. For example, before the privatisation of the British coal mining industry, British Coal and the National Union of Miners functioned respectively as the *monopsony buyer* and *monopoly seller* of labour, with coal miners' wages being determined in a process of bilateral bargaining undertaken by the monopsonist and the monopolist. Before we examine such a situation, we shall first assume that there are a large number of workers in the monopsonistic labour market and that they each act independently and have not formed a trade union.

In terms of economic analysis, such a monopsony labour market is very similar to the monopoly goods market which we studied in Chapter 7. In much the same way that the market demand curve facing a monopoly supplier of a good is also the monopolist's average revenue curve, so in a monopsony labour market, the **market supply curve of labour** is the firm's **average cost of labour curve (AC_L)**. The market supply curve of labour or AC_L curve shows the different wage rates which the monopsonist must pay to attract labour forces of different sizes. For example, Fig. 11.4 shows a monopsony employer hiring ten workers at a weekly wage or AC_L of £100 each. The wage or AC_L would rise to £110 per week were the employer to take on an extra worker and increase the labour force to eleven.

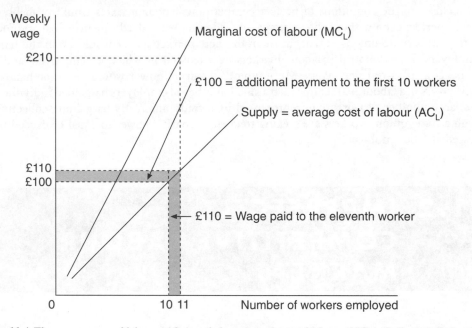

Fig. 11.4 The average cost of labour (AC_L) and the marginal cost of labour (MC_L) in a monopoly market

You should note that the supply curve, or AC_L curve, shows the wage which must be paid to *all* workers at each size of employed labour force, to persuade the workers to supply their services. However, in a monopsony labour market, the AC_L curve is *not* the marginal cost curve of labour (MC_L). As explained in the previous paragraph, at any size of total employment, the monopsonist must raise the wage rate to attract extra workers, in the absence of wage discrimination paying the higher wage to *all* its workers. In this situation, the MC_L incurred by employing an extra worker includes the total amount by which the wage bill rises, and not just the wage paid to the additional worker hired. The MC_L curve of labour which is illustrated in Fig. 11.4 is thus *above* the AC_L or supply curve (just as in the goods market, a monopolist's MR curve is *below* its AR curve). The MC_L incurred by the firm as a result of employing the eleventh worker is £210, made up of the £110 weekly wage paid to this worker, *plus* the £10 extra per week now paid to each of the other ten members of the labour force.

Both the equilibrium wage and the equilibrium level of employment in a monopsony labour market are shown in Fig. 11.5. As in a perfectly competitive labour market, the firm's equilibrium level of employment is determined where MRP = MC_L, at point A in Fig. 11.5. However, the equilibrium wage is *below* A and less than the MRP of labour, being determined at point B on the supply curve of labour. Although the monopsonist could pay a wage determined at A and equal to the MRP of labour, without incurring a loss on the last worker employed, he has no need to. The monopsonist can employ all the workers he requires by paying the wage W_1, determined at point B. If the firm were to pay a wage higher than W_1, it would inevitably incur unnecessary production costs, and could not maximise profits. Thus, profit maximisation in the goods market requires a wage no higher than W_1 in the labour market. (Once again, note the similarity of the proceeding analysis with the theory of monopoly in the goods market. As we saw in Chapter 7, Fig. 7.5, the monopolist could reduce price below P_1 and still make profits, but such action would of course, fail to maximise profits.)

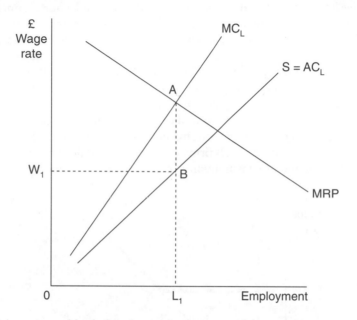

Fig. 11.5 Equilibrium wage and level of employment in a monopsony labour market

The effect of introducing a trade union into a perfectly competitive labour market

A **trade union** is an association of workers formed to protect and promote the interests of its members. A major function of a union is to bargain with employers to improve wages and other conditions of work – though many UK employers now refuse to recognise and bargain with the unions to whom their employees belong. For the purposes of our analysis, we shall regard a trade union as a **monopoly supplier of labour**, which is able to keep non-members out of the labour market and also to prevent its members from supplying labour at below the union-determined wage rate. In real life a union may not necessarily have these objectives, and even if it does, it may not be able to attain them. We shall make another unrealistic assumption that a union can fix any wage rate it chooses, and that employment is then determined by the amount of labour employers will hire at this wage.

Given these assumptions, we can show the possible effects resulting from the formation of a union in a previously competitive labour market in Fig. 11.6. In the absence of a union, the *competitive wage* would be W_1, with the market supply of labour shown by the curve S_1. If we assume that a trade union is formed and that the union succeeds in raising the minimum wage to W_2, the market supply curve of labour becomes the kinked line W_2XS_1. For all sizes of labour force to the left of or below both L_3 and the kink in the supply curve at point X, the supply curve of labour is horizontal or perfectly elastic, lying along the minimum wage W_2 set by the trade union. However, if the firms ever wished to employ a labour force greater in size than L_3 at point X, they would have to offer a wage which is higher the union-set minimum of W_2 in order to attract the required supply of labour. For these higher levels of employment beyond L_3 and point X, the supply curve of labour resumes its upward slope. This is largely academic since, given the positions of the market demand curve for labour and the kinked market supply curve of labour shown in Fig. 11.6, the equilibrium or market-clearing level of employment will be at L_2, which is below the competitive level of employment at L_1. There is thus an **excess supply of labour** equal to L_3-L_2 at the union-determined wage rate of W_2, which means that unemployment exists in the labour market since there are more workers wishing to work than there are jobs available at this wage. Such unemployment is called **real wage unemployment**, reflecting the fact that the wage rate is too high, and that market imperfections prevent the wage from falling to price the unemployed into work.

This theory is sometimes used to justify the argument that any attempt by a union to raise wages must inevitably be at the expense of jobs, and that if unions were really interested in reducing unemployment, they would accept wage cuts. However, many economists – especially those of a Keynesian and left-of-centre persuasion – dispute such a conclusion. In the first place we have assumed that the conditions of demand for labour are unchanged, which is very often an unrealistic assumption to make. By agreeing to accept technical progress by working with new capital equipment and new methods of organising work, and by improving the skills of their members – for example through training – a union may be able to ensure, with the co-operation of management, that the MRP curve of labour shifts rightwards. In these circumstances, increased productivity creates scope for both increased wages and increased employment. Both wages and employment may also rise when a union negotiates for higher wages in an expanding market, since increased demand for outputs creates increased demand for inputs. Indeed, rising real wages throughout the economy are likely to increase the aggregate demand for the output of all firms producing consumer goods, because wages are the most important source of consumption expenditure in the economy.

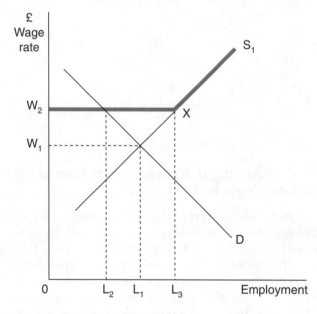

Fig. 11.6 The effect of introducing a trade union into a perfectly competitive labour market

Note: this diagram also illustrates the effect of minimum wage legislation

The effect of introducing a trade union into a monopsonistic labour market

The assertion that unions raise wages at the expense of jobs is also heavily dependent on the assumption that, before the union was formed, the labour market was perfectly competitive. In the case of a monopsony labour market, it is theoretically possible for a union to raise both the **wage rate** and **employment**, even without the MRP curve shifting rightwards. Such a situation is illustrated in Fig. 11.7. As in Fig. 11.5, the equilibrium wage would be W_1 in a non-unionised labour market, with the equilibrium level of employment at L_1. We shall now suppose that a union is formed which fixes the wage rate at W_2.

With the wage set by the union at W_2, the kinked line W_2XS_1 becomes the labour supply curve facing the monopsonist employer, just as in Fig. 11.6. The kinked line W_2XS_1 is also now the average cost of labour curve, but it is *not* the monopsonist's marginal cost of labour curve, which is represented instead by the double kinked line W_2XZV. We explain this in the following way. Providing the monopsonist employs a labour force smaller than L_2, the MC_L of employing an extra worker equals both the AC_L and the union–determined wage of W_2. Beyond L_2 and point X in Fig. 11.7, the monopsonist must offer a higher wage in order to persuade additional workers to supply labour. In this situation, with all the workers now being paid the higher wage, the MC_L curve lies above the supply curve or AC_L curve. The upward-sloping line ZV drawn in Fig. 11.7 shows the MC_L of increasing employment beyond L_2. But between the horizontal section of the MC_L curve for levels of employment below L_2, ending at point X, and the upward-sloping section of the curve ZV, is a vertical line or discontinuity, XZ. In Fig. 11.5, in the absence of a union, the equilibrium wage in a monopsony labour market would be W_1 and the equilibrium level of employment L_1. Fig. 11.7 shows that at the union-fixed wage of W_2, equilibrium employment rises to L_2 – which is the level of employment at which the MRP curve intersects the vertical section of the MC_L curve between X and Z. Thus the union increases both the wage rate and the level of employment compared to the situation without a union.

We can use Fig. 11.7 to show that the union, providing it possesses the necessary bargaining power, can increase the wage beyond W_2 and still increase employment. Wage rates can be increased, along with employment, up to levels shown at point Y, where the wage is W_3 and employment is maximised at L_3. If the union increases wages beyond W_3, some of the extra employment is lost. Finally, any attempt to increase the wage rate beyond W_4, shown at point A, can be achieved only by reducing employment below L_1, namely the level of employment before the union was formed.

In Fig. 11.7 the shaded area between the wages of W_1 and W_4 is sometimes called the **zone of bargaining**, reflecting the fact that in an imperfect labour market a union may sometimes trade-off between higher wage rates and higher employment levels, without having to accept a reduction in employment below L_1. In the absence of a trade union, the zone of bargaining shows the **monopsony profit** (the exact equivalent of monopoly profit in the goods market) which the monopsonist gains at the expense of the workforce by reducing the wage to W_2. By forming a trade union with sufficient bargaining power to counter the market power of the employer, the workers can divert some of this monopsony profit away from the employer to increase both the wage rate and employment.

Note: See the tutorial note for the essay question at the end of the chapter which explains how this theory can be applied to the analysis of the effects of a minimum national wage.

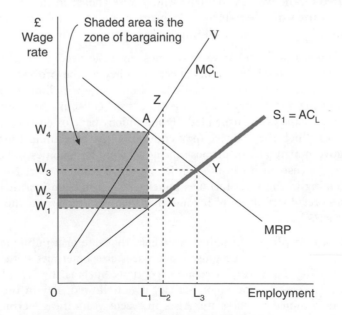

Fig. 11.7 The effect of introducing a trade union into a monopsonistic labour market.

Note: This diagram also illustrates the effect of minimum wage legislation.

METHODS OF WAGE DETERMINATION IN THE UK

In distribution theory it is generally assumed that wages are determined by individual negotiation between workers and employers and that market forces eventually bring about a ruling market wage. When trade unions are introduced into this analysis, it is assumed that firms decide how much labour to employ at a wage level determined by the union acting as a monopoly supplier of labour. The actual process of wage and salary determination in the UK is both more complicated and more varied.

Collective bargaining

In 1993 there were 9.5 million trade union members in the UK, though this represents a significant fall in union membership as compared to the peak year of membership in 1979 when there were 13.3 million members. Less than half of the labour force are now trade union members. The pay of many trade union members is determined by collective bargaining. The union represents its members' interests collectively by bargaining with employers to improve pay and other conditions of work.

Individual negotiation

This generally takes place in non-unionised parts of the economy. Highly paid managers, executives and consultants who offer specialist professional services will normally negotiate on an individual basis. At the other extreme, unorganised low-paid workers such as fruit-pickers and other casual workers also negotiate individually. In these circumstances the employer usually has much more bargaining power than the individual worker. Consequently the wage may effectively be determined by the employer on a 'take it or leave it' basis.

State determination

There are various ways in which the state can intervene to influence both market forces and the collective bargaining process:

❶ **Protecting low-paid workers** In low-paid industries such as catering, trade unions are difficult to organise and they tend to be ineffective.
Wages councils were established to determine minimum rates of pay in these industries, but the Conservative government now intends to abolish wages councils and allow a free-for-all. Wages councils, which were abolished in 1993, represent a form of **minimum wage legislation**. In many countries, a minimum wage has been established by law, to cover all industries.

❷ **Statutory incomes policies** At various times since the Second World War, British governments have imposed a statutory incomes policy on the process of wage determination. An incomes policy usually lays down an upper limit to wage settlements. During a statutory incomes policy, 'free' collective bargaining is either constrained or perhaps even suspended. Trade unions have often been suspicious of incomes policies which they believe may undermine the bargaining function of a union. The government's main purpose in introducing an incomes policy has usually been to attack the cost-push causes of inflation which result in part from the nature of wage bargaining in the UK. Incomes policies have also been justified as a method of ensuring a fairer distribution of income than that resulting from the collective bargaining process.

❸ **The state as an employer** In industries where the state or a public authority is the employer, unions are usually recognised and wages are sometimes determined by collective bargaining. However, there are exceptions, such as the armed forces and the police, where normal trade union activity is not allowed. Pay in the armed forces is effectively determined by the state. Also, in recent years the government has suspended collective bargaining for some public sector workers such as teachers. **Pay review boards** have been set up to advise the government on how workers such as teachers and nurses should be paid, usually on the basis of comparability with private sector workers.

④ **Arbitration and conciliation** In the process of free collective bargaining, a trade union will often demand a pay rise which is greater than the increase the employer is initially prepared to pay. Bargaining is a process in which each side modifies its offer or claim until agreement is reached. The vast majority of agreements are reached without a breakdown in the bargaining process and without dispute. Occasionally, however, agreements cannot be reached and a dispute either occurs or is threatened. Many collective agreements contain negotiating procedures to be followed when the next round of bargaining takes place. The procedural arrangements commonly specify the stage in the breakdown of bargaining at which outside arbitrators or conciliators should be brought in to help both sides reach agreement. In 1975 the Employment Protection Act established the Advisory Conciliation and Arbitration Service (ACAS). If both sides in a dispute agree to it, ACAS may be called in to try to settle a dispute.

Chapter roundup

The process of wage determination in particular labour markets is an important part of inflation theories (see Chapter 15). The shape of the supply curve of labour is crucial to the 'supply-side' theory explained in Chapter 16; whilst in Chapter 17, the different views of Keynesians and monetarists are discussed concerning the labour market and the wage determining process.

Illustrative questions and answers

1   Essay Question

Most European Union governments have agreed to introduce legislation guaranteeing minimum wage levels and improved employment rights for workers. So far the United Kingdom government has refused to introduce this type of legislation.

(a) Explain the economic arguments in favour of a guaranteed minimum wage and improved employment conditions for workers. (10)

(b) In the light of these arguments, discuss the economic reasons for the refusal of the UK government to introduce this type of legislation. (15)   *AEB*

Tutorial note

In recent years the case for and against a national minimum wage has been a favourite examination topic at A Level, and it is likely that it will remain so in the immediate future. Two factors which have contributed to the popularity of guaranteed minimum wages as an examination topic have been: (i) the Social Chapter of the **Treaty on European Union** negotiated at **Maastricht** in 1991 which came into effect in 1993; and (ii) the abolition by the Conservative Government of **wages councils**, also in 1993. A further factor has been the growing threat faced by all European countries from the emergence of industrial competitors in the so-called *tiger* economies of Asia and the Pacific Rim.

The Social Chapter of the Maastricht Treaty aims to deter *social dumping*, whereby some member countries of the EU Single Market (e.g. the United Kingdom) deliberately try to reduce wages and relax employment conditions below those of other EU countries, so as to attract firms and jobs away from their neighbours. The Social Chapter created minimum requirements throughout the EU for the protection of workers' health and safety, and established the principle of equal pay for men and women for work of equal value. In Britain, however, the Conservative Government opted out of the Social Chapter, arguing that its provisions would raise business costs and destroy competitiveness and jobs.

Before 1979, successive UK governments believed in the need to use the powers of the state to protect low-paid workers in industries such as catering and agriculture, where trade unions are ineffective and difficult to organise. Wages councils were established in these industries to determine minimum rates of pay. The powers of the wages councils were restricted in the 1980s and the councils were finally abolished by the Conservative Government in 1993. There is evidence that, since their abolition, wages and other conditions of service have deteriorated, sometimes alarmingly, for the workers they previously protected. Supporters of a national minimum wage claim that, following the abolition of the wages councils, good employers have been undercut by the bad, and the bad have been undercut by the downright exploitative.

To earn a high mark for this question, it is necessary to base your answer firmly on economic theory, though extra merit can of course be earned if you make relevant use of the evidence provided by recent UK and EU experience. (You might also make use of evidence provided by other countries. For example, supporters of a minimum wage claim that the introduction of a minimum wage in the American state of New Jersey increased rather than reduced employment in the fast food industry, though this conclusion has been hotly contested.) It is important for you to realise that the economic theory explained in the chapter, about the effects of introducing a trade union into perfectly competitive and monopsony labour markets, can also be used for analysing the effects of a minimum wage. When answering part (a) of the question, draw a diagram for a monopsony labour market similar to Fig. 11.7. Then explain how in the context of this diagram, far from reducing employment, the imposition of a minimum wage above the free-market wage could lead to more rather than fewer jobs. For part (b) use Fig. 11.6, which suggests that when introduced into a competitive labour market, a wage set above the market-clearing wage rate must reduce employment.

Suggested answer

- Explain the meaning of a guaranteed minimum wage, and briefly relate the introduction of a minimum wage to European Union policy.

- The main argument in favour of a minimum wage relates to the principal of **equity**, fairness or justice. A minimum wage is necessary to reduce inequalities or to prevent even greater inequalities emerging. Supporters of a guaranteed wage argue that the level at which the minimum wage is set is critical. They accept that if minimum wage is set at too high a level (e.g. a £10 hourly wage rate in the UK), the costs of the policy would certainly exceed the benefits. However, if the wage rate was set at a more realistic level (e.g. £4 an hour), there would be few if any costs, whilst the benefits would be significant.

- A guaranteed minimum wage may redress the balance of market power between employers and workers.

- Draw a diagram to show a monopsony labour market, and explain how in this market structure, increasing the wage rate can also increase employment.

- A guaranteed minimum wage may also boost the economy by increasing aggregate demand.

- If you have sufficient time, support these arguments with evidence from EU countries e.g. falling wages in industries such as catering in the UK following abolition of Wages Councils.

- Move on to the second part of the question by stating that UK Conservative governments have rejected these arguments, believing instead that the main effect of a minimum wage would be to raise employers' costs, leading to an increase in unemployment.

- Use a supply and demand diagram of a competitive labour market to explain this argument.

- Expand the argument by relating it to the need to keep competitive with newly industrialising economies, particularly the *tiger* economies of the Far East.

2   Data Question

(a) To what extent do the data in the tables below indicate an improvement in the living standards of *either* male manual *or* female non-manual workers over the period 1981 to 1986? (6)

(b) Account for the differences in average weekly earnings and average hours of work per week in 1986 between:

(i) manual and non-manual workers; (8)

(ii) male and female workers. (6)

ULEAC

Table 1

	Average weekly earnings and average hours of work per week (Full-time workers)			
	1981		1986	
	Earnings (£)	Hours	Earnings (£)	Hours
Male				
All	136.50	41.7	203.40	41.8
Manual	118.40	44.2	170.90	44.5
Non-manual	161.20	38.4	243.40	38.6
Female				
All	89.30	37.2	134.70	37.3
Manual	2.10	39.4	104.40	39.5
Non-manual	95.60	36.5	144.30	36.7
All adults	121.60	40.3	181.20	40.4

Table 2

	Retail Price Index						
	1980	1981	1982	1983	1984	1985	1986
Index	100.0	111.9	121.5	127.1	133.4	141.5	146.3

(Source: Annual Abstract of Statistics, *CSO, 1988)*

Tutorial note

(a) Table 1 shows *nominal* earnings, which you need to convert – with the aid of the Retail Price Index data in Table 2 – into details of *real* earnings, i.e. data which shows the *purchasing power* of the workers' nominal earnings. Proceed in the following way:

(i) for your chosen category of worker (either male manual or female non-manual) divide average earnings in 1981 by the RPI for 1981 (111.9), and then multiply by 100, which is the price index for the base year (1980).

(ii) repeat for 1986, dividing average earnings in 1986 by the RPI for 1986 (146.3) and again multiplying by 100. You now have two figures which show average weekly real earnings for 1981 and 1986 for your chosen category of worker. You are now in a position to assess whether standards of living have risen. However, to make a fuller assessment, divide the figures you have just calculated by average weekly hours worked to calculate whether real *hourly* wage rates increased between 1981 and 1986. And if there is time, you might mention that the data do not indicate whether earnings have become more or less equal *within* the category of male manual or female non-manual workers, and they do not allow you to assess other contributing factors to standards of living such as the value people place on leisure time and quality of life factors.

(b) (i) and (ii) Start your answers by briefly stating what the differences were: non-manual workers, both men and women, earned significantly more than manual workers, but worked fewer hours a week; while males (in aggregate) also earned significantly more than women, but in this case they worked slightly longer hours. Then suggest at least one possible reason for each of the four differences that the question requires you to explain.

Question bank

1 It often seems that the highest pay is given to occupations that are most agreeable, such as senior civil servants and university lecturers, whilst those occupations that are most unpleasant, such as road-sweeping and rubbish collection, receive low pay.

Discuss the extent to which economic analysis supports this view. (25)

Cambridge

Pitfalls

This is an example of a type of question which is frequently set at A Level: you are asked to discuss the reasons why workers in a particular occupation earn considerably more than lowly-paid workers in other occupations. Two possible dangers with this type of question are: (i) drifting into a discussion of whether senior civil servants ought to be paid much more than road sweepers; and (ii) writing at length about real or apocryphal cases of workers being highly or lowly paid, e.g. the chief executive of British Gas or students working for Burger King.

Key points

You should explain the concept of a worker's net advantage which comprises the utility of the wage paid to the worker, plus the job satisfaction (or minus the job dissatisfaction) the worker experiences. Then explain that, other things being equal, the more pleasant the job and the greater the job satisfaction, the lower is the amount of monetary compensation (i.e. the wage or salary) needed to persuade a person to supply his or her labour. However, all other things are seldom equal, so you need to discuss a number of other determinants of wages which could explain the wage differences mentioned in the question. Explain how differences in productivity, factors contributing to inelastic supply, and institutional and cultural factors all help to explain why some groups of workers earn more than others. Make sure that overall, you emphasise the roles of supply and demand.

2 Discuss whether wages are determined by marginal revenue product. (25)

Cambridge

Pitfalls

With an unstructured question such as this, there is a danger that you will write an answer which is too narrowly focused. Only about half of the 25 marks are awarded for discussing marginal revenue product; the other marks are earned for discussing supply factors, and influences upon wages such as social and institutional factors. Also, you must avoid the temptation to write all you know about marginal productivity theory, without discussing whether marginal productivity actually determines wages.

Key points

You must carefully explain the meaning of the marginal revenue product of labour and how, in a competitive labour market, the MRP curve functions as a firm's demand curve for labour. Make the point that for each firm, MRP determines the level of employment and not the wage, since the wage is determined by market demand and supply. However, the overall productivity of labour force is an important determinant of market demand for labour, and hence of the wage. You can extend your answer in a number of relevant ways, e.g. by introducing monopsony labour markets, the supply of labour, the role of trade unions etc.

3 (a) What does the demand curve for labour of an individual firm show? (5)

(b) Explain why this demand curve is likely to be sloping downwards from left to right in the short-run. Why is the firm's demand curve for labour likely to be more elastic in the long-run than in the short-run? (12)

(c) If the price of capital used by a firm falls, why is it uncertain how this will affect the firm's demand for labour in the long-run? (8)   *NICCEA*

Pitfalls

There is a danger of not getting the balance right in your answers to the first two parts of this question. Part (a) can be answered with a simple statement that the demand curve for labour shows more labour being demanded at low wage rates than at high wage rates, accompanied by an appropriate diagram. With part (b), you should bring in marginal productivity theory to explain the shape of the demand curve. Make sure you don't write inadvertently about the demand for goods rather than the demand for labour!

Key points

Marginal revenue productivity is the key concept for the first two parts of the question. It is useful to be aware of the difference between, and the link between, market demand for labour and a firm's demand for labour. Most of your answer to part (b) should be devoted to explaining why a firm reduces its demand for labour as the wage rate rises, in response to the declining marginal revenue productivity of labour as more labour is employed. It becomes unprofitable to employ workers with a low MRP when wage rates rise. For the second part of (b), explain that the longer the time period in question, the greater a firm's ability to respond to a wage increase by substituting capital for labour. This then leads into part (c). The main point to make here is that a fall in the price of capital (either through cheaper plant and machinery, or a reduced interest rate or cost of borrowing), is likely to boost economic growth. Overall, the demand for labour might increase, despite the fact that firms adopt more capital intensive methods of production.

MONEY AND MONETARY POLICY

Units in this chapter

12.1 *Money and the banking system*
12.2 *Monetary policy*

Chapter objectives

The economy we live in is a **monetary economy** in which most of the goods and services produced are traded or exchanged via the intermediary of money. The first unit of this chapter examines the nature and functions of money in a modern monetary economy, before going on to explain how most modern money takes the form of **bank deposits** which are created by the private enterprise banking system. The second unit explains the meaning of **monetary policy** and identifies the **policy objectives** and the **policy instruments** through which monetary policy is implemented. The chapter concludes by introducing the significant changes which have taken place in recent years in UK monetary policy, which will be discussed further in Chapter 17.

12.1 MONEY AND THE BANKING SYSTEM

WHAT IS MONEY?

For most people, money is both so desirable and so central to everyday life, that the question *what is money?* seems hardly to merit a second thought. The answer seems obvious: in the UK money is **coins** issued by the Royal Mint, Bank of England **notes**, and any **funds on deposit in banks**. Residents of Northern Ireland and Scotland might emphasise that the banknotes issued by such private enterprise banks as the Royal Bank of Scotland are also money, and these days, there would also probably be general agreement, that **funds deposited in building societies** (as well as in banks) are certainly money. But where do we draw the line in our definition of money? Should a **National Savings Certificate** be regarded as money? Or a **credit card**? Or a **foreign currency** such as the American dollar or the Indian rupee, given the fact that we may not be able to spend or even always to exchange a foreign banknote or coin in the UK? Clearly, the more we ponder the question, the more complex the question of meaning and definition can become.

THE FUNCTIONS OF MONEY

Economists cut through these rather complex issues by defining money in terms of the **two principal functions** they believe money performs in the economy. These are:

- **The medium of exchange function.** The economy we live in is a monetary economy in which most of the goods and services produced are traded or exchanged via the intermediary of money, rather than through barter. Whenever money is used to pay for goods or services, or for the purpose of settling transactions and the payment of debts, it is functioning as a means of payment or medium of exchange.

- **The store of value (or store of wealth) function**. Instead of spending money, a person may decide to store his or her personal wealth in the form of money rather than in other forms of wealth, like property or financial assets such as stocks and shares. By deciding to *store* rather than *spend* money, the purchasing power of money is transferred into the future, though this may of course be eroded by inflation.

Money also has two other functions. These are as:

- **A unit of account.** Money is the unit in which the prices of goods are quoted and in which accounts are kept. The unit of account function of money allows us to compare the relative values of goods even when we have no intention of actually spending money and buying goods, for example when we 'window shop'.

- **A standard of deferred payment**. Money's function as a standard of deferred payment allows people to delay paying for goods or settling a debt, even though goods or services are being provided immediately. Money acts as a standard of deferred payment whenever firms sell goods **on credit**, or draw up contracts specifying a monetary payment due at a later date.

THE HISTORICAL DEVELOPMENT OF MONEY

Commodity money

In order to function as money, an asset must be an acceptable medium of exchange and a possible store of value. Early forms of money which replaced barter were commodities, such as beads, shells, cattle and slaves, usually with an intrinsic value of their own. Gradually the precious metals, gold and silver, replaced other forms of commodity money because they possessed to a greater degree the other desirable characteristics necessary for a commodity to function as money: relative **scarcity**, **portability**, **durability**, **divisibility**, and **uniformity**.

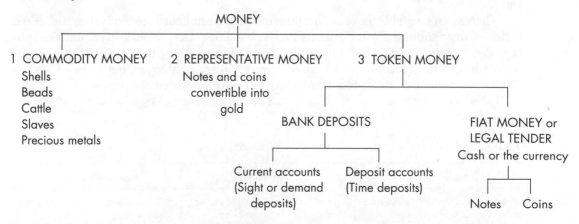

Fig. 12.1 Historical and present-day forms of money

Representative money

Nevertheless gold and silver are vulnerable to theft and difficult to store, and it became the custom for precious metals to be deposited with goldsmiths for safekeeping. The goldsmiths developed into banks, and the **gold receipts** which they issued became **bank-notes** or **paper money**. The notes were acceptable as a means of payment since they could be exchanged for gold on demand. Although relatively worthless in itself, the money represented ownership of commodities with an intrinsic value.

Token money

Banks discovered that they could increase their profits by issuing notes to a value greatly in excess of the gold deposits which they held. Imprudent banks would over-expand the note issue, and depositors suffered in the crashes which periodically occurred when banks could not meet demands by the public to convert notes into gold. As a direct result of these bank crashes, the 1844 Bank Charter Act largely removed from English and Welsh banks the right to issue their own notes, though some banks continued to issue notes on a limited scale until the last 'country' bank merged in 1921. This change in the law encouraged a new development in banking, the **creation of deposit money**. Instead of issuing its own notes when a customer requested a loan, a bank would make a ledger or book-keeping entry, crediting the customer's account with a loan or bank deposit. Such a bank deposit is obviously a store of value. However, a bank deposit is also a medium of exchange if it is customarily accepted that payment can be made by shifting ownership of the deposit, for example through the medium of a cheque.

Bank deposits are of course **token money**. They are **customary money** rather than **legal tender**, and generally accepted as money because of people's confidence in the banks and the monetary system. Bank deposits make up by far the largest part of modern money, between about two-thirds and 85 per cent of the money supply, depending on how money is defined. In contrast, **cash** (notes and coins, or the currency) is just the 'small change' of the system. Nowadays the state has a monopoly of the issue of cash, in England and Wales at least, and cash has gradually developed to become purely token money, just like a bank deposit. Unlike a bank deposit, however, cash is usually legal tender – 'fiat money' made legal by government decree – which must be accepted as a medium of exchange.

MONEY, NEAR MONEY, AND MONEY SUBSTITUTES

It is generally agreed that bank **current accounts** (**sight deposits** or **demand deposits**) function as money. They are both a store of value and a medium of exchange since cheques can be drawn on the deposit and are accepted in payment of a debt. Nowadays many people use credit cards as a medium of exchange. However, a **credit card** is not a store of value, and its use merely delays the settling of a debt through a cash transaction or the shifting of a bank deposit. A credit card is a **money substitute** rather than a form of money in its own right.

Whereas a money substitute is a medium of exchange but not a store of value, the reverse is true of **near money**. Financial assets such as building society deposits were until recently regarded as near monies. A building society deposit is a substitute for a bank current account or a cash holding as a convenient form of storage for wealth or value, but it does not serve directly as medium of exchange unless cheques can be drawn on the deposit.

Table 12.1 summarises the distinctions between money, near money and money substitutes.

Table 12.1 *Money, near money and money substitutes*

Near money	Money	Money substitutes
store of value but insufficiently liquid to be a medium of exchange, e.g. National Savings securities	medium of exchange and store of value, e.g. cash, bank and building society deposits	medium of exchange but not a store of value, e.g. credit cards and charge cards

THE PROBLEM OF DEFINING THE MONEY SUPPLY

Thirty years ago, neither economists nor politicians gave much attention to the precise definition of the money supply, since it was generally accepted that 'money did not matter' in the macroeconomic management of the economy. As we shall see in later chapters, this is no longer the case. According to the **monetarists**, money does matter, and the control of the money supply is an important part of monetarist economic management in general, and monetary policy in particular. Even if it is accepted that monetarist theory is correct (we shall later see that Keynesians dispute this) practical monetarism may be impossible if the money supply is a 'will-o'-the wisp' which cannot by its nature be controlled. Suppose that the monetary authorities (the Bank of England and the Treasury) decide either to restrict the rate of growth of the money supply or to reduce the absolute size of the money stock. The more successful they appear to be in controlling whatever they define as the money supply, the more likely it is that near monies, outside the existing definition and system of control, will take on the function of money as a medium of exchange. The phenomenon is related to **Goodhart's Law**, which states that as soon as a measure of the money supply (e.g. M4) is adopted as a target for monetary control, any apparently stable, former relationship between it and the price level will break down, rendering the measure useless as a control variable. In this sense, 'money is as money does'! Keynesians sometimes argue that the money supply is impossible to control, since it passively adapts to whatever level is required to finance the transactions which are desired at the existing price level. We shall examine the implications of this argument in the context of monetary policy later in this chapter and inflation in Chapter 15.

Whether or not this view on the impossibility of controlling the money supply is completely accepted, it does help to explain why policy makers have commonly used more than one definition of the money supply. The '**narrow definition**' favoured in Britain used to be **M1**, comprising cash and bank sight deposits. However, wealthy individuals and companies will normally hold interest-earning deposit accounts or time deposits alongside their current accounts or sight deposits. Should time deposits be defined as money? Unlike a sight deposit, the ownership of a time deposit cannot be shifted by cheque; hence a time deposit is not a medium of exchange. But to compete with the building societies, the banks have allowed deposit accounts to become increasingly more liquid. A customer may keep a very low balance in a current account, upon which cheques can be drawn; when a large payment is due to be made, part of the deposit account is simply shifted into the current account. Bank customers therefore treat their deposit accounts as money, a practice encouraged by the banks in order to attract funds away from building societies and National Savings Certificates. For this reason, time deposits are included in the wider measure of money M3. But because building society deposits have become as liquid as bank deposits, M1 and M3 have now given way to **M2** and **M4** (which include building society deposits) as the main measures of **narrow** and **broad money** respectively.

Table 12.2 *The monetary aggregates in the United Kingdom*

M0	Notes and coin in circulation; the banks 'till' money and their 'operational' (or working) deposits with the Bank of England
M1	Notes and coin in circulation; UK private sector sterling bank deposits
M2	Non-interest bearing component of M1; private sector interest-bearing 'retail' sterling bank deposits; private sector holdings of retail building society shares and deposits and National Savings Bank ordinary accounts
M3	M1 plus private sector holdings of sterling bank deposits and sterling bank Certificates of Deposit (CDs)
M3c	M3 plus private sector holdings of foreign currency bank deposits
M4	M3 plus private sector holdings of building society shares and deposits and sterling CDs less building society holdings of bank deposits, bank CDs and notes and coin
M5	M4 plus holdings by the private sector (excluding building societies) of money market instruments (bank bills, Treasury bills, local authority deposits), certificates of tax deposit and National Savings instruments (excluding certificates, SAYE and other long-term deposits)

Narrow money (M2) and Broad money (M4)

The definition of **M2** is based upon the distinction between **retail** and **wholesale** deposits. Retail deposits are liquid – or relatively liquid – deposits held by the general public which are likely to be spent. They include a range of building society deposits, as well as bank sight deposits. By contrast, wholesale deposits are normally owned by banks and financial institutions themselves, and held in other banks and financial institutions. They reflect asset portfolio management decisions of banks and other financial institutions and have relatively little effect upon the retail spending decisions of the general public. Therefore wholesale deposits, and any other deposits which are unlikely to be translated quickly into spending power, should be excluded from measures of the money supply which are designed primarily to monitor retail conditions. This is the logic behind the creation of M2, which includes retail deposits held in all financial institutions – building societies as well as banks – but excludes both wholesale deposits held by banks in other banks, and also long-term deposits. **M4**, which has replaced M3 as the favoured measure of broad money, includes long-term as well as short-term or retail bank and building society deposits, but excludes wholesale deposits (which do however figure in M5, the widest of the official measures of money).

M0 or the Cash base

Although M1 and M2 have conventionally been regarded as **narrow money**, in 1983 an even narrower measure, **M0**, was created by the United Kingdom monetary authorities. The definition of M0 is limited largely to cash in circulation with the general public. M0 is a measure of the **cash base** to the monetary system (sometimes called the **monetary base**). Although as we noted earlier, cash is the 'small change' of the monetary system, it is significant as the one part of the money supply over which the authorities – since they alone issue cash – can exercise a monopoly control.

THE CREATION OF BANK DEPOSITS

Bank deposits form the largest part of both M2 and M4. Bank deposits are the main form of money because banks possess the ability to create new deposits or credit. We shall restrict the analysis to a very simple model of credit creation in an economy in which there is just one commercial bank which has a monopoly of all bank dealings with the general public. For our purposes a **bank** is defined as an institution which:

1 accepts deposits which can be transferred by cheque; and

2 makes advances (which can be either overdrafts or term loans).

We shall further assume that the commercial bank aims to maximise profits, but is required to hold a reserve of 10% cash against its total deposit liabilities. The 10% cash ratio may be a reserve requirement of the central bank, or it may be chosen for prudential reasons by the bank itself.

Suppose that a member of the public now makes a new deposit of £1000 in cash. From the bank's point of view £1000 is both a liability and an asset, and will be recorded as such in the bank's balance sheet:

Liabilities	Assets
Deposits £1000	Cash £1000

As things stand, all the bank's deposit liabilities are backed with cash. If this remained the position, the 'bank' would simply be a safe-deposit institution. However, the bank can increase profits by crediting £9000 to the account of a customer who has requested a loan.

On the assets side of the balance sheet this will be shown as an **advance** of £9000 – whether the loan is an overdraft or a term loan granted for a definite period or term of years does not matter. Since the bank must honour any cheques which are drawn on the account up to the value of £9000, **deposit liabilities** have increased by exactly the same amount as **interest-earning assets**:

Liabilities	Assets	
Deposits £10 000	Cash	£1000
	Advances	£9000

Both the customer who made the original deposit and the customer in receipt of the advance can draw cheques to a combined value of £10 000 on their deposits. The initial £1000 has expanded deposits, and hence the money supply, to £10 000. As we are assuming a monopoly bank, there is no danger of customers drawing cheques payable to customers of other banks. Nevertheless, there could be a cash drain from the bank, if customers decide always to keep some proportion of their money assets in the form of cash. A cash drain would limit the bank's ability to create deposits to a figure somewhat below that illustrated in our example.

Deposits will be expanded whether the bank expands advances or purchases interest-earning assets such as securities or bonds from the general public. Suppose the bank creates £6000 of advances and purchases £3000 of bonds. The bank pays for the bonds with a cheque for £3000 drawn on itself, thereby increasing total deposit liabilities to £10 000 when the payment is credited to the account of the person who sold the bonds. The spectrum of assets owned by the bank is different from the previous position, but the deposit liabilities, which represent the creation of money, are the same as in our last example:

Liabilities	Assets	
Deposits £10 000	Cash	£1000
	Bonds	£3000
	Advances	£6000

Of course, the assumption of a monopoly commercial bank is completely unrealistic, but it does illustrate the central principle of credit creation – that **the banking system as a whole can create an expansion in bank deposits (and thus the money supply) which is a multiple of the liquid reserves held by the banks**. Because, in our example, cash is the only liquid asset or reserve held to back fractionally the bank's deposit liabilities, the ability of the banks to expand deposits is dependent on the cash ratio. The **money multiplier** measures the maximum expansion of deposits (or **low-powered money**) which is possible for a given increase in cash (or **high-powered money**) deposited in the banking system. Assuming that there is no cash drain, for our model we can write:

$$\text{money multiplier} = \frac{1}{\text{cash ratio}}$$

British banks have usually kept some form of **liquid assets ratio** or **reserve ratio**, rather than the simple cash ratio of our model. (Liquid assets are those assets possessed by the banks which can be quickly converted into cash.) It is useful, therefore, to write the money multiplier more generally as:

$$\text{money multiplier} = \frac{1}{\text{liquid assets ratio}}$$

When we assume a **multi-bank** system, similar to that in the UK, the general conclusions of our model still hold. If the increase of £1000 in cash deposits is spread over all the banks, deposits can expand to £10 000 providing that every bank is prepared to create deposits to the full extent the cash ratio allows. However, if only one bank is willing to expand deposits to the full, it will soon face demands for cash which it cannot meet. Customers will draw cheques on their deposits which will be paid into the accounts of the customers of the banks that have refused to expand credit. When the cheques are cleared, the bank must pay cash to the other banks, equal to the shift in deposits. To avoid this possibility, the bank will restrict the extent to which it is prepared to expand deposits. However, if all banks expand credit to the full, payments to customers of other banks will largely cancel out. The banking system as a whole can expand deposits to £10 000, though some banks may gain business at the expense of others.

THE DEMAND FOR MONEY

It is usual to identify three reasons or motives to explain why people wish to hold money balances. These are summarised in the following table:

Table 12.3 *The three motives for wishing to hold money*

The demand for active money balances	❶ The **transactions demand for money** is explained by the general public's need to hold money balances to finance planned expenditure in the near future	These stem from the medium of exchange function of money
	❷ The **precautionary demand for money** is explained by the need to hold money balances to finance unplanned expenditure, e.g. for an unexpected house repair.	
The demand for passive or idle money balances	❸ The **speculative demand for money** is explained by people's decisions to hold their personal wealth in money, rather than in interest-earning alternatives to money, i.e. non-money financial assets	Stems from the store of value function of money

As the table indicates, the **transactions** and **precautionary** demands for money stem from the fact that people wish to hold money for the essentially active purpose of financing planned expenditure which they intend to undertake in the near future (the transactions demand), or emergency purchases (the precautionary demand). Economists usually assume that the transactions and precautionary demands for money are unaffected by changes in the rate of interest. This assumption is illustrated in Fig. 12.2(a), where we have added together the transactions and precautionary demands for money – to form the demand for **active money balances** – which is depicted as a vertical line plotted against the rate of interest.

The **speculative demand** for money stems from money's function as as a wealth asset or passive store of value. By contrast with the transactions demand and the precautionary demand, the speculative demand for money is affected by the rate of interest offered on **non-money financial assets** such as government bonds. It is affected by speculation about *future* changes in the rate of interest as well as by current changes, and it is this which explains the rather puzzling label: speculative demand. Fig. 12.2(b) shows that, as the *current* rate of interest on government bonds falls, people decide to hold larger speculative money balances. People find it more attractive to hold money as wealth, rather than bonds. They prefer liquidity, hence this theory is often called **liquidity preference theory**.

The overall **demand for money (M$_D$) curve** is illustrated in Fig. 12.2(c). This curve, which is also called the liquidity preference curve, is obtained by summing the transactions, precautionary, and speculative demands curves for money in (a) and (b) of the diagram. The *slope* of the demand for money curve is explained by the speculative demand for money, (and by liquidity preference); its *position* is determined by the transactions and precautionary demands. An increase in the demand for active money balances, resulting for example, from an increase in real income, causes the M$_D$ curve to shift rightwards. This is known as an increase in liquidity preference, showing that people wish to hold larger money balances at all interest rates.

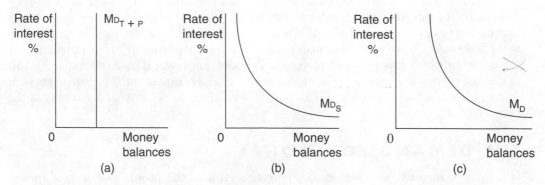

Fig. 12.2 The demand for money: (a) the transactions demand for money, (b) the speculative demand for money, (c) the demand for money or liquidity preference curve

THE UK BANKING SYSTEM

So far, we have defined a bank rather loosely as an institution which both accepts deposits from the general public and which creates deposits, for example by making loans or advances. Until 1979, there were no legal restrictions in the UK to prevent any institution calling itself a bank. Officially, however, the UK banking sector comprised all the listed banks which recognised a uniform reserve ratio, together with the banking department of the Bank of England (the country's central bank), and the institutions which make up the London discount market.

Since the passing of the 1979 Banking Act, it has been an offence for any person or institution to take deposits unless authorised to do so by the UK central bank, the Bank of England. The **authorised listed banks** operating in the UK can be divided into three main groups: **British banks, overseas banks** and **consortium banks**, with the British banks being further subdivided into groups such as **retail banks** and **merchant banks** (or **wholesale banks**). There has been recent rapid growth in the operations in the UK of overseas banks and consortium banks, and also of the more specialised British banks. (A consortium bank is a bank which is owned by a group of other banks, including at least one overseas bank, but no one bank owns more than 50% of the share capital.)

In response to this growth, banking regulations which only applied to the UK banks have been applied to all listed banks. However, because the British banking system now exists within a **global financial system** in which business is mobile and in which the major centres such as London, Tokyo and New York are in fierce competition with each other, the UK monetary authorities have, on the whole, relaxed rather than increased the degree of control and regulation exercised on banks and other financial institutions operating within the UK. They have done this to allow British banks to compete in world-wide markets and to attract overseas and consortium banks into the London financial markets.

Retail and wholesale banks

All banks, with the exception of the central bank, are **commercial banks** in the sense that their ultimate objective is to make a profit for their owners. The **retail banks** – and in particular the **UK clearing banks** who operate a system for the daily clearing of cheques – are the most important commercial banks in the UK, with the cheque and time deposits which they accept and create forming the most important part of the money supply. The retail banks are **general purpose banks**, most of whose business is retail banking with the individuals and firms which make up the general public. Because retail banking business in sterling within the UK has been growing more slowly than both large-scale wholesale lending of deposits between banks in what is known as the **inter-bank market**, and also overseas lending of sterling and other currencies in the **eurocurrency market, merchant banks** which specialise in **wholesale** and international banking business have tended to grow at a faster rate than the UK clearers. Merchant banks are based in the City of London, where most of their work is located, operating in wholesale and international money markets and in the other financial services they offer. As they are not involved in extensive retail business with the general public (and with the clearing of cheques which gives the clearing banks their name), the merchant banks do not need large networks of branches spread across the country. As a result, the merchant banks do not incur the considerable overhead costs suffered by the clearing banks from maintaining their expensive branch networks. (Currently the high street clearing banks are closing thousands of branches in an attempt to cut overhead costs. The banks are encouraging the general public to move towards a **cashless society** by making greater use of hole in the wall **cash machines, direct debit cards** and **credit cards**, which enable the **electronic transmission of funds** to replace more costly paper-shifting.)

In recent years, the distinction between retail and clearing banks has become blurred. Many, if not most, of the previously independent merchant banks have been taken over, either by UK retail banks such as the Nat West, or by overseas banks. Major clearing banks such as the Midland Bank have also been taken over by overseas banks. These changes reflect the growth world-wide of massive highly-diversified financial conglomerates, each operating in a large number of increasingly globalised financial markets. Typically these days, a bank owns a string of subsidiaries undertaking a range of financial activities, such as investment banking and arranging take-overs, stock broking or share dealing, and the selling of insurance.

The discount market

One of the specialised financial markets in which banks operate is the discount market, which is an important money market. The clearing banks and a group of specialised financial institutions called **discount houses** buy and sell **bills** on the discount market. Bills are highly liquid financial assets. There are two main types: **commercial bills** or **bills of exchange,** which are issued by commercial banks, and **Treasury bills,** sold by the Bank of England on behalf of the government.

The Bank of England

The Bank of England, which is the United Kingdom's **central bank**, is technically a nationalised industry, owned and ultimately controlled by the government. It is organised in two departments, the **Issue Department** responsible for note issue, and the **Banking Department** which conducts the Bank of England's banking business. The most important, or wider function of the Bank of England is to implement the government's monetary policy. We examine this aspect of the Bank of England's activities in 12.2. Here, we shall describe the narrower or specific banking functions of the Bank of England. These are that the Bank of England is:

❶ **Banker to the clearing banks and other banks in the monetary sector**. Just as ordinary members of the general public hold bank accounts in clearing banks such as Barclays or Lloyds, so the commercial banks in their turn deposit any 'spare' cash they possess into their balances at the Bank of England. These working balances allow the banks to settle indebtedness between themselves by shifting the ownership of a balance or deposit from one bank to another, and they also provide a channel through which new note issue and cash gets into circulation.

❷ **Banker to the government**. The Bank of England keeps the government's principal bank accounts, receiving tax and other revenue and making payments with respect to government expenditure. The bank also **manages the National Debt** on behalf of the government, selling new issues and redeeming maturing Treasury bills and government bonds (**gilt-edged securities** or **gilts**).

❸ **Holder of the country's stock of gold and foreign currency reserves**. The Bank of England manages the nation's foreign exchange reserves, implementing the government's exchange rate and balance of payments policy and any **exchange control regulations** which are in force. The Bank is most active in this respect when committed to buying and selling pounds and reserves to support a **fixed exchange rate,** for example from 1990 to 1992 when the £ was tied to the EU **Exchange Rate Mechanism (ERM)**.

❹ **Banker to other countries**. The Bank of England acts as banker to those overseas countries that wish to hold their foreign currency reserves in sterling on deposit in London.

❺ **General banking supervisor**. The Bank of England decides who can operate as a bank in the UK and the ways in which banks must operate to protect depositors. Recent banking legislation and a growing need to oversee the orderly integration of UK banks into the world financial system have greatly expanded this function though, as we have already noted, international financial competition has caused the Bank of England to relinquish regulations which would reduce the competitive ability of British-based banks in the new global market. Financial scandals, such as the Bank of Credit and Commerce International (BCCI) scandal in 1991, have also cast doubt on the effectiveness of the Bank of England's regulation of overseas banks operating in the UK.

❻ **Lender of last resort**. Traditionally, the Bank of England has been prepared to supply cash to the banking system in order to maintain liquidity and confidence, and to prevent bank failures.

12.2 MONETARY POLICY

THE MEANING OF MONETARY POLICY

All governments have a variety of **economic objectives**, such as full employment, economic growth and low inflation, which contribute towards, or are necessary to achieve, the ultimate economic objective of **increased welfare and living standards**. A number of different types of economic policy can be used to achieve these objectives, including monetary policy and fiscal policy (we examine fiscal policy in the next chapter). We can define monetary policy as any deliberate action undertaken by the government or the central bank to achieve the government's economic objectives using **monetary instruments** such as controls over bank lending and the rate of interest.

THE MONETARY AUTHORITIES

Monetary policy is implemented by the country's monetary authorities, namely the government's **finance ministry** and the **central bank**. In the UK, these are the **Treasury** and the **Bank of England**. In practice the direction and broad objectives of UK monetary policy are decided upon jointly by the Treasury and the Bank of England, with the Treasury – in the event of any dispute – in principle having the final say. Once the broad aim of policy has been decided, the Bank of England then implements the policy details.

INDEPENDENT CENTRAL BANKS

Although technically subordinate to the Treasury (and bound by the nationalisation statute of 1946 which require the Bank to obey any directives issued by the government), the Bank of England operates in the knowledge that the Treasury is unlikely to enter into open conflict with the Bank, because of the damaging effects on confidence which would probably result. As a result, the Bank of England has claimed to operate with a considerable degree of independence from Treasury interference. Throughout the world, the trend is towards greater **central bank independence** from government control, and the Bank of England is currently the least formally independent of the major European Union central banks. Thus the question of whether or not to give the Bank a much greater degree of formal independence from political interference has become quite a significant monetary policy issue in the UK in recent years.

THE INSTRUMENTS AND OBJECTIVES OF MONETARY POLICY

To understand economic policy, it is useful to distinguish between **policy objectives** and **policy instruments**, which are the means used to try to achieve the objectives. Since the 1970s, the ultimate objective of UK monetary policy has been to **control inflation**, in order to create the conditions in which the true ultimate objective of policy, improved economic welfare, can be attained. For part of the period, up to around 1985, UK monetary policy could be described as **monetarist**. Monetarists believe that (via the quantity theory of money which is explained in Chapter 15) inflation is caused by a prior increase in the stock of money (or money supply), and that therefore to control inflation, the growth of the money supply must first be controlled. In a strictly monetarist monetary policy, the money supply (or more correctly the rate of growth of the money stock), becomes the **intermediate objective** or policy target, but it is impossible to control the money supply directly. In order to hit an intermediate target specified in terms of the money supply, the authorities must first aim to control an immediate or operational target of monetary policy, such as the liquid assets possessed by the banking system or the rate of interest. As we saw earlier in this chapter, bank deposits form the largest part of the money supply, and the private enterprise banking system creates bank deposits to a multiple of the cash and liquid assets possessed by the banks. Thus, by controlling the liquid assets of the banks as an immediate policy target, monetary policy can, in principle, control total bank deposits and hence the money supply. This was the way UK monetary policy was implemented in the early 1980s: it was intended to influence the ability of banks to create deposits for their customers.

Since 1985 however, the basic strategy of UK monetary policy has been rather different. While the control of inflation continues to be the ultimate policy objective, the authorities have attempted to control monetary growth by influencing the *demand* for bank loans, rather than the banks' ability to *supply* deposits and loans. The **rate of interest** is now the main instrument of monetary policy. The authorities raise or lower interest rates in order to influence the general public's demand to hold money balances.

CONTROLLING THE ABILITY OF BANKS TO CREATE DEPOSITS

As already noted, in recent years UK monetary policy concentrated almost exclusively on influencing the demand for credit by raising or lowering interest rates. Nevertheless a number of policies have been used in the past – and could be used in the future – to influence the banks' ability to create or supply bank deposits. These include **direct controls** and **open market operations**.

Open market operations

This describes the **buying or selling of government securities by the Bank of England on the open market** (i.e. the capital market), in order to influence the banking system's ability to create credit and bank deposits. In principle, a sale of government securities (gilts) to the general public should lead, via the **money multiplier**, to a multiple contraction of credit and total assets, and to an equal fall in total deposits. Contractionary open market operations proceed through the following stages:

❶ The Bank of England sells gilts to the general public, who purchase the securities with cheques drawn on their deposits in the clearing banks.

❷ When the cheques are paid into the Bank of England, the balance sheets of the clearing banks will show an equal fall in customers' deposits (on the liabilities side of the balance sheet), and balances at the Bank of England (on the assets side).

❸ Because customers' deposits have fallen, the gilt sale has reduced the money supply. There may, however, be a secondary and much larger fall in the money supply if the banks now have to take action to reduce total bank deposits in order to restore their cash or reserve asset ratios which have been squeezed by the gilt sale. If the banks were initially operating close to their desired reserve or liquid assets ratios, they must reduce lending (shown on the assets side of the balance sheet) and total deposits (on the liabilities side) to restore the ratios.

Given the money multiplier as:

$$\frac{1}{\text{liquid assets ratio}}$$

then, according to the theory of open market operations, total bank deposits will fall or contract by the size of the initial fall in liquid assets × the money multiplier.

CONTROLLING THE DEMAND FOR BANK LOANS OR CREDIT

The technique of monetary control just described, operates on the ability of the retail banks to **supply** credit and to create bank deposits. By contrast, **manipulating interest rates**, attempts to influence the growth of credit and bank deposits through an indirect route, by acting on the general public's **demand** for bank loans. Whereas the direct controls on bank lending ration the quantity or supply of credit available, by raising or lowering interest rates, the monetary authorities can seek to **ration demand via price**. As we have also noted, this has been the main way that monetary policy has operated in the UK in recent years.

One of the ways in which the authorities can influence interest rates is by raising or lowering the **discount rate** or **lending rate** at which the Bank undertakes the **lender of last resort function** of supplying cash to the banking system through the discount market. Changes in the Bank of England's lending rate affect interest rates in two ways. In the first place, a change in the lending rate usually has an immediate effect upon the **bill discount rate** at which banks buy bills from the discount houses, and then upon other short-term interest rates. The Bank of England can force the bill discount rate down by reducing its own lending rate, while conversely an increase in the Bank of England's lending rate also allows the bill discount rate to rise. Secondly, but less tangibly, changes in the Bank of England's lending rate tend to act as a **psychological signal** to financial institutions and markets that the Bank of England wants interest rates to move in a particular direction.

Fig. 12.3 illustrates how, by raising or lowering interest rates, the authorities may hope to control the stock of money or money supply in the economy. Until quite recently, when interpreting a diagram such as Fig. 12.3, it was usual to assume that monetary policy acts directly on the supply of money depicted by the vertical money supply curve (labelled Ms) depicted in the diagram. For example, by shifting the money supply from Ms_1 to Ms_2, the authorities could use monetary policy to raise the level of interest rates from r_1 to r_2. Under this interpretation, it is the money supply which determines interest rates rather than vice versa, but given the way that monetary policy has operated in recent years, this may be the wrong way of looking at things. Instead of regarding the money supply as the policy instrument which the authorities use to determine interest rates within the supply and demand framework shown in Fig. 12.3, we should reverse our assumptions. Instead of the money supply being used as an **exogenous** policy instrument to determine an **endogenous** rate of interest objective, in actual monetary policy the rate of interest has been used as the policy **instrument** with the **money supply** becoming the **policy objective**. Thus the money supply is treated as endogenous within the money market illustrated in Fig. 12.3, its equilibrium value being determined by sliding the exogenous policy instrument, the rate of interest, up or down the general public's demand curve for money balances. Suppose for example, that the authorities aim to hit a money supply target of Ms_2 in Fig. 12.3 when the actual stock of money in the economy is MS_1. By raising the rate of interest from r_1 to r_2 the money supply can be reduced to Ms_2. At the higher rate of interest r_2, the general public reduce their demand for money. This then causes the money supply to shrink to equal the reduced money balances which the general public now wish to hold.

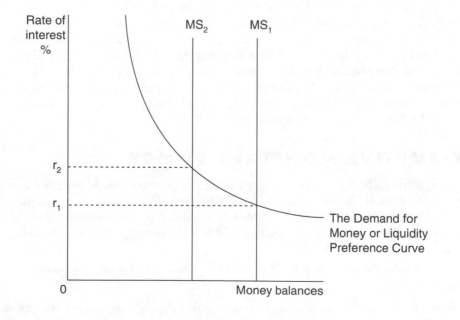

Fig. 12.3 The rate of interest and monetary policy

MONETARY POLICY AND EXPECTATIONS OF FUTURE INFLATION

In the preceding sections, it has been implied that the money supply has been the main intermediate target of recent UK monetary policy. While this was certainly true in the monetarist period of the late 1970s and early 1980s, it is no longer true. The policy of first announcing a target rate of growth of the money supply (e.g. for M4), and then operating monetary policy to try to hit the target, was abandoned in the mid-1980s. Before we describe how monetary policy changed after 1985, we shall first draw attention to an important feature of the monetary policy of the early 1980s which has continued to be significant.

In the monetarist period of the early 1980s, domestic monetary targets were supposed to provide a source of **counter-inflationary discipline**, encouraging workers and firms within the domestic economy to reduce their expectations of future inflation and to behave generally in a less inflationary way. Using the theory of **rational expectations** (which is explained in Chapter 15), the monetarists argued that if people believe that a tough government means business in reducing inflation, they will immediately begin to behave in a less-inflationary way, which in itself will reduce inflation. The policy was designed to 'talk-down' the rate of inflation by causing workers and firms to reduce their inflationary expectations.

THE EXCHANGE RATE AND MONETARY POLICY

After 1985, the exchange rate replaced measures of the domestic money supply such as M0 and M4 as the main target and source of counter-inflationary discipline in UK monetary policy. The authorities now believed that, if the government announced a **high exchange rate target**, together with a firm commitment to operate monetary policy so as to hit the target (i.e. never to devalue), then inflation would fall for two reasons. Firstly, by making imports less expensive, the high exchange rate would directly reduce the rate of inflation within the domestic economy. Secondly, and indirectly, the government hoped that the high exchange rate – like the setting of money supply targets a few years earlier – would cause workers and firms within the UK economy to alter their expectations and change their economic behaviour. Once they realised that the government meant business in maintaining a high exchange rate, UK firms would quickly understand that unless they reduced price rises to fall in line with competitors in countries such as Germany, they would lose markets and face bankruptcy. At the same time, their workers would quickly learn to moderate pay demands or risk pricing themselves out of jobs and into unemployment.

For the first few years in which UK monetary policy was based on the exchange rate rather than a domestic money supply target, the £ remained outside the **Exchange Rate Mechanism (ERM)** of the European Monetary System (EMS). At this time, UK monetary policy was based on **shadowing the Deutschmark**, which meant that the authorities set interest rates and bought and sold £s on the foreign exchange market to maintain an unofficial exchange rate target for the £ against the DM. In 1990, this policy was formalised when the £ entered the fixed exchange rate system of the ERM.

PRE-EMPTIVE MONETARY POLICY

The period during which the exchange rate was used as the intermediate target for monetary policy was quite short. It lasted from the mid-1980s until 1992, when the £ was forced out of the ERM (see Chapter 20). Since 1992, UK monetary policy has changed once again, though four of the most significant features of 1980s' monetary policy have been retained. These are:

- control of inflation continues to be the ultimate objective of monetary policy;
- policy objectives are still announced;
- it is assumed that the success of monetary policy depends on influencing favourably peoples' expectations of inflation;
- the rate of interest is still the main, and indeed the only monetary policy instrument used to achieve these aims.

However, with a fixed exchange rate no longer available to function as the intermediate objective of monetary policy, *all* intermediate policy targets have been dropped. Instead, monetary policy has been directed explicitly at a **published inflation rate target**. Immediately after leaving the ERM in 1992, the government set a specific target for the underlying rate of inflation of between 1% and 4%. In 1993, the government stated that the longer term objective was to bring the inflation rate down to 2.5% or less by 1997.

Current policy has been called **pre-emptive monetary policy**. The authorities believe that by monitoring a large number of economic indicators, including various measures of the money supply such as M0 and M4, they can accurately detect inflationary pressures which might emerge many months ahead. The authorities have announced that they are prepared to raise interest rates even when there is no immediate sign of accelerating inflation, to anticipate and pre-empt a rise in the inflation rate that would otherwise occur many months ahead. Also, in an attempt to influence inflationary expectations favourably and reduce the temptation for the government to override the Bank of England for short-term political reasons, the formation of monetary policy has been made more open or transparent. The Bank of England now regularly publishes an inflation report, and the minutes of the regular policy meetings attended by the Chancellor of the Exchequer and the Governor of the Bank of England are also published shortly after each meeting. These changes have increased the degree of independence in the formation and implementation of monetary policy enjoyed by the Bank of England, without going the full way towards creating an independent central bank.

Chapter roundup

Monetary policy is only one of the economic policies available to a government in the pursuit of its economic objectives, though in recent years monetary policy has probably been the most important. The next chapter examines fiscal policy, while supply-side policies and various forms of interventionist policy, such as incomes policy, are explained in Chapters 16 and 17. Chapter 17 on Keynesianism and monetarism also explains the Medium-Term Financial Strategy which has provided the policy framework for UK monetary and fiscal policy in recent years. Finally, the relationship between monetary policy and the exchange rate is explored in greater detail in Chapter 20.

Illustrative questions and answers

1   Essay Question

(a) Why are there several definitions of money in the UK? (30)

(b) What issues arise for the monetary authorities in controlling the supply of money?

(70)

ULEAC

Tutorial note

The proliferation of definitions or measures of the money supply reflects the period when pure or technical monetarism became increasingly influential in the UK from about 1970 to around 1985. From 1976 onwards, the government needed a precise measure of money because anti-inflation policy in general, and monetary policy in particular, was based upon the automatic policy rule of announcing a target rate of growth for the money supply, for a medium-term period of about three years ahead, together with a firm commitment to implement monetary policy so as to 'hit' the target. But as we have explained in this chapter, the operation of Goodhart's Law meant that as soon as the monetary authorities (i.e. the Bank of England and the Treasury) used a particular measure of money, say M3, as the operational target for monetary policy, any previously stable relationship between the measure and inflation broke down. For example, other financial assets which were not included in the definition of the targeted measure of money, would begin to function as money. For a few years the monetary authorities responded to this situation by 'inventing', and then targeting, ever-wider measures of money, for example M2 and M4, in response to the fact that the nature of money was changing. We have also explained how the authorities reacted to this situation in the opposite way: designating M0 as the narrowest measure of money, on the basis that the authorities can, in principle, completely control the cash which is the major component of M0.

Around 1985 the UK government abandoned the pure or technical monetarism which we have described, largely because it was not working and because the credibility upon which the policy depended to have any chance of success had evaporated. (To mark this event, the headline 'Monetarism, it's dead; Official!' appeared in *The Times* newspaper.) Thus the need for ever-more measures of the money supply (a proliferation which in its time was nicknamed 'monetary madness') has now diminished – unless of course the UK monetary authorities once again come under the influence of strict monetarists such as Professor Sir Alan Walters.

Suggested answer

- Explain that a narrow measure of money such as M1 or M2 takes account of the medium of exchange function of money, whereas broader measures such as M3 and M4 reflect the store of value function.

- Relate the proliferation of measures of money to the period of relatively pure or technical monetarism, pre-1985, when counter-inflation policy and monetary policy were based on trying to control the growth of the money supply.

- Introduce the implications of Goodhart's Law which suggests that such a policy is unlikely to be successful in controlling both monetary growth and inflation.

- If monetary growth cannot be controlled by acting *directly* on the *supply* of money, one alternative is to aim at *indirect* control by using interest rates to influence the *demand* for money.

- A further alternative (embodied in ERM membership in 1990) is to abandon 'domestic monetary targetry' as the main weapon of counter-inflation policy, and switch instead to using a fixed exchange rate as the main policy instrument to control inflation.

2 Data Question

High interest rates are damaging for a number of reasons. First, by adding to industrial costs they make goods and services more expensive and they can push the over-borrowed company into bankruptcy. Secondly, they crush the enterprising spirit: if you can earn so much simply lending your money, why go to the trouble
5 of expanding your business? Thirdly, they suck into Britain large sums from the international money markets and this reinforces support for the pound, which many industrialists think is overvalued. Fourthly, they push up the cost of mortgages and it is this that works through more quickly than anything else in demands for higher wages.
10 High interest rates, therefore, are inflationary and counter-productive, in that they undermine other economic objectives of the Government. They can, in the short term, actually increase the money supply since borrowers will tend to borrow more to cover their higher loan charges. The need for some more effective control of credit creation is not a matter of economic principle; it is a question
15 of judgement and management. The Government and the banks do need some more effective levers, whether in the form of a monetary base control or some more immediate control on personal borrowing. Such measures by their very nature need not be permanent and could be eased when there are signs of a continuous slowing down in the money supply. There will be many who would
20 say this won't work, but then the present system isn't working at all well. The existing high level of interest rates is putting into jeopardy the economic, social and political objectives of the Government.

(Source: Lord Rippon in a letter to The Times, *11 October 1989)*

(a) Explain why the author suggests that 'high interest rates are inflationary'. (4)

(b) Why would high interest rates 'suck into Britain large sums from the international money markets' (lines 5 and 6)? Explain carefully why this might be undesirable. (6)

(c) How might high interest rates 'undermine other economic objectives' (line 11)? (5)

(d) The author suggests the need 'for some effective control of credit creation', other than interest rates (lines 13 and 14). Examine the effectiveness of alternative controls available to the authorities. (5) *ULEAC*

Tutorial note

(a) High interest rates can be both deflationary and inflationary. By reducing consumption and investment demand, high interest rates dampen demand-pull inflationary pressures in the economy; but they also contribute to cost-push inflation. As Lord Rippon indicates, high interest rates add to production costs for firms who have to borrow; they raise import costs via a higher exchange rate brought about by the capital inflows they attract; and they add to the living costs of house owners with mortgages, which can then lead on to inflationary wage demands.

(b) This question develops a point we have already made. As Chapters 19 and 20 explain, owners of 'foot-loose' capital funds (often known as 'hot money'), switch their funds between currencies so as to earn the highest interest rate on offer. Thus if sterling interest rates are higher than those on offer for other currencies, capital funds will be placed in sterling deposits within the UK banking system. In part, this may be undesirable for the reason indicated in the answer to part (a): namely as a result of the high interest rates needed to 'suck in' the capital flows and their effect on firms' production costs. Even more damaging, however, is the likely contribution of the overvalued exchange rate to de-industrialisation. Finally, 'hot money' flows are extremely unstable; what flows in can just as easily flow out, and a massive capital outflow can trigger a full-blown sterling crisis.

(c) The overall effect of high interest rates is deflationary rather than inflationary; this undermines the domestic economic objectives of pursuing growth and full employment.

(d) As we have explained in the chapter, monetarist and free-market critics of credit controls argue that they are (i) inefficient, reducing the competitiveness of the banking system, and (ii) ineffective – in the absence of foreign exchange controls, credit controls simply do not work as people can borrow abroad. Keynesians reply by arguing that (i) credit controls do work in some other EU countries, and (ii) it is possible to devise new forms of control such as higher required monthly repayments on credit card debt that would be effective in controlling consumer credit.

Question bank

1 (a) With the aid of a numerical example, explain how banks create credit and bank deposits. (10)

(b) Discuss the factors which limit the ability of banks to create credit and bank deposits. (15) *AEB*

Pitfalls

You must state the assumptions you are making, indicating clearly whether you are explaining a monopoly bank model of deposit and credit creation (similarly to the one explained in the chapter) or a multi-bank model. To earn full marks it is not necessary to introduce both models into your answer, though you must obey the instruction to illustrate your answer with a numerical model. With part (b), you must develop your answer beyond a simple list. Also, make sure you don't rewrite the question as *discuss how monetary policy limits the ability of banks to create credit and bank deposits*.

Key points

In part (a) you must explain how, every time a bank advances a loan to a customer, it simultaneously creates a deposit liability. Also explain how, in pursuit of profit, deposits can be created as a multiple of the cash and other reserve assets held by the banking system. Factors to discuss in part (b) include: the constraints imposed by the need to maintain cash and reserve asset ratios; the supply of reserve assets; the availability of credit-worthy customers; and the impact of monetary policy.

2   What are the functions of the Bank of England? Discuss whether or not there would be any advantage in the Bank of England being independent of the government in the formulation and implementation of monetary policy. (25)   *NEAB*

Pitfalls

The danger here would be to concentrate too much on describing the narrower functions, such as note issue and supervising the banking system, and to ignore the Bank's broader function of implementing monetary policy.

Key points

You should devote only about a third of your answer to listing and briefly describing the narrow functions of the Bank of England. Devote the second third to outlining the Bank's function, along with the Treasury, in formulating and implementing monetary policy, taking care not to get too bogged down in describing different aspects of monetary policy. Finally, in the last part of your answer, you must address the issue of independence posed by the question. You should outline at least one advantage and one disadvantage of independence, and come to some conclusion on whether the advantage(s) exceed the disadvantage(s). Advantages of independence include: limiting the ability of governments to reduce interest rates to gain a short-term political advantage just before a general election; and increasing creditability that monetary policy targets will be achieved, thereby favourably influencing inflationary expectations. Disadvantages are: possible gimmickry; the introduction of unnecessary deflationary bias into policy making; and the removal of political accountability.

3   (a) For what purpose do people demand money? (12)
      (b) Discuss the possible consequences of an increase in the **supply** of money. (13)
                                                                                        Cambridge

Pitfalls

With part (a), the main danger lies in writing about the four functions of money without relating money's functions to peoples' motives in wishing to hold money balances. With part (b) there is a danger of confusing *causes* and *effects* or consequences.

Key points

The transactions, precautionary and speculative motives for holding money should provide the focus of your answer to part (a). Briefly explain each motive, and outline its determinants. Your answer to part (b) might centre on the quantity theory of money, which is explained in Chapter 15. Depending on the assumptions made when specifying the quantity theory, an increase in the money supply may reflate the economy, inflate the price level, or be absorbed in idle money balances which people hold rather than spend.

CHAPTER 13

TAXATION, PUBLIC SPENDING AND FISCAL POLICY

Units in this chapter

Chapter objectives

This chapter begins by explaining the nature of **public expenditure** and of the **taxes** which governments must levy in order to finance their spending programmes. We then explain the meaning of **fiscal policy**, and outline the most significant changes taking place in UK fiscal policy in recent years. The chapter concludes by relating fiscal policy to the overall budgetary position of central government and the wider public sector, introducing the link between the **budget deficit** and the **public sector borrowing requirement (PSBR)**. It explains how the PSBR may constrain the government's freedom of action, not only in fiscal policy but in other areas of economic policy such as monetary policy.

13.1 TAXATION AND PUBLIC SPENDING

PUBLIC EXPENDITURE

Public expenditure is undertaken by the public sector of the economy. In the UK, the public sector can be divided into three parts: central government; local government; and nationalised industries, though as a result of privatisation, few nationalised industries now remain. In any case, much of the spending by nationalised industries, such as the Post Office, is excluded from the definition of public spending on the grounds that it is financed by revenue raised from the sale of the industries' output, and is not dependent on finance from the taxpayer.

Spending by central and local government taken together is known as **general government expenditure**. Perhaps more significant than the absolute totals of public expenditure, is the ratio of public expenditure to national income or output, which indicates the share of the nation's resources taken by the government. In the financial year 1994–95 general government expenditure was £287.8 billion, or nearly 43% of national output.

Apart from the periods from 1914 to 1918 and from 1939 to 1945 which saw very rapid, but temporary, increases in government spending to pay for the First and Second World Wars, the twentieth century has witnessed a steady but relatively slow increase in government expenditure from around 10% to over 40% of GDP, reaching 47.25% in 1975-76. The ratio remained around 45% in the early 1980s, despite the election in 1979 of a monetarist Conservative Government committed to reducing the share of both public spending and taxation in national output. The ratio of public expenditure to national output did fall to 38% in the late 1980s, before rising above 40% again in the early 1990s. In successive budgets in the mid-1990s, the Conservative Government confirmed that it wished to reduce public expenditure to below 40% once again. Whether public spending will succeed in falling below 40% of national output will depend partly on which political party forms the government. It will also depend on how well or badly the UK economy performs. As explained later in the chapter, public spending and taxation tend to rise as proportions of national output when the economy is in recession, even though their absolute totals may fall. Conversely, when the economy is doing well, public spending and tax revenue fall as a percentage of national output.

The ratio of total government expenditure to national output is an accurate measure of the share of the nation's total financial resources under the command of the government. However, because a large part of government expenditure is upon **transfers** – such as unemployment pay and welfare benefits – the ratio is a misleading indicator of the share of national output produced by government itself. Transfers do not involve a claim by the government on national output, or a diversion of resources by the government away from the private sector. Rather, they merely redistribute income and spending power from one part of the private sector to another – from taxpayers to recipients of state benefits and pensions. When transfers are excluded, government spending falls from over 40% of national output to between only 20% and 30%. This figure is a more accurate measure of the share of national output directly commanded by the state – and thus unavailable for use in the private sector – to produce the hospitals, roads and other goods and services which government collectively provides and finances for the most part out of taxation.

Fig. 13.1 shows the pattern of public expenditure planned by the Conservative Government for the financial year 1995-96. As in most years, welfare benefits or social security, health, social services and education account for around 60% of total expenditure.

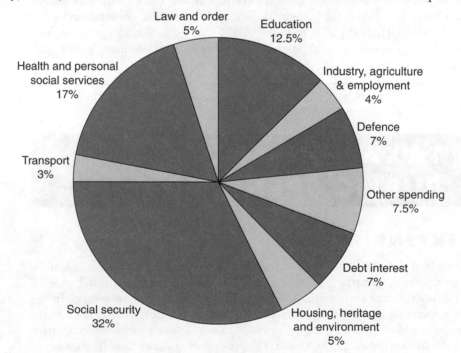

Fig. 13.1 The Pattern of Public Expenditure in the United Kingdom 1995–96

TAXATION AND OTHER SOURCES OF GOVERNMENT REVENUE

Taxation is of course the principal source of government and public sector revenue. In the financial year 1995–96, the government expected to raise £222 billion through taxation, out of a total government revenue of £284 billion. Taxation accounted for approximately 78% of total revenue, rising to nearly 95% if National Insurance contributions (which were expected to be £47 billion) are included as a form of taxation. Although in strict legal terms, National Insurance contributions are not a tax, from an economic point of view they are certainly a form of taxation since they are a compulsory levy on employers, employees and the self-employed to pay for unemployment pay and welfare benefits provided by the state.

Besides taxation and National Insurance contributions, the other forms of revenue available to the UK government include:

● the profits of nationalised industries;

● interest and dividend income on loans granted by the government to individuals, firms and nationalised industries within the domestic economy and also on international loans to foreign governments;

● dividend income paid on state-owned shareholdings in private enterprise companies;

● privatisation proceeds or the income from the sale of state-owned assets;

● income from the sale of government services;

● rents from leasing government-owned buildings and land.

Most of these are included in the *other financing* item in Fig. 13.2, though rather confusingly, the UK government classifies the privatisation income from asset sales as *negative expenditure* rather than *revenue*.

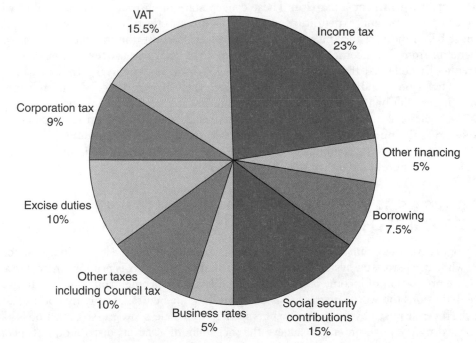

Fig. 13.2 Sources of Government Revenue, including borrowing, in the United Kingdom 1995–96

TYPES OF TAXATION

A **tax**, which is a compulsory levy charged by a government or public authority to pay for its expenditure, can be classified in a number of ways:

❶ **According to who levies the tax** Most taxes are levied by central government in the UK, but the council tax and the uniform business rate are examples of local government taxation.

177

❷ **According to what is taxed** The major categories here are taxes on income, expenditure and capital, though other categories include pay-roll taxes. Personal income tax is the most important tax on income in the UK, though employees' National Insurance contributions (NIC) and corporation tax (a tax on company income or profits) are other examples. The Inland Revenue is the department of the civil service mainly responsible for collecting taxes on income and capital, whereas the Board of Customs and Excise collects expenditure taxes. Expenditure taxes are usefully divided into *ad valorem* or percentage taxes such as value-added tax (VAT), and specific taxes (or unit taxes) which include the excise duties on tobacco, alcohol and petrol. A specific tax on, for example, wine is levied on the quantity of wine rather than on its price. Thus a bottle of expensive vintage claret bears the same tax as a bottle of cheap table-wine. Similarly, a user tax such as a television licence or motor vehicle tax is levied irrespective of either the price or the current market value of the TV set or car.

From 1989/1990 until 1993, a poll tax temporarily replaced the local rates as the main form of local taxation in the UK. Prior to its short life in the early 1990s, a poll tax, which is a tax 'on being a human being', was last levied in the United Kingdom in the 14th century, when it triggered a peasants' revolt that caused its hasty withdrawal! Viewed as a 'community charge', a poll tax was classified as an expenditure tax levied to pay for local government services provided. Taxes on wealth and capital have never been significant in the United Kingdom. The main current capital tax is inheritance tax, a tax on gifts from the dead to the living. Finally, amongst a number of miscellaneous taxes, are employers' National Insurance contributions, a form of pay-roll tax in which the amount of tax paid varies with the number of workers employed.

❸ **Direct and Indirect Taxation** These concepts are often used interchangeably with taxes on income and expenditure, though it is not strictly true that a tax on spending must be an indirect tax. Income tax is a direct tax because the income receiver, who benefits from the income, is directly liable in law to pay the tax (even though it is frequently collected through the PAYE scheme from the employer). In contrast, most taxes on spending are indirect taxes since the seller of the good, and not the purchaser who benefits from its consumption, is liable in law to pay the tax. Nevertheless, as we shall see later, the seller usually tries to pass on the incidence of the tax to the purchaser by raising the price of the good by the amount of the tax! There are, however, examples of direct taxes on expenditure, such as the stamp duty paid by the purchaser rather than by the seller of a house.

PROGRESSIVE, REGRESSIVE AND PROPORTIONATE TAXATION

In a progressive tax system a progressively larger proportion of income is paid in tax as income rises, while in a regressive system a smaller proportion is paid. A tax is proportionate if exactly the same proportion of income is paid in tax at all levels of income. You should note that in these definitions the word progressive is completely 'value neutral', implying nothing about how the revenue raised by the government is spent. Nevertheless, progressive taxation is likely to be used by the government to achieve the social aim of a 'fairer' distribution of income. However, progressive taxation cannot by itself redistribute income – a policy of transfers in the government's public spending programme is required for this. Progressive taxation used on its own will merely reduce post-tax income differentials compared with pre-tax differentials. Progressive, regressive and proportionate taxes can also be defined in terms of the marginal and average tax rates. The marginal tax rate measures the proportion of the last pound paid in tax as income rises, whereas the average tax rate at any level of income is simply the total tax paid as a proportion of total income. In the case of a progressive income tax, the marginal rate of tax is higher than the average rate, except when no tax at all is paid on the first band of a person's income. If income tax is regressive, the marginal rate of tax is less than the average rate, while the two are equal in the case of a proportionate tax.

THE PRINCIPLES OF TAXATION

Adam Smith's **four principles or canons of taxation** are commonly used as the starting-point for analysing and evaluating the operation of a tax system. Adam Smith suggested that taxation should be **equitable, economical, convenient** and **certain**, and to these we may also add the canons of efficiency and flexibility:

❶ **Equity** A tax should be based on the taxpayer's ability to pay. This principle is sometimes used to justify progressive taxation, since the rich have a greater ability to pay than the poor. A tax system should be fair, but there are likely to be different and possibly conflicting interpretations of what is fair or equitable.

❷ **Economy** Collection of a tax should be easily and cheaply administered so that the yield is maximised relative to the cost of collection.

❸ **Convenience** The method of payment should be convenient to the taxpayer.

❹ **Certainty** The taxpayer should know what, when, where and how to pay, in such a manner that tax evasion is difficult. (Tax evasion is the illegal failure to pay a lawful tax, whereas tax avoidance involves the arrangement of personal or business affairs within the law to minimise tax liability.)

❺ **Efficiency** A tax should achieve its intended aim without side-effects. If, for example, the raising of the top rate of income tax in order to raise revenue results in increased disincentives to work, then the tax is inefficient. Since it is usually impossible to avoid all the undesirable side-effects of a tax, the tax system should attempt to minimise them.

❻ **Flexibility** If the tax system is used as a means of economic management then, in order to meet new circumstances, certain taxes may need to be easily altered.

THE INCIDENCE OF TAXATION

The **formal incidence** of a tax refers to which particular taxpayer is directly liable to pay the tax to the government. In the case of indirect taxes upon expenditure such as VAT, the question arises whether the seller of the good who bears the formal incidence can **shift the incidence** or burden of the tax onto the purchaser by raising the price by the full amount of the tax. A firm's ability to shift the incidence of a tax depends upon price elasticity of demand. Fig. 13.3 illustrates the situation where demand is relatively elastic and only a small proportion of the tax can be successfully shifted.

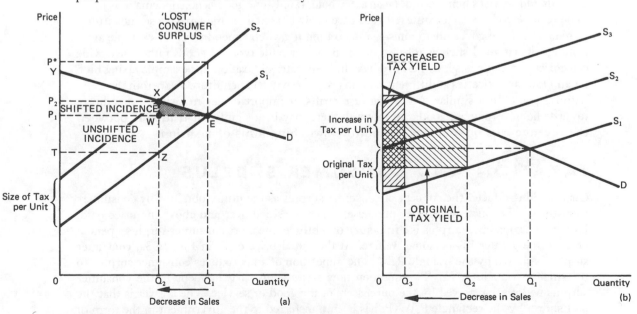

Fig. 13.3 Elasticity and taxation (a) the ability of a supplier to shift the incidence of an expenditure tax depends upon elasticity of demand (b) an example of a tax increase producing a fall in the government's tax revenue when demand and supply are both relatively elastic

179

The imposition of a tax raises a supplier's costs; thus at each price the firm is prepared to supply less. If the tax is a specific or unit tax charged at the same rate irrespective of the good's price, the supply curve will shift upwards, from S_1 to S_2, the vertical distance between the two curves showing the tax per unit. If all the tax is to be successfully shifted, the price must rise to P*. This will only happen if demand is completely inelastic. In any other circumstance, some consumers will reduce their purchases as the price rises. However, many consumers will still want the good and so the price is bid up from P_1 to P_2. The size of the government's tax revenue is determined by the amount bought and sold at the new equilibrium (Q_2) multiplied by the tax per unit. This is shown by the rectangle TZXP$_2$. You should now note that the part of the tax rectangle above the initial equilibrium price, P_1, represents the successfully shifted incidence of the tax, whereas the part of the tax rectangle below P_1 cannot be shifted and must be borne by the supplier. When demand is relatively elastic, only the smaller proportion of the tax can successfully be shifted.

We leave as an exercise for the reader the tasks of drawing appropriate diagrams to show what happens when demand is inelastic and to show the converse effects resulting from the imposition of a unit subsidy paid to the supplier.

THE TAX YIELD

If the principal aim of a tax is to raise revenue, the government will wish to maximise the tax's yield. In the case of taxes upon expenditure the government needs to consider the price elasticities of both demand and supply of the goods upon which taxes are levied. When a tax is first introduced, it will produce a positive yield provided that at least some of the good is bought and sold after the imposition of the tax. However, the quantity bought and sold will usually fall after the imposition of a tax, so the government may not receive the revenue it was expecting. If the size of the tax is increased, the absolute size of the government's revenue may rise, fall, or indeed stay the same, depending on the elasticities of supply and demand. Fig. 13.3b illustrates the effects of an increase in taxation when demand and supply are both relatively elastic. In this case the tax yield falls. Although the government receives a larger tax revenue from each unit bought and sold at the new equilibrium, the loss in revenue resulting from the fall in sales more than offsets the revenue gain. When demand and supply are relatively inelastic, however, government revenue will increase.

Some important public policy implications result from this analysis. If the government wishes to maximise revenue it should tax as many goods and services as possible. Not only will this **widen the tax base**, but it will also reduce the elasticity of demand for the bundle of goods and services being taxed, taken as a whole. If only one good is taxed, demand is likely to be relatively elastic since untaxed goods are likely to contain some fairly close substitutes! Conversely, if the government aims to use taxation to switch expenditure, for example away from a demerit good such as tobacco, it should tax specific types of goods rather than wide categories. On this basis it could introduce different rates of taxation, for example taxing high tar and low tar cigarettes at different rates in order to switch expenditure away from the more harmful good. In a similar way, it can use tariffs or import duties to switch expenditure towards home-produced goods. In this way there may be a significant **trade-off between the revenue-raising and the expenditure-switching aims of taxation**.

TAXATION AND CONSUMER SURPLUS

Chapter 3 introduced the concept of consumer surplus as the utility obtained by consumers from the goods and services they purchase, which is valued over and above the price paid. Essentially, consumer surplus is a **measure of welfare**: the more consumer surplus a person obtains, the greater his personal welfare. At the initial price of P_1 in Fig. 13.3a, consumer surplus is shown by the triangle P_1EY. The imposition of a tax reduces consumer surplus to the smaller triangle P_2XY. The question now arises as to what happens to the consumer surplus no longer received by the purchasers of the good or service. The answer is that the part shown by the rectangle P_1WXP$_2$ has been transferred to the government in the form of tax revenue, but the part represented by the small triangle WEX is completely 'lost'. On the basis of this analysis, economists have argued in favour of reducing taxes to as low a level as possible; the lower the rate of taxation, the smaller the loss of consumer surplus.

However, the conclusion is not as clear-cut as is suggested by this analysis. Low-income groups are likely to obtain a greater utility from an extra pound of income (or from the goods and services an extra pound can purchase) than high-income groups. Correspondingly, the welfare loss experienced by a rich person who loses a pound in taxation is likely to be smaller than the welfare gain accruing to a poor person receiving the same pound in the form of a transfer payment. This argument can justify progressive taxation and the redistribution of income through transfer payments. (The effect of taxation upon consumer surplus is very similar to what happens when the formation of a monopoly raises the price of a good. Part of the consumer surplus is transferred to the monopolist as a monopoly profit, but part is 'lost' to everyone.)

OTHER ASPECTS OF TAXES ON INCOME AND EXPENDITURE

❶ Taxation and incentives It is often argued that a progressive income tax damages the economy through its effects on personal incentives. After all, the most obvious way legally to avoid an income tax is to work fewer hours, or even to stop working altogether. It is argued that expenditure taxes are preferable to income tax because they have no effect on the choice between work and leisure. Instead, expenditure taxes affect the choice between saving and spending, and they also switch expenditure into the consumption of untaxed goods and services.

Nevertheless, economic theory does not prove that an increase in income tax inevitably must have a disincentive effect upon personal effort. If the **supply curve of labour is upward-sloping**, a disincentive effect will result, since a tax increase is equivalent to a wage cut and less labour is supplied as wages fall. But in circumstances where workers aspire to a 'target' disposable income, when the **supply curve of labour is perverse** or **backward-bending**, a tax rise will mean that people have to work longer to achieve their desired target income. The tax may cause people to work harder, though it is more likely to promote tax evasion and black economy activity.

❷ Fiscal drag and fiscal boost Fiscal drag occurs in a progressive income tax structure when the government fails to raise tax thresholds or personal tax allowances at the same rate as inflation. Suppose that prices and all money incomes double. In the absence of taxation real incomes will remain the same. However, real disposable incomes will fall if inflation drags low-paid workers, who previously paid no tax, across the tax threshold to pay tax for the first time. In a similar way, higher-paid workers may be dragged deeper into the tax net, possibly into higher tax bands where they will pay tax at steeper marginal rates. In these circumstances the government's total revenue from income tax will rise faster than the rate of inflation, even though the tax structure has not been changed.

Conversely, in times of inflation fiscal boost is likely to reduce the real value of specific expenditure taxes (but not of *ad valorem* taxes such as VAT). Unless the government adjusts the rate of specific taxes to keep pace with inflation, their nominal value will stay more or less the same, but their real value will decline.

The simultaneous occurrence of fiscal drag and fiscal boost (such as occurred in the period of rapid inflation in the UK in the 1970s) shifts the structure of taxation away from taxes on expenditure and towards taxes on income. This can be avoided either by replacing progressive income tax with a proportionate tax, and specific expenditure duties with ad valorem taxation, or by indexing personal tax allowances, income tax bands, and the rates at which specific duties are levied.

❸ The poverty trap and the unemployment trap The vulnerability of the tax structure in the UK to the process of fiscal drag is closely related to the emergence of a phenomenon known as the poverty trap. The poverty trap occurs because the tax threshold at which income tax is paid overlaps with the ceiling at which means-tested welfare benefits cease to be paid. If a low-paid worker is caught within this zone of overlap, he not only pays tax and National Insurance contributions on an extra pound earned, but he also loses part or all of his right to claim benefits. The resulting marginal tax rate may be very high indeed, sometimes over 100 per cent.

The existence of the poverty trap supports the argument that the major disincentives to personal effort resulting from the structure of taxation and welfare benefits in the UK are experienced by low-paid rather than by highly paid workers. Not only is the effective marginal tax rate paid by the lower income groups frequently higher than the top rate of 40 per cent paid by the well-off; poorly paid workers are likely to experience less job satisfaction and to have less scope for perks and fringe benefits. Indeed the low-paid may be tempted to escape from the poverty trap either by avoiding tax through not working at all and living off benefits, thus becoming trapped in unemployment, or by evading tax through working in the untaxed hidden economy or black economy.

The poverty trap is undoubtedly made worse when fiscal drag draws low-paid workers into the tax next. Amongst the policies which could eliminate or reduce the effects of the poverty trap are the raising of tax thresholds and the replacement of **means-tested benefits** either by untaxed or universal benefits granted as of right (such as child benefit) or by benefits subject to tax 'clawback'. In the latter case, the government grants a benefit as of right and without a means test, but 'claws back' a fraction of the benefits through the income tax system from recipients who are above the tax threshold. Alternatively, the introduction of a **negative income tax** (**NIT**) has been suggested to merge the existing income tax and benefits structures. In a NIT scheme there would be a single tax threshold, above which people would pay (positive) income tax, and below which they would receive payments from the Inland Revenue (negative income tax) in lieu of welfare benefits. Amongst possible disadvantages of a NIT scheme are its tendency to reinforce the means-testing principle (though some may consider this an advantage), and the argument that civil servants in the Inland Revenue Department are not the most appropriate 'experts' to assess welfare needs. Avoid confusing the poverty trap with the **unemployment trap**. Low-waged people in work are caught in the poverty trap whereas the unemployment trap affects some of the unwaged or unemployed people. As we have noted, the low-waged may escape the poverty trap by choosing voluntary unemployment instead, thus entering the unemployment trap. Also avoid confusing the poverty trap with real poverty. Low-income families in the poverty trap are relatively poor but the real poor are not in work.

HOW PROGRESSIVE IS THE BRITISH TAX SYSTEM?

Over the years, the poverty trap and occasional fiscal drag have tended to reduce the advantages to the low-paid accruing from the progressive structure of British taxation. In any case the British income tax structure is probably much less progressive than is commonly supposed. Employees' National Insurance contributions are generally a regressive tax falling most heavily as a proportion of income on low-paid and middle-income groups, while the degree of progression in the upper reaches of the income tax structure is greatly reduced by the possibilities of legal tax avoidance open to the better-off. On the expenditure side, some excise duties such as tobacco duty are probably regressive whereas others, including petrol duty, are progressive. Value-added tax is probably slightly progressive since some necessities are currently excluded from the tax, but this may be countered by the fact that the low-paid spend a larger fraction of their income than the well-off, their savings being correspondingly lower. Moreover, extension of VAT to fuels such as gas and electricity, was a regressive move.

13.2 FISCAL POLICY

THE MEANING OF FISCAL POLICY

Fiscal policy is the part of a government's overall economic policy which aims to achieve the government's economic objectives through the use of the **fiscal instruments** of **taxation**,

public spending and the **budget deficit** or **surplus**. As an economic term, fiscal policy is often associated with **Keynesianism**. These days, the Keynesian fiscal policy based on the management of aggregate demand which was implemented in the UK in the three decades before 1979, has been superseded by a very different fiscal policy, related to **monetarism** and **supply-side economics**. Before explaining the instruments and the objectives of this more free-market fiscal policy, we shall first look at the main features of the **demand-side** fiscal policy pursued by Keynesian governments in the years before 1979.

KEYNESIAN FISCAL POLICY

The period from the 1930s to the 1970s is often called the **Keynesian era**. This is because many of the economic policies pursued during these decades were based on economic theories put forward in the 1920s and 1930s by the great British economist, **John Maynard Keynes**. In the Keynesian era, fiscal policy came to mean the use of the overall levels of public spending, taxation and the budget deficit to manage the level of aggregate money demand (AMD) in the economy, so as to achieve full employment and stabilise the business cycle. Keynesian fiscal policy, which was implemented with varying degrees of success in the decades before 1979, included the following main elements:

1 A belief that, left to itself, an unregulated market economy results in unnecessarily low economic growth, high unemployment and volatile business cycles.

2 By deliberate **deficit financing**, the government can – through using fiscal policy as a demand management instrument – inject demand and spending power into the economy to eliminate deficient demand and achieve full employment.

3 Having achieved full employment, the government can then use fiscal policy in a **discretionary** way (i.e. changing tax rates and levels of public spending to meet new circumstances) to **fine-tune** the level of **aggregate demand**. For much of the Keynesian era, the Keynesians believed that fiscal policy could achieve full employment, while avoiding an unacceptable increase in the rate of inflation.

FISCAL POLICY IN RECENT YEARS

In the Keynesian era, fiscal policy played a central role in the UK in the creation of a mixed economy based on the political consensus that the British economy should contain a mix of market and non-market economic activity and public and private ownership. In the years since 1979, along with policies such as privatisation and deregulation, fiscal policy has been used to break up the mixed economy by increasing the role of markets and of private sector economic activity and by reducing the economic role of the state.

The main elements of the fiscal policy implemented by the Conservative Government in the United Kingdom between 1979 and the mid-1990s included:

1 The rejection of the use of taxation and public spending as **discretionary** instruments of demand management. Under monetarist and supply-side influence, the Conservative Government believed that a policy of stimulating or reflating aggregate demand to achieve growth and full employment is, in the long run, at best ineffective and at worst damaging. Monetarists have argued that any growth of output and employment resulting from an expansionary fiscal policy is short-lived, and that in the long term, the main effect of such a policy is **inflation** which quickly destroys the conditions necessary for satisfactory market performance and wealth creation (see Chapters 15, 16 and 17).

2 **Reducing** public spending, taxation and government borrowing as proportions of national output. Besides wishing to reduce what they see as the inflationary effects of big government spending, monetarists and supply-side economists believe that the increased high levels of government spending, taxation and borrowing of the Keynesian era led to the **crowding-out** of the private sector. This is explained in 13.3. In order to free resources for the private sector and reduce the burden of taxation upon businesses and individuals, recent UK governments have tried (with only limited success) to reduce the proportions of national output taken in taxation and transferred in welfare benefits.

3 **Microeconomic fiscal policy** replaces macroeconomic fiscal policy. The more macroeconomic elements of fiscal policy which were dominant during the Keynesian era, have given way to a much more microeconomic fiscal policy. Marginal rates of income tax have been cut in order to create incentives to work hard, save and be entrepreneurial, and welfare benefits have been reduced so as to encourage the unemployed to accept low-paid jobs rather than state handouts.

4 **Subordinating** fiscal policy to the needs of monetary policy. The macroeconomic elements of fiscal policy also became subservient to the needs of monetary policy. This is explained in Chapter 17.

FISCAL POLICY AND THE CORRECTION OF MARKET FAILURE

Fiscal policy can be used to achieve a number of other economic objectives, besides the ones outlined in the previous two sections. Some of the most important involve the correction of market failure. For a detailed explanation, you should refer back to Chapter 9. In summary, a government might use taxation to: tax monopoly profits; finance the collective provision of public goods and merit goods; discourage the consumption of demerit goods and the discharge of negative externalities such as pollution; and alter the distribution of income, either in pursuit of greater equity when taxes and transfers are used to reduce inequalities, or to promote greater economic efficiency through tax and benefit cuts.

AUTOMATIC STABILISERS

So far we have assumed that the fiscal policy choice facing a government lies between discretionary demand management, Keynesian-style, and balancing the budget as advocated by many monetarists and supply-side economists. There is, however, an alternative approach which lies between these extremes, in which a government bases fiscal policy on the operation of **automatic stabilisers** which dampen or reduce the multiplier effects resulting from any change in aggregate demand within the economy. (Multiplier effects are explained in the next chapter).

Suppose, for example, that a collapse of confidence or export orders causes aggregate demand to fall. National income then also begins to fall, declining by the initial fall in demand × the multiplier, but as national income falls and unemployment rises, demand-led public spending on unemployment pay and welfare benefits also rises. At the same time, if the income tax system is progressive, the government's tax revenues fall faster than national income. In this way, increased public spending on transfers and declining tax revenues inject demand back into the economy, thereby stabilising and dampening the deflationary impact of the initial fall in aggregate demand, and reducing the overall size of the contractionary multiplier effect.

Automatic stabilisers also operate in the opposite direction to dampen the expansionary effects of an increase in aggregate demand. As incomes and employment rise, the take-up of means-tested welfare benefits and unemployment pay automatically falls, while at the same time tax revenues rise faster than income. Again, the size of the multiplier is reduced.

13.3 THE PSBR

THE PSBR AND THE GOVERNMENT'S BUDGETARY POSITION

A **budget deficit** occurs whenever **government spending exceeds revenue** from taxation and from the other sources such as the sale of government services. Conversely, a **budget**

surplus results when **government revenue exceeds expenditure**. A third possibility is a **balanced budget**. Using the symbols G for government spending and T for taxation and other sources of revenue, the three possibilities are:

G = T: balanced budget
G > T: budget deficit
G < T: budget surplus

We can measure the budget deficit (or surplus) for central government alone, or for central and local government taken together, in which case it is known as the general government budget deficit (or surplus), or indeed for whole of the wider public sector including nationalised industries as well as government.

It is important not to confuse the *elimination* of a budget deficit with the *financing* of a deficit. A budget deficit can be eliminated by cutting public spending or by raising taxation, both of which can balance the budget or move it into surplus. Assuming the deficit persists, it must be financed by **borrowing**. The borrowing which finances the deficit of the whole of the public sector is known as the public sector borrowing requirement or PSBR. A deliberate policy of running a budget deficit financed by borrowing, is known as **deficit financing**.

The PSBR is the other side of the coin to the budget deficit. Whenever there is a budget deficit there will be a *positive* borrowing requirement. By contrast, a budget surplus means that the government can use the excess of revenue over expenditure to repay previous borrowing. In this situation, the Public Sector Debt Repayment (PSDR), which is associated with a *negative* borrowing requirement, is perhaps a more appropriate measure of the government's net borrowing position than the PSBR.

THE COMPONENTS OF THE PSBR

Central government is the most important part of the public sector, but as noted earlier in the chapter, the public sector also includes local government or local authorities, and the few remaining nationalised industries which have escaped privatisation. The PSBR is made up of three components: the borrowing of central government (CGBR) and local authorities (LABR), which together form the general government borrowing requirement (GGBR), and public corporations (PCBR) or:

$$\text{PSBR} \equiv \text{CGBR} + \text{LABR} + \text{PCBR}$$

CHANGING ATTITUDES TO THE PSBR

Before the Keynesian era, British governments usually aimed for the sound finance or financial orthodoxy of a balanced budget, believing budget deficits to be morally bad and destructive of confidence. Deficit financing became an important part of macroeconomic policy during the Keynesian decades of the 1950s, 1960s and 1970s. In these years, Keynesian-inspired governments deliberately used the budget deficit to inject spending power into the economy, as a part of a wider policy to manage aggregate demand in order to achieve full employment and to stabilise the business cycle. During most of the years of Keynesian deficit financing, the PSBR was positive and growing both in absolute terms and as a percentage of national output or GDP.

In the 1980s, under the influence of monetarist and free-market supply-side thinking, deliberate deficit financing was once again rejected and the Government used fiscal policy to reduce the size of the budget deficit and move towards the fiscal neutrality of a balanced budget. The PSBR fell from nearly £10 billion in 1979/80 (or approximately 5.25% of GDP) to £3.4 billion in 1986/87 (0.75% of GDP). In 1987/88 buoyant tax revenues and the proceeds of privatisations caused the budget to move into surplus, with the PSBR becoming negative in 1987/88 as buoyant tax revenues caused the budget to move into surplus. From 1987/88 to 1990/91 there was a Public Sector Debt Repayment (PSDR), surplus tax revenues being used to redeem or buy back government debt from the private sector.

RECENT CHANGES IN THE PSBR

It is generally agreed that the government's budget deficit and the PSBR are best measured not by their money or nominal values (such as £32.2 billion outcome in 1995–96), but as ratios of the total size of the economy's output or national income. Fig. 13.4 shows how the PSBR has changed as a proportion of national income in the UK since the 1970s and how it is expected to change up the year 2001. The diagram also shows actual and projected changes in government spending and revenues, again measured as percentages of national income.

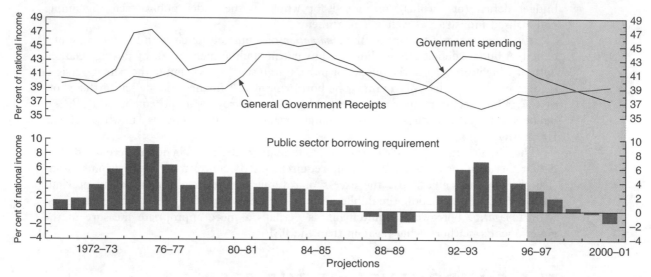

Fig. 13.4 Changes in government spending, revenue and the PSBR in the United Kingdom as proportions of national income

You will see from Fig. 13.4, that at the end of the Keynesian era of deficit financing in the 1970s, Keynesian deficit financing had caused the PSBR to grow to nearly 6% of GDP, but the main feature to note is the cyclical nature of government spending, tax revenues and also the PSBR. In the downswing of the business cycle, government spending rises and tax revenues fall as proportions of national income. The opposite happens in the recovery period when the economy is doing well. Consequently the the PSBR grows when the economy is doing badly, and declines when the economy recovers from recession. Cyclical factors therefore provide another very important explanation for the budget surplus and positive PSBR experienced in the late 1980s.

They also help to explain why the government's budget moved back into deficit and the PSBR again became positive in 1990/91, reflecting falling tax revenues and increased spending on unemployment pay as the UK economy once again entered recession. At this time, the government announced a policy change of aiming to balance the budget over a whole business cycle. The Conservative Government accepted once again the Keynesian argument that a budget deficit and positive PSBR can justifiably function as automatic stabilisers during a recession to reduce the volatility of the business cycle.

THE STRUCTURAL AND CYCLICAL COMPONENTS OF THE PSBR

In the light of the arguments presented in the previous two sections, it is useful to divide the budget deficit and the PSBR into two elements: the cyclical and the structural deficit and borrowing requirement. The **cyclical deficit** is that part of the overall budget deficit which rises and falls with the downswings and upswings of the business cycle, as automatic stabilisers take effect. Much of the growth of the budget deficit and borrowing requirement in the early 1990s can be related to the fall in tax revenues and increased spending on unemployment pay in the recession, just as in the 1980s an improvement in the government finances accompanied the boom years. Now, if *all* the growth of the PSBR is cyclical, the problem of a growing budget deficit disappears as the UK economy recovers from recession, providing the recovery is sufficiently buoyant and sustained. However, prospects will be much more gloomy if – as seems to be the case – a significant part of the growth of the PSBR is structural rather than cyclical. Growth in the **structural component** of the budget deficit and PSBR relates to the changing structure of the UK economy. In recent years a series of trends ranging from the de-industrialisation of the UK economy which has eroded the tax base, through to an ageing population and the growth of single parent families dependent on welfare benefits, have all contributed to the growth of the structural budget deficit and PSBR. The rather dispiriting message carried by the deterioration in the state of the public sector finances is that if a government of whatever political complexion seriously wishes to reduce or eliminate the structural deficit, it will have to introduce significant tax increases or public spending cuts, or both.

FUNDING THE PSBR

When the government borrows to finance its budget deficit, it can borrow either from the banking system (largely by selling Treasury bills) or from the general public (largely by selling gilt-edged securities). The latter is known as funding the PSBR. Fully funding the PSBR means that the government sells just sufficient new long-dated debt to cover its borrowing requirement. The general public buy illiquid securities from the government, paying for them with bank deposits. The bank deposits borrowed recirculate back to the general public when spent by the government, with the result that the overall effect on the money supply of fully funding the PSBR is neutral rather than contractionary.

Overfunding and underfunding the PSBR, and the monetary effects of the PSBR

Overfunding the PSBR means that the government sells more new long-dated debt than is needed to fully-fund its current borrowing requirement. Overfunding the PSBR is really the same thing as contractionary open market operations explained in Chapter 12. Overfunding the PSBR has a contractionary effect on the money supply. The opposite process is underfunding the PSBR, which takes place when the government sells insufficient long-dated securities to fully-fund the borrowing requirement. In this situation the government has to make up the difference by borrowing from the banking system, probably through Treasury bill sales. Underfunding the PSBR expands the money supply, firstly because the banks create deposits which are lent to the government to finance its spending programme, and secondly because the sale of Treasury bills increases the liquid assets held by the banks, allowing a possible multiple expansion of deposits to take place. In some circumstances, the government may deliberately choose to underfund the PSBR, for example in a severe recession when the government may wish to expand the money supply and boost aggregate demand. In this situation a policy of deliberately underfunding the PSBR is equivalent to expansionary open market operations. At other times, when the government simply cannot sell enough long-dated debt to fully fund a huge budget deficit and borrowing requirement, a policy of underfunding the PSBR may be forced on the government against its will.

The full-fund rule

In the early 1980s the UK government deliberately overfunded the PSBR. At this time, overfunding was the main plank in the government's monetarist strategy of trying to control the growth of the money supply, but it was abandoned in 1985, largely because a policy of systematic overfunding undertaken over several years, had caused undesirable distortions and inefficiencies to emerge in the financial system. After 1985, the UK government adopted instead a **full-fund rule**, in which the PSBR is financed through the sale of gilts, and other long-dated debt outside the banking system, so that government borrowing has a neutral effect on the money supply. In its budget in March 1993, the government slightly relaxed the full-fund rule, including the sale of long-dated debt to the banking system within the official definition of the full-fund rule.

CROWDING OUT

Although the methods of borrowing described earlier do not expand the money supply, monetarists argue that they **crowd out** the private sector by causing investment by firms to fall. Suppose for example, that the government increases public spending by £20 billion, financing the resulting budget deficit with a sale of gilt-edged securities. In order to persuade the general public to buy the extra debt, the guaranteed annual interest rate offered on new issues of gilts must be raised. This in turn raises interest rates generally and crowds out or displaces private sector investment by making it more expensive for firms to borrow or raise funds on the capital market through new issues of corporate bonds and shares. As a result, the size of the government spending multiplier with respect to real output is likely to be close to zero, rendering fiscal policy ineffective as a method of stimulating levels of activity and employment in the economy.

Financial crowding out and resource crowding out

The process just described, in which the government competes with private sector businesses for the supply of household savings and funds, is known as **financial crowding out**. **Resource crowding out** is a more general term which relates to those most fundamental of economic concepts: **scarcity** and **opportunity cost**. Resource crowding out simply means that real resources such as land capital and labour cannot be employed simultaneously in both the private and public sectors. Therefore, the opportunity cost of employing more resources in the public sector inevitably involves the sacrificed opportunity to use the same resources in private employment. However, this implicitly assumes full employment of all resources. When spare capacity and unemployed labour exist in the economy, it may often be more correct to describe the opportunity cost of increased government spending in terms of the foregone opportunity for resources to remain idle.

THE NATIONAL DEBT

The budget deficit and the borrowing requirement, which are examples of economic **flows** (and which are the difference between the two much larger flows of government or public sector expenditure and revenue), must not be confused with the National Debt, which is a **stock** concept. The National Debt is a rather misleading term. It is *not* the debt of the whole of the nation, or even of the whole of the public sector, and it is largely unrelated to the balance of payments deficit with which it is sometimes confused. It is simply the **total stock** of central government debt – the **accumulated stock of borrowing** which has built up over the years and which the government has not yet paid back.

IS THE NATIONAL DEBT A BURDEN?

In the Keynesian era, when almost continuous deficit financing led to a steadily accumulating National Debt in the UK, the reduction of the overall size of the National Debt was not a fiscal policy objective. In more recent years – and related to the Conservative Government's aim of trying to reduce the levels of both public expenditure and the PSBR as proportions of national output – National Debt reduction has become part of the Government's supply-side orientated fiscal policy.

The question of whether fiscal policy should aim to reduce the absolute size of the National Debt relates closely to the issue of whether the National Debt is a burden – both for the government and its freedom to pursue the economic policy of its choice, and for the nation as a whole. We shall now look at some of the ways in which the UK National Debt may or may not represent a burden for the government and the nation.

The nominal debt and the real debt

It is important to avoid confusing the *nominal* or *absolute* size of the National Debt with the *real* National Debt. In so far as the National Debt imposes a burden upon the government – and indirectly upon the nation as taxpayers who must finance interest payments on the debt – it is the real debt that is significant. The nominal National Debt is simply the accumulated money value of all central government debt. The real National Debt is measured by the nominal debt as a proportion or ratio of GDP or national output. Thus:

$$\text{Real National Debt} = \frac{\text{Nominal National Debt}}{\text{GDP at market prices}}$$

The real value of the UK National Debt has actually fallen , despite the fact that the nominal value of the debt has risen in all years except when there has been a budget surplus. In the 1950s and 1960s the fall in the real National Debt could be explained by economic growth. The economy grew in real terms faster than the rate at which successive budget deficits added to the nominal National Debt, thereby reducing in real terms the overhang of debt accumulated during the Second World War. In the 1970s and 1980s, inflation and *not* economic growth was the most important single cause of the falling real value of the UK National Debt. If the rate of inflation is greater than the rate at which the CGBR adds to the National Debt, the money value of the debt as a proportion of money GDP usually falls. Also, if the rate of inflation is greater than the nominal interest rate the government pays to debt-holders, the government gains and debt-holders lose.

The servicing burden

Although, until recently at least, inflation reduced the real value of the National Debt, it contributed to an increased **cost of servicing** the National Debt. This – represented by **interest payments to debt holders** – is not really a burden upon the nation taken as a whole, providing the debt is held internally by people living in the country. When the debt is internally held, servicing costs – apart from management costs – are really just a transfer from taxpayers (whose taxes are higher than they would be in the absence of debt interest payments) to debt-holders who have lent to the government. However, in times of rapid inflation, savers or debt-holders begin to realise that they have lost out by lending their savings at negative real interest rates. In these circumstances, the government may experience considerable difficulty in persuading the general public to buy new debt, at least at current interest rates. The government will have to raise interest rates both to finance the current CGBR and also to replace existing debt as it matures. In the 1980s the cost of servicing the UK National Debt was quite high, even though the real debt had fallen to less than 50% of GDP. Savers had learned the lesson of the rapid inflation and negative real interest rates experienced in the 1970s and were reluctant to lend to the government unless nominal rates of interest were well above the rate of inflation, thus ensuring an attractive real return on their savings. The resulting high real interest rates caused by the government's need to sell debt may then have led to the crowding out process.

Constraints upon economic policy

The National Debt is a burden, or more accurately a constraint, if it is large and the accompanying servicing or interest costs limit the government's freedom of action in other important aspects of economic policy. In the Keynesian era the UK government's monetary policy was often determined by the need to secure conditions in which new debt could easily be sold and in which servicing costs would not be too high. Monetary policy could not be used to pursue other possible policy objectives.

The externally-held debt

If part of the National Debt is held *externally*, by residents of other countries, it can represent a burden since part of current income and output must flow overseas as interest payments. This may reduce living standards within the country, and large quantities of externally-held debt can also constrain domestic economic policy, since policies unpopular with overseas debt-holders may trigger the mass selling of both the externally-held debt and then the country's currency. A foreign exchange crisis could then ensue. However, the externally-held debt should not be regarded as a significant burden on the United Kingdom, since less than 4% of the National Debt is currently owned overseas. Unfortunately, the same is not true for many developing countries because external holdings of government debt form a major part of the Third World debt problem.

The deadweight debt and the reproductive debt

There are many ways of classifying a country's National Debt, for example into the **internally-held debt** and the **externally-held debt**, and into the **floating debt** (short-term debt such as Treasury bills) and the **funded debt** (long-term debt such as gilts). These should not be confused with the **deadweight debt** and the **reproductive debt**. Suppose that the government sells gilts and uses the revenues to build a motorway or some other capital project. Although the government is borrowing for a period of many years, the resulting liability is matched by a wealth-producing asset, the motorway. This type of reproductive borrowing is not a burden on future generations, since interest payments on the debt are in essence paid for out of the motorway's contributions to future national output. In contrast, any long-term borrowing used to finance current spending, for example on unemployment pay, can be regarded as a burden on future generations whose taxes will be required to pay interest on the deadweight spending indulged in by the government today.

Chapter roundup

This chapter links with topics covered in both earlier and subsequent chapters. Public spending and taxation can best be understood in the context of the public and private sectors of the economy, and the changing role of government in the economy. These are covered in Chapter 1 on economic systems and Chapter 8 which describes the government's privatisation policies. One of the principal reason why governments levy taxation is to correct market failure – the subject of Chapter 9. Fiscal policy can be viewed as both a complementary policy and as an alternative policy to monetary policy, which is covered by Chapter 12. Public finance and fiscal policy issues also figure strongly in the chapters which follow, particularly in the context of supply-side economics (Chapter 16) and Keynesianism and monetarism (Chapter 17).

Illustrative questions and answers

1   Essay Question
How should the services currently provided by local authorities be financed? (25)

AEB

Tutorial note

The reform of local government finance has been extremely topical in recent years and looks likely to remain so through the rest of the 1990s. In 1992 when this question was set, the poll tax or community charge had replaced property rating as the tax levied by local authorities to pay for their spending (though under both systems transfers or grants from central government had grown to be by far the main source of finance for local authority spending). During its short life, the poll tax was unpopular and it became increasingly unworkable. Therefore the poll tax was replaced in 1993 by a council tax, which like the old system of local authority rates is based on property values. Houses have been divided into groups according to their estimated market values; local authorities now levy the council tax according to the property band that a household occupies. Because property values were estimated before the worst of the slump in house prices that took place in the early 1990s, the new tax has been criticised for treating the South East of England unfairly. Property values fell by more than a third in the South East in the early 1990s, while holding up much better in the northern parts of Britain. However it must be remembered that house buyers in the South East had fared much better than their northern counterparts during the 1980s boom in house prices, benefiting to a greater extent from untaxed capital gains (because house prices increased most in the South East) and from income tax relief on their mortgages (because their mortgages were larger).

Back in 1981, The Conservative government published a Green Paper inviting discussion on various options for financing local government: a poll tax; a local sales tax; a local income tax, and a property tax in the guise of reformed domestic rates. The Green Paper also briefly considered but rejected other possibilities such as: local duties on petrol, alcohol and tobacco; a local vehicle excise tax; and a local payroll tax. Very much in line with such *canons of taxation* as *economy*, *efficiency* and *equity*, the Green Paper assessed each potential tax against seven criteria:

(i)   Is it practical?
(ii) Is it fair?
(iii) Does it make councillors, who take decisions on local expenditure, accountable to the local tax payers?
(iv) Are the administrative costs acceptable?
(v)   Are the implications for the rest of the tax system acceptable?
(vi) Does it encourage proper financial control? and
(vii) Is it suitable for all tiers of local government?

This particular question has been worded so as to allow a variety of possible responses. You could adopt a service by service approach, perhaps arguing that services such as parks and libraries should be financed in a different way from the police. (The distinction between services provided as *public goods* and *merit goods* could be relevant here.) Or you could introduce a long list of possible sources of finance, including some that we have not previously mentioned, for example the sale or commercialisation of local authority services such as admission to leisure centres, with or without the privatisation of the actual provision of the services. At the other extreme you might compare just two sources of finance, say a poll tax and a property tax. We suggest that you select say three or four alternative sources of finance, and then base your assessment against the type of criteria we listed in the previous paragraph. When we compare a poll tax and a property tax for example, a poll tax, (at least in an 'uncapped version') scores quite well in terms of accountability but much less well when measured against the criteria of economy and equity. In the early 1990s, the poll tax proved to be about three times more expensive to collect than the property tax (the local rate) which it had replaced. And although property taxation can be regressive in particular instances (e.g. when a single person and several income earners live next door to each other in identical accommodation), on average the poll tax was much more regressive. The old local rating system promoted various inefficiencies (for example, deterring home improvement), but so has the poll tax. The poll tax has encouraged the inefficient use of housing; retired people continuing to live in large houses after their families have grown up and moved away. It also has promoted widespread evasion and deregistration from electoral roles. For these and other reasons , the 1981 Green Paper came out strongly against a poll tax, but this did not stop the government which commissioned it from introducing such a tax!

Suggested answer

- Briefly set out the historical background to the question.
- Specify a number of alternative methods of finance such as: a revival of the poll tax; a return to the rating system (note: part of the rating system remains, i.e. the business rate levied on commercial property); the council tax; local income and sales taxes. Mention also, that other alternatives might include: an extension of central government funding of local authorities; or an abolition of local government with its activities being taken by central government or non-governmental bodies such as Urban Development Corporations; or commercialisation and possibly also privatisation of local authority services.
- Select, say, three of the alternative sources you have listed.
- State the criteria against which you are going to assess the alternatives: e.g. efficiency; economy; equity; accountability, etc.
- Carefully assess each alternative against these criteria, perhaps making the point that different forms of finance may suit different services. By all means mention the political context, but don't drift into political abuse.
- Reach an argued conclusion.

2 Data Question

We have reached an important position as regards fiscal policy. This is also very different from what was believed in the early eighties. It was then thought that a prudent fiscal policy which involved reducing the PSBR to a small percentage of GDP, or perhaps zero, would avoid 'crowding out' of private sector investment
5 and leave sufficient resources in the economy to be devoted to the accumulation of wealth. We were asked to believe that monetary policy would ensure that there would be no inflationary excess of demand over output and that a prudent fiscal policy would ensure that this demand was properly distributed between consumption and investment. The PSBR is now forecast to be about minus £14.2
10 billion which is about minus 3 per cent of GDP and roughly similar to last year; but last year many observers were saying that this fiscal policy was too lax! Why such a change?

The reason for this is the behaviour of private sector spending. Keynesian economists (who ran for cover in the early 1980s) have always known that there
15 is no such thing as a 'prudent fiscal policy' in the abstract; fiscal policy can only be said to be prudent in the light of the private sector's decisions. And, in the United Kingdom recently, these have been historically abnormal.

The fundamental reason is the behaviour of consumer spending. The personal sector savings ratio, now 5 per cent, was as low as 3 per cent in mid
20 1988. This compares with 10–15 per cent in the late 1970s. This personal sector savings ratio is not only abnormally below the levels witnessed through much of the last two decades, but it is also worrying that at present the British private sector does not want to save to make resources available for investment. This is why the government needs to run a large surplus.

(Adapted from: David Vines, 'Is the "Thatcher Experiment" still on course?',
The Royal Bank of Scotland Review, December 1989

(a) (i) Explain what is meant by the 'PSBR' (lines 3 and 9). (3)
  (ii) In your own words, explain and comment upon what, according to Vines, was regarded as a 'prudent' fiscal policy in the early eighties (lines 7 and 8). (6)
(b) (i) Using lines 18–24, explain how the behaviour of the private sector in the late 1980s differed from that of the late 1970s. (3)
  (ii) What would you expect to be the economic consequences of this change in behaviour, and why would they be 'worrying' (line 22)? (3 and 4 marks)
(c) In the light of the changed behaviour discussed in (b), how would Keynesian economists expect a prudent fiscal policy to change (lines 18–24)? (6)

Oxford

Tutorial note

(a) Provided that economic agents in the private sector (households and firms) are underspending their incomes, there is a case for the public sector to run a budget deficit of more or less the same size (to be financed by public sector borrowing – the PSBR) so as to prevent deficient aggregate demand emerging and depressing economic activity. Any larger public sector deficit and borrowing requirement would be imprudent because it would divert productive resources away from the 'wealth-creating' private sector to the supposedly 'wealth-consuming' public sector (to use the 'monetarist' parlance that was fashionable in the early 1980s). At the time, monetarists also argued that a large PSBR was imprudent for a second reason besides 'crowding out', namely that it leads to excess monetary expansion and inflation. However, this argument is not mentioned in the passage.

(b) (i) During the 'Lawson boom' in the late 1980s, the private sector departed on a spending spree or binge, 'overspending' its income. In these circumstances it could be argued that a prudent fiscal policy involves the public sector running a budget surplus and negative PSBR to take excess demand out of the economy.

(ii) One consequence of the change in behaviour is mentioned in the passage: investment no longer being financed by domestically generated savings. As a further consequence, UK investment had to be financed by capital inflows from abroad. This brings us to the consequences for the balance of payments: instead of saving, the private sector was spending on imports, leading to a massive deterioration in the current account of the balance of payments, which was financed in the capital account by the capital inflows we have just mentioned. This was 'worrying' because it raised the question of whether the UK could continue to pay its way in the world and/or whether the rest of the world would continue to be willing to supply the capital flows to make good the shortfall of UK-generated savings. The behaviour of the private sector has also proved 'worrying' because arguably, the severe recession of the early 1990s has been a 'debt recession' directly induced by the overspending of the late 1980s. To finance their spending, households and firms borrowed far too much and accumulated too much debt during the 'Lawson boom'. In the early 1990s they reduced spending and increased saving so as to reduce indebtedness as a ratio of income. Thus the 'overshoot' of the late-80s boom triggered an equal overshoot on the downside of the economic cycle, but this time in the direction of a collapse in confidence and a debt-induced recession.

(c) Firstly, a Keynesian would argue that there is a case for the government allowing the public sector finances to move 'naturally' into deficit during the recession, acting as an 'automatic stabiliser' to reduce the fluctuations in the business cycle. (By 1991, the Conservative Government had partially accepted this argument.) Secondly, by 1992, many Keynesians were arguing that the debt-induced recession had become so serious and severe, that 'prudent fiscal policy' would involve a massive but selective increase in public spending directed at industry to restore business confidence. (The Japanese government apparently accepted the logic of this argument, but not the Conservative Government in the UK.)

Question bank

1 (a) How might the government use fiscal policy to influence the economy? (12)

   (b) Discuss the view that the government ought to balance its budget. (13)   *AEB*

Pitfalls

Two key words in the question are *might* and *ought*. In part (a), you don't have to write about the actual fiscal policy implemented by UK governments, but don't define fiscal policy too narrowly, e.g. solely in terms of demand management. Do make sure you restrict your answer to fiscal policy, i.e. don't drift into other areas of economic policy such as monetary policy. With part (b) there is a danger of confusing a balanced budget with the balance of payments.

Key points

In part (a), you must first define fiscal policy. Outline possible policy objectives, and then describe the underlying strategy and particular fiscal policy instruments (such as new taxes or changed tax rates) that might be used to achieve the desired policy objective(s). Start your answer to part (b) by defining a balanced budget and relate the term to budget deficits and surpluses. Explain two reasons for running an unbalanced budget, i.e. Keynesian deficit financing or demand management, and the automatic stabilising role of the budget. Then present the counter-arguments of monetarist and supply-side economists, namely that budget deficits lead to crowding out and/or excessive monetary growth and inflation. Conclude by giving your own opinion on the issue.

2 (a) Distinguish between direct and indirect taxation, and give an example of each. (10)

(b) What theoretical arguments exist to justify a movement from direct to indirect taxation? (15)

Oxford & Cambridge

Pitfalls

Although part (a) carries quite a large number of marks, the answer can be quite short. There is a danger of drifting into a generalised and largely irrelevant account of the tax system, but you must briefly explain why the taxes you list (e.g. income tax and value added tax) are examples of direct and indirect taxation. With part (b), you must obey the instruction to use economic theory; there is a danger of writing an anecdotal answer insufficiently underpinned by economic theory. Note that the question does not ask you to explain theoretical arguments *against* shifting the structure of taxation towards indirect taxation. Don't introduce these arguments, except perhaps to indicate briefly that not everyone agrees that the structure of taxation should be changed.

Key points

Part (a) requires accurate definitions of direct and indirect taxation, supported by suitable examples. The main theoretical arguments you should use in the second part of your answer relate to personal incentives and the shape of the supply curve of labour (see Chapter 11 on the labour market). You should clearly explain that supply-side economists, rather than Keynesians, support the case for increasing the importance of indirect taxation and reducing the role of direct taxes.

3 (a) How might the increase in UK public expenditure in real terms over the last ten years be explained? (30)

(b) Why might a government wish to reduce real public expenditure? (30)

(c) Contrast the macroeconomic effects of a reduction in defence expenditure with those of a reduction in state retirement pensions. (40)

ULEAC

Pitfalls

With part (a), there is a danger of explaining the *nominal* growth of public spending (in terms of the effects of inflation) rather than the *real* growth. Your answer to part (b) must be firmly based on monetarist and supply-side theory; avoid writing an answer that states only that Conservative governments wish to reduce public expenditure to enable tax cuts to be made. While this point is relevant, your explanation must be developed further. Make sure in your answer to part (c) to discuss (and contrast) *macroeconomic* rather than *microeconomic* effects.

Key points

Your answer to part (a) could centre on cyclical factors (the effects of the business cycle) and structural factors, such as the growing number of retired people in the economy. Make sure that you define real expenditure. Start your answer to part (b) by explaining how, if public expenditure grows in real terms faster than the economy as a whole, taxation and/or borrowing must also rise in real terms. Outline the possible adverse effects on the economy, e.g. destruction of personal incentives, inflation and crowding out. Develop your answer by explaining that monetarist and supply-side economists believe the adverse effects exceed any benefits increased public spending may have. Recent UK governments have been strongly influenced by supply-side theory, and have tried either to reduce public spending in real terms or to reduce its growth relative to the economy as a whole. Part (c) asks for a contrast rather than a discussion of similarities, but you should briefly make the point that the two policies are similar in that they will both lead to a reduction in aggregate demand. A cut in pensions will have an immediate effect on the distribution of income, increasing inequalities. A reduction in military expenditure might increase unemployment in defence-related industries and reduce the demand for capital goods. A reduction in military commitments overseas might improve the balance of payments by saving on invisible imports (see Chapter 19). Both policies could free resources for use elsewhere in the economy.

NATIONAL INCOME

Units in this chapter

Chapter objectives

Microeconomics – the subject matter of the early chapters of this book – is concerned with the individual markets that make up the economy, and the behaviour of individual economic agents such as consumers and producers. For the remaining chapters, we switch attention away from the little bits of the economy towards such questions as *What determines the average price level?* and *How do we explain the overall levels of employment and unemployment in the economy?* These are the concern of **macroeconomics**, the part of economics that attempts to explain how the **whole economy** works. Macroeconomics examines the determination of **aggregate** levels of output, income, prices, employment and unemployment, and the trade flows that make up the balance of payments. Unit 14.1 introduces the concepts of **national income, expenditure**, and **output**. Having looked at the **use and misuse of national** income statistics, the unit concludes by explaining the concept of **equilibrium national income**, which is a key concept used in the analysis of macroeconomic problems and policy. The remaining units of the chapter investigate three important elements of the income-expenditure model: the determinants of **consumption** and **saving**, **investment** and the **national income multiplier**.

14.1 NATIONAL INCOME

NATIONAL WEALTH, CAPITAL AND INCOME

Fig. 14.1 illustrates the very important relationships and distinctions between national income, wealth and capital. **National wealth** comprises all the physical assets or things that have value, owned by the nation's residents. The **national capital stock** is the part of national wealth capable of producing more wealth. It includes all the **capital goods** and raw materials owned by the country's residents, as well as **social capital** such as the roads, hospitals and schools which are owned by the state, but it excludes consumer goods which are a part of national wealth but not national capital. All capital is wealth, but the reverse is untrue: not all wealth is capital. Wealth and capital are both examples of economic **stocks** and are thus distinguished from **income** which is a **flow**. **National income** is the flow of new wealth resulting from the productive use of the national capital stock. Being part of a continuous flow, national income is measured per time period: monthly, quarterly, or more usually yearly.

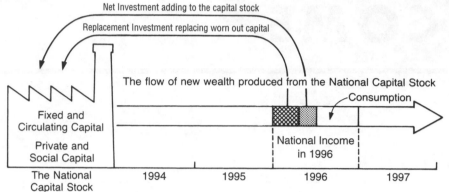

Fig. 14.1 National income as an economic flow

NATIONAL INCOME, NATIONAL PRODUCT AND NATIONAL EXPENDITURE

Three different methods can be used to measure national income or the flow of new wealth produced by an economy. They are:

- **The product method.** The money value of all the goods and services, or output, produced in the economy are added together. The final total is called national product, which we shall represent by the symbol Q.

- **The income method.** The money values of the incomes received by factors of production employed in producing the output are added together. This is national income, represented by Y.

- **The expenditure method.** The money values of all spending upon output are added up. The total is national expenditure, shown by the symbol E.

Since these are simply three methods of measuring the same thing, namely the flow of new wealth or output produced, national income, product and expenditure must be identical! This can be expressed as the accounting identity:

national income ≡ national product ≡ national expenditure, **or:** $Y \equiv Q \equiv E$.

THE SYSTEM OF NATIONAL INCOME ACCOUNTS

The principal function of the national income accounts is to provide the basic data for economic policy-making, particularly at the macroeconomic level, and for economic forecasting. $Y \equiv Q \equiv E$ is the most fundamental of all the identities in the system of national income accounts, which are published officially by the government a few months after the end of the year to which they apply. It is important for A Level students to be familiar with some of the most important national income accounting terms, and with some of the uses and limitations of national income figures.

As Fig. 14.1 shows, part of the national capital stock will be worn out producing this year's national income. Assuming that the capital stock is being run at full capacity, part of this year's national income must be invested to restore the capital stock to its previous size, if the economy is to remain capable of producing the same size of output next year. **Gross national product (GNP)** measures national output before allowing for capital consumption or depreciation. By contrast, **net national product (NNP)** measures the goods and services available after replacing worn out capital stock.

You should also understand the distinction between market prices and factor cost. **GNP at market prices** measures the value of output at the prices which consumers pay. Since prices paid by consumers include expenditure taxes such as value added tax, GNP at market prices overstates the true value of output, and subsidies paid to producers result in undervaluation. To convert GNP at market prices into **GNP at factor cost**, which accurately measures the value of output, expenditure taxes must be deducted and subsidies added.

In the British national accounts, the term national income is always presented net of depreciation, whereas national product is presented both gross and net − before and after depreciation is subtracted. Thus as an accounting identity:

national income ≡ net national product at factor cost.

Another important distinction is that between national product and domestic product. **Gross domestic product (GDP)** measures the incomes received and the outputs produced by factors of production actually employed within the United Kingdom economy, or within United Kingdom national boundaries. GDP is not the same as gross national product (GNP) because part of domestically generated incomes flows overseas to foreign owners of companies operating in the United Kingdom, and to residents of other countries who own shares in British companies. Similarly, United Kingdom residents receive dividend incomes and profits remitted on assets they own abroad. GDP is thus converted into GNP by adding the **net property income from abroad**, which results from such profit and dividend flows. A positive figure for net property income from abroad indicates that UK residents receive more profits from assets owned in other countries than overseas residents receive from the assets they own in the United Kingdom.

THE USE AND MISUSE OF NATIONAL INCOME STATISTICS

Since national income statistics are the main source of data on what has happened and what is happening in the economy, they are frequently used as indicators of economic growth, economic and social welfare, and for purposes of comparison with other countries. In order to be useful for these purposes, it is important that national income statistics are accurately constructed. Income is a payment for productive services rendered by the factors of production. Transfer payments such as unemployment pay, welfare benefits and pensions must be excluded from the measurement of national income since they are simply a transfer, via taxation and government spending, from one group of people to another, without the recipients adding to production. If such transfers were wrongly added to the national income total, the error of **double counting** would occur, leading to an over-estimate of national income. Double counting would also occur if the value of all goods, including capital goods and raw materials, were included in the total for national output when calculating national product. Only the money values of final goods and services sold to consumers must be totalled. Alternatively, we can measure the value added by all industries, including producers of raw materials and other capital goods, at each stage of production.

National income statistics are also based on a number of rather arbitrary judgments on what is and is not productive work. In any economy a certain amount of production takes place in the **non-monetised economy**, without money incomes being received for production undertaken. The non-monetised economy is, of course, most significant in developing economies, but within developed economies such as the United Kingdom, housework and do-it-yourself home improvement take place within the non-monetised economy. Any measurement of national income must therefore, either estimate or ignore the value of production undertaken in the non-monetised economy. The United Kingdom accounts can be criticised for estimating the value of some but not all the production taking place in the non-monetised sector of the economy. Imputed rents are estimated for the housing services received by owner-occupiers from the houses they live in, based on an estimate of the rent which would be paid if the house owners were tenants of the same properties, but house-keeping allowances paid within households are not estimated, implying that housework − most of which is undertaken by women − is unproductive!

Official statistics tend to underestimate the actual volume of economic activity that occurs, not only because various activities occurring in the non-monetised economy are ignored, but also because illegal activities are omitted. A major reason for this is the existence of the so-called hidden or underground economy, sometimes popularly known as the **black economy**. This refers to all the economic transactions conducted in cash which are not recorded in the national income figures because of tax evasion. A study published in the *Economic Journal* in 1990 estimated that Britain's black economy fell from a peak of more than 11% of GDP in the late 1970s to 7.6% in the mid-1980s. This is a relatively low figure in comparison to many other countries. In 1993 *The Economist* magazine estimated that the black economy accounted for as much as 30% of GDP in Greece, 25% in Spain and 20% in Italy and Portugal.

Comparisons over time

1 Money national income is a misleading indicator of economic growth. For the growth rate to be calculated, money national income of each year, expressed in current prices of that year, must be deflated to show real income in the constant prices of a single year. An index number, such as the Retail Price Index, used to deflate GNP to constant prices is known as a GNP deflator.

2 Population usually grows over time, so real GNP per head of population (per capita) is a better indicator of living standards than the aggregate real GNP figure.

3 The quality of goods and services available is likely to change over time, presenting a particularly difficult problem in the use of GNP statistics.

4 More generally, the GNP figures cannot measure changes in intangibles, which affect the quality of life and the general level of welfare in society. Externalities, including both external benefits and costs, usually escape measurement in national income statistics, as do such intangibles as the value people place on leisure time and living close to work. When externalities are measured, what is in effect a welfare loss may appear as a welfare gain! For example, if motorists spend more time each day sitting in congested traffic, they will regard this as a welfare loss. However, as far as the national income statistics are concerned it will appear as extra consumption expenditure on the outputs of the vehicle and petroleum industries.

Comparisons between countries

1 We have already mentioned how comparisons of GNP per head between countries are misleading if the relative importance of the non-monetised economy is greatly different.

2 Further problems occur in the comparison of real income per head if different commodities are consumed. For example, expenditure on fuel, energy and building materials is likely to be greater in a country with a cold climate than in a warmer climate.

3 A reliable comparison of real GNP per capita requires the accurate deflation of money GNP figures to constant prices in each country. There are considerable differences in statistical method and sophistication between countries, in the construction of both national income accounts and price indices. In addition, artificially managed exchange rates may distort comparison of internal price levels within countries, and even if exchange rates reflect the prices of goods which are traded internationally, they will not reflect the prices of goods and services which do not enter into international trade.

EQUILIBRIUM NATIONAL INCOME

It is important not to confuse the topic of national income accounting which we have just surveyed, with the concept of equilibrium national income. This is one of the most important macroeconomic concepts which you must understand.

In Chapter 2 we introduced the concept of **equilibrium** in the context of a single market within an economy. We defined equilibrium as a state of rest, or a condition in which the plans of all the economic agents in the economic model are fulfilled and consistent with each other. We shall continue to use this concept of equilibrium in examining the conditions necessary to achieve an equilibrium level of national income or output within the goods market of an economy. Nevertheless, equilibrium is a state towards which the economy is heading; the equilibrium will not necessarily be reached. It is more realistic to think of the economy as being in a state of disequilibrium, tending, in the absence of outside disturbances or shocks, towards the equilibrium level of national income. Essentially, national income and output will be in equilibrium when the planned or intended aggregate money demand (AMD) of all the economic agents in the economy in the current period equals the output (or income) produced in the previous period.

THE 45° LINE

Before examining in more detail the concept of equilibrium national income, we must first explain the significance of a line drawn on a graph at 45° to origin. Providing that the axes of the graph are measured in the same units and the same scale, a line drawn at 45° to origin allows a distance measured along the horizontal axis to be shown also as the vertical distance between the horizontal axis and the 45° line. In Fig. 14.2 the horizontal distance (oa) equals the vertical distance (ab) because the two distances are sides of the same square.

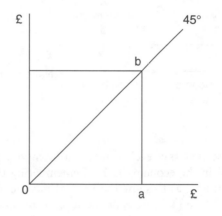

Fig. 14.2 The 45° line

AGGREGATE EXPENDITURE

Aggregate expenditure in the economy comprises the **planned expenditure upon output** of all the economic agents in the economy. The following identity shows the various components of aggregate expenditure:

$$\text{Aggregate expenditure} \equiv C + I + G - T + X - M$$

C represents **planned consumption spending** by households, and **I** represents **planned investment spending** by firms, both of which are examined later in the chapter. The other components of aggregate expenditure measure, respectively, the net planned expenditure of the government sector and the overseas sector. G–T measures the extent to which the government or public sector is injecting demand into the economy via a budget deficit, or taking demand out of the economy by running a budget surplus. **G** and **T** respectively measure **government spending** and revenues (mostly **taxation**). X – M measures the extent to which expenditure by the rest of the world on the country's **exports (X)** exceeds expenditure by the country's residents on **imports** produced by other countries **(M)**. X – M also shows the state of the **balance of payments**. When X > M, there is a balance of payments surplus, with the overseas sector functioning as a positive source of demand for the country's output. In the case of a balance of payments deficit when exports are less than imports (X < M), the overseas sector is responsible for a net leakage of demand out of the economy.

EQUILIBRIUM NATIONAL INCOME
ILLUSTRATED ON A 45° DIAGRAM

Fig. 14.3 shows aggregate expenditure in the economy at different levels of national income or output. The diagram shows that as national income rises, aggregate expenditure (shown by the line labelled C + I + G – T + X – M) also rises, but at a slower rate than income. (You should see 14.2 on consumption for an explanation of this.)

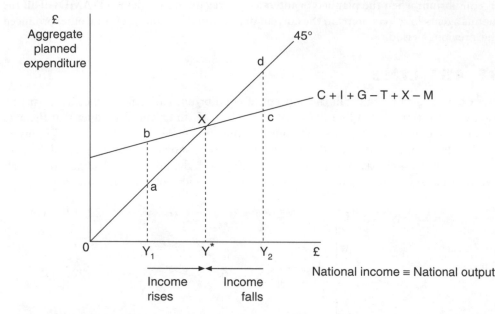

Fig. 14.3 Equilibirum national income

We shall now suppose that the level of nominal or money national income or output currently being produced in the economy is Y_1. Remembering the property of the 45° line, we can use the vertical line (Y_1a) to show the level of income Y_1. At this level of income, aggregate planned expenditure (Y_1b) exceeds the level of income or output available (Y_1a). Firms could react to this situation in one of three ways. In the immediate period, firms might be able to meet the level of demand by **de-stocking**, i.e. by running down stocks of previously accumulated unsold goods. Clearly, the ability of firms to meet demand in this way is limited by the size of any previously accumulated stocks or inventories. Indeed, the depletion of stocks may itself create an incentive for firms to consider one of the other ways of meeting the excess demand, by increasing real output, or by raising prices. Either way, nominal income or money national income will rise. The level of income Y_1 is therefore a disequilibrium level of national income.

By using similar reasoning, we can show that levels of income such as Y_2 also represent disequilibrium in the goods market. When the level of income is Y_2, planned expenditure is less than the income or output available at the current price level. Firms will find themselves unable to sell all their current output and an amount equal to (cd) will accumulate as an unsold stock. Firms may react to this **unintended stock accumulation** by reducing real output or prices. Nominal income Y thus falls, so Y_2 cannot be an equilibrium level of income.

Disequilibrium conditions apply

if, when: Y < C + I + G – T + X – M   Y tends to rise,
and when: Y > C + I + G – T + X – M   Y tends to fall,

it follows that only when: Y = C + I + G – T + X – M   will Y remain unchanged.

Y = C + I + G – T + X – M is therefore the **equilibrium equation** which sets out the conditions which must be met for the goods market of the economy to be in a state of rest or equilibrium. In Fig. 14.3 the equilibrium level of national income or output is shown at Y*, where the aggregate expenditure curve crosses the 45° line at point (x). Only at Y* are the market plans of households and firms fulfilled and consistent with each other. At any other level of nominal income or output, the unintended accumulation or running down of stocks creates an incentive for firms to change the level of nominal output (Y) they are producing, by changing either real output or prices, or both output and prices.

THE CIRCULAR FLOW OF INCOME

Fig. 14.4, which is an example of a **circular flow diagram**, illustrates equilibrium income in terms of the flows of income and expenditure around the economy. The solid lines in the diagram show the real flows occurring in the economy between households and firms. Households supply labour and other factor services or inputs in exchange for real goods and services, but in a monetary economy, real flows shown by the sold lines will generate money flows of income and expenditure shown by the broken lines.

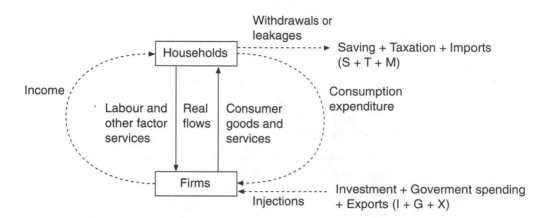

Fig. 14.4 The circular flow of income

When households consume all the income they receive, the circular flow of income is complete and the level of income circulating between households and firms represents an equilibrium, but if households plan to save part of the income received, the circular flow is broken. In Fig. 14.4 saving is shown as a leakage or withdrawal of demand from the circular flow of income, whereas investment spending by firms is shown as an injection of demand into the flow. Government spending and exports are also injections of demand, while taxation and imports are additional leakages or withdrawals from the circular flow of income.

Fig. 14.4 shows that the circular flow of income is complete, and thereby in equilibrium, only when withdrawals of demand out of the circular flow equal injections into the flow i.e. when: saving + taxation + imports = investment + government spending + exports or:

$$S + T + M = I + G + X$$
(planned withdrawals   (planned injections)
or leakages)

$S + T + M = I + G + X$ is the alternative way of writing the equilibrium equation for national income.

Fig. 14.5 illustrates what happens when planned injections into the circular flow of income do not equal planned withdrawals or leakages of demand out of the system. The upper panel of the diagram is identical to Fig. 14.3, but the lower panel includes two lines which show leakages or withdrawals of demand out of, and injections of demand into, the circular flow of income. Equilibrium income Y^* is shown where the withdrawals curve (W) crosses the injections curve (J). At the income level Y_1, injections of spending into the flow of income exceed leakages out of the flow (W < J). The net injection of demand causes the income circulating round the economy to rise. Conversely, when W > J as at income level Y_2, the net withdrawal of demand drains income from the system. The flow of income around the economy thus rises or falls (depending on whether W < J or W > J) until equilibrium is attained at income level Y^*, where W = J.

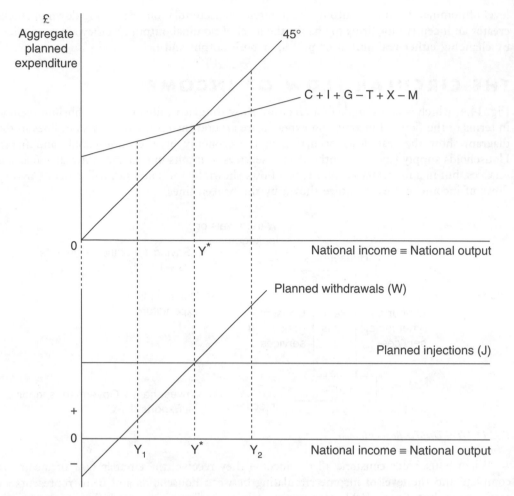

Fig. 14.5 The two ways of showing equilibrium national income
(a) In the upper panel: $Y = C + I + G - T + X - M$
(b) In the lower panel: $S + T + M = I + G + X$ or $W = J$

MONEY NATIONAL INCOME AND REAL NATIONAL INCOME

So far we have assumed that both aggregate expenditure and national income (Y) are measured in money or nominal terms. We now need to distinguish money national income from real national income. We shall follow the convention of using upper case or capital letters for nominal variables, and lower case letters for real variables. **Real national income (y)** is the physical output of new goods and services produced in the economy in a year. **Nominal or money national income (Y)** measures this real income or output at the current price level (P). The relationship between nominal and real income is expressed in the identity:

$$y \equiv \frac{Y}{P} \quad \text{or:} \quad Y \equiv Py$$

Nominal national income (Y) can rise either if real output increases, usually causing employment to increase as well, or if the price level rises and inflation takes place.

14.2 CONSUMPTION AND SAVING

CONSUMPTION AND THE LEVEL OF INCOME

If you refer back to Fig. 14.3 in the first unit of this chapter, you will see that aggregate expenditure rises as income increases, but it does so at a slower rate. One of the main explanations for this lies in the behaviour of aggregate consumption spending in the economy. Consumption is the main component of aggregate expenditure, accounting for around 70% of total demand in the economy. It follows that the factors which influence aggregate consumption spending by households must be the most important determinants of the overall level of aggregate expenditure in the economy.

There is general agreement that income, and particularly disposable income, is a major determinant of consumption. In his *General Theory* published in 1936, Keynes wrote: '*The fundamental psychological law, upon which we are entitled to depend with great confidence... is that men are disposed, as a rule and on average, to increase their consumption as their income increases, but not by as much as the increase in their income.*' Using functional notation, we may state the **Keynesian consumption theory** in the following equation:

$$C = f(Y)$$

More specifically, Keynes believed that although **aggregate planned consumption (C)** rises as income rises, it rises at a slower rate than income so that at high levels of income planned consumption is less than income and planned saving is positive.

AUTONOMOUS AND INCOME-INDUCED CONSUMPTION

The equation $C = f(Y)$ is very general, telling us no more than that consumption is assumed to be determined mainly by income. We shall now write the consumption function in more detail as :

$$C = a + cY$$

Written in this way, the equation for the consumption function shows aggregate consumption as comprising two elements: autonomous consumption and income-induced consumption. **Autonomous consumption** is the part of total consumption which is unaffected by the level of income, i.e. it is constant at all levels of income. The value of autonomous consumption is thus determined by influences upon consumption other than the level of income. We explain these at the end of this unit. In Fig. 14.6 the value of autonomous consumption is indicated by the distance (**a**) drawn on the vertical axis of the diagram. **Income-induced consumption** is measured by (**cY**), **c** being the slope of the consumption function. Income-induced consumption is the part of consumption that varies with the level of income.

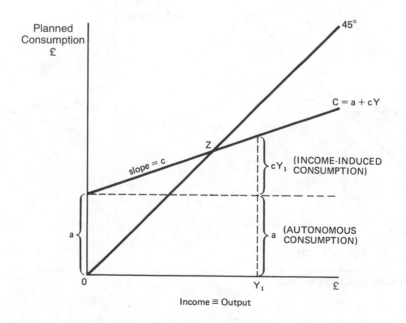

Fig. 14.6 The Keynesian consumption function

THE PROPENSITY TO CONSUME

At this point it is useful to introduce the terms the propensity to consume and the propensity to save which economists use to measure **planned consumption and saving as a ratio of income**. At any level of income (Y), the **average propensity to consume (APC)** measures total planned consumption (C) as a ratio of the level of income. Likewise, the **average propensity to save (APS)** measures total planned saving (S) as a ratio of income.

Since it is very easy to confuse the average propensity to consume or APC with the **marginal propensity to consume (MPC)**, make sure that you learn the distinction between the two concepts. The MPC measures a **change in planned consumption as a ratio of change in the level of income**. The **marginal propensity to save (MPS)** measures the **change in planned saving as a ratio of a change in income**. To illustrate the propensities to consume and save, consider a man who plans to spend £8 out of an income of £10. In these circumstances his APC is 0.8 and his APS is 0.2. If the man's income increases to £11 and he plans to spend 60 pence of the additional pound, his MPC and MPS will be respectively, 0.6 and 0.4.

Fig. 14.7 shows the average propensity to consume falling as income rises. At low levels of income such as Y_1, households plan to consume an amount which exceeds their income; hence the APC is greater than unity (APC > 1). For all levels of income at which the consumption function lies above the 45° line, the APC exceeds unity. You will notice that as income rises, the APC falls to unity at Y_2, the level of income at which the consumption function crosses the 45° line, before falling below unity at all higher levels of income where the consumption function lies below the 45° line. Although in Fig. 14.7a, the average propensity to consume falls as income rises, the marginal propensity to consume remains constant. This is because the **marginal propensity to consume is the slope of the consumption function**, represented by the symbol (c) in the equation of the consumption function:

$$C = a + cY$$

A linear (i.e. straight line) consumption function, which Fig. 14.7a depicts, has a constant slope at all levels of income. This is not very realistic. It is probably more realistic to expect a rich person to consume a smaller percentage of an extra £ of income than a poor person, in which case the marginal propensity to consume should fall as income rises. If this is the case the consumption function will be non-linear or curved as in Fig. 14.7b.

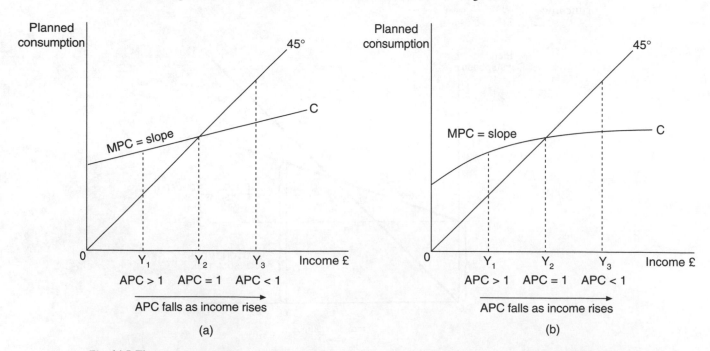

Fig. 14.7 The average propensity to consume (APC) and the marginal propensity to consume (MPC): (a) for a linear consumption function, (b) for a non-linear consumption function

THE SAVINGS FUNCTION

Saving is defined as income not consumed. If households plan to consume a smaller part of their income, the proportion they plan to save must rise. Fig. 14.8 shows how a savings function can be derived from a Keynesian consumption function by subtracting planned consumption from income at every level of income. The equation of the linear savings function is:

$$S = -a + s\,Y$$

The term ($-a$) represents **autonomous (negative) saving** or **dissaving**, while (**s**), the slope of the savings function, is the **marginal propensity to save**. At levels of income below Y_2, households plan to dissave – either by borrowing or by running down previously accumulated stocks of saving – in order to finance consumption plans which are in excess of the level of income. Y_2 is the level of income at which planned consumption equals income and planned saving is zero. Notice that the savings function crosses the zero axis at Y_2 immediately below the point at which the consumption function crosses the 45° line. At all levels of income above Y_2, planned savings are positive (i.e. greater than zero) because at these higher levels of income, households no longer intend to spend all their income on consumption.

The average propensity to save (APS) thus rises as income rises, becoming positive as saving replaces dissaving, but the marginal propensity to save (MPS) or the slope of the savings function remains constant, providing the consumption and savings functions are linear. We would need a non-linear savings function, with the slope becoming steeper as income rises, to show that the marginal propensity to save increasing at higher levels of income.

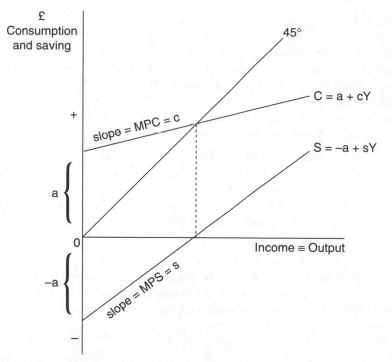

Fig. 14.8 Deriving a savings function from a consumption function

THE LIFE-CYCLE THEORY OF CONSUMPTION

The Keynesian consumption theory just described explains consumption and saving in terms of *current* income, i.e. income received this year. However, it is more realistic to assume that an individual makes consumption and savings decisions taking into account some notion of *expected income* over a much longer time period, perhaps extending over the individual's remaining lifetime. Many people save early in their working lives to finance house purchase, and then continue to save to finance retirement or to protect dependents against the financial problems that would result from the saver's early death. This type of saving is called **contractual saving** which occurs when an individual makes a contract to save regularly with a financial institution such as a pension fund. Contractual saving is usually undertaken with a **long-term motive** in mind. For many people contractual saving takes place at regular intervals over a number of years, to be followed in later years by dissaving when a house is purchased or upon retirement. People plan their contractual savings on the basis of a long-term view of expected life-time income, and of likely spending plans over the remaining length of an expected life-cycle. Temporary fluctuations in yearly income generally have little effect on the contractual savings that are regularly contributed to pension schemes and to the purchase of life insurance policies.

OTHER INFLUENCES UPON CONSUMPTION AND SAVING

There are many other influences upon consumption and saving besides current and expected income. These include:

❶ **The distribution of income**. As we saw earlier, the marginal propensity to consume is likely to be greater at lower levels of income. At any overall level of aggregate income, a redistribution of income from rich to poor is therefore likely to increase consumption and to reduce saving.

❷ **The rate of interest**. This is the reward for saving. The higher the rate of interest, the greater the attraction of saving and foregoing present consumption. Therefore saving increases at higher rates of interest and consumption falls.

❸ **Wealth**. The stock of personal wealth, as well as the flow of income, influences consumption and saving decisions. As people become wealthier, their consumption increases. The state of **consumer confidence** is a closely related factor. People usually consume a larger fraction of their income, and save less, when they feel optimistic about the future. This is the so-called feel-good factor which can encourage consumption and reduce saving in the upswing of the business cycle. Conversely, when people are pessimistic about the future, as in a recession, a feel-bad factor operates, which tends to depress consumption.

❹ **Expectations of future inflation**. The uncertainty caused by rising inflation can increase precautionary saving and reduce consumption. Sometimes however, people's expectations of higher future inflation may have the opposite effect. Households may decide to bring forward consumption decisions by spending now on consumer durables such as cars or TV sets, thereby avoiding expected future price increases.

❺ **The availability of credit**. Besides the rate of interest, other aspects of monetary policy, such as controls on bank lending and hire-purchase controls affect consumption. If credit is easily and cheaply available, consumption is likely to increase at all levels of income as people supplement current income by borrowing on credit created by the banking system. A tight monetary policy, on the other hand, will reduce consumption.

14.3 INVESTMENT

THE DISTINCTION BETWEEN INVESTMENT AND SAVING

In everyday speech, the two terms investment and saving are often used interchangeably, as if the words mean the same thing. The word investment is often used to describe a situation in which a person invests in stocks or shares, paintings or antiques. Economists, however, use the two words in different ways. As we noted in the previous unit, **saving** is simply income which is not consumed. **Investment** must involve the purchase – usually by firms – of real resources which form part of the economy's **capital stock** and **productive potential**. Since investments in second-hand shares, or in most works of art, involve merely the transfer of ownership of existing assets from one person to another, and *not* the production of new productive assets, they should not be regarded as investment in the economist's meaning of the word.

Economic investment can be of two types:

- **investment in fixed capital**, such as new factories or plant and **social capital** such as roads or publicly-owned hospitals;

- and **inventory investment** in stocks of raw materials or **variable capital**.

Unit 14.1 explained that capital is a **stock** concept, and investment is a **flow**. The **national capital stock** can be measured at any particular point of time. It represents the total of all the nation's capital goods, of all types, which are still in existence and capable of production. By contrast, we measure the flow of investment over a period of time, usually a year. A country's **gross investment** includes: replacement investment (or depreciation) which simply maintains the size of the existing capital stock by replacing worn-out capital, and net investment which adds to the capital stock, thereby increasing productive potential. A country's net investment is the engine of economic growth.

THE MARGINAL EFFICIENCY OF CAPITAL

Investment is a much more volatile or unstable component of aggregate demand in the economy than aggregate consumption expenditure. Changes in investment spending by firms are a major cause of the cyclical fluctuations in output known as the **business cycle**. The **marginal efficiency of capital (MEC)** theory helps to explain why investment spending is so volatile.

Fig. 14.9 illustrates how the aggregate level of investment is determined according to the MEC theory. The two main determinants of investment in the MEC theory are the **expected future productivity** of investment projects not yet undertaken, and the **cost of borrowing** or rate of interest. At any point of time, there will be thousands, if not millions, of potential investment projects not yet undertaken in the economy. Each of these potential investment projects will have its own expected future rate of return or productivity, measured by the symbol **i**. If this expected rate of return were to be calculated for each and every possible capital project available to all the business enterprises in the economy, we could, in principle, rank the investments in descending order of expected future yields. The resulted downward-sloping curve drawn in Fig. 14.9 is known as the **marginal efficiency of capital curve**.

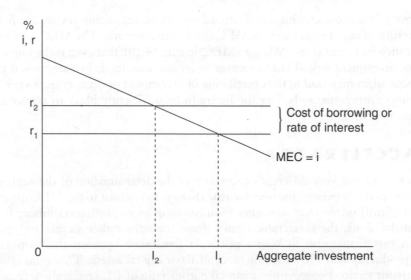

Fig. 14.9 The marginal efficiency of capital theory of investment

We now assume that the cost of borrowing or rate of interest is determined in the money markets by forces outside the control of businessmen. Taking the rate of interest as given at r_1, the equilibrium level of aggregate investment I_1 is determined in Fig. 14.9 at the point where the marginal efficiency of capital equals the cost of borrowing, i.e. where: $i = r$. If conditions in the money market change and the rate of interest rises to r_2, the equilibrium level of investment falls from I_1 to I_2. Potential investment projects considered just worthwhile at r_1 become unprofitable at higher rates of interest such as r_2.

The position of the MEC curve (as distinct from its slope) is determined by businessmen's expectations of an unknown and possibly uncertain future. In his *General Theory*, Keynes stated in colourful language, that in his view, the animal spirits of businessmen are perhaps the key determinant of the level of aggregate investment in the economy. If *animal spirits* are high and business confidence improves, entrepreneurs revise upwards their expectations of future profits yielded by the investments they are considering. The expected rate of return for each prospective investment project improves, and for the economy as a whole, the MEC curve shifts outwards. Fig. 14.10 shows the aggregate level of investment increasing from I_1 to I_2, following a rightward shift of the MEC curve from MEC_1 to MEC_2.

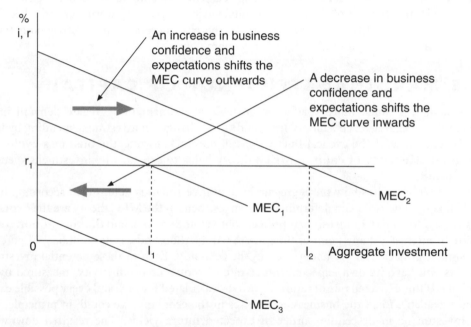

Fig. 14.10 Shifts of the MEC curve in response to changing moods of business optimism and pessimism

If a collapse of business confidence or animal spirits occurs, firms revise downwards the expected return of each project and the MEC curve shifts inwards. The MEC curve may shift inwards to such an extent (from MEC_1 to MEC_3 in Fig. 14.10), that even if the rate of interest fell to zero, investment would fail to recover to its previous level. In a depressed economy, business pessimism may lead to the cancellation of investment projects even at very low costs of borrowing. Entrepreneurs believe the future to be sufficiently bleak to render almost all investments unprofitable.

THE ACCELERATOR

There is a second and very different explanation of the determination of the aggregate level of investment in the economy: the **accelerator theory**. In contrast to the MEC theory, which is based very firmly on the microeconomic foundations of how a profit-maximising firm makes investment decisions, the accelerator theory stems from the rather simple and mechanical assumption that firms wish to keep a relatively fixed ratio between the output they are currently producing and their existing stock of fixed capital assets. This ratio is called the **capital output ratio**. For example, a capital output ratio of 4:1, or simply 4, means that at constant prices £4 of capital is required to produce £1 of output.

In the accelerator theory, the level of current net investment in fixed capital depends on the change in income or output in the previous year:

$$I = v(\Delta Y)$$

or

$$I_t = v(Y_t - Y_{t-1})$$

where I_t is net investment this year, Y_t is current national income, Y_{t-1} is national income last year and v is the capital output ratio. As explained shortly, the capital output ratio, v, is also known as the **accelerator coefficient**, or simply as the **accelerator**.

To illustrate the accelerator principle, we shall assume that no replacement investment is needed and that the average capital output ratio in the economy is 4. Let us now consider the following numerical example:

Year	Net Investment			Current income		Last year's income
t = 1995:	£40m	=	4	(£100m	–	£90m)
t = 1996:	£40m	=	4	(£110m	–	£100m)
t = 1997:	£80m	=	4	(£130m	–	£110m)
t = 1998	£40m	=	4	(£140m	–	£130m)

In each of the four years shown in this example national income grows. Between 1994 (which is year$_{t-1}$ in row 1) and 1995, we have assumed that income grows by £10 million. Via the capital output ratio (4), this growth of income of £10 million induces net investment of £40 million. This level of investment is required to increase the capital stock so that the desired capital output ratio can be maintained at the now higher level of income. In row 2 income continues to grow in 1996 by the same absolute amount, £10 million, thereby inducing a constant level of investment (compared to 1995) of £40 million. But when in 1997, in row 3, the growth of income speeds up or accelerates – from an absolute rise of £10 million to £20 million – the level of investment doubles. This is because, to maintain the ratio between the size of capital stock and the flow of output, the capital stock must be £80 million larger in 1997 than it was in 1996. Finally, we have assumed in row 4 that the growth of income falls back again to £10 million in 1998. Although income is still growing, net investment now declines back to its previous level of £40 million.

This very simple illustration shows how the accelerator theory derives its name. It is **the rate of growth of income and output** rather than the fact that output is growing, that determines whether investment is growing, falling, or at a constant level. According to the acceleration principle:

❶ if income is growing by a **constant** amount each year, net investment is also constant;

❷ if the rate of growth of income speeds up or **accelerates**, net investment increases; and

❸ if the rate of growth of income slows down or **decelerates**, net investment declines.

Relatively slight changes in the rate of growth of income or output can cause quite large absolute rises and falls in investment as firms adjust their capital stocks to the required level. The acceleration principle therefore provides a second explanation (the MEC theory having provided the first explanation) of why investment in capital goods is a more volatile or unstable component of aggregate demand than consumption.

Limitations of the accelerator theory

❶ **The accelerator theory is too mechanical.** It assumes that all firms react to increased demand for their output in the same way. Some firms may wait to see if the higher level of demand is maintained, whilst others may order more plant and machinery than is immediately required.

❷ **The acceleration principle assumes that there is no spare capacity or unused capital.** If when demand for their output increases, firms already possess excess capacity left over from a previous boom in demand, the firms could increase output by utilising this spare capacity, without the need to invest in additional fixed capital.

❸ Demand may increase at a time when the capital goods industries are themselves at full capacity and unable to meet a higher level of investment demand. In this situation, the price of capital goods is likely to rise, and reinforced by the unavailability of capital goods, this creates an incentive for firms to economise in the use of capital and switch to more labour-intensive methods of production. The value of the capital output ratio will fall, with the result that firms can increase output to meet the new levels of demand without necessarily investing in much more capital.

OTHER INFLUENCES UPON INVESTMENT

Perhaps the best approach to explaining investment is to accept that no one single theory can completely explain why businessmen invest in certain capital projects and not in others. Other determinants of investment (besides the acceleration principle, the cost of borrowing and the role of business expectations) might include

- the **relative prices of capital and labour**;
- the **nature of technical progress**;
- the **adequacy of financial institutions** in the supply of investment funds; and
- the **impact of government policies** and activities upon investment by the private sector.

14.4 THE NATIONAL INCOME MULTIPLIER

THE MEANING OF A MULTIPLIER

In this final unit of the chapter, we explain an important way in which the level of national income responds to a change in aggregate demand or expenditure. A **multiplier** exists whenever a change in one variable induces or causes **multiple and successive stages of change** in a second variable. Each succeeding stage of change is usually smaller than the previous one so that the total change induced in the multiplier process comes effectively to an end when further stages of change approach zero. We can calculate the value of a multiplier by dividing the total change induced in the second variable by the size of the initial change in the first variable. For example, a multiplier of 8 tells us that an increase in the first variable will cause successive stages of change in the second variable which are eight times greater in total than the initial triggering change.

THE SIMPLE MULTIPLIER

In order to illustrate the multiplier process, we shall assume for convenience that the values of all the components of aggregate demand are fixed in the sense that they don't vary with the level of income and output in the economy. The one exception is consumption which varies positively with income. We shall also assume that the marginal propensity to consume (MPC) is 0.8 for all households at all levels of income. This of course means that the marginal propensity to save (MPS) must be 0.2. **Saving** is thus the only **income-induced leakage** or withdrawal of demand in our economy, and whenever income increases by £10, consumption spending increases by £8 and £2 is saved. Finally, we shall assume that a margin of spare capacity and unemployed labour exists in the economy which the government wishes to reduce.

According to Keynesian theory, the government can increase real income and output, and reduce unemployment, by deliberate deficit financing. As Chapter 13 explains, deficit financing occurs when the government increases public sector expenditure so that government spending exceeds income from taxes and other sources of revenue. The government could, for example, increase unemployment pay, welfare benefits and other transfer incomes, or transfers to industry such as regional aid. Alternatively, it might invest in public works or social capital, for example in hospital building or road construction. Fig. 14.11 illustrates an increase in public spending of £1 billion, spent for example on the renewal of sewage systems or on a similar urban infrastructure regeneration programme.

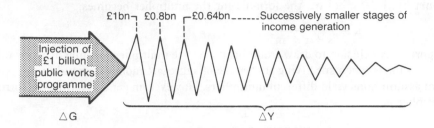

Fig. 14.11 The multiplier process when the marginal propensity to consume is 0.8

We shall assume that the increase in public spending is received as income by building workers who, like everybody in the economy, spend eighty pence of every pound of income on consumption. Since we are assuming that imports and taxation are constant at every level of income, this means that at the second stage, £800 million of the £1 billion income initially received by the building workers is spent within the economy on consumer goods and services, with the remaining £200 million leaking into unspent savings. At the third stage, people employed in the consumer goods industries spend 0.8 of the £800 million incomes received at the second stage of income generation. Further stages of income generation then occur, with each successive stage being 0.8 of the previous stage. Each stage is smaller than the preceding stage to the extent that part of income leaks into savings. Assuming that nothing else changes in the time taken for the process to work through the economy, the eventual increase in income resulting from the initial injection of government spending is the sum of all the stages of income generation. The sum of the successive stages is, of course, greater than, or a multiple of, the initial increase in government spending which triggered the multiplier process. The value of the government spending multiplier equals:

$$\frac{\text{change in income}}{\text{initial change in government spending}}$$

Providing that consumption is the only income-related component of aggregate demand (with saving being the only income-induced leakage of demand from the circular flow of income), the value of the multiplier depends on the values of the marginal propensities to consume and save. In this example, the formula for the multiplier is:

$$k = \frac{1}{1 - c}$$

where **k** is the symbol for the multiplier and **c** is the marginal propensity to consume (MPC)

or:
$$k = \frac{1}{s}$$
where **s** is the marginal propensity to save (MPS)

The formula reflects the fact that at each succeeding stage of the multiplier process, a fraction of income, determined by the MPS, leaks into saving and is not available for consumption at the next stage of income generation. The larger the MPC (and the smaller the MPS), the larger is the value of the multiplier. In our example, the value of the multiplier is 5

(i.e. $\frac{1}{1 - 0.8}$ or $\frac{1}{0.2}$)

indicating that an initial increase in government spending of £1 billion, financed by a budget deficit, will subsequently increase money national income by £5 billion in total.

A MORE REALISTIC MULTIPLIER

When deriving the simple multiplier, we assumed that saving is the only leakage of demand which varies with the level of income, i.e. which is income-induced. This is unrealistic. The other two leakages of demand out of the circular flow of income, taxation and imports, are also likely to vary with income. The amount of income leaking out of the circular flow and not being spent on consumption, will depend not only on saving and the MPS, but on the marginal rate at which income taxes are levied and the marginal propensity to import. If we represent the **marginal rate of income tax** by the symbol **t** and the **marginal propensity to import** by the symbol **m**, the formula for the multiplier becomes:

$$k = \frac{1}{s + t + m}$$

One important conclusion to draw from this is that the multiplier formula depends upon the assumptions made when specifying the nature of aggregate money demand in the economy. Different assumptions yield different multipliers. However, in general terms, the formula for the multiplier is:

$$k = \frac{1}{\text{marginal change in net income-induced leakages of demand}}$$

DIFFERENT NATIONAL INCOME MULTIPLIERS

So far a multiplier process resulting from an initial change in government spending has been explained. This is often called the **government spending multiplier**. It is important to note, however that a change in *any* of the components of aggregate money demand can induce multiple stages of change in the level of money national income or output. The national income multiplier is a generic term, covering the multiplier effects arising from a change in any of the components of aggregate demand. Besides the government spending multiplier, we can recognise the **autonomous consumption multiplier**, the **investment multiplier**, the **tax multiplier**, the **export multiplier**, and the **import multiplier**, as examples of specific national income multipliers. The government spending and tax multipliers are sometimes called **fiscal policy multipliers**, and the export and import multipliers are called **foreign trade multipliers**.

MULTIPLIER-ACCELERATOR INTERACTION

By bringing together the **multiplier theory** and the **accelerator theory** of investment, it is possible to construct a **dynamic macroeconomic theory** which models changes in income and output through time. Writing the investment multiplier relationship as:

$$\Delta Y = k\,(\Delta I)$$

and the accelerator relationship as

$$I = v\,(\Delta Y)$$

where **k** is the investment multiplier and **v** is the accelerator, we can bring the two together in a **multiplier-accelerator dynamic model** of output growth. In essence:

An initial multiplier effect, triggered by some event increasing investment (or by some other event leading to an increase in aggregate demand) causes income to rise, which in turn induces, via the accelerator, a feed-back to investment leading to a further multiplier effect, and so on. Continuing multiplier-accelerator interaction allows us to plot the dynamic growth path of the economy. Multiplier-accelerator interactions also provide a method of explaining the business cycles which are a feature of most modern economies.

Chapter roundup

This chapter has introduced and explained one of the two macroeconomic models of the economy that A Level candidates need to know: the Keynesian income-expenditure model of the economy. The main features of this model can be illustrated on 45° line and circular flow diagrams. Chapter 16 introduces and explains a second macroeconomic model of the economy, the aggregate demand/aggregate supply model (AD/AS model), which in recent years has tended to replace the income–expenditure model as the main framework for analysing macroeconomic problems and policy. Check the syllabus of your examining board: most syllabuses still require knowledge of both models, but the ULEAC and AEB syllabuses now only specify the AD/AS model. However, you could still use the income–expenditure model to answer generally worded questions, for example on the effects of an increase in government expenditure upon the economy.

Illustrative questions and answers

1 Essay Question

'GNP statistics are useful for comparing the economic welfare of developed countries, but not for comparisons of welfare between developed and less developed countries.' Discuss.

(25)

Oxford

Tutorial note

In the chapter we have briefly surveyed some of the limitations of national income statistics, both with regard to comparisons over time and between different countries. We have indicated how comparisons of GNP per head between countries are misleading if the relative importance of the non-monetised economy is greatly different. Related to this are differences in the degree of statistical sophistication in the collection of data, particularly between developed and developing countries, and a lack of international uniformity in methods of classifying and categorising the national accounts. As we have also indicated, further problems occur when making comparisons because different commodities are consumed in different countries.

A common method of comparing GNP per capita in different countries is to convert the GNP figures for each country into a common currency such as the US dollar. However, this calculation suffers from the assumption that the exchange rates between local currencies and the $ are correctly valued in the sense that a dollar's worth of output in one country becomes immediately and accurately comparable with a dollar's worth of output in another country. This can never be so. The purchasing power of a currency over domestically produced goods and services which do not enter into international trade or compete domestically with imports, may be completely different from the currency's purchasing power over imported goods. Exchange rate changes only reflect the price changes of internationally traded goods such as automobiles. Thus, in so far that there is a much wider gap in developing countries than in developed countries between price changes of internationally traded and non-traded goods, GNP figures measured in US dollars tend to underestimate real levels of income and output in developing economies. A solution to this problem is to make comparisons of GDP figures between countries using specially constructed exchange rates that take into account differences in the internal price levels of non-traded goods and consumption patterns.

Suggested answer

- Briefly explain the meaning of GNP and related concepts, and indicate your interpretation of the term 'economic welfare'.

- Explain why GNP statistics are used as a measure of welfare and standards of living, but describe their limitations.

- Suggest that these limitations or weaknesses become greater, so even more caution must be used, when making comparisons between countries.

- Explain the factors which make comparison of GDP statistics of developed and developing economies especially misleading.

2 Data Question

Table 1

	Total personal disposable income (£bn)	Consumers' expenditure (£bn)	Saving ratio %
1978	113.1	100.2	11.4
1979	35.7	118.7	12.6
1980	160.0	137.9	13.8
1981	176.1	153.6	12.8
1982	191.3	168.5	11.9
1983	206.1	184.6	10.4
1984	220.9	197.5	10.6
1985	238.8	215.5	9.7
1986	256.9	237.4	7.6
1987	275.7	259.3	5.9
1988	303.4	289.8	4.5

(Source: *An Economic Profile of Britain, 1989*, Lloyds Bank)

Table 1 gives data relating to personal income, expenditure and saving in Great Britain.

(a) What is meant by the term 'total personal disposable income'? (2)

(b) Calculate the average propensity to consume in 1978. (2)

(c) Calculate the marginal propensity to consume between 1987 and 1988. Comment on your result. (4)

(d) (i) What do you understand by the term 'saving ratio'? (2)
    (ii) Analyse the factors which may have influenced the trends in saving and consumption during the period 1978–88. (6)

(e) Examine the possible effects of the falling saving ratio on:
    (i) the rate of inflation;
    (ii) the Balance of Payments. (4)

ULEAC

Tutorial note

(a) In the UK national income statistics, the distinction is made between *original, gross, disposable* and *final* income. Initially households receive *original income* from various sources, mainly employment, occupational pensions which are really deferred pay, and investments in shares, etc. The addition of cash benefits or *transfers* given by the state, such as the state pension and unemployment pay, gives *gross income*. The subtraction of direct taxes such as income tax and National Insurance contributions, and the council tax, would yield *disposable income.*' Total personal disposable income' is therefore the aggregation of the disposable income of all UK residents – but individuals, not companies in the 'corporate sector' of the economy. (In fact we can take the classification two stages further: deducting indirect taxes such as VAT from *disposable income* yields *post-tax income*. *Final income* is then calculated by adding the imputed value of the benefits people receive from services consumed 'in kind', such as education and health care, provided by the state.)

(b) There is in fact a minor inaccuracy in questions (b) and (c). As we have explained in this chapter, *propensities* to consume and save are '*ex ante*' concepts, i.e. they measure what people *wish* or *plan* to do, before the event. But the data in the table are '*ex post*', i.e. a measurement after the event of how much households *have ended up* consuming (*actual* or *realised consumption*). Nevertheless, since by their nature, the average and marginal propensities cannot be measured directly, '*ex post*' data such as that in the table are often used for their calculation. Thus, the ratio of consumers' expenditure (column 2) to total personal disposable income (column 1), gives an estimate of the APC for each of the years, after the deduction of income tax.

(c) Calculate the MPC in a similar way, except make sure you first deduct the 1987 levels of consumers' expenditure and personal disposable income from their 1988 levels. This gives you the changes between the two years from which you can complete the calculation of the MPC. You will find that, according to the data, the MPC was greater than 1 between 1987 and 1988 indicating that consumption was rising by a greater absolute amount than income.

(d) (i) Unlike the '*ex ante*' average propensity to save, the 'saving ratio' is an '*ex post*' concept, measuring total realised savings as a ratio of total personal disposable income. But for the reason we have explained (in the context of consumers' expenditure and the APC), the savings ratio is often used as a measure of the APS.

    (ii) Explain how high inflation influenced saving around 1980: people needed to save to restore the real value of their stock of accumulated saving which was being eroded by high inflation. Also, high inflation added to uncertainty, which promoted saving. Go on to explain how saving fell during the Lawson boom of the late 1980s.

(e) In the late 1980s, the falling savings ratio boosted consumer demand (as your calculation of the MPC in 1988 indicates). This would have added to demand-pull inflationary pressures during the 'Lawson boom', and it also 'sucked' imports into the economy via the marginal propensity to import, contributing to a rapidly deteriorating balance of payments on current account.

Question bank

1 (a) What are the main determinants of consumption in an economy? (15)

    (b) Discuss the possible effects of an increase in consumption upon an economy.
(10)
WJEC

Pitfalls

Do not confuse aggregate consumption with the microeconomic theory of demand for a particular good or service which was explained in Chapter 3. With part (a), there is a danger of restricting your answer to a list of determinants; you must explain briefly the various points you introduce. Also, do not confuse causes (the subject of part (a)) with effects (the subject of part (b)).

Key points

Define consumption, and briefly state its main determinants: current income, expected future income, wealth, the rate of interest etc. Expand on at least two of these, for example current income and the rate of interest. With part (b) explain that the effects will depend on the supply side of the economy. If there is little spare capacity, inflation may be the main effect; otherwise there may be desirable reflationary effects which stimulate output and employment. You might make relevant use of the multiplier theory.

2 (a) What factors influence investment? (12)

    (b) In November 1992 it was reported that the French government cut basic interest rates in the hope of stimulating investment in a weak economy. Assess the likely effects on an economy of stimulating investment. (13)   *Cambridge*

Pitfalls

As mentioned in the chapter, there is a danger of confusing investment with saving. Despite the scenario, part (b) is not actually about the French economy. You need no specialist knowledge of France or indeed of any other economy, though an ability to use evidence to back up the points you make will be an advantage.

Key points

Structure your answer to part (a) in much the same way as you dealt with consumption in the previous question, explaining at least one theory of investment (e.g. the marginal efficiency of capital theory) and briefly stating other influences upon investment. An immediate effect of stimulating investment will be to reduce current consumption. Also develop the likely long-term effects of faster economic growth, improved competitiveness, and the potential for higher levels of consumption and living standards in the future.

3 (a) Explain what is meant by the equilibrium level of national income. Describe the multiplier process as national income changes. (13)

   (b) How would the outcome of the multiplier process be affected by (i) an increase in the level of savings and (ii) an increase in the level of exports? (12)   *Cambridge*

Pitfalls

You must not confuse the national income multiplier (the subject of this question) and the money multiplier. Both are of great significance for economic policy. The money multiplier, which is significant in the analysis of monetary policy, measures the relationship between a change in the supply of notes and coins or cash to the banking system and the resulting change in total bank deposits in the economy. As a broad generalisation, the size and stability of the money multiplier influences the power and effectiveness of monetary policy, whereas the size of the national income multiplier is significant for the government's fiscal policy.

Key points

State that national income is in equilibrium when aggregate planned expenditure equals the level of national income or output, then briefly explain the process through which disequilibrium is eliminated and equilibrium attained. Introduce the multiplier, defining the concept, before explaining how a change in aggregate demand disturbs a previously-attained equilibrium, causing the level of national income to rise or fall until equilibrium has been restored at a new level of national income. With part (b), you must explain that saving is a leakage of demand, while exports are an injection. An increase in saving will reduce the equilibrium level of national income via the multiplier, while an increase in exports will trigger a positive multiplier effect. A change in the marginal propensity to save would also alter the value of the multiplier.

CHAPTER 15

UNEMPLOYMENT AND INFLATION

Units in this chapter

Chapter objectives

Over the last thirty years, large scale **unemployment** and **inflation** have been two of the most serious economic problems facing governments throughout the world. Accelerating and highly variable rates of inflation caused acute problems in almost every developing and developed country in the non-Communist world in the 1970s. Although the rate of inflation fell considerably in developed economies during the 1980s, inflation climbed again in the UK in the mid-1980s, and fears of a return to rapid inflation persist and continue to influence economic behaviour and government policy. Unacceptably high inflation rates are also endemic in many countries of the developing world, but while in countries such as the United Kingdom, the problem of inflation lessened in the recession of the early 1990s, large scale unemployment grew to levels not seen since the Great Depression of the 1930s. This chapter examines the causes of unemployment and inflation and investigates the policies recommended by Keynesian and free-market economists for reducing and possibly eliminating these twin evils.

15.1   UNEMPLOYMENT

KEYNESIAN AND FREE-MARKET APPROACHES TO UNEMPLOYMENT

The main types of unemployment which economists have identified will now be surveyed. We must realise however, that there is considerable disagreement, particularly between Keynesian economists and their opponents, about the significance and even the existence of some of the types of unemployment which we list.

From a Keynesian perspective of employment, an important distinction is made between the concepts of **voluntary** and **involuntary unemployment**. Keynesians explain at least a part of mass unemployment in terms of **deficient aggregate demand**, which is outside the influence and control of workers. Keynesians believe demand-deficient unemployment to be involuntary. By contrast, economists of the neo-classical or free-market school, who include most modern **monetarists** and **supply-side economists**, reject the possibility of demand-deficient unemployment, except possibly as a temporary phenomenon which is soon corrected by market forces, providing only that markets are sufficiently competitive. For these anti-Keynesian economists, much of modern unemployment is voluntary, explained by workers choosing higher wages and fewer jobs.

CAUSES OF UNEMPLOYMENT

Frictional unemployment

Frictional unemployment results from frictions in the labour market which create a delay or time-lag during which a worker is unemployed when moving from one job to another. Note that our definition of frictional unemployment assumes that a job vacancy exists and that a friction in the job market, caused by either the **geographical** or the **occupational immobility of labour**, prevents an unemployed worker from filling the vacancy. It follows therefore, that the number of unfilled job vacancies which exist can be used as a measure of the level of frictional unemployment in the economy. In recent years, neo-classical or anti-Keynesian economists have revived the theory of frictional unemployment, arguing that much current and recent unemployment in the UK is frictional in nature. They believe that the availability and level of welfare benefits provided by the state, encourages newly laid-off worker to be unrealistic in their wage demands. Instead of accepting work, albeit at lower rates of pay, and filling the job vacancies that exist in the labour market, the newly unemployed often decide to remain frictionally unemployed, living off the state safety net of welfare benefits.

Casual and seasonal unemployment

Casual unemployment is really just a special case of frictional unemployment, which occurs when workers are laid-off on a short-term basis in trades such as tourism, agriculture, catering and building. When casual unemployment results from regular fluctuations in weather conditions or demand, it is called seasonal unemployment.

Structural unemployment

This type of unemployment results from the **structural decline of industries**, unable to compete or adapt in the face of either changing demand and new products, or changing ways of producing existing products and the emergence of more efficient competitors in other countries. The **growth of international competition** has been a particularly important cause of structural unemployment. During the post-Second World War era from the 1950s to the 1970s, structural unemployment in the UK was regionally concentrated in areas where industries such as textiles and shipbuilding were suffering structural decline, so structural unemployment was largely regional. Such **regional unemployment** caused by the decline of sunset industries was more than offset by the growth of employment elsewhere in the UK in sunrise industries which took the place of the declining industries. However, in the severe recession of the early 1980s and again in the early 1990s, structural unemployment affected almost all regions in the UK as the **de-industrialisation process** spread right across the manufacturing base. Structural unemployment has become perhaps the major cause of large scale unemployment in the 1980s and 1990s.

Technological unemployment

This can be regarded as a special case of structural unemployment which results from the successful growth of new industries using labour-saving technology such as **automation**. In contrast to mechanisation which has usually *increased* the overall demand for labour, automation can lessen the demand for labour because it means that machines (such as robots) rather than men, operate other machines. Whereas the growth of **mechanised industry** increases employment, **automation** of production can lead to the shedding of labour even when industry output is expanding.

Real-wage or classical unemployment

Free-market or neo-classical economists believe that a large part of the high level of unemployment in the 1920s and 1930s was caused by excessively high real wages in labour markets which were insufficiently competitive for market forces to eliminate the problem. In recent years the view that a large part of modern unemployment in the UK, especially **youth unemployment**, has been caused by too high a level of real wages has been an important part of the supply-side explanation of unemployment. We examine this cause of unemployment in more detail later in this unit.

Keynesian or demand-deficient unemployment

Keynesian economists believe that **deficient aggregate demand** was a major cause of persistent mass unemployment in the 1920s and 1930s. Economists generally agree that temporary unemployment (called **cyclical unemployment**) may be caused by a lack of demand in the downswing of the business cycle. However, Keynesians go further, arguing that the economy can settle into an **under-full employment equilibrium** caused by a continuing lack of effective aggregate demand.

Residual unemployment

This is rather a 'catch-all' category covering any other possible cause of unemployment. Residual unemployment may include the **unemployable** and the **workshy**. It is now recognised in the UK that long-term unemployment in itself may make a worker unemployable when job-skills and work habits are eroded and when employers perceive that workers with more recent job experience present fewer risks. The existence of the workshy represents a form of voluntary unemployment. In recent years an **unemployment trap** (which we explained in Chapter 13) has been identified in the United Kingdom. Low-skilled workers become trapped in unemployment when they are better-off living off state benefits than in a poorly-paid job paying tax and National Insurance contributions. In these circumstances it can be perfectly rational for someone with only poor job and wage prospects to choose unemployment and welfare benefits instead.

THE UNEMPLOYED, THE NON-EMPLOYED AND THE ECONOMICALLY INACTIVE

When unemployment is measured, it is usually assumed that the unemployed are economically active in the sense that they want to work and make at least some effort to look for jobs. Since 1979 however, there has been a sharp drop in **male labour force participation** in most of the older or mature developed economies in western Europe and North America. The decline of employment in industries which have traditionally employed male manual workers has been largely to blame, the decline being caused by automation and by the growth of manufacturing in the Newly Industrialising Countries (NICs) of the developing world. In the UK the emergence of the unemployment trap has been an additional contributory factor. As a result of this trend, it has been suggested that those of the registered unemployed who claim unemployment benefit but have given up the search for work should no longer be classified as unemployed. Instead, the **non-employed** – comprising all workers without jobs – should be sub-divided into the **unemployed**, namely those who are available and actively looking for work, with the remainder classified as the **economically inactive**.

SEARCH THEORIES OF UNEMPLOYMENT

The existence of the workshy and of the unemployment trap is closely related to an explanation of frictional unemployment that has become very popular amongst free-market and supply-side economists in recent years. This is the **search theory of unemployment**.

Suppose that a worker earning £500 a week in a skilled occupation loses his job. There are few existing vacancies in his occupation, but we shall assume that there are plenty of vacancies for unskilled workers, with each vacancy offering a wage of around £150 a week. Given this information about the state of the job market, the worker is likely to choose to remain unemployed, at least to start with, rather than to fill a lower-paid vacancy. This is a perfectly rational decision because the wage, and perhaps also the conditions of work and status associated with the job, do not meet his aspirations, and he is uncertain whether better-paid and higher status vacancies exist which he does not know about. The voluntary unemployment the worker chooses can be viewed as a search period spent, hopefully, scanning the labour market for a job which meets his aspirations. There are at least two sets of circumstances that can end both the search period and the worker's voluntary unemployment. On the one hand the worker may find a vacancy for which he is qualified and which meets his initial aspirations. The vacancy might have been there all the time, with the worker unaware of its existence until he had searched the job market, or alternatively, the vacancy might have arisen during the worker's search period, perhaps as a result of a general improvement in the labour market. On the other hand the worker's period of voluntary unemployment may come to an end when he realises that his initial aspirations were too high and that he must settle for a lower-paid and less attractive job.

The longer the search that unemployed workers are prepared to undertake, the greater will be the size of frictional unemployment in the economy. Free-market economists argue however, that as unemployed workers run down their stock of savings, the threat of poverty creates incentives both to search the job market more vigorously, and to reduce personal aspirations more quickly. We have already noted that, in the free-market view, the existence of a state safety net of unemployment pay, redundancy payments and welfare benefits increases frictional unemployment by allowing an unemployed worker to finance a longer voluntary search period. Thus supply-side economists generally recommend the reduction of the real value of welfare benefits for the unemployed, together with the restriction of benefits to those who can prove that they are genuinely looking for work, so as to create incentives for workers to reduce aspirations more quickly and hence to shorten search periods. Cutting the real value of welfare benefits also serves to widen the gap between disposable income in and out of work, thereby reducing or eliminating the unemployment trap. In response to the various arguments presented, the UK government has now restricted the availability of unemployment benefit (renamed **jobseekers' allowance**) to newly-unemployed workers genuinely looking for work. The period during which the unemployed can claim the allowance has also been reduced from one year to six months.

The weakness of the search theory lies in the assumption that unfilled vacancies exist. Although the search theory of unemployment may explain some of the growth of unemployment in the UK in recent years, it cannot explain all unemployment, especially in the parts of the country where industries have collapsed, and it carries the political implication that reductions in welfare benefits will cure unemployment. However, the growth of structural unemployment resulting from the de-industrialisation of manufacturing industry has probably been the most important single cause of the massive growth in unemployment from one million to around three million which occurred in the UK in the early 1980s, and again at the beginning of the 1990s.

THE INSIDER/OUTSIDER THEORY OF UNEMPLOYMENT

Another explanation of unemployment that has become very fashionable in recent years, particularly amongst free-market and supply-side economists, is provided by the insider/outsider theory of the labour market. Trade union members are the **insiders**, while unemployed workers, especially those who allowed their union membership to lapse on losing their jobs, are the **outsiders**. The theory is based on the assumption that unionised workers enjoy higher wages than non-unionised workers, but that this **union mark-up** is achieved at the expense of fewer jobs. Thus the insider/outsider theory is really an extension of the real wage theory of unemployment. The theory argues that however much trade union pay negotiators claim to be concerned about job losses and the prospects of their unemployed members, this is mere lip service. In reality the unions care only about the employment prospects of insiders, i.e. those of their members who are currently employed; they don't really care about the outsiders. The insider/outsider theory suggests that unions may be prepared to push for higher real wages even when unemployment is high, basically because they are unbothered about the outsiders amongst the unemployed.

A CLOSER LOOK AT THE REAL-WAGE OR CLASSICAL THEORY OF UNEMPLOYMENT

We have already noted that before the Great Depression of the 1930s, economists explained unemployment largely in terms of the classical or real-wage theory of unemployment. In more recent years, the real-wage theory has been revived by supply-side economists to explain the high level of unemployment which has persisted in the UK economy. The theory is illustrated in Fig. 15.1, which shows the economy's aggregate labour market. In this diagram, full employment is determined at the wage W_{FE}, where the aggregate demand for labour equals the aggregate supply. Suppose however, that the wage is above W_{FE}, for example at the level W_1. At this wage, employers wish to hire L_1 workers, but a greater number of workers, equal to L_2, would like to supply their labour at this wage. Unless the wage falls, real-wage unemployment equal to $L_2 - L_1$ results.

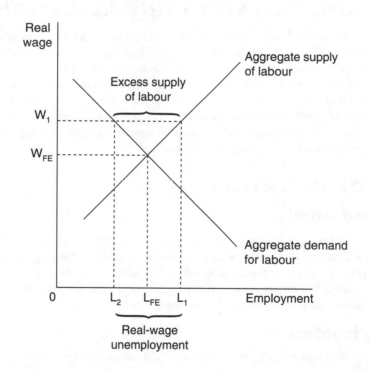

Fig. 15.1 The real-wage theory of unemployment

The real-wage theory explains unemployment in terms of an excess supply of labour at the wage rate prevailing in the market. Free-market economists believe that, as long as the labour market is competitive, classical or real-wage unemployment should only be temporary. Market forces will bid wages down in response to the excess supply of labour, until the number of workers willing to work equals the number that firms wished to hire. However, if the labour market is insufficiently competitive, labour market rigidities may prevent the market mechanism from eliminating real-wage unemployment. Free-market economists argue that trade unions exercising their power as monopoly suppliers of labour, together with the excessive level of (and ease of access to) unemployment benefits, have prevented wages from falling so as to price the unemployed into jobs.

THE NATURAL LEVEL OF UNEMPLOYMENT

Another important element in the explanation of employment and unemployment favoured by anti-Keynesian free-market economists, centres on the concepts of the **natural levels of employment** and unemployment. Fig. 15.1 illustrates the natural level of employment occurring at L_{FE}. However, economists have always accepted that there will be some frictional and structural unemployment in the economy, even when the labour market clears and real-wage unemployment has been eliminated. This minimum level of frictional and structural unemployment is called the natural level of unemployment, though sometimes the term is restricted to frictional unemployment alone, excluding structural unemployment from the definition. It has also been called the **full employment level of unemployment**. The more competitive and adaptable the economy is, then the lower will be this minimum level of unemployment. We shall return to the natural level and rate of unemployment when we cover inflation later in this chapter.

15.2 INFLATION

INFLATION, DEFLATION AND REFLATION

Inflation is usually defined as a **persistent or continuing tendency for the price level to rise**. Although **deflation** is strictly the opposite – a persistent tendency for the price level to fall – the term is usually used in a rather looser way to refer to a reduction in the level of activity or output. In this sense, a deflationary policy reduces the level of aggregate demand in the economy. Some economists find the terms **disinflation** and **disinflationary policy** preferable. Likewise, **reflation** refers to an increase in economic activity and output, and a reflationary policy stimulates aggregate demand. In a sense, inflation is reflation gone wrong, increasing the price level rather than real output.

TYPES OF INFLATION

Suppressed inflation

Although inflation involves the *tendency* for the price level to rise, it is not inevitable that prices will actually rise. Strong governments may successfully introduce tough price controls which prevent the price level from rising, without at the same time abolishing the underlying inflationary process. The **suppression of rising prices** diverts the inflationary process into quantity shortages, queues, waiting-lists and black markets.

Creeping inflation

The inflation rate experienced by most industrialised countries in the 1950s and early 1960s was fairly stable from year to year, averaging less than 5%. However, throughout the period it gradually crept upwards, developing into a stratoinflation in many countries in the late 1960s and early 1970s. In the early 1990s, the UK government had to take care lest the low rate of inflation, achieved by deflating the economy, began to creep upwards once again.

Stratoinflation

Whereas creeping inflations were typical of industrial countries in the postwar period, **stratoinflation** was the experience of developing countries, particularly in Latin America. In a stratoinflation the inflation rate ranges from about 10% to several hundred per cent, and it may be particularly difficult to anticipate.

Hyperinflation

The transition from a creeping inflation to a stratoinflation in the early 1970s raised fears of an acceleration into a **hyperinflation**. The famous German inflation of 1923 was a hyperinflation, and similar but less publicised hyperinflation occurred in other countries in central and eastern Europe at the end of both World Wars and have recently occurred in Eastern Europe, following the break up of the USSR. However, hyperinflations are usually short-lived and they should not be regarded as typical. A hyperinflation usually occurs in a severe political crisis when a government turns to the printing press to create money to pay its debts. Inflation can accelerate to a rate as high as several thousand per cent a year. During hyperinflation, money ceases to be a medium of exchange and a store of value, and normal economic activity may completely break down.

Stagflation (or Slumpflation)

In the 1970s and early 1980s the incidence of both relatively high rates of inflation and increasing unemployment in the developed world led economists to coin the word **stagflation**. It combines stagnation in the economy (low or negative increases in output) with price inflation. As we shall see, its existence made conventional Keynesian demand management policies seem inappropriate and politically damaging as a means of controlling either unemployment or inflation. In the recession of the early 1990s, there was once again a fear of a renewed stagflation affecting the UK economy.

THE ADVERSE EFFECTS OF INFLATION

The seriousness of the adverse effects of inflation greatly depends on whether the inflation is **anticipated** or **unanticipated**. It was relatively easy to anticipate more or less fully the creeping inflation of the 1950s and 1960s. Indeed in these years it was sometimes argued that a mild amount of inflation was harmless or even perhaps beneficial. This was because creeping inflation accompanied an expanding economy and became associated by businessmen with growing markets and healthy profits. This view may well explain why the control of inflation was regarded as a relatively minor policy objective. In contrast, it is very difficult for people fully to anticipate a stratoinflation as the actual inflation rate varies substantially from year to year. The adverse effects will be much more severe and may completely destabilise the economy. Generally speaking, the main adverse effects of inflation are:

❶ It can be unfair. Weaker social groups in society such as old people on fixed pensions lose, while others in stronger bargaining positions gain. This is an example of how inflation affects the distribution of income and wealth. Nevertheless the indexing of pensions has reduced this particular disadvantage of inflation. In the absence of indexation, inflation also raises the average rate of taxation through the process of **fiscal drag** (see Chapter 13).

❷ A second important distributional effect occurs between borrowers and lenders. Inflation tends to redistribute wealth from lenders or creditors to borrowers or debtors. In an inflation the rate of interest may well be below the rate of inflation. This means that lenders are really paying a negative real interest rate to borrowers for the doubtful privilege of lending to them! The biggest borrower of all is usually the government. Inflation can be thought of as a hidden tax that redistributes wealth to the government and reduces the real value of the national debt. This suggests that governments may not always be as keen as they pretend to control inflation completely!

❸ Inflation distorts many types of economic behaviour and imposes costs upon economic agents. It can distort consumer behaviour by causing people to bring forward their purchases if they expect the rate of inflation to accelerate. This would probably affect sales of consumer durables such as washing machines and it might also lead to the hoarding of goods such as groceries. If this were the case the savings ratio might be expected to fall as people borrowed or used up savings in order to finance consumption. However, an interesting feature of the inflation in the 1970s was the sharp rise in the savings ratio. This suggests that greater uncertainty may have caused people to save more. A large part of savings is intended to finance old age and retirement. If the inflation rate suddenly accelerates, existing planned savings become inadequate to finance retirement and people increase their savings to top up or supplement their existing stock of accumulated savings, in an attempt to restore the real value of accumulated savings. However, in response to a much lower and more stable inflation rate, the savings ratio fell dramatically in 1983, causing a rapid growth in consumer expenditure that fuelled, for a time at least, the growth of output and economic recovery. At the beginning of the 1990s, the savings ratio rose again in a 'return to thrift', causing a reduction in consumption spending, which contributed to the severity of the recession experienced in the UK.

④ **Similar uncertainties affect the behaviour of firms and impose costs upon them.** Long-term planning becomes very difficult. Firms may be tempted to divert investment funds out of productive investment into commodity hoarding and speculation. Profit margins may be severely squeezed in a cost inflation and firms can attempt to avoid this by making capital gains on property, land and even fine art and antiques rather than by using their funds in normal production.

⑤ **Shoe leather and menu costs.** In a period of rapid inflation, consumers spend more time and effort shopping around checking on which prices have or have not risen. The extra costs incurred are called *shoe leather* costs. By contrast, *menu* costs are incurred by firms or producers as a result of having to adjust, for example, the costs of revising and reprinting price lists, adjusting slot machines and issuing new catalogues.

⑥ **In a severe stratoinflation money becomes less useful as a medium of exchange and a store of value.** More money may be needed to finance the buying of goods at higher prices, but this is countered by the disadvantages of holding money which is falling in value. In a hyper-inflation the use of money may completely break down and be replaced by less efficient barter. This imposes extra costs on most transactions.

THEORIES OF INFLATION

Table 15.1 provides a summary of the historical development of the major theories of inflation, which will now be examined.

Table 15.1 *The theories of inflation*

1	18th Century to the 1930s: The old **quantity theory of money**
2	1930s: Keynes's *General Theory* explains **deflation** in terms of deficient aggregate demand
3	1940s: Keynes develops his *General Theory* to explain how, in conditions of full employment, excess demand can pull up the price level in a **demand-pull inflation**
4	1950s/1960s: Many Keynesians switch to the **cost-push** or **structuralist theory of inflation**
5	1950s/1960s: Keynesian **demand-pull v cost-push debate** conducted with the aid of the **Phillips curve**.
6	1950s: The early **monetarist theory of inflation**: Milton Friedman's revival of the **quantity theory of money** (the **modern quantity theory**)
7	1968: The incorporation of the role of **expectations** into the inflationary process in the monetarist theory of inflation: the role of **adaptive expectations** in Milton Friedman's **theory of the expectations-augmented Phillips curve**
8	1970s: The apparent breakdown of the Phillips relationship
9	1970s/1980s: The incorporation of the role of **rational expectations** into the inflationary process: the **New Classical school**
10	The current controversy: cost-push or structural explanations of inflation, e.g. post-Keynesian or neo-Keynesian explanations v monetarist and New Classical explanations.

The quantity theory of money

Old theories seldom die; they reappear in a new form to influence a later generation of economists and politicians. This is certainly true of the **quantity theory of money**, which is the oldest theory of inflation. From the 18th century to the 1930s, it was *the* theory of inflation. The quantity theory went out of fashion in the Keynesian era, but modern monetarism has restored the quantity theory to a central place in the current controversy on the causes of inflation.

Early or 'naive' versions of the quantity theory are usually distinguished from the revival of the quantity theory in a more sophisticated form by Milton Friedman in the 1950s. However, all versions of the quantity theory, old and new, form a **special case of demand inflation** in which rising prices are caused by excess demand. The distinguishing characteristic of the quantity theory is the location of the source of excess demand in **monetary** rather than **real forces** – in an excess supply of money created or condoned by the government.

At its simplest, the quantity theory is often stated as 'too much money chasing too few goods'. Indeed to some this is a definition of inflation, though as a definition it rather begs the question of the cause of a rising price level. The theory can also be written as a simple equation:

$$MV = PT$$

This says that the **money supply** times the number of times money changes hands (the **velocity of circulation**) equals the **price level** times the total number of **transactions**. This is the famous **Fisher equation of exchange**, devised by the American economist Irving Fisher. In the Fisher equation, T includes second-hand purchases of goods and services. Strictly these should be omitted from a measure of national income or output, so it is usually better to rewrite the equation of exchange as:

$$MV = Py$$

in which y is a measure of transactions involving currently produced output or real national income. Py is thus money national income. In this form the equation of exchange is known as the **Cambridge equation**.

The equation of exchange illustrates the very important difference between an identity and a behavioural equation. As the equation stands, it is merely an identity or truism implying very little more than that the amount bought always equals the amount sold. To convert the equation into the quantity theory, two strong assumptions have to be made and the theory stands or falls with these assumptions: The price level is determined by the money supply and not vice versa, or:

$$P = f(Ms)$$

where Ms is the money supply, to be distinguished from the demand for money (Md). Keynesians in particular have attacked this assumption. They argue that the money supply passively adapts or accommodates itself to finance the level of transactions taking place at the current price level. To generalise, monetarists believe that the money supply actively determines the price level, whereas Keynesians have argued that the price level determines the money supply. Keynesians agree with what they consider to be the trivial point that an expansion of the money supply is needed if inflation is to occur, but they argue that if the money supply is restricted so that current level of transactions cannot be financed, then a drop in output and employment will occur. Near monies may take on the function of money, thus rendering control of the money supply ineffective. This (extreme?) Keynesian view of **reverse causation** can be summarised as:

$$Ms = f(P)$$

Rewriting the Cambridge equation as:

$$Ms = \frac{1}{V}Py$$

and accepting the first assumption, it is easy to see that an increase in the money supply Ms will feed through to an increase in the price level P provided that V and y are relatively constant. Keynesians have attacked the quantity theory by attacking this assumption. They have argued that even if the assumption that the money supply influences the price level is correct, then the influence could be very small if an increase in the supply of money was absorbed in a lower velocity of circulation, V, rather than in an increase in the price level. However, in response to evidence that V has slowed down in recent years, monetarists now argue that the velocity of circulation need only be predictable, and not necessarily constant.

This dispute extends into an argument about the **transmission mechanism** through which an increase in the money supply is supposed to increase the price level. Modern versions of the quantity theory are usually stated in terms of the demand for money:

$$Md = \frac{1}{V}Py$$

Monetarists believe that the demand for money is a stable function of the level of money income, money being required solely for transactions purposes (the transactions demand for money). When the government increases the money supply, people find themselves possessing larger money balances than they wish to hold. They simply spend their excess money holdings, thereby providing the mechanism by which prices are pulled up. Keynesians attack this **cash balance mechanism**, arguing that since people hold money for speculative reasons – the speculative demand for money – it does not automatically follow that an increase in the money supply is spent. If the demand for money is unstable, the effects of an increase in the money supply are unpredictable.

Even if it is agreed that the velocity of circulation is constant and that the demand for money is a stable function of money income, Keynesians have a third line of attack. An expansion of the money supply may increase **real output**, y, rather than the **price level P**, particularly if there is substantial spare capacity in the economy. Thus the Keynesians stress the reflationary potential of monetary policy, though because it is unpredictable it should be used as a supplement or 'back-up' to fiscal policy. Milton Friedman has admitted that monetary expansion can increase real output, but he argues that the effect is short-lived and that the main long-term effect is on the price level.

The Keynesian demand-pull theory of inflation

In an influential pamphlet published at the beginning of the Second World War, Keynes adapted his theory of deficient demand in a depressed economy to explain how inflation could be caused by excess demand in a fully employed economy.

The theory is illustrated in Fig. 15.2 in which the maximum level of real output the economy is capable of producing with existing capacity is Y_{FE}. However, the level of aggregate money demand exercised by the various sectors in the economy, shown by E_1, is greater than the output that can be produced. Excess demand pulls up prices, resulting in an equilibrium level of money national income at Y_1. A sustained reduction in aggregate demand to E_2 is necessary to close the inflationary gap so as to achieve full employment without inflation.

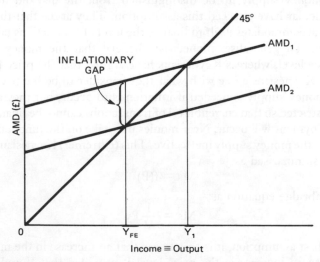

Fig. 15.2 The Keynesian Demand-Pull theory of inflation

Although the monetarist and the Keynesian theories are both demand theories of inflation, the Keynesian theory locates the engine of inflation firmly in the 'real' economy. Taken together, the combined claims on output of households, firms, the government and the overseas sector are greater than the output that can be produced. Thus inflation is explained by the real forces which determine how people behave. In the British economy of the postwar years in which governments were committed to pursue the objective of full employment, people could behave both as workers and as voters in an inflationary way. As workers, they could bargain for money wage increases in excess of any productivity increase without the fear of unemployment, while in the political arena they could add to the pressure of demand by voting for increased public spending and budget deficits. We have already noted how, in a trivial sense, Keynesians admit that inflation is a monetary phenomenon, since the money stock must expand to accommodate and sustain a rising price level. But Keynesians dispute that inflation is caused by a simple prior increase in the money supply; they believe that the real causes lie much deeper.

Cost theories of inflation

During the postwar years, **creeping inflation** continued, even in years when there was little or no evidence of excess demand in the economy. This prompted many Keynesians to switch their allegiance away from the **demand theory** of inflation to **cost-push** or **structuralist** theories which explain inflation in terms of the structural and institutional conditions which prevail on the supply side of the economy. Such Keynesians are sometimes called **post-Keynesians** or **neo-Keynesians**.

Cost-push theorists argue that growing monopoly power in both labour and goods markets has caused inflation. Strong trade unions are able to bargain for money wage rises in excess of any productivity increase. Monopoly firms are prepared to pay these wage increases partly because of the costs of disrupting modern continuous-flow production processes, and partly because they believe they can pass the increased costs on to the consuming public in higher prices. It is often assumed in the cost-push theory that prices are formed by a simple **cost-plus pricing rule**. This means that monopoly firms add a standard profit margin to their costs when setting their prices.

The cost-push theory has become a very popular theory with newspapers and the general public. It suggests the simple conclusion that **trade union pushfulness** and perhaps big business are responsible for inflation. However, the question is often begged as to why unions became more militant in the 1960s and 1970s. **Marxist** versions of the cost-push theory locate the reason for increased labour militancy in a defensive struggle by workers to restore their real wages which are being squeezed by capitalists attempting to maintain the rate of profit. Some Marxists regard inflation as the outcome of a distributional struggle within the crisis of capitalism. Other cost-push theorists argue that changed conditions in the labour market in the era of full employment led to aggressive rather than defensive union behaviour. The guarantee of full employment by the state in the postwar years and the provision of a safety net of labour protection legislation are said to have created conditions in which unions could successfully be more militant.

In explaining inflation, cost-push theorists place great emphasis on the roles of **pay relativities** and **different rates of productivity growth** in different industries. Suppose there are two sectors within an economy: one with a fast rate of growth of labour productivity and the other with a zero rate. Firms in the high productivity sector are prepared to pay wage increases equal to the rate of growth of productivity. Cost inflation need not therefore occur in this sector. However, workers with similar skills in the zero growth sector bargain for the same wage increases in order to maintain their comparability or to restore the differential relative to less skilled workers. Cost inflation thus occurs in the sector with zero productivity growth as the firms pass the increased wage costs on to consumers in higher prices.

A **wage-price spiral** is unleashed as each group of workers attempts in a **leap-frogging process** to maintain or improve its real wage and its position in the pay league table. Cost-push theorists essentially view the labour market not as one large competitive market but as a collection of non-competitive and separated markets for different trades and skills. Although workers realise that if all wages rise at the same rate as productivity, then inflation will probably fall, they also realise that what is in the interest of workers *collectively* need not be in the interest of a *single* group acting in isolation. A group that accepts a wage increase lower than the current rate of inflation will probably suffer if other workers do not behave in a similar fashion. Thus a group acts to preserve its relative position in the pay pecking order, even if its members know that by fuelling inflation a large money wage increase may be only a small real wage increase or even a decrease.

THE RISE OF THE PHILLIPS CURVE

In the late 1950s and the early 1960s a great deal of energy was spent by economists in debating whether inflation is caused by excess demand or by cost-push forces. After 1958 the debate was conducted with the aid of a recently discovered statistical relationship, the **Phillips curve**, which is illustrated in Fig. 15.3. The Phillips curve purported to show a stable but non-linear relationship between the rate of change of wages (the rate of wage inflation) and the percentage of the labour force unemployed. Taking the rate of growth of productivity into account, Phillips estimated that in the UK an unemployment level of about 2.5% was compatible with price stability (or zero inflation), and that an unemployment level of 5.5% would lead to stable money wages. Economists grasped on the supposed stability of the Phillips relationship over a period of nearly one hundred years to argue that it provided statistical support for the existence of a trade-off between inflation and employment. Using the Phillips curve, economists believed that they could advise governments on the **opportunity cost in terms of inflation** of achieving any **employment target**. In offering this advice, the non-linearity of the curve was significant. At low levels of unemployment a further reduction in unemployment would incur a much greater cost in terms of increased inflation than a similar reduction at a higher level of unemployment. Indeed, the Phillips curve appeared to justify the Keynesian view than an unemployment rate of about $1\frac{1}{2}$% should be regarded as full employment; any lower level of unemployment, or 'over-full employment' would be associated with an excessive cost in terms of inflation.

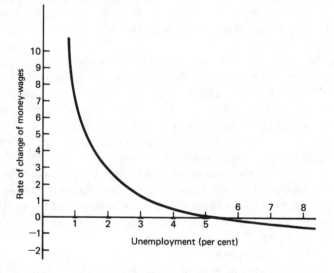

Fig. 15.3 The Phillips curve

Nevertheless, the Phillips curve was never, in itself, a theory of inflation. In its early years the Phillips curve was most often used by Keynesians of the demand-pull school, including Phillips himself, to illustrate how the rate of inflation varied with the amount of excess demand in the economy. In the **demand-pull interpretation**, the level of unemployment was used as a measure of excess demand which served to pull up money wages in the labour market. However, the Phillips curve was also accommodated in the **cost-push theory**, the level of unemployment being interpreted as a measure of trade union pushfulness. The Phillips curve could illustrate and provide statistical support for both theories of inflation, but it could not decide between the two.

THE FALL OF THE PHILLIPS CURVE

Around 1970 a growing level of unemployment accompanied by a much higher rate of inflation appeared to signal the breakdown of the Phillips relationship. According to the monetarists, this greatly damaged the credibility of both the cost-push theory of inflation and the demand-pull theory, at least in its Keynesian version. It is worth noting, however, that many Keynesians now claim that the Phillips curve was never a true part of Keynesianism, merely excess baggage added on, the rejection of which does not destroy essential Keynesian theory. Nevertheless, neither the demand-pull nor the cost-push theorists had predicted the emergence of the stagflation or slumpflation of the 1970s. Yet a leading monetarist, Milton Friedman, had predicted the breakdown of the Phillips relationship a number of years before it actually happened. It is not surprising, therefore, that the simultaneous appearance of increased unemployment and accelerating inflation greatly boosted monetarism.

There are at least two competing theories of what has happened to the Phillips relationship. In the version favoured by some cost-push theorists, the inverse relationship between inflation and unemployment still exists, but the trade-off is now at much higher rates of inflation and levels of unemployment. The continuing growth of non-competitive forces in the structure and institutions of the economy are blamed for a rightward shift of the Phillips relationship. The cost-push school favours the use of an incomes policy as the only method which can once again achieve both a lower inflation rate and a lower level of unemployment.

In contrast, monetarists argue that even at the height of the Keynesian era there was never a stable relationship allowing a long-term trade-off between inflation and employment. The statistical relationship identified by Phillips is at best short-run and unstable. According to monetarists, the true long-term relationship between unemployment and the rate of inflation lies along a vertical line, on which no trade-offs are possible, running through the **natural rate of unemployment** also known as the **non-accelerating inflation rate of unemployment** (NAIRU). This is shown in Fig. 15.4. To understand this conclusion we need to introduce two theories, one old and one relatively new, to help explain the monetarist view of how the economy works. The old theory, the monetarist theory of aggregate employment, is essentially the pre-Keynesian employment theory discussed earlier in the chapter, whilst the new theory introduces the role of expectations into the inflationary process. According to the monetarist theory of employment, the natural levels of employment and unemployment (U^* in Fig. 15.4) are determined at the equilibrium real wage at which workers voluntarily supply exactly the amount of labour that firms voluntarily employ. Since monetarists do not recognise demand-deficient unemployment it follows that, at the natural rate, unemployment is composed largely of frictional and structural unemployment.

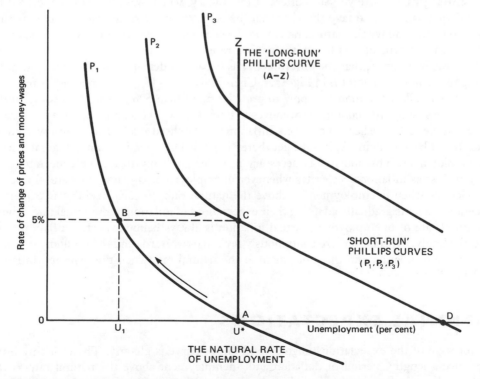

Fig. 15.4 The expectations-augmented Phillips curve

We now introduce the **role of expectations** into the inflationary process. In order to keep the analysis as simple as possible, we shall assume that the rate of productivity increase is zero. Thus, the vertical axis in Fig. 15.4 measures the rate of increase both of money wages and of prices. Suppose that the economy is initially at point A. Unemployment is at the natural rate U*, and the rates of increase of prices and money wages are zero and stable. In these circumstances, workers may expect the future inflation rate also to be zero. If the government is dissatisfied with the level of unemployment at U* and expands demand, it may believe that it can successfully trade-off along the Phillips curve P_1 to a point such as B. The cost of achieving U_1 appears to be an inflation rate of 5% . But will the new situation be stable? Not so, say the monetarists. Workers are only willing to supply more labour beyond the natural level of employment if the real wage rises, but a rising real wage causes employers to demand less labour! Initially, more workers may enter the labour market in the false belief or illusion that a 5% increase in the money wage is also a real wage increase. We call this **money illusion**. Similarly, if firms falsely believe that revenues are rising faster than labour costs, they will employ more labour. In other words, an increase in employment beyond the natural rate can only be sustained if workers and employers suffer permanent money illusion in equal but opposite directions!

Gradually, both workers and employers will realise that they have confused money quantities with real quantities and that they have suffered from money illusion. Without permanent money illusion, employment can only stay above the natural level if inflation accelerates to keep employees' expectations about the rate of inflation consistently below the actual rate. As workers continuously adjust their expectations of future inflation to the actual rate and bargain for ever-higher money wages, the short-run Phillips curve shifts outward from P_1 to P_2 and so on. Thus a level of unemployment below the natural rate can only be sustained if the government finances and accommodates the accelerating inflation by expanding the money supply. But even in these circumstances the inflation will eventually accelerate into a hyperinflation and into a breakdown of economic activity, causing unemployment to rise above the natural rate. According to this logic, any attempt to reduce unemployment below the natural rate involves the short-run cost of accelerating inflation, whilst eventually having the perverse effect of increasing unemployment above the natural rate to an unnecessarily high level.

The theory just described is sometimes known as the theory of the **expectations-augmented Phillips curve**. Supporters of this theory, which was originally conceived by Milton Friedman, tend to take the view that the economy must suffer rather a long period of unemployment above the natural rate to rid the economy of the effect of expectations built up while unemployment was below the natural rate.

Suppose, once again, that the government has expanded demand and the money supply, moving the economy to point B in Fig. 15.4. Unemployment is U_1. It now realises its mistake, and refuses to allow the money supply to grow by more than 5% a year. According to the Friedmanite school, the economy now moves to point C as workers and employers gradually realise that the real wage has not changed. Inflation has stabilised at 5%. But if the government wishes to get back to point A, it must get there via point D, which is at a much greater level of unemployment. This journey is necessary in order gradually to reduce expectations of inflation. Just as inflation accelerates whenever unemployment is below the natural rate, so it decelerates when unemployment is above the natural rate. In each case this is explained by economic agents gradually adapting their expectations of inflation to the actual rate. Above the natural rate of unemployment, actual inflation is always below expected inflation.

Accordingly, expectations are continuously revised downwards and the economy can only return to zero inflation and unemployment at the natural rate when the expected inflation rate has fallen to zero.

RATIONAL EXPECTATIONS

The message of the expectations-augmented Phillips curve is gloomy. The economy must experience a lengthy period of deflation and unemployment above the natural rate as the penalty to be paid for an irresponsible reduction in unemployment below the natural rate.

However, in recent years many monetarists have tacked on to the Friedmanite concept of the natural rate of unemployment, an alternative theory of how expectations are formed.

According to this theory, it is unrealistic to assume that a rational economic agent acting in its self-interest will form expectations of future inflation only on the basis of past or experienced inflation. If economic agents on average correctly forecast the results of events taking place in the economy now, it is in their self-interest quickly to modify their economic behaviour so that it is in line with their expectations. Thus if workers believe that the government means business in reducing the money supply and the rate of inflation, they will immediately build a lower expected rate of inflation into their wage-bargaining behaviour. In this way, inflation can be reduced relatively painlessly without a lengthy period of unemployment above the natural level.

In recent years an important division has developed between **monetarists of the Friedmanite school** and those of the **rational expectations or new classical** school. According to the Friedmanites, governments can reduce unemployment below the natural rate as long as workers and employers suffer illusion. However, according to the rational expectations school, workers and employers instantly realise their mistakes and see through any attempt by an irresponsible government to reflate the economy; thus demand management policies can never succeed in reducing unemployment below the natural rate, even in the short run. Monetarists of both schools usually agree that although the government cannot in the long run reduce unemployment below the natural rate, it can reduce the natural rate itself by policies designed to make the labour market more competitive, hence policies to reduce trade union power and to abolish the closed shop, together with other supply-side policies.

Summary: the three stages in the development of the monetarist theory of inflation

❶ **Mark I** of the monetarist theory of inflation was the revival by Milton Friedman in the 1950s of the **quantity theory of money**. This explained inflation as a purely monetary phenomenon, caused by the government creating or condoning excess monetary growth.

❷ **Mark II**: the incorporation of the **theory of adaptive expectations** into the inflationary process. The weakness of the Mark I theory is that it fails to explain why a government might be prepared to expand the money supply on a continuing basis to finance an inflation. Milton Friedman's theory of the expectations-augmented Phillips curve provides an explanation and also, we should note, explains inflation in terms of the 'real' economy rather than purely as a monetary phenomenon.

❸ **Mark III**: the 'new classical' school. Whereas the Mark II explanation of inflation is based on a **theory of adaptive expectations**, the new classical school has replaced this with the theory of rational expectations. In the adaptive expectations theory, workers and employers slowly change or adapt their expectations of future inflation to the current rate of inflation. By contrast, in the new classical explanation of inflation, it is rational for economic agents instantly to adapt their expectations of the future to all the up-to-date information that is available.

Chapter roundup

In this chapter we have used the income-expenditure macroeconomic model, first introduced in Chapter 14, to explain unemployment and inflation in terms of the state of aggregate demand and expenditure in the economy. The next chapter, (Chapter 16), examines unemployment and inflation within the framework provided by the aggregate demand/aggregate supply (AD/AS) macroeconomic model, relating the natural level of unemployment to the economy's natural or equilibrium level of output. This then leads into Chapter 17 which, among other issues, contrasts Keynesian and monetarist approaches to employment and inflation.

Illustrative questions and answers

1 Essay Question

(a) What do economists mean by the 'natural' rate of unemployment? (10)

(b) How might 'demand-side' and 'supply-side' economic policies affect the 'natural' rate of unemployment? (15)   AEB

Tutorial note

As we have explained, the term the 'natural' rate of unemployment was first introduced by the leading monetarist Milton Friedman, when putting forward the theory of the 'expectations -augmented' Phillips curve in the late 1960s. However the 'natural' rate or level of unemployment is really just a revival of the old neoclassical or pre-Keynesian belief that a competitive market economy automatically self-adjusts to an 'equilibrium' level of unemployment made up of frictional and possibly structural unemployment. It is the level of unemployment that exists at the equilibrium real wage which equates the aggregate demand for labour with the aggregate supply and clears the labour market, i.e. all 'classical' or 'real wage' and 'demand -deficient' unemployment has been eliminated. Related terms are the 'non-accelerating inflation rate of unemployment' (NAIRU) and the 'full employment rate of unemployment'.

Monetarist and 'supply-side' economists believe that 'demand-side' policies in the sense of expanding aggregate demand to try to reduce unemployment, cannot reduce the 'natural' rate of unemployment. Indeed if the government expands demand to try to reduce unemployment below the economy's 'natural' rate, or if demand management leads to the neglect of the economy's 'supply side', such policies may in fact have the long term effect of increasing the 'natural' rate of unemployment. They argue that free-market or 'anti-interventionist' 'supply-side' policies (which we describe in the next chapter) should be used as the only way of reducing the 'natural' rate of unemployment. By contrast, Keynesians argue that there is still a role for demand management, and also for 'interventionist' 'supply-side' policies as well as for the more 'free-market' variety.

Suggested answer plan

1 Explain the 'natural' rate of unemployment, illustrating the concept on a diagram to show the aggregate demand for, and aggregate supply of , labour, or on a Phillips curve diagram.

2 With the aid of a Phillips curve diagram, show the effects of an expansion of demand which reduces unemployment below its 'natural' rate.

3 Explain the monetarist or 'supply-side' argument that 'free-market' 'supply-side' policies are needed to reduce the 'natural' rate of unemployment.

4 Summarise the Keynesian counter view in favour of more interventionist 'supply-side' policies and in support of at least some demand management.

2 Data question

Study the data below which relate to unemployment, inflation and savings.

Figure 1 Unemployment and inflation

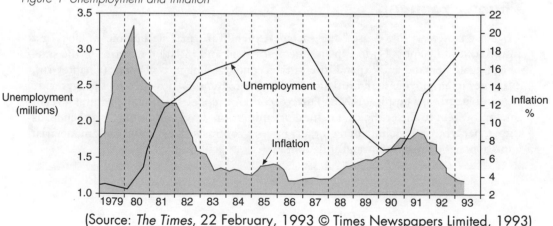

(Source: *The Times*, 22 February, 1993 © Times Newspapers Limited, 1993)

Figure 2 Unemployment and savings

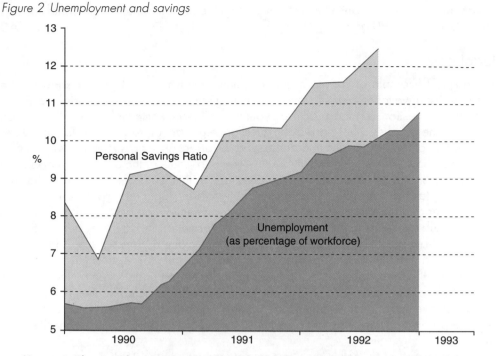

(Source: *The Sunday Times*, 21 February 1993 © Times Newspapers Limited, 1993)

Figure 3 Growth and recession
% change in GDP (quarter by quarter)

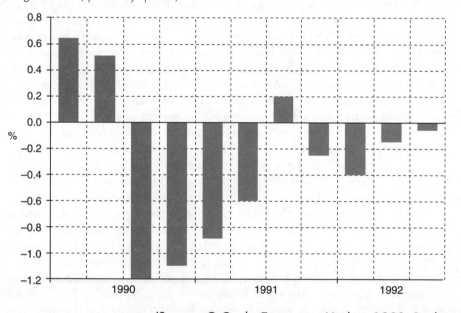

(Source: G Cook, *Economics Update 1993*, Sterling Books)

(a) Using the data from both Figures 1 and 2, estimate the size of the workforce at the end of 1992. Show your calculations. (3)

(b) (i) What does Figure 1 suggest about the relationship between inflation and unemployment? (3)

(ii) Using economic analysis, explain the relationship which you have identified in (b) (i). (5)

(iii) Mr. Norman Lamont (then Chancellor of the Exchequer) said in May 1991 that unemployment was 'a price worth paying in order to achieve a low rate of inflation'. In the light of this statement, examine **two** benefits of a low rate of inflation. (4)

(c) Examine possible reasons which might explain the movement of the personal savings ratio between 1990 and 1992. (5)   *ULEAC*

Tutorial note

This is a good example of a data question which includes several graphs showing the changes which have taken place in recent years in a number of economic variables. Some parts of such a question, e.g. part (b) (i) test your understanding of the information contained in just one of the graphs. Other parts of the question, e.g. part (a), require you to draw upon more than one of the data series in order to write a correct answer. When answering part (a), you must show your workings to make sure you earn some of the available marks even if you make a slip in the calculation. With questions of this type, one or more of the sub-questions may test the skill of synthesis, i.e. the ability to bring together disparate information from a number of different sources to back up an argument or line of reasoning. Note that none of the sub-questions ask explicitly about the information in Figure 3, but this figure, which shows how output varies according to the phase of the business cycle, is there for a purpose: relevant use of it can improve your answers to parts (b) (ii) and (c).

In part (c), the personal savings ratio measures the saving undertaken by the personal sector of the economy as a ratio of total personal sector disposable income. The personal sector is, however, a rather misleading term, containing not just individuals and households, but unincorporated businesses such as partnerships and organisations such as charities and universities.

No explanation of the fall in the personal savings ratio in the 1980s – or its rapid rise around 1990 – could be complete without some discussion of the housing market and of house price inflation in determining people's spending and savings decisions in the UK in recent decades. Fifty years ago only a minority of UK households owned the property they lived in; most paid rent either to a private landlord or the local authority owning the council house or flat in which they lived. This is still true in many other European countries. However, the UK now has one of the highest rates of owner occupancy of its housing stock in the world. Most owner occupiers borrow large sums of money on a mortgage to finance house purchase. During periods of rapid house price inflation as occurred in the 1980s, the value of the house rises, but the mortgage does not. In fact the real value of mortgage debt falls as it is eroded by inflation. In the 1980s, with rising house values and declining financial liabilities, owner-occupiers grew wealthier, though their wealth was locked up in the bricks and mortar or equity of the houses they lived in. As their net wealth increased, many house owners decided to convert a fraction of their wealth into money they could spend. This process, which is called *equity leakage* or *equity withdrawal,* began to happen on a large scale in the newly-liberalised or deregulated UK financial markets in the 1980s. Some house owners simply increased their borrowing, or dissaved, using the value of their houses as security. In effect such households geared-up or increased the gearing ratio of debts or borrowing to capital or wealth, just as a firm increases its gearing ratio whenever it borrows. Other households, believing that house prices would continue to rise faster than the average inflation rate, decided to borrow more in order to purchase a more expensive house. Borrowing is the opposite of saving (i.e. it represents negative saving or dissaving) so, as people borrowed more in the 1980s either to get on the 'housing ladder' for the first time, or to trade up to a bigger house, or simply to convert housing equity into spending power, the personal savings ratio fell.

A particularly significant feature of the UK housing market in the 1980s was the belief apparently held by many households, that house prices could only go up and never down. Certainly, the experience of the UK housing market since the 1950s seemed to give considerable support to this view. House owners probably also concluded that UK political parties would generally do as much as they could to support house prices, if only because British governments depend heavily on the votes of owner-occupiers to return them to office. However, as British people came increasingly to regard house purchase as a risk-free one-way bet and the easiest way to increase personal wealth, the ratio of house prices to average earnings and the debt service burden for first-time house buyers rose to their highest ever levels in 1989 and early 1990.

As the UK economy entered recession in 1990, the inflated level of house prices became unsustainable. The house price bubble burst in 1990, and the rapid fall in house prices which followed created the problem of *debt overhang* for those owner occupants who had borrowed heavily to buy houses at or near the peak of house price inflation in the late 1980s. Many of these households now experienced *negative equity*, i.e. their debt or liabilities (largely mortgage debt owed to a bank or building society) exceeded the value of their assets (largely the declining value of the property bought at the peak of the 1980s housing boom). This has probably been the most important single factor explaining the return to thrift and the rise in the personal savings ratio in the early 1990s. Households who had borrowed heavily in the 1980s in the expectation that ever-rising property prices and inflation would quickly reduce the real value and burden of their debt, decided to use current income to pay-off and reduce the resulting debt overhang, to try to restore their ratio of debt to income to a more prudent and sustainable level.

The decision to save rather than to consume is also affected by uncertainty. In the recessionary years of the early 1990s, growing insecurity in the job market and fear of unemployment became the main cause of peoples' uncertainty about the future and a further factor explaining the growth of the personal savings ratio.

Suggested answer plan

(a) Approximately three million people were unemployed at the end of 1992 (Figure 1), or 10.8% of the labour force (Figure 2). Divide three million by 10.8 and multiply by 100.

(b) (i) The data suggests a Phillips curve relationship, or an inverse relationship between unemployment and inflation. Back up this assertion with a couple of statistics selected from Figure 1.

(ii) There is a danger that you will be deflected into discussion of the expectations-augmented Phillips curve. Don't be over-ambitious! Restrict your answer to a theoretical explanation of the basic Phillips curve relationship, explaining how falling unemployment leads to excess demand (and demand-pull inflation) and/or to increased labour bargaining power (and cost-push inflation). You might also make use of the information in Figure 3, relating your answer to the phases of the business cycle.

(iii) A low rate of inflation means that the economy does not suffer significantly from the distortive effects of inflation upon economic activity. Give two examples e.g. in terms of the distribution of income and the direction of saving into productive investment rather than speculation. A good answer might be based on the argument favoured by monetarist and supply-side economists: that price stability is a necessary condition for the efficient functioning of a market economy. Whatever you do, don't get waylaid into making spurious political points about Mr. Norman Lamont!

(c) Begin your answer by defining the personal savings ratio and describe briefly how the ratio changed between 1990 and 1992. Then draw on the explanation we have provided in the tutorial note to explain the fall and subsequent rise in the ratio shown by the data.

Question bank

1 Explain how the monetarist approach to the analysis and cure of inflation differs from the Keynesian approach. Discuss, on the basis of UK experience, which approach may be said to be more effective. (25)   *NEAB*

Pitfalls

You must avoid the temptation to write all you know about inflation, or to restrict your answer to praising or criticising government economic policy towards inflation. Since this is an unstructured question (i.e. not divided into parts (a) and (b) with the mark allocation indicated), it is probably best to assume that each part carries equal marks and to divide your time relatively equally between the two halves of the question.

Key points

Define inflation and state briefly that as almost all governments regard excessive inflation as an economic problem, control of inflation is an important policy objective. Then carefully explain that the monetarist analysis of inflation centres on excess monetary growth pulling up the price level in a demand-pull inflation, and the role of expectations in the inflationary process. By contrast, Keynesian economists generally explain inflation in terms of cost-push factors, and market imperfections in the goods and labour markets. For the second part of your answer, you must draw on evidence from the UK economy, perhaps contrasting the effects of the Keynesian incomes policies pursued in the 1970s to control cost-push inflation with the monetarist policies implemented in the 1980s.

2 'Controlling inflation is easy. Controlling inflation whilst maintaining a high level of employment is impossible.'
Discuss in the light of recent United Kingdom experience. (25)   *Oxford*

Pitfalls

Again this is an unstructured question, but it is rather more discursive than Question 1. There is a danger that you will write an answer which is too general and lacking in structure. Again you must draw on evidence from the British economy to back up the points which you make.

Key points

Your answer should centre on the Phillips curve trade-off between unemployment and inflation. You must explain why government policies which reduce unemployment might be expected to increase the rate of inflation. Thirty years ago the position of the Phillips curve meant that by carefully managing demand, governments could achieve an acceptable combination of relatively low inflation and unemployment. From the 1960s onwards, the Phillips relationship shifted outwards so that more recently, the trade-off has taken place at higher rates of inflation and levels of unemployment.

You could argue that it is not necessarily easy to control inflation. You might say that the growth of a psychology of inflation in the UK contributed to this. In the 1960s and 1970s, British people assumed that inflation was normal and that they should expect their wages and house prices to rise each year. This in turn affected their economic behaviour and contributed to further price rises.

If you agree that inflation can be controlled easily, you could make the point that if a government has the political resolve, it can control inflation simply by depressing aggregate demand and deflating the economy sufficiently. However, the costs in terms of bankrupting industries and increasing unemployment may be politically unacceptable, but high unemployment may arguably be a price worth paying for controlling inflation. This view is based on the proposition that control of inflation is a necessary condition for a market economy to function efficiently, and for economic growth and fuller employment to be delivered in future years. High unemployment now might be needed to create the price stability necessary for more jobs in the future.

3 The costs of inflation used to be stated in terms of income distribution. Now the adverse effects of inflation are seen more in terms of employment and output.

(a) Explain what is meant by inflation and consider the impact of a high rate of inflation on the distribution of income in an economy. (13)

(b) Discuss why a high rate of inflation might have an adverse effect on output and employment. (12)   *Cambridge*

Pitfalls

In part (a), you must not drift into an account of all the disadvantages of inflation. You must concentrate solely on the distributional effects. Part (b) is more difficult because it is less well covered in standard textbooks. You must show an understanding of the arguments used by monetarist and supply-side economists about the adverse effects of inflation.

Key points

Having defined inflation as a persistent or continuing rise in the average price level, explain the distributional effects of inflation, for example between employees in strong bargaining positions and pensioners on fixed incomes, and between debtors and creditors. In your answer to part (b), you should explain how, by distorting normal economic activity, creating inefficiencies and shortening decision makers' time horizons, inflation contributes to the malfunctioning of a market economy. The adverse effects on economic performance are greatest when inflation is unanticipated and highly variable.

CHAPTER 16

SUPPLY-SIDE ECONOMICS

Units in this chapter

Chapter objectives

We have already encountered the term supply-side economics in earlier chapters of this book. This chapter, explores the meaning of **free-market** supply-side economics in greater depth, in both its microeconomic and macroeconomic aspects. We shall also note how many Keynesian economists – previously associated with demand management and the demand side of the economy – now claim to attach importance to the supply side, though arguably their supply-side economics is much more **anti-market** and **interventionist** than that of the **radical right** economists with whom the term is most usually associated.

16.1 SUPPLY-SIDE ECONOMICS

THE BACKGROUND TO SUPPLY-SIDE ECONOMICS

The term supply-side economics was first used in 1976 by Professor Herbert Stein of the University of Virginia in the United States, later coming into prominence in 1980 to describe the economic policies promised by Ronald Reagan in his successful campaign for the American presidency. Supply-side economics then became associated with **Reaganomics**, which was the nickname given to the American Government's economic programme in the early 1980s. The ideology and policies of other free-market orientated governments were also strongly influenced by supply-side theories in the 1980s, in particular the Conservative administrations of Margaret Thatcher in the United Kingdom from 1979 to 1990, for which the nickname **Thatcherism** was coined.

Supply-side economics has also influenced Labour or socialist administrations in Australia and New Zealand, but it is more usually associated with the emergence of the radical right or **New Right** in a **neo-classical revival**, and with the **decline of Keynesianism**. There are many diverse and often competing schools of economic and political theory within the neo-classical revival, including various schools of monetarism which will be explained in the next chapter. Although there is some disagreement over points of both emphasis and detail, all members of the radical right believe in the **virtues of capitalism and free market forces**, a belief which is matched by a distrust and **dislike of** big government and the role of **state intervention** in the economy.

The strict meaning of supply-side economics

In its original meaning, as developed by the radical right, supply-side economics describes a particular way at looking at the effects of the government's **fiscal policy** upon the economy. During the Keynesian era, most economists had regarded fiscal policy, and especially the government's use of taxation, as affecting the economy almost solely at the macro level through its effect on aggregate demand. For Keynesians, the size of the government's budget deficit, or surplus, was the key to fiscal policy, regardless of whether a deficit resulted from higher levels of public spending or from tax cuts. The impact of public spending increases or tax changes upon the economy at the micro level was largely ignored.

By contrast, supply-side economics is concerned with the microeconomic effects of taxation and public spending. In many respects, supply-side economics is simply a revival of the old classical public finance theory that disappeared from view during the Keynesian era. Central to supply-side economics is the idea of a tax cut (not to stimulate aggregate demand Keynesian-style) but to create incentives by altering relative prices, particularly those of labour and leisure, in favour of work, saving and investment. **Professor Arthur Laffer**, a prominent American supply-sider (and adviser to President Reagan in the 1980s), has described supply-side economics as

> providing a framework of analysis which relies on personal and private incentives. When incentives change, people's behaviour changes in response. People are attracted towards positive incentives and repelled by the negative. The role of government in such a framework is carried out by the ability of government to alter incentives and thereby affect society's behaviour.

A broader interpretation of supply-side economics

As we have just explained, in its original meaning supply-side economics relates exclusively to fiscal policy and tax cuts, and their effects upon incentives. However, it is useful to conceive of supply-side economics in broader terms than fiscal policy alone. In this looser interpretation, we can define supply-side economic policy as **the set of government policies which aim to change the underlying structure of the economy and improve the economic performance of markets and industries and of individual workers and firms within markets.** Supply-side policies are **microeconomic** rather than **macroeconomic**, since they aim to improve general economic performance by acting on the motivation and efficiency of individual economic agents within the economy. Supply-siders, together with other radical-right economists, believe that while the economy is always close to its natural levels of output and employment, these natural levels can be unnecessarily low because of distortions (often blamed on 'twenty-five years of Keynesian policies') which reduce both an individual's willingness to supply labour and a firm's willingness to employ labour and supply goods. Supply-siders therefore recommend the use of microeconomic policies which they believe will remove these distortions, improve incentives and generally make markets more competitive. In the Keynesian era, microeconomic policy (along with macropolicy) usually extended (rather than reduced) government interventionism in markets, in fields such as **regional policy, competition policy** (or anti-monopoly policy), **labour market policy** and other aspects of **industrial policy**. By contrast supply-side microeconomic policy centres on a rolling back of the functions of the state and a reduction of the level of government intervention in the economy. Along with tax cuts (to create incentives to work, save and invest) and welfare benefit cuts (to reduce the incentive to choose unemployment), supply-side economic policy, in its wider interpretation, includes policies of **privatisation**, **marketisation** and **deregulation** (described in detail in Chapter 10). Supply-siders – and other schools within the free market revival (be they self-styled monetarists or New Classical economists) wish to create an **enterprise economy**, through the promotion of entrepreneurship and **popular capitalism**; to replace the **dependency culture** and **statism** they see as the legacy of several decades of Keynesianism and a misguided consensus around the supposed virtues of a mixed economy. Indeed, for supply-siders, and other members of the radical right, the mixed economy is better described as a mixed-up economy!

SUPPLY-SIDE ECONOMICS AND THE SUPPLY CURVE OF LABOUR

Supply-side theory depends crucially upon the assumption that the supply curve of labour is upward-sloping and not backward-bending, and that increases in income tax create disincentives for the further supply of labour. (Refer back to Chapter 11 at this stage for an explanation of the supply curve of labour.) An upward-sloping supply curve of labour implies that increases in the marginal rates of income tax, being equivalent to cuts in wage rates, have a disincentive effect upon the supply of labour. Workers decide to supply less labour (choosing more leisure time instead) and they may also prefer the untaxed supply of labour in the informal black or underground economy to the more formal supply of taxed labour in the overground economy.

SUPPLY-SIDE ECONOMICS AND UNEMPLOYMENT

Supply-siders, and other more free-market orientated economists, argue that the growth of **voluntary unemployment** explains much of the high level of unemployment occurring in the UK since the 1970s. Workers do not necessarily voluntarily leave their jobs and choose unemployment, but once unemployed (for whatever reason) they choose to remain unemployed for a much longer period than was previously the case. In part, this may be a 'discouraged worker' effect: repeated job rejections, in conditions of high unemployment, may discourage further attempts to find a job. **Search theories**, explained in the previous chapter, have also been used to explain a growth in voluntary frictional unemployment. Search theorists argue that such voluntary frictional unemployment has increased because, in the Keynesian era, the state created for the unemployed a 'safety net' of welfare benefits such as unemployment pay. A higher real level of welfare benefits could then be used by the unemployed to finance a longer search period, thus delaying the decisions to reduce aspirations and fill a vacancy. Highly relevant here is the **replacement ratio**; the ratio of disposable income when unemployed to disposable income in work. An increase in the replacement ratio, caused perhaps both by higher welfare benefits available to the unemployed, and also by fiscal drag and higher taxation affecting the low-paid, encourages workers with few skills to offer in the job market, to choose unemployment in preference to work. This is the **unemployment trap**, to which we referred in Chapter 13.

Since supply-side economists, such as Professor Patrick Minford, have argued that much recent and current unemployment in the UK is voluntary frictional, it is not surprising that they recommend free-market orientated supply-side policies as the appropriate remedy. Such policies include cuts both in marginal income tax rates and in welfare benefits, together with a tightening of rules to make benefits more difficult to claim. Supply-siders claim that tax cuts increase the incentive to work, while reducing the real value of benefits decreases the incentive to choose unemployment. Neo-Keynesians reply by arguing that tax and benefits cuts involve an unacceptable and socially divisive increase in inequality. They also believe that only a small part of current unemployment is of the voluntary frictional kind, so free-market supply-side policies will not have much affect on the rump of involuntary structural unemployment resulting from the deindustrialisation process, from the effects of an overvalued exchange rate, decades of under-investment both by the private sector, and by the state in social capital or infrastructure.

THE LAFFER CURVE

The assumption by supply-siders of an upward-sloping supply curve of labour leads on to the supply-side argument that high rates of income tax and the overall burden of income tax upon taxpayers create disincentives which eventually, as taxation increases, diminish national income and cause total tax revenue to decline. This can be illustrated by a Laffer curve, which we have drawn in Fig. 16.1:

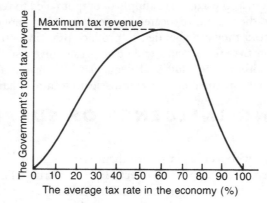

Fig. 16.1 A Laffer curve

The Laffer curve shows the government's total tax revenue as the average tax rate increases from 0 to 100%. Tax revenue is zero when the tax rate is 0 per cent; and it is assumed also to be zero at an average tax rate of 100% (there being no incentive to produce output other than for subsistence if any extra output is completely taxed away). In between these limiting rates, of 0 and 100%, the Laffer curve shows tax revenue first rising and then falling as the average rate of taxation is increased. Tax revenue reaches its maximum at the highest point on the Laffer curve, after which any further increase in the average tax rate becomes counter-productive as total tax revenue falls.

Supply-siders have argued that the increase in the burden of taxation, that took place in the Keynesian era in the UK and USA, to finance the growing government sector, raised the average tax rate towards or beyond the critical point on the Laffer curve at which tax revenue is maximised. If this was the case, then the policy of tax cuts recommended by the supply-siders would have the paradoxical effect of actually raising tax revenues. A growing national output, stimulated by lower tax rates, would yield higher total revenues despite the reduced tax rates, and the effect would be reinforced by a decline in tax avoidance and evasion as these activities became less worthwhile at less penal rates of taxation.

THE CHOICE BETWEEN CONSUMPTION AND SAVING

As we have already noted, the central idea of supply-side economics is that fiscal policy works by changing relative prices or incentives. So far we have drawn attention to the **labour/leisure choice**, developing the policy implication of the Laffer curve that income tax cuts can stimulate the supply of labour, with the government actually benefiting from higher total tax revenues, despite lower tax rates, at a higher resulting level of national output. However, it is too simplistic to explain supply-side economics solely in terms of the theory that across the board personal income tax reductions are self-financing; and that the prime aim of supply-sidism is to secure more revenues for the government and to improve its budgetary position. Rather, the essence of 'supply-sidism' is the overcoming of the economy's inability to grow without a rapid rise in inflation, together with a reversal of the declining competitive position of industry.

Supply-siders argue that a second choice, facing individual economic agents, is as important as the labour/leisure choice. This is the choice between consumption and saving. The cost, to an individual, of spending a £ of income on consumption is the future income stream given up by not saving and investing the £. The present value of the income stream is in part determined by marginal tax rates. The higher the marginal tax rate on investment income, the lower is the value of the income stream that savings will yield. Thus, high rates of taxation levied on investment income, make current consumption of income cheap in terms of the investment income foregone. As a result, savings and investment decline. Supply-siders argue that the increased public spending and deficit financing of the Keynesian era stimulated aggregate demand; but that the Keynesians completely ignored the adverse effects we have just described of the higher levels of taxation that accompanied the Keynesian expansionism. As a result, expansionary Keynesian fiscal policies, designed to boost output and employment, led only to rising inflation, as the aggregate supply of output failed to respond to the demand stimulation. By contrast, the tax cuts advocated by supply-siders are not designed to stimulate aggregate demand. Instead they are intended to produce price incentives which encourage households to save rather than to consume; and businesses to invest so that the growth of the economy can proceed without the additional demand which results from higher incomes hitting the wall of stagnant national output and dissipating into inflation.

THE GROWING INFLUENCE OF SUPPLY-SIDE ECONOMICS

Today, many economists who would not regard themselves as supply-siders claim that their analysis has always incorporated supply-side effects. However, true believers in supply-sidism would dispute this claim. Be that as it may, few economists or politicians of whatever persuasion or *ism*, now call for large budget deficits as the way to achieve full employment; while almost all voice agreement with the idea that the tax structure should be used to create incentives for work, saving and investment. Arguably, by the 1990s, supply-sidism has become a more significant part of the now-dominant neoclassical revival than monetarism (since for many, monetarism has been discredited by the apparent breakdown in its central postulated relationship between the rate of growth of the money supply and inflation).

The heyday of supply-side economics probably occurred – in the UK at least – in the mid and late 1980s. During these years, government ministers claimed that their free-market supply-side policies had produced a British economic miracle, characterised by sustained economic growth and increased industrial competitiveness. Recessions, if they ever occurred again, would be mere 'blips' – short and shallow, over almost before they began. But in the light of the severe and deep recession which hit the UK economy in the early 1990s, the confidence of the supply-siders and other free-market economists has been severely dented. This has been matched by the growing confidence of Neo-Keynesians calling for much more interventionist supply-side policies to aid British industry, in particular the manufacturing sector.

16.2 AGGREGATE DEMAND AND AGGREGATE SUPPLY

THE KEYNESIAN INCOME/EXPENDITURE MODEL REVISITED

Perhaps the most serious weakness of the **Keynesian income/expenditure model**, examined in Chapter 14, is the model's lack of a proper supply-side. Within the model, the 45° line illustrated on a Keynesian cross diagram, such as Fig. 14.3, represents the Keynesian aggregate supply function. Following any increase or decrease of aggregate expenditure, the aggregate supply of output adjusts upwards or downwards to equal the level of aggregate expenditure at a new equilibrium level of national income. However, the model tells us little about a key question of interest: how much of the adjustment to the new equilibrium level of income will be a change in **real output** and how much will be represented by a change in the **price level**? Because of this inadequacy within the basic Keynesian model, another macroeconomic model, known as the **aggregate demand/aggregate supply model (or AD/AS model)**, has come into prominence in recent years.

THE AGGREGATE DEMAND/AGGREGATE SUPPLY MODEL

The main differences relating to the nature of aggregate supply which separate Keynesians and supply-siders (together with most monetarists and other members of the radical right), can be explained using the AD/AS model illustrated in Fig. 16.2. In this figure we show aggregate demand for, and aggregate supply of, real output as functions of the price level. For the most part, there is little disagreement between Keynesians and supply-siders about the nature and shape of the aggregate demand curve; it is the **aggregate supply curve** that is the centre of dispute and interest.

The AD curve, which is illustrated in Fig. 16.2, shows the total quantities of real output that all economic agents – households, firms, the government and the overseas sector – plan to purchase at different levels of domestic prices, when everything other than the price level is held constant. If there is a change in any of the factors held constant, the curve will shift rightward or leftward, depending on whether there has been an increase or a decrease in aggregate demand. For example, an increase in consumer or business confidence would shift the AD curve rightward, via the effect on consumption or investment. Expansionary monetary and fiscal policy would also bring about a rightward shift of the AD curve. Contractionary policy or a collapse in consumer or business confidence would cause the AD curve to shift leftward.

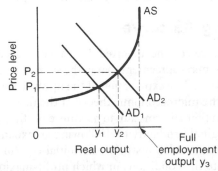

Fig. 16.2 The AD/AS model

Two factors explain the *slope* of the AD curve, as distinct from a *shift* of the curve. The first is a **real balance effect** or **wealth effect**. Assuming a given nominal stock of money in the economy, a decrease in the price level increases people's stocks of real money balances, i.e. the same amount of money will buy more. Thus people feel wealthier and demand more goods. Secondly, increased real money balances cause the rate of interest to fall, further stimulating consumption and investment spending.

INTRODUCING AGGREGATE SUPPLY

Just as the AD curve shows the total quantities of real output that economic agents plan to purchase at different levels of domestic prices, so the AS curve shows the quantities of real output that businesses plan to produce and sell at different price levels. There are, however, a number of possible shapes for the AS curve. These different shapes result from different assumptions about how the economy works, and they carry different implications for macroeconomic policy.

The inverted L-shaped AS curve

Fig. 16.3 illustrates an inverted L-shaped AS curve based on the Keynesian view of how the economy works which was prevalent through much of the Keynesian era in the 1950s, 1960 and early 1970s.

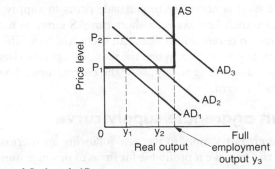

Fig. 16.3 The inverted L-shaped AS curve

243

According to Fig. 16.3, an expansion of aggregate demand will reflate real output rather than inflate prices, providing there is unemployment and spare capacity in the economy. Following an expansion of aggregate demand, which shifts the aggregate demand function from AD_1 to AD_2, real output increases from y_1 to y_2 but the price level does not change. This is explained by two (rather unrealistic) Keynesian assumptions. Firstly, it is assumed, that while there is unemployment, workers will be prepared to supply more labour at the going money wage rate to enable more output to be produced. Secondly, a constant marginal productivity of labour is assumed. Taken together these assumptions mean that marginal production costs remain constant as output is increased, until full employment is reached. Firms are therefore prepared to respond to increased demand by increasing output, without requiring an increase in the price level to induce an increased supply. In effect, Say's Law is reversed: instead of supply creating its own demand, demand is assumed to create its own supply. Once full employment is reached, at the level of real output y_3, any further increase in aggregate demand (e.g. to AD_3) causes prices and not output to rise.

The upward-sloping AS curve

Almost all economists now reject the inverted L-shaped AS curve which we have just described. Instead, there is general agreement that in the short run at least, the AS curve slopes upward as depicted in Fig. 16.4. The explanation of the upward-sloping AS curve stems from two important elements of the microeconomic theory of the firm, which we first came across in Chapter 4: the assumption that all firms aim to maximise profits, and the law of diminishing returns or diminishing marginal productivity. Following an expansion of aggregate demand from AD_1 to AD_2 in Fig. 16.4, which disturbs and initial equilibrium in the economy, the price level must rise to create the conditions in which profit-maximising firms are willing to supply more output. This is because firms face a declining marginal productivity of labour

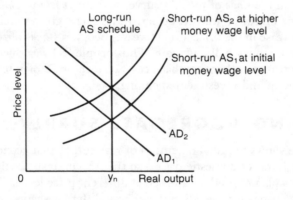

Fig. 16.4 Long-run and short-run aggregate supply curves

as they increase output in the short run. In this situation, the real wage rate paid by firms must fall (to match the declining marginal product of labour), in order to persuade firms it is profitable to demand more labour and to increase the supply of output. Given a constant money wage rate (which is assumed for all short-run AS curves), a rise in the price level (for example to P_2) reduces the real wage rate and produces the conditions necessary for firms to employ more labour and supply more output. The upward-sloping short-run AS function shows that a rise in the price level is necessary to persuade firms to supply more output!

It is important to emphasise that, because each short-run AS curve is drawn under the assumption that the money wage rate remains unchanged, there will be a different short-run AS curve for each and every money wage rate. When the money wage rate rises, firms reduce the the quantity of output they are willing to supply at the current price level. As a result, the short-run AS curve shifts leftward.

The vertical long-run aggregate supply curve

We have just seen that for aggregate supply to increase following an increase in aggregate demand, the price level must rise to make it profitable for firms to produce more output. This means that, at the going money wage rate, real wage rates fall. What happens next depends upon how workers respond to this cut in real wage rates. If they refuse to supply the extra labour needed to produce the extra output, output will fall back to the equilibrium level (y_n in Fig 16.4) prevailing before the rightward shift of the AD curve. However, if workers respond to the higher price level by pushing up money wage rates to restore their real wage rates, then the short-run AS curve will shift leftward from AS_1 to AS_2. The net effect is that the new AD and AS curves (AD_2 and AS_2) once again intersect at the original equilibrium level of output y_n. For supply-side economists, y_n is the natural level of output towards which market forces and a flexible price mechanism eventually adjust; it represents the long-run equilibrium level of output or production potential associated with the natural levels of employment and unemployment of labour which we investigated in Chapter 15. The vertical line drawn in Fig. 16.4, between the intersections of each pair of short-run AD and AS curves at this natural or equilibrium level of output is the long-run AS curve. It carries the message that the short-run expansionary effect on output and employment, resulting from the government increasing aggregate demand, is negated in the long run by the way the supply side of the economy responds to the demand stimulus.

SOME FURTHER DEVELOPMENTS OF THE AD/AS MACROECONOMIC MODEL

The explanation of the AD/AS model which we have given in the last two sections represents the way the model was first developed a few years ago, but the model has been modified and reinterpreted in a number of important ways in recent years. In the first place, the AD curve will only be downward sloping, showing aggregate demand falling as the price level rises, if we assume the money supply to be exogenously determined (i.e. the monetary authorities determine the money supply). This may be unrealistic. Many economists argue that the money supply is endogenously determined (i.e. passively adapting to the general public's demand to hold money balances). With an **endogenously-determined** stock of money in the economy, the AD curve is vertical rather than downward sloping.

The most significant developments of the AD/AS model concern aggregate supply rather than aggregate demand. When the AD/AS model was first developed, Keynesian economists generally rejected the vertical long-run AS curve, along with its message that an expansion of demand cannot increase output and employment permanently. By contrast, many modern Keynesians (sometimes called **new Keynesians** or **neo-Keynesians**), now accept that the AS curve will be vertical in the long run. However, there are significant differences in the new Keynesian and modern supply-side explanations of the vertical long-run AS curve which are explained below.

The new Keynesian explanation of aggregate supply

To understand the new Keynesian theory of aggregate supply, we must first understand the Keynesian theory of wage determination. Keynesian economists stress that wage rates are usually negotiated and set for a contract period, customarily for the year ahead. This is so, whether wages are set through collective bargaining or through individual negotiation. As a result of the system of wage setting, wage rates adjust only sluggishly to new conditions. They are characterised by what Keynesians call wage stickiness. When the price level rises, money wages lag behind, not catching up until the current contract period runs out. During this period, the real wages fall, and the aggregate supply of output increases. However, contract renewal gives workers the opportunity to negotiate an increase in the money wage sufficient to restore the real wage to its previous level. This raises production costs and reduces profits, causing firms to reduce the output they are prepared to supply, i.e. the short-run AS curve shifts leftward. In summary, in the new Keynesian analysis, short-run AS curves relate to the period during which wages are in effect preset, the long-run AS curve relates to the longer period in which all wage contracts have been revised to take account of price changes. When prices rise while wages are fixed, employment and output rise. Over the longer period, money wages adjust to higher prices and the long-run AS curve is vertical.

The new classical explanation of aggregate supply

Free-market economists believe in the virtues of competition and free markets. One such group of economists is known as the **new classical** school, already mentioned in the context of the theory of rational expectations in Chapter 15. The key belief, which separates new classical economists from other generally free-market orientated economists, centres on the nature of markets. New classical economists assume that market prices are highly flexible, instantly adjusting to balance supply and demand, but if markets continuously clear and are always effectively in equilibrium, it should be impossible to distinguish between short-run and long-run aggregate supply: they should both be represented by the same vertical AS curve. Following **Professor Robert Lucas**, however, new classical economists do distinguish between an upward-sloping short-run AS curve and the vertical long-run AS curve. Professor Lucas, who is perhaps the most eminent of the new classical economists, explains the new classical short-run AS curve in the following way. Although markets and prices are highly flexible, individual firms have imperfect information about the general price level. When the price of their own product rises, they do not know whether it is a relative price rise of their product alone, or whether it is a part of a general price rise of all goods and services. Only a *relative* price rise justifies an expansion of output. If the general price level rises unexpectedly, new classical economists call this a **price surprise**. Initially, producers believe this to be a rise solely in their own relative price. In the short run therefore, each firm increases its output and the aggregate supply of output increases. When firms realise that general prices, rather than their own relative prices, have risen, the short-run AS curve shifts leftward and aggregate output falls back to its natural level.

THE VERTICAL AGGREGATE SUPPLY CURVE AND ECONOMIC POLICY

Whichever theoretical explanation of the the vertical LRAS curve is used, the curve is located at the natural or equilibrium level of real output, which is the level of output consistent with the natural rate of unemployment in the labour market. Because output and employment are assumed to be at their natural or equilibrium levels, any expansion of aggregate demand, for example from AD_1 to AD_2 in Fig. 16.4, causes the price level to rise, with no long-term effect upon the levels of real output and employment.

Supply-side economists conclude that it is irresponsible for governments to use expansionary fiscal or monetary policies to try to increase national output and employment. While such policies may succeed in the short run, at the expense of inflation, they are doomed eventually to fail. In the long run, output and employment fall back to their equilibrium or natural levels, which are determined by the economy's production potential or ability to supply. Thus, instead of expanding demand to reduce unemployment below its natural rate, supply-side economists believe that the government should use microeconomic supply-side policies to reduce the natural rate itself. It should introduce market-orientated supply-side policies with the aim of improving incentives and the performance of individual economic agents and markets. Only in this way can the government improve the economy's production potential by shifting the LRAS curve rightwards and increasing the natural levels of output and employment. In the supply-side view, there is no case for demand management, except when unemployment is well above its natural level and output well below its natural level. Macroeconomic policy in general should be subordinated to the needs of a supply-side orientated microeconomic policy which aims to increase the economy's production potential and shift the LRAS curve rightwards.

SUPPLY-SIDE POLICIES: A SUMMARY

Supply-side policies can be defined as those free-market and anti-interventionist government policies which increase the economy's production potential by improving competition and the efficiency of markets and resource allocation. If successful, such microeconomic policies have a macroeconomic effect also, through shifting the aggregate supply curve rightwards, thereby increasing the equilibrium or natural levels of output and employment and reducing the natural level of unemployment. Supply-side economic policies include:

1. **Industrial policy measures** such as privatisation, contractualisation, marketisation, deregulation and the creation of internal markets where the state continues to provide economic services such as health care and education.

2. **Tax reforms** including reducing the overall burden of income tax, cutting the marginal rate of income tax, and replacing the taxation of income with expenditure taxes.

3. **Reform of the welfare state** including reducing state welfare benefits to create an incentive to choose low-paid employment rather than unemployment, thereby reducing the unemployment trap.

4. **Labour market measures**, including improving the training of labour, removing protection for workers in low-paid industries, reducing the powers of trade unions, replacing collective bargaining with individual wage negotiation, restricting the right to strike, introducing short-term contracts to replace 'jobs for life', introducing profit-related and performance-related pay, and encouraging more flexible pension arrangements.

5. **Financial and capital market measures**, including deregulating financial markets and promoting greater competition amongst banks and building societies, encouraging saving with special tax privileges, encouraging wider share ownership, promoting entrepreneurship, popular capitalism and an enterprise culture, reducing public spending and the PSBR so as to free resources for private sector use and avoid crowding out.

Chapter roundup

Supply-side economics developed in the 1970s and 1980s as part of the wider neo-classical revival and attack upon the previously dominant Keynesian economics. The aggregate demand/aggregate supply (AD/AS) model has become the principal framework in which the theoretical and policy issues which separate free-market and Keynesian economists are analysed. Monetarists and supply-siders, both being part of the wider neo-classical revival and resurgence of free-market economics, share many similar views. Some of the major conflicts and controversies separating monetarists and Keynesians, which relate closely to the content of this chapter, are explored in the next chapter. Also of relevance are Chapter 10 on privatisation and related policies, Chapter 11 on the labour market, Chapter 12 on monetary policy and Chapter 13 which covers taxation, public spending and the PSBR.

Illustrative questions and answers

1   Essay Question

'There can be no doubt that the transformation of Britain's economic performance in the 1980s ... is above all due to the supply-side policies we have introduced to allow markets of all kinds to work better.' (Nigel Lawson, Chancellor of the Exchequer, July 1988). Discuss.
(100)
ULEAC

Tutorial note

By the time Nigel Lawson expressed this view in July 1988, the UK economy had benefited from seven years of continuous economic growth, starting from the depths of a severe recession which had lasted from 1979 to 1981. While accepting that growth was to be expected during the upswing of the business cycle, the Conservative Government went further and claimed that its supply-side policies were responsible for significantly improving the economy's long-term growth trend. The Government claimed that the abandonment of Keynesian demand management and interventionism had paved the way for a supply-side led British economic miracle. At the time the UK had moved close to the top of an EC league table measured in terms of the growth in productivity and employment, the fewest days lost in strikes etc.

But by 1991, the picture was much less rosy. 1990 saw the collapse of the Lawson boom and the UK economy entered the longest (if not the deepest) recession since the 1930s. Initially the Conservative Government believed that the recession would be a mere 'blip', interrupting only temporarily the continuation of growth and economic success brought about by its supply-side revolution. However, with the recession fast developing into a more severe slump or depression, Keynesian economists have argued that it was the boom years of the mid and late 1980s that constituted the true 'blip', temporarily disrupting the on-going and depressing story of low growth, de-industrialisation and declining competitiveness that have afflicted the UK economy since at least the 1970s. The Keynesians further argue that the 1980s boom, far from being the result of successful supply-side policies, was largely caused by a massive and irresponsible boost to demand, brought about by tax cuts and the removal of controls on bank lending – policies introduced by the Chancellor of the Exchequer Nigel Lawson himself.

Suggested answer plan

- Briefly describe the state of the UK economy in the late 1980s.
- Explain how, in principle, supply-side policies could have brought about the economic success experienced at the time.
- Discuss whether the evidence supports the view that supply-side policies were responsible for this success.
- Introduce the possibility that demand expansion rather than supply-side policies were responsible for the 1980s boom.
- Draw an overall conclusion, and indicate that whatever the truth, the economic success did not continue into the early 1990s, though supply-siders claim further success for their policies in the mid-1990s.

2 Data Question

Table 1 *Distribution of the workforce*

| | Thousands | | | |
	1979	1983	1986	1989
Employees in employment:				
Manufacturing	7 253	5 252	5 227	5 191
Services	13 580	13 501	14 297	15 427
Other	2 340	2 024	1 863	1 835
Self-employed persons	1 906	2 221	2 627	2 986
Unemployed	1 312	3 127	3 312	1 842

(Source: *Annual Abstract of Statistics* 1990 edition *Social Trends* (20) 1990 edition)

Table 2 *Gross domestic product at current prices*

| | £ million | | | |
	1979	1983	1986	1989
Whole economy	172 804	260 399	324 031	394 787
Manufacturing	48 714	61 299	76 485	93 433

(Source: *Annual Abstract of Statistics* 1990 edition)

Table 3 Output per person employed

Index numbers 1985 = 100				
	1979	1983	1986	1989
Whole economy	89.1	96.7	102.9	107.4
Manufacturing	79.9	91.8	103.1	115.7

(Source: *Economic Trends Annual Supplement* 1990 edition)

Table 4 Visible trade of the United Kingdom

	1979	1983	1986	1989
Volume index numbers 1985 = 100				
Exports	83.1	87.6	104.0	110.7
Imports	83.5	87.0	107.1	129.5
Value (£ million)				
Visible balance	−3 444	−1 509	−9 364	−20 826

(Source: *Annual Abstract of Statistics* 1990 edition)

(a) (i) Describe the main changes in the distribution of the United Kingdom's workforce between 1979 and 1989, as shown in Table 1. (4)

(ii) Examine the possible causes of the changes you have described. (7)

(b) To what extent do the data support the view that the United Kingdom economy has gone through a period of deindustrialisation? (5)

(c) Discuss the significance of the changes which have occurred in United Kingdom manufacturing industry for the performance of the economy. (9)   AEB

Tutorial note

(a) (i) The data shows the growing importance of employment in the tertiary or service sector and the decline of employment in manufacturing and primary industries (the 'others' category). Note also the growth of self-employment.

(ii) You can argue that the growth of service employment reflects the increased demand for services as income increases; the reduced scope for both productivity increases and labour-shedding in the service sector compared to manufacturing; and the relative protection of many service industries from import competition. The decline of employment in the primary sector was probably concentrated in the decline of the coal mining industry, while the growth of self-employment reflected government encouragement of small businesses and the fact that some of the workers who were laid-off in the recession of the early 1980s started their own small businesses. The decline of employment in manufacturing reflects the de-industrialisation process which we discuss below.

(b) You must draw on the information in all four tables for your answer to this question, and not just Table 1. Start your answer by stating what you understand by deindustrialisation, and then look for evidence of the process in the data. Beware of Table 2! At first sight, Table 2 implies that manufacturing output rose throughout the period shown by the data, though not as rapidly as total output. However the table shows nominal output (at current prices) before the effects of inflation have been taken into account. Since no data on inflation has been included in the question, you cannot calculate the changes in real manufacturing output.

For the most part, the data covers the upswing in the business cycle and the Lawson boom in the economy in the middle and late 1980s. And while the tables cover the recession which affected the UK economy in the early 1980s, the data ends just before the second very severe recession which hit the UK economy in 1990. In fact this question provides an excellent illustration of an important skill which data response questions can test: namely *your ability to separate the long-term trend in the economy from cyclical variations around the trend*. At the height of the Lawson boom, the Conservative Government and its supporters were claiming that its free-market supply -side policies had brought about a British economic miracle. Manufacturing output had in fact climbed back from the depths of the earlier recession, rising past its 1979 level, supporting the argument, so the Government claimed, that a *re-industrialisation* rather than *de-industrialisation* of Britain was taking place. The data on labour productivity in Table 3 and the shedding of labour indicated by Table 1 might support this view. But Keynesians claim that the Government did indeed make the mistake of confusing the cyclical upswing with the long-term trend, and that while the credit-led extended boom of the 1980s masked the deindustrialisation process (though the import penetration implied by the trade figures in Table 4 provide some continuing evidence of deindustrialisation), deindustrialisation returned with a vengeance to scourge the UK economy in the early 1990s.

(c) For this part of the question you should develop the points we have just made in the guidance notes to part (b); for example does manufacturing matter, and can, and are, service industries taking the place of manufacturing in the UK economy?

Question bank

1 Explain the basis for supply-side measures to cure unemployment. Discuss whether or not the principal measures taken by the Government to deal with unemployment in recent years have been successful. (25)   *NEAB*

Pitfalls

With the first part of the question, there is a danger of *describing* the various supply-side measures such as privatisation and income tax cuts. Lengthy description is not required; instead you must explain that supporters of supply-side policies believe they are more effective than demand-management policies in promoting the growth of output and employment. For the second part, you must write a balanced answer and avoid a polemical approach either for or against supply-side economics.

Key points

Start off by explaining the meaning of supply-side policies, giving *brief* examples of particular supply-side measures. Then address the basis of supply-side measures, in terms of the supposed inappropriateness of demand-side measures and the effect of supply-side measures in improving the economy's efficiency, competitiveness and overall performance. For the last part of your answer, you must draw on the experience of the UK in recent years. Indicate the criteria by which you are judging success, and conclude by giving your opinion on whether supply-side measures have achieved the objectives set by the policy makers.

2 (a) Explain what is meant by the 'natural rate of unemployment' (also known as NAIRU). (30)

  (b) Evaluate the effects of demand-side and supply-side policies on the natural rate of unemployment. (70)   *ULEAC*

Pitfalls

There is a danger of writing too short an answer to part (a). This part of the question carries almost a third of the available marks, so you must expand your answer beyond a basic definition. Although the question does not instruct you to draw a diagram, it would be a good idea to make relevant use of a Phillips curve diagram. The key word in part (b) is *evaluate*; you will not score highly if you simply *describe* the various policies, or if you restrict your evaluation solely to demand-side or supply-side policies.

Key points

Start by defining the natural rate as the rate of unemployment consistent with non-accelerating inflation, and with market clearing in the aggregate labour market. Illustrate the concept on an expectations-augmented Phillips curve diagram. Alternatively you could explain the natural rate with the aid of a supply and demand diagram for the aggregate labour market, showing the natural or equilibrium level of employment. For part (b), firstly define demand-side and supply-side policies, then explain their likely effects, and then conclude your answer by assessing which is preferable.

3 (a) What factors determine the level of aggregate supply in an economy? (40)

    (b) To what extent may reductions in unemployment benefit and income tax rates affect the general level of unemployment. (60)   *ULEAC*

Pitfalls

The question does *not* ask for an account of the AD/AS model or for an explanation of the shape of the aggregate supply curve. You don't have to give a definitive answer to part (b); however you should display an awareness that different causes of unemployment require different remedies.

Key points

Define aggregate supply, and then divide your answer to part (a) equally between a discussion of the underlying determinants of aggregate supply (e.g. the resource base, the availability and quality of labour and capital etc) and the factors which influence the output decisions of profit-maximising entrepreneurs. For part (b), you may argue that the policy measures specified in the question might reduce frictional and real-wage unemployment, but would not reduce some types of unemployment, e.g. demand-deficient unemployment. The extent to which the measures will reduce unemployment must depend on the relative significance of the various possible causes of unemployment. Make sure you use appropriate theory to back up the arguments you make.

CHAPTER 17

KEYNESIANISM AND MONETARISM

Units in this chapter

Chapter objectives

In this chapter we bring together many of the themes and strands of argument which have been developed in the previous chapters on macroeconomics. In Chapter 15, we saw how it has proved difficult for governments to achieve two of the most important goals of economic policy: **full employment** and **price stability**, and in Chapter 16 we have looked in some depth at free-market **supply-side economics** which is closely related to monetarism. We shall now conclude our coverage of macroeconomies in the domestic economy, by presenting a more general overview of **Keynesian** and **monetarist economic goals** or **objectives**. We shall continue to develop the instruments and objectives approach to economic policy which we have used on occasion in previous chapters, explaining how different **policy instruments**, for example fiscal and monetary policy, have been used by economists of the two schools to try to achieve their desired objectives.

17.1 MACROECONOMIC POLICY

THE OBJECTIVES OF MACROECONOMIC POLICY

Macroeconomics involves the study of the whole economy, or the economy at the aggregate level. Macroeconomic policy is concerned with improving and stabilising the aggregate levels of output, employment and prices in the economy, and the trade and capital flows that make up the balance of payments. At the risk of over-simplification, it is useful to think of macroeconomic policy as a problem of **assigning separate policy instruments to particular objectives or goals**. Since the Second World War, governments in industrial mixed economies such as the UK have faced the same broad range of objectives, namely to:

1. create and maintain **full employment**;

2. achieve **economic growth** and **improved living standards**;

3. achieve a fair or **acceptable distribution of income and wealth**, between regions and different income groups in society;

4. to limit or **control inflation**, or to achieve some measure of **price stability**;

5. to attain a **satisfactory balance of payments**, usually defined as the avoidance of an external deficit which might create an exchange rate crisis.

The order in which we have listed these objectives is not accidental. There is general agreement amongst economists of all schools, free-market and monetarist as well as Keynesian, that objectives (1) to (3) are the **ultimate objectives** of economic policy – though there is considerable disagreement both on the nature of full employment and social fairness, and on how to attain them. Objectives (4) and (5) are **intermediate objectives** or possibly constraints in the sense that an unsatisfactory performance in controlling inflation or the balance of payments can prevent the attainment of one or other of the ultimate policy objectives.

THE INSTRUMENTS OF MACROECONOMIC POLICY

At a general level, we can divide the instruments of economic policy into **monetary policy**, **fiscal policy** and the use of **direct controls** which constrain or limit the freedom of market forces and of economic agents, such as firms or workers, to behave and make decisions in the way they would otherwise wish. **Incomes policy** and the **imposition of regulations** are examples of policies based on direct controls. In Chapter 13 we defined **fiscal policy** as economic policy to achieve the government's economic objectives using fiscal instruments such as government spending, taxation and the budget deficit. Chapter 12 defined monetary policy in terms of monetary instruments such as the money supply, the rate of interest and controls over bank lending. It is often appropriate to disaggregate broad labels such as fiscal policy and monetary policy and look in a more detailed fashion at specific policy instruments encompassed within them, such as changes in particular taxes and types of government spending (in fiscal policy), changes in interest rates (as a monetary policy instrument) and the use of the exchange rate as a macro-policy instrument. As a generalisation, in the Keynesian era policy instruments of all kinds were used at the macro-level in a discretionary way, to manage aggregate demand or the **demand-side** of the economy. This means that governments were prepared to change such instruments as tax and interest rates from year to year – and sometimes almost from month to month – in pursuit of the short-term management of demand and of economic activity.

Under the influence of monetarism and free-market theory, the reverse has been true. Economic policy has been aimed largely at improving supply-side performance, and at creating a stable and competitive environment in which markets can function efficiently. Since the decline of Keynesianism, macroeconomic policy has been used primarily to stabilise the price level. Macroeconomic policy is now less important than it used to be in the government's overall economic policy. Supply-side policies which aim to improve the performance of individual economic agents, industries and markets, have grown in relative importance.

THE MEANING OF FULL EMPLOYMENT

During the Keynesian era (from the 1940s to the late 1970s), successive UK governments were committed to achieving full employment, which was the principal objective of economic policy. At the time, full employment was often defined as occurring when about 3% of the labour force were unemployed. Now, in the mid-1990s, there are about 27 million people in the UK labour force. According to this definition, full employment would occur in the UK if 800,000 people were unemployed. However, monetarist and supply-side economists usually define full employment in terms of the **natural level** or rate of unemployment which was explained in Chapters 15 and 16. Currently, most monetarists estimate the natural rate of unemployment in the UK to be around 2 million, though a leading monetarist, Professor Patrick Minford, has argued that the natural rate is about 800,000, and therefore currently consistent with the earlier Keynesian measure of full employment.

IS FULL EMPLOYMENT STILL A POLICY OBJECTIVE?

Since 1979, unemployment in the UK has seldom been below 2 million. Indeed, in the recessions of the early 1980s and 1990s, unemployment rose above 3 million. Many people claim that, if unemployment were correctly measured, the total would be significantly above the official figure which measures the number of people actually claiming benefits. If governments are still committed to achieving full employment, they have been unsuccessful – assuming we define full employment in terms of 3% of the labour force unemployed. Some Keynesian economists argue that under the influence of monetarist and supply-side theory, recent UK governments have abandoned the previous commitment to full employment. A few go even further, arguing that governments have deliberately used high unemployment as a policy instrument to batter the labour force into submission, in pursuit of policy objectives such as price stability and higher business profitability. Free-market economists deny this. They argue that only entrepreneurs and markets, and not governments can create jobs. Thus, the government should restrict its role to creating the conditions in which the private sector can deliver growth and eventual full employment. These conditions include price stability and competitive, efficient markets, free of the burden of high taxation and excessive government regulation. Temporarily high unemployment is an unavoidable cost of putting the economy right, but once competitive and flexible markets are in place and prices are stable, the **enterprise economy** should deliver growth and fuller employment.

17.2 KEYNESIANISM AND MONETARISM

KEYNESIANISM

Keynesianism is a label attached to the theories and policies of those economists who claim to have inherited the mantle of the great English economist, J M Keynes. In *The General Theory of Employment, Interest and Money* published in 1936, Keynes created a theory of the working of the whole economy, and from this foundation modern macroeconomics developed. Keynes argued that no automatic tendency exists for unregulated market forces to bring about full employment and that persistent mass unemployment could be caused by deficient demand. Before his death in 1946, Keynes adapted his **theory of deflation and deficient demand** to the **problem of inflation caused by excessive demand**. However, although he did not live to see it, the true Keynesian era dawned in the years after 1945 when, in the United Kingdom in particular, Keynesianism became the new economic and political orthodoxy. Essentially, Keynesianism became associated with an increased level of government intervention in the economy, especially through **budget deficits** and **fiscal policy**, to **fine-tune or manage aggregate demand** to a level consistent with achieving relative full employment and economic growth without excessive costs in terms of inflation or balance of payments crises.

MONETARISM

Monetarism takes its name from the belief held by all monetarists that inflation is explained by the quantity theory of money; according to strict monetarism all inflation is caused by a prior expansion of the money supply. In fact, monetarism means rather more than this, extending to encompass a large part of the **pre-Keynesian** or **classical** view of how the economy works. Indeed, **the new classical macroeconomics** is probably a better descriptive label than monetarism of the true roots of the views held by many members of the monetarist school.

SOME FUNDAMENTAL ISSUES OF DISPUTE

Later in the chapter we shall examine some of the issues of dispute between Keynesians and monetarists on particular aspects of government policy. First, however, we shall look at some rather more fundamental differences in the views held by the two schools on the nature of the economy:

1 The separation of real and monetary forces

Many monetarists appear to accept the old classical view (known as the **classical dichotomy**) that real and monetary forces in the economy are separate. Via the quantity theory of money, an increase in the money supply causes the price level to rise, but it leaves unaffected the equilibrium values of relative prices and levels of output and employment. This view, which is generally rejected by Keynesians, carries the implication that a policy of monetary expansionism will in the long run increase prices but not output and employment, though in the short run (a period of up to five or ten years according to Milton Friedman) some monetarists agree that monetary changes can primarily affect output.

2 The stability of market forces

Monetarists see a market economy as a calm and orderly place in which the market mechanism, working through incentives transmitted by price signals in competitive markets, achieves a better or more optimal outcome than can be attained through government interventionism. In essence, risk-taking businessmen who will gain or lose through the correctness of their decisions in the market-place know better what to produce than civil servants and planners cocooned by risk-free salaries and secured pensions. And provided that markets are sufficiently competitive, what is produced is ultimately determined by the wishes of consumers, who also know better than governments what is good for them. According to this philosophy the correct economic function of government is an **enabling** function rather than a **providing** function, to act as 'nightwatchman' by maintaining law and order, to provide public goods where the market fails, and generally to ensure a suitable environment in which wealth-creating private enterprise can function in competitive markets subject to minimum regulation.

This view of the correct economic role of government leads monetarists generally to **reject discretionary intervention** in the economy as a means of achieving goals such as reduced unemployment. At best, such intervention will be ineffective, at worst it will be destabilising and damaging. To ensure that such intervention does not take place, governments should adopt, if necessary by law, fixed or automatic policy rules. In the past monetarists have recommended the adoption of a **fiscal** rule to **balance the budget** or **reduce the PSBR** to a fixed percentage of GDP; a monetary rule to expand the money supply in line with the growth of real GDP; and an **exchange rate rule** either to keep to a fixed exchange rate or to allow the exchange rate to float freely. (The debate between Keynesians and monetarists on the respective merits and demerits of discretionary policy and automatic rules is sometimes conducted in terms reminiscent of a motor manual. Thus Milton Friedman argued the advantage of a 'fixed throttle' increase in the money supply, rejecting the fine-tuning of demand advocated by the Keynesians.)

In contrast, Keynesians adopt a rather different view of the functioning of an unregulated market economy. In particular, they stress:

- the **imperfect nature of generally uncompetitive markets**, the growth of monopoly power and producer sovereignty, and the importance of uncertainty about the future and lack of correct market information as potentially destabilising forces;

- the **possible breakdown of money linkages between markets**. In market economies money is used as a means of payment for market transactions, but people receiving money incomes from the sale of labour in the labour market may not necessarily spend their income on the purchase of goods and services in the goods market. Instead they may decide to hold idle money balances. Thus Say's Law that 'supply creates its own demand' breaks down and deficient demand causes involuntary unemployment of labour and other resources.

Thus monetarists emphasise the optimal aspects of a competitive economy in a state of general (and fully employed) equilibrium, and the role in attaining such an equilibrium of private economic agents reacting to price signals in conditions of near-perfect market information. In competitive markets the market mechanism working through **flexible** prices will move the economy towards a full employment equilibrium. In contrast, the Keynesians emphasise the **inflexible** nature of prices and particularly wages. They also see the economy in terms of **disequilibrium** rather than **equilibrium**. The economy is subject to the uncertainty of random shocks or autonomous changes which, by inducing destabilising multiplier effects, hold no guarantee of a smooth and orderly movement to a full employment equilibrium. By managing the level of demand the government can 'know better' than unregulated market forces. It can anticipate and counter the destabilising forces existent in the market economy, achieving a better outcome than is likely in an economy subject to market forces alone.

In summary, therefore, monetarists lay great stress on the essentially stabilising properties of market forces, seeing discretionary government intervention as destabilising and inefficient. Conversely, Keynesians justify discretionary interventionism on the grounds that it stabilises an inherently unstable market economy.

17.3 POLICY ISSUES

KEYNESIAN OBJECTIVES AND INSTRUMENTS

In order to explain the principal points of difference between Keynesian and monetarist policies, we shall adopt an **objectives and instruments approach**. First we must identify the objectives, goals or targets which governments or their policy-makers wish to achieve. Once we have specified the objectives, the next stage is to assign a particular policy instrument to a particular objective.

In the earlier part of the Keynesian era, and especially in the 1950s and early 1960s, the Keynesian policy-makers in the United Kingdom relied on one principal policy instrument – the use of discretionary fiscal policy. Fiscal policy was used to achieve three policy objectives: **full employment, a satisfactory balance of payments** (and the protection of a fixed exchange rate), and **control of inflation**. In order to create full employment, tax cuts and increases in public spending resulting in a budget deficit were used to expand demand. However, an increased level of demand also raised imports and pulled up the price level. Eventually, either a balance of payments crisis or an unacceptable rise in the inflation rate, or both, would cause the policy-makers to initiate a reversal of policy in which fiscal policy would be used to deflate demand in order to protect the exchange rate or to reduce inflation. Thus Keynesianism became associated with stop-go management of the economy.

It is worth noting that in this era discretionary **fiscal policy** was used as the principal tool of demand management, partly because the Keynesians believed it to be more effective than discretionary monetary policy, but also because **monetary policy** was in the main assigned to another objective, that of **National Debt management**. Nevertheless, the role of monetary policy was not absolutely clear; it was also used as a supplementary tool of demand management to back up fiscal policy, and as a means of protecting the exchange rate through high interest rates in the recurrent balance of payments crises of the era. In a credit squeeze, demand would be deflated through the use of monetary policy instruments such as open-market operations and the raising of interest rates.

During this first period of Keynesian management of the British economy, successive British governments were committed to preserving a fixed exchange rate. The **exchange rate** was thus a **target** rather than an **instrument** of the policy. But in the latter part of the Keynesian era in the later 1960s and the early 1970s, many Keynesians came to the conclusion that if stop–go was to be avoided a separate policy instrument must be assigned to each of the three principal objectives of policy. Accordingly, the Keynesian assignment rule became:

INSTRUMENT		OBJECTIVE
Fiscal policy	:	Full Employment and Growth
Exchange Rate policy	:	Balance of Payments
Incomes policy	:	Control of Inflation
Monetary policy	:	National Debt Management

KEYNESIANS AND THE EXCHANGE RATE

The Keynesians believed that their ability to achieve sustained full employment and economic growth by means of expansionary demand management policies was severely constrained by the tendency of the balance of payments to go into serious deficit whenever full employment was approached. Increasingly in the early 1960s, Keynesians argued in favour of abandoning the commitment to maintain a fixed exchange rate. **Devaluation** should be used as a policy instrument to look after the balance of payments, leaving fiscal policy free to pursue the objective of full employment. (You should refer to Chapters 19 and 20 for a detailed explanation of the effects of a change in the exchange rate on the balance of payments.) The ideas of **export-led growth** and of the existence of a **virtuous circle** became fashionable amongst Keynesians in the 1960s. They argued that a devaluation (or downward float) of the exchange rate improves the competitive position of exports and worsens that of imports. The improved balance of payments position then stimulates growth which in turn stimulates productivity. The competitive position of exports then further improves as a result of falling average costs of production. The process continues, with exports stimulating growth, stimulating competitiveness and so on. Conversely, it was believed that an overvalued exchange rate could explain Britain's predicament in the 1960s, trapped in a **vicious circle** of uncompetitive exports, slow growth, and a worsening balance of payments position.

Nevertheless, neither the 1967 devaluation of the £ nor its floating in 1972 succeeded in achieving for Britain the 'miracle' of export-led growth. Against this background, economists of the Keynesian persuasion increasingly turned their attention to **incomes policies**, and even to **import controls**, in the search for additional policy instruments with which to manage the economy successfully.

KEYNESIANS AND INCOMES POLICY

As it became increasingly clear that, on its own, discretionary fiscal policy or demand management was unable to secure both full employment and price stability, Keynesians, or post-Keynesians, of the cost-push school turned their attention to incomes policy as the appropriate instrument to reduce inflation. However, many economists dispute the idea that an incomes policy should be regarded as a well-defined policy instrument. They argue that incomes policy has become a label for a wide variety of statutory and voluntary, short-term and long-term policies for the freezing, restraint or planned growth of wages, incomes, and even prices. Incomes policies can vary from emergency ad hoc measures, usually of short duration in response to a panic or crisis, to the long-term forward planning of the growth of incomes, based on some social consensus.

Other economists take the view that the control of inflation is not necessarily the main objective of an incomes policy. Many Marxists argue that its main function is to squeeze wages so as to alter the distribution of income in favour of profits. A popular view is that incomes policies should be used to pursue a 'social fairness' policy in which job evaluation replaces market forces as the determinant of wages. One result of this proliferation of interpretations as to what is meant by incomes policy is that it is exceedingly difficult to evaluate the effectiveness of incomes policies in controlling inflation. This is because it is almost impossible to compare a 'policy-on' period with a period of 'policy-off' as no one can agree on what exactly constitutes an incomes policy.

MONETARIST INSTRUMENTS AND OBJECTIVES

While the Keynesians have consistently searched for an ever-wider range of policy instruments with which to conduct the management of the economy, the monetarists have argued that the correct role of government is to **minimise its intervention in the economy**. While monetarists usually believe that discretionary monetary policy has a more powerful influence on the level of money national income than fiscal policy, it is wrong to draw the conclusion that monetarists advocate its use in the management of the level of demand. Not only would a discretionary monetary policy be unpredictable in its effects, the main effect of monetary expansion would be a rising price level rather than a growth of real output. Monetarists usually reject the use of discretionary economic management policies of any kind – **fiscal policy**, **monetary policy**, **incomes policy** and **exchange rate policies**. Instead, they argue that the economic function of government is to create the conditions in which market forces, working through price signals and private incentives, can properly operate. Nevertheless, it is still useful to analyse monetarist economic policy in terms of instruments and objectives, even though the monetarists prefer the announcement of firm policy rules to a discretionary intervention in the working of the economy:

❶ The **ultimate objective** of monetarist policy is to create conditions in which market forces and private enterprise can ensure full employment and economic growth.

❷ Control of inflation is seen as a necessary condition or **intermediate objective** which must be achieved before market forces can work properly.

❸ Monetarists believe that inflation is caused by an excessive rate of growth of the money supply. Therefore control of the money supply is a necessary **intermediate (or immediate) objective** of policy. Nevertheless, control of the money supply may be difficult to achieve. Some monetarists believe that it should be regarded as a general indicator of whether or not the policy is 'on course', and used in conjunction with other indicators or intermediate targets such as the exchange rate and the rate of growth of Money GDP.

❹ Monetary policy cannot be separated from the **fiscal stance** adopted by the government. At the root of monetarism is the belief that the levels of public spending and the PSBR must be used as a **policy instrument** to achieve control over the rate of growth of the money supply. A tight fiscal stance and the reduction of both public spending and the PSBR as a proportion of GDP will also reduce undesirable **crowding out** in the economy by freeing a greater volume of resources for use and employment in the private sector. Some monetarists recommend a **balanced budget fiscal policy rule**.

❺ Monetarists place considerable emphasis on **supply-side** or **microeconomic policies** which have the general objective of making markets more competitive. Competition policy and industrial relations policy (perhaps a euphemism for anti-trade union policy) are examples, together with cuts in income tax rates to promote supply-side incentives.

MONETARISTS AND THE EXCHANGE RATE

Practical monetarism thus involves the adoption of two automatic policy rules:

❶ A **fiscal rule** to balance the budget or to reduce public spending and the PSBR as proportions of GDP;

and

❷ A **monetary rule** to allow the money supply to grow at some predetermined rate, for example based on the rate of growth of real GDP.

There is much less agreement amongst monetarists on the form of a third rule to be adopted for the exchange rate. Monetarists generally fall into one of two camps, advocating either a **fixed** or a **freely floating** exchange rate. Those monetarists who have studied the inflationary process in a regime of fixed exchange rates such as existed before 1972 are sometimes called **international monetarists** or **global monetarists**. In such a system, the **world inflation rate** is determined by the rate of growth of the **world money supply**. For a country like the UK, the domestic inflation rate must converge with the world inflation rate to maintain the fixed exchange rate. The domestic money supply responds endogenously to accommodate, or finance, the rate of inflation imported from the rest of the world. Thus, instead of changes in the domestic money supply causing inflation, with fixed exchange rates, the imported rate of inflation changes the domestic money supply. This is the reverse of the traditional theory of monetarism, developed originally by Milton Friedman as appropriate either for a closed economy or for a system of floating exchange rates. Nevertheless, in a fixed exchange rate system, the rate of world inflation is still caused by world monetary growth.

At the beginning of the monetarist experiment in the early 1980s, many monetarists seemed to prefer a completely **free** or **cleanly floating exchange rate** because this is consistent with their view that market forces and not the government should determine as far as possible the level of activity within the economy. As in the case of other forms of government intervention, many monetarists believe that an attempt by government to manage the exchange rate will create distortions and inefficiencies and is in any case in the long run unable to defy market forces. (The £'s brief experience in the **Exchange Rate Mechanism** of the European Monetary System, from 1990 to 1992, gives considerable support to this view. We develop this theme in Chapter 20.) Additionally, a floating exchange has the advantage, in theory at least, of isolating the economy from international inflationary pressure. As has just been explained, with a fixed exchange rate, a country may import inflation from the rest of the world. Many monetarists, and also many Keynesians, argue that this is what happened in the 1960s when the USA expanded its domestic economy and built up a huge balance of payments deficit against the rest of the world. Because the dollar was the cornerstone of the Bretton Woods system of fixed exchange rates that existed at the time, the Americans managed to persuade other countries to maintain their fixed exchange rates against the dollar and to accept dollars in payment for US imports from the rest of the world. The resulting outflow of dollars from America into the reserves of the rest of the world greatly swelled international demand and, in the monetarist interpretation, added to the excessive rate of growth of the world money supply. If, instead, other exchange rates had freely floated against the dollar, the rest of the world would not have imported the dollars created by the American authorities. The American balance of payments deficit would simply have resulted in an excess supply of dollars on foreign exchange markets which would then have caused the exchange rate of the dollar to fall until the US deficit had been eliminated.

Nevertheless, the experience of floating exchange rates in the 1970s and 1980s has convinced many monetarists – and Keynesians as well – that a floating exchange rate contributes to the inflationary process. They argue that a completely fixed exchange rate provides a source of discipline for workers and business enterprises within the domestic economy. If, for example, workers bargain for wage increases of 10% when the average rate of growth of productivity is only 4%, then the domestic price level is almost sure to rise. But in a regime of freely floating exchange rates, international competitiveness need not be adversely affected. The exchange rate may simply fall to maintain the initial relative price of British goods compared with foreign goods. But the inflation process does not stop here. Workers may respond to the rising money price of imports by demanding even higher money wages in an attempt to increase the real wage. This causes a further rise in prices, followed by a fall in the exchange rate and further wage increases in a vicious inflationary spiral accompanied by a plummeting exchange rate.

The floating of the exchange rate may also remove a source of discipline from the behaviour of governments. Indeed, the acceleration in the rate of inflation experienced simultaneously by many countries in the 1970s has been explained in terms of the breakdown of the Bretton Woods system of fixed exchange rates in 1971 and 1972. Governments apparently felt free to reflate demand, hoping that a floating exchange rate would 'look after' the balance of payments. They also hoped that in a regime of floating exchange rates there would no longer be a need periodically to deflate demand in order to support the exchange rate. As a result, simultaneous reflation by many countries in the early 1970s caused a world-wide increase in demand which world output was incapable of meeting, and inflation resulted.

By the mid-1980s many economists, both monetarist and Keynesian, had swung round to the opinion that a fixed exchange rate was needed to impose the necessary counter-inflationary discipline upon the behaviour of workers and firms in the setting of wages and prices, and upon government in avoiding the temptation to reflate demand irresponsibly. This was perhaps the most significant reason why the £ joined the fixed exchange rate system of the ERM in 1990. But ERM membership at the high parity at which the £ was fixed, provided not so much a source of discipline as a straitjacket. Monetary policy in general – and interest rates in particular – had to be set to attract capital flows into the £ to support the overvalued exchange rate. As a result, the government lost almost all its freedom to pursue an economic policy aimed at protecting the domestic economy from the recession which hit the UK economy in 1990. Opponents of fixed exchange rates and also supporters of the ERM who believed that the £ should have entered the system at a much lower parity, now agree that ERM entry at an overvalued exchange rate in 1990 caused the UK recession in the early 1990s to be much longer and deeper than would have been the case if the £ had stayed out of the ERM.

MONETARISTS AND INCOMES POLICIES

Most monetarists completely oppose the use of an incomes policy except as an informal policy to control pay increases in the public sector, where the state is the employer. As we have explained, monetarists accept the neoclassical tradition of the allocative efficiency of market forces and retain a suspicion of the economic power of the state. Incomes policies are undesirable because they interfere with and distort the working of the market mechanism, and extend the economic role of the state. Nevertheless, some economists take up a more eclectic or pragmatic position between the extremes adopted by cost-push Keynesians and monetarists. The eclectics argue that an incomes policy may sometimes have a useful role in reducing inflationary expectations, without at the same time greatly distorting market forces.

Although monetarists and supply-side economists reject a formal, and especially a **statutory** incomes policy, they certainly incorporate a policy towards incomes – or an informal incomes policy – into their overall policy aim of improving the competitiveness of the labour market. We can identify four distinct aspects of this monetarist policy towards incomes. These are the:

❶ **reduction of trade union monopoly power** over the supply of labour;

❷ **removal of labour restrictive practices** in labour markets;

❸ **education of workers in the reality of the market place**; and

❹ **direct imposition of wage restraint in the public sector** where the state is the employer, for example the annual public sector pay increase ceiling of 1.5% imposed by the Conservative Government in 1992 and the following years.

A FURTHER LOOK AT MONETARIST MONETARY POLICY

In the United Kingdom, the framework within which monetary policy has been conducted in recent years has been the **Medium Term Financial Strategy (MTFS)**, adopted by the Conservative Government in its 1980 budget. Initially, the MTFS was based almost exclusively on the monetarist belief that a firm announcement of a money supply target for a medium-term period, stretching several years ahead, would itself bring down the rate of inflation through its effect on **expectations of future inflation**. On its introduction in 1980, the Conservative Government stated that the MTFS *plots the path for bringing inflation down through a steady reduction in the rate of growth of the money supply secured by the necessary fiscal policies.* The objective of the MTFS was to bring about a gradual reduction in the growth of money GDP (or the nominal value of domestic output), in the belief that this would result in lower inflation, whilst leaving the growth of real GDP unaffected. Central to the strategy in the monetarist period of the early 1980s, was the announcement of medium-term targets for the growth of the money supply, designed to talk-down the rate of inflation by causing workers and firms to reduce their inflationary expectations. The monetarists argued that if people believe that a tough government is serious about reducing inflation, it will immediately begin to behave in a less-inflationary way, which in itself will reduce inflation.

Monetarists also emphasise the **interdependence of monetary and fiscal policy**. They believe that at the macro level, fiscal policy must be subordinate to, and consistent with, the needs of monetary policy. Governments must reduce the overall level of the PSBR, and use methods of borrowing or financing the PSBR, which are compatible with the monetary policy objective of preventing excess growth of the money supply. (You should refer back to Chapters 12 and 13 for an explanation of how various methods of financing a budget deficit and the PSBR affect the money supply.)

Chapter roundup

In this chapter, which concludes our main section on macroeconomic theory and policy, we have attempted to draw together many of the themes introduced in earlier units from Chapter 12 to Chapter 16. The essentials of the Keynesian national income-expenditure model are covered in Chapter 14. Chapters 12 and 13 cover areas of monetary and fiscal dispute between Keynesians and monetarists, including the topical issue of the importance of the PSBR and its effects upon the economy. Chapter 15 concentrates on the dispute about the causes of unemployment and inflation, while Chapter 16 surveys the main elements of supply-side economics which, along with monetarism, forms an important part of the neoclassical revival.

We have made some mention in this chapter of the impact that the balance of payments and the exchange rate have on the task of domestic economic management. This theme is developed in more depth in Chapter 19 on the balance of payments and Chapter 20 on the exchange rate.

Illustrative questions and answers

1   Essay question

(a) Explain and evaluate the monetarist view on the causes of inflation. (15)

(b) How does this explanation affect monetarists' attitudes towards

    (i)   the Public Sector Borrowing Requirement (PSBR)? (5)

    (ii) direct Government control of wages and prices? (5)   *WJEC*

Tutorial note

Unlike many essay questions, the first part of this question carries most marks, so you must develop your answer to part (a) at some length. Draw on the coverage of inflation theory in Chapter 15. As the chapter explains, the monetarist theory of inflation centres on the role of the money supply. Via the quantity theory of money, an expansion of the money supply leads, after a lag, to an increase in the price level. Basing your answer on the equation of exchange $(MV = Py)$, carefully explain the quantity theory. You can evaluate the theory either in the light of Keynesian criticisms of the theory, or by appealing to evidence. Does UK experience in the 1980s and 1990s support the theory?

Monetarists believe that PSBR growth leads either to excess monetary growth, and thence to inflation, or to financial crowding out of the private sector. Since monetarists believe that both these consequences of a large PSBR are undesirable, it follows that at the macro level, monetarist fiscal policy centres on controlling the growth of the PSBR.

The main body of this chapter explained how, in the Keynesian era, UK governments imposed income policies which involved the direct control of wages and prices. Monetarists, along with other free-market orientated economists, reject wage and price controls, arguing that they are distortive, inefficient and damaging. Far from using wage and price controls to contain inflation, monetarists advocate the removal of any existing controls which constrain the freedom of the labour market. Public sector wages provide the one exception; monetarists believe that when the state is the employer, wage rises should be limited to a rate consistent with the government's inflation target.

Suggested answer plan

(a) (i) Explain that monetarists believe that inflation is caused by a prior increase in the money supply.

(ii) Expand your explanation by outlining the quantity theory of money.

(iii) Introduce Keynesian criticisms of the quantity theory.

(iv) Evaluate the monetarist explanation of inflation, in the light of the Keynesian criticisms.

(v) Assess whether evidence provided by the UK economy supports the monetarist view.

(b) (i) State that monetarists believe that PSBR control is a necessary precondition for control of the money supply.

(ii) Explain the link between PSBR growth and money supply growth which underpins this view.

(iii) State that monetarists reject wage and price controls imposed on the private sector.

(iv) Explain that monetarists believe that such controls store up higher inflation for the future, and damage the economy.

2 Data Question

The rehabilitation of market forces in the early 1980s was seen at first as an aberration from the postwar consensus, and one that was likely to be short-lived. But I have little doubt that, as a longer perspective develops, history will judge that intervention and planning were the aberration, and that the market economy is the normal, healthy way of life.

Needless to say, belief in the system of free markets does not imply that markets are infallible, any more than examples of irrational market behaviour in any way undermine belief in the market system. What matters is that free markets bring greater benefits and fewer (and more readily corrected) costs than statism.

This is a truth increasingly recognized throughout the world: the lesson that the way to economic success is through the market place.

(Source: N. Lawson, *The State of the Market*, IEA Occasional Paper 80, 1988)

(a) What did Mr Lawson mean in referring to the 'postwar consensus'? (6)

(b) Critically appraise the statement that 'free markets bring greater benefits and fewer (and more readily corrected) costs than statism'. (14)

(c) What examples might Mr Lawson have had in mind in support of his case in favour of market forces? (5)

ULEAC

Tutorial note

At the economic level, the '**postwar consensus**' referred to the wide measure of agreement amongst economists (during the three decades after 1945) on the virtues of Keynesianism and the mixed economy. At the political level, this was the '**Butskellite consensus**', named after two centrist politicians, one Conservative (Rab Butler) and the other Labour (Hugh Gaitskell), who were influential in ensuring that every British government, from 1950 until the election of Mrs Margaret Thatcher's Conservative administration in 1979, subscribed to the 'postwar consensus'. The mix of private and public ownership and market and non-market provision of goods and services were regarded as 'about right for

Britain'. The election of a Labour government might extend the state sector at the margin, via some extra nationalisation, while conversely a Conservative administration (prior to 1979) might tinker with denationalisation; but there was general agreement on the virtues of Keynesian-inspired management of aggregate demand and of state provision of public and merit goods such as education and the National Health Service.

The second part of the question calls for a discussion of whether the benefits of free (and presumably competitive) markets, in terms of consumer sovereignty and the various types of efficiency we have explained at length earlier in this book, exceed the disadvantages resulting from the many examples of market failure we have also explained. Under '**statism**', market failure is regarded as so serious that state intervention completely replaces the market. Nigel Lawson probably had in mind a much different role for the state: essentially a **minimalist 'enabling' role** to create the competitive conditions in which markets can function efficiently. The examples Nigel Lawson might have had in mind (in 1988), in support of his case in favour of market forces, would include any benefits he believed had resulted from the programmes of privatisation and deregulation pursued in the 1980s. Since 1988 many of the economic changes taking place in Eastern Europe might also be cited; though the move towards the marketisation of formerly Communist and 'statist' economies, has also exposed some of the deficiencies of exclusive reliance on the virtues of the market.

Question bank

1 Explain what constitutes macroeconomic policy. Outline the broad changes which British macroeconomic policy has undergone since the 1970s and evaluate the success of current measures. (25) *NEAB*

2 (a) Outline the changing priorities of United Kingdom macroeconomic policy during the 1990s. (40)

(b) Discuss whether monetary policy alone is sufficient to achieve current macroeconomic priorities. (60) *ULEAC*

Pitfalls

The first part of both questions are broadly similar, but take care to note the dates specified in each question. Question 1 requires knowledge of the 1980s and 1990s, whereas Question 2 relates only to the 1990s. To write a good answer to the second part of Question 1, you must avoid the temptation simply to *describe* current economic policy. You must *evaluate* the success of the policy, particularly in terms of the main stated policy objective: the control of inflation. Part (b) of Question 2 requires only a brief description of monetary policy.

Key points

Start your answers to both questions by defining macroeconomics and by outlining the standard objectives of macroeconomic policy. Develop your answer to Question 1 by relating these objectives to policy instruments, then describe how Keynesian macroeconomic policy gave way to monetarist and free-market objectives and instruments over the period since the 1970s. Judge the success of recent policy by whether it has achieved its objectives. For 2(b), you should explain that monetary policy and fiscal policy are not independent of each other. To achieve its monetary policy objectives, a government must adopt an appropriate fiscal policy. You might also argue that appropriate supply-side policies are necessary to increase employment and economic growth, even though supply-side measures tend to be microeconomic rather than macroeconomic.

3 (a) Explain the argument that restricting the money supply should help to reduce inflation. (12)

(b) What are the problems of trying to use money supply control as a method of reducing inflation? (13)

WJEC

Pitfalls

For part (a), you must explain the monetarist theory of inflation. Don't debate whether the quantity theory of money provides a correct explanation of inflation in this part of your answer. You can debate this issue in your answer to part (b), but your answer will be too narrow if this is the only point you make.

Key points

The argument that restricting the money supply should help to reduce inflation assumes that inflation is caused by the growth of the money supply. If excessive monetary growth causes inflation, it follows that to control inflation, the growth of the money supply must be slowed down. Using the equation of exchange (MV = PT or MV = Py), develop this argument further. For part (b), you should introduce at least two arguments. Firstly, you could outline the difficulties involved in hitting a particular money supply target. Secondly, you could explain Goodhart's law. This states that as soon as a government uses money supply targets in order to control inflation, any previously stable relationship between the particular measure of the money supply targeted and inflation breaks down, rendering the policy ineffective.

TRADE

Units in this chapter

Chapter objectives

Previous chapters have examined the nature and the functioning of economic processes *within* a single economy – and in particular within the British economy – without devoting much attention to economic relations between countries. This chapter describes and explains the reasons for the **international specialisation** of production *between* countries and the resulting **trade** or **exchange of goods and services** that takes place. After examining the case for **tariffs** or **import duties** and other forms of **protectionism**, and assessing the **costs and benefits** of protectionism, **patterns of world trade**, past and present are described and explained. The chapter concludes with a brief survey of **free trade areas** and **customs unions**, considering whether such **trading blocs** promote or hinder the development of world trade.

18.1 THE CASE FOR TRADE

THE GENERAL CASE FOR SPECIALISATION AND TRADE

The general case for specialisation and trade centres on the proposition that countries or regions can attain levels of production, consumption and economic welfare which are beyond the production possibilities open to them in a world without trade. Assuming full employment of all factors of production, a country can only increase the production of one good or service by diverting resources away from the production of other goods. Whenever resources are scarce, the opportunity cost of increasing the output of one industry is the alternative output foregone in other industries in the economy. If, however, a country concentrates scarce resources and factors of production into producing the goods in which it is most efficient, total world production can increase. **Gains from specialisation** and trade are possible if countries can agree to exchange that part of the output which they produce that is surplus to their needs. Having stated the general case for trade, we shall now examine some more specific arguments in favour of specialisation and trade.

The benefits of competition

In Chapter 7 we explained how market forces operating in a perfectly competitive market economy can, subject to rather strong assumptions, achieve a state of **economic efficiency**, defined as a combination of **productive** and **allocative efficiency**. Within an isolated and relatively small economy, markets may be too small to be competitive and monopoly may predominate. Exposure to international competition is likely to make markets more competitive and hence more efficient.

The benefits of economies of scale and division of labour

The **benefits of division of labour** were first recognised in the 18th century by the great classical economist Adam Smith. Smith discussed the division of labour in the context of workers **specialising in different productive tasks** within a factory which itself specialised in producing a particular type of product. He then went on to extend the analysis to **specialisation between regions and countries**. Thus, it should be stressed that there are many different levels at which the benefits of the division of labour can be attained: **division of labour within a plant**; **division between plants** within a firm; **division between firms** within an industry; division **between industries** within a country; and finally **division of labour between countries**.

Adam Smith suggested three reasons why division of labour increased production and efficiency:

❶ workers become better at a particular task – **practice makes perfect**;

❷ **time**, which would be lost when workers move between tasks, is saved;

❸ **more and better capital** can be employed in production.

The latter advantage cited by Smith is particularly important, since it is closely related to the benefits of economies of scale. If a country specialises in producing the goods in which it is already most efficient, a large scale of production may allow it to benefit from **increasing returns to scale** and **economies of scale**. In other words, its industries become even more efficient, when, for example, long production runs allow firms to introduce more advanced forms of machinery and improved technology. In the absence of international trade, the limited extent of the domestic market may prevent a country from benefiting from economies of scale. Thus, by **extending the market**, international trade and specialisation allows the full benefits of the division of labour and economies of scale to be achieved (though we should also note that the possibility of diseconomies of scale and other disadvantages of the division of labour form the basis of a case against trade).

Increasing the range of choice

The international immobility of some factors of production and the unique allocation of natural resources in each country mean that **the production possibilities open to each country are different**. In the extreme, the production of some goods or services may be exclusive to a particular country. A simple example will show in this situation how wider choice can result from trade. If there are just two nations (A and B) and one can only produce bread and the other jam, then if each country's production exceeds its needs, both countries can gain by trading their surplus rather than letting it rot. Thus the welfare of each nation is increased as they both have bread and jam, rather than bread or jam.

ABSOLUTE ADVANTAGE

The benefits of the division of labour suggest that if each of the world's countries, with its own endowment both of natural resources such as soil, climate and minerals, and of man-made resources such as capital, know-how and labour skills, specialises in *what it does best*, total world output or production can be increased compared to a situation without specialisation. In economic terms, being better at producing a good or service means that a country can **produce a particular output** of the good at the **lowest cost in terms of resources used** (factors of production or inputs); in the language of Chapter 7, the country is **technically** and **productively efficient** in producing the good. We can say that if a country is best at or most technically efficient at producing a good or service, it possesses an **absolute advantage** in the good's production, whereas if it is not the best, the country suffers an **absolute disadvantage** when compared to other more technically efficient producers.

To illustrate absolute advantage (and the more subtle concept of comparative advantage), we shall construct a highly simplified model of the 'world' economy, by assuming just two countries A and B, each with just two units of resource (for example man-years of labour) that can produce just two commodities, bread and jam.

We shall also assume:

- Factors of production are perfectly mobile within each country and they can be instantly switched between industries. However, factors are immobile between countries, though final goods and services can be traded.
- There are constant returns to scale and constant average costs of production in both industries in both countries.
- Both commodities, bread and jam, are in demand in both countries.
- The limited resources and factors of production in each country are fully employed.

Suppose now that each country has equal resources and devotes half of its limited resources to bread production and half to jam. The production totals are:

	Bread (units)	Jam (units)
Country A	10	5
Country B	5	10
'World' total	15	15

The relative or **comparative cost** of bread production is lower in country A than in country B, but the position is reversed in the production of jam. Country A has an absolute advantage in bread production, whereas the absolute advantage in jam production lies with country B. If each country specialises in the production of the commodity in which it is most efficient and possesses the absolute advantage, we get:

	Bread (units)	Jam (units)
Country A	20	0
Country B	0	20
'World' total	20	20

The gains from specialisation and trade equal 5 units of bread and 5 units of jam, provided that there are no transport costs.

COMPARATIVE ADVANTAGE

It is less obvious that specialisation and trade are also worthwhile even when a country can produce all goods more efficiently at a lower absolute cost than other countries. This phenomenon is explained by the principle of **comparative advantage**, or a comparison of the **relative** efficiency of production in different countries rather than their **absolute** efficiency.

Suppose that country A becomes more efficient in both bread and jam production. If each country devotes half its resources to each industry, the production totals are:

	Bread (units)	Jam (units)
Country A	30	15
Country B	5	10
'World' total	35	25

Country A possesses an absolute advantage in both industries, but whereas A is six times as efficient in bread production, it is only 50% more efficient in jam production. Nevertheless, if country B produces an extra unit of jam, it need give up only half a unit of bread. In contrast, country A must give up two units of bread in order to increase production of jam by one unit. We say that **a country's comparative advantage lies in the good which it can produce relatively cheaply**, at a **lower opportunity** cost than its trading partner. Country A (which has the absolute advantage in both commodities) possesses a comparative advantage in bread production, whereas country B (with an absolute disadvantage in both) has the comparative advantage in jam production.

If each country specialises completely in the activity in which it possesses a comparative advantage, the production totals are:

	Bread (units)	Jam (units)
Country A	60	0
Country B	0	20
'World' total	60	20

You will notice that compared with the situation without specialisation and trade in which each country devoted half its resources to each industry, there is a gain of 25 units of bread, but a loss of 5 units of jam. Thus, in the case where one country is more efficient in both activities, we cannot say, without some knowledge of demand and the value placed on consumption of bread and jam by the inhabitants of the two countries, whether a welfare gain will result from **complete specialisation**. We can be more sure of a welfare gain if at least as much of one good and more of the other results from specialisation and trade. We can obtain this result by devising a situation in which country A, the country with the absolute advantage in both goods, decides not to specialise completely, but to devote some of its resources to jam production. For example, if country A produces 5 units of jam with one-sixth of its resources and 50 units of bread with the other five-sixths, then the production totals are:

	Bread (units)	Jam (units)
Country A	50	5
Country B	0	20
'World' total	55	25

Compared with the situation without specialisation and trade, there is a gain of 15 units of bread.

THE TERMS OF TRADE

The rate of exchange of bread for jam, or the **terms of trade**, will determine the benefits of trade for these trading partners. The limits to the exchange are set by each country's **opportunity cost ratio**. In the example where country A has an absolute advantage in the production of both goods, country A will be prepared to give up no more than 2 units of bread for 1 unit of jam, whilst country B will require at least $\frac{1}{2}$ a unit of bread for 1 unit of jam if trade is to be worthwhile. Thus the terms of trade must lie between $\frac{1}{2}$ unit of bread and 2 units of bread for 1 unit of jam. The exact rate of exchange, or the relative price of the two commodities, will be determined by the strength of demand.

In the real world where millions of goods and services are traded, a nation's average terms of trade are measured with index numbers. The average prices of exports and imports are calculated using weighted indices and the export index is divided by the import index to give the **terms of trade index**. A rise in the index shows an improvement in a nation's terms of trade, indicating that a given quantity of exports now pays for more imports than previously. We shall examine the causes and effects of changes in the terms of trade in greater detail in Chapters 19 and 20. It is worth noting, however, that a rise in the exchange rate of the £ and a domestic inflation rate higher than that of our trading partners, can both 'improve' the terms of trade, but that the effects of the 'improvement' are not necessarily beneficial in other respects.

18.2 PROTECTIONISM

METHODS OF PROTECTION

The decision to protect is made deliberately by a government. The method chosen may affect demand, supply or price. The demand for goods can be influenced by **tariffs**, **subsidies** and exchange controls. Supply can be manipulated by **embargoes, quotas, administrative restrictions** and **voluntary agreement**.

Tariffs

Tariffs, which may be specific or ad valorem, are taxes placed on imported, but not on domestic, goods. The ability of a tariff to reduce imports depends upon its size and upon the elasticity of demand for the imported good. If the country which imposes the tariff produces close substitutes, demand for imports is likely to be price elastic. In these circumstances, a tariff will reduce imports by switching demand towards the domestically produced substitutes. Conversely, if demand for imports is price inelastic, the main effect of the tariff will be on import prices rather than on the quantity of imports. (Refer back at this stage to the analysis in Chapter 13 on the various effects which follow an increase in expenditure taxes. A tariff is simply an example of an expenditure tax.)

Subsidies

These are provided in many, often clandestine, forms to avoid GATT restrictions on subsidies and dumping. The provision of export credit, VAT remission and regional aid may reduce total costs for exporters and thereby distort trade by affecting market prices. Support can be given to exporters by government agencies, such as the Export Credit Guarantee Department. At the same time, subsidies to domestic producers enable them to compete more easily with imported goods.

Exchange Control

Some nations control the amount of currency which can be used for buying imports. Usually foreign currency earnings (from exports) are deposited with the central bank, which authorises the withdrawals for the buying of imports. In this way, selective control of imports can be achieved. In Britain, up to 1979 when **exchange control** was abolished, transfers of cash and overseas investment were limited to protect the balance of payments.

Embargoes

As we have already mentioned, some goods are completely banned from entry into a country. This encourages smuggling and the development of black markets.

Quotas

The import of a certain quantity of goods may be allowed, usually via licensing arrangements, for example footwear into the UK. Although acting on supply rather than demand, a **quota** has the same effects as a tariff in that it raises prices and domestic output whilst cutting the volume of imports.

Administrative restrictions

These are used by many nations as a **covert method of protection**. A Japanese trading practice, considered by other countries to be unfair, has been the withholding of information on product specifications from foreigners but warning domestic producers of changes well in advance. Similarly, Britain has refused to admit poultry from countries which use vaccination rather than slaughter as the means of controlling foul pest.

Voluntary agreements

One government may try to persuade another to pressurise its exporters into limiting supplies to certain markets, for example Japanese government restraint over Japanese car exports to the UK and other EU countries. In April 1993, Japan agreed a voluntary cut in car exports to EU countries of 9.4% for 1993 (excluding the production of cars from 'transplant' factories armed by Nissan, Toyota and Honda in the UK). However, as car sales were expected to fall by a greater amount in the recession-hit EU market, European car manufacturers claimed that the agreement was in fact a sell-out that would increase the overall share of Japanese imports in the EU market.

THE CASE FOR PROTECTIONISM

The case for specialisation and trade is based on the proposition that all countries taken together will gain in terms of increased production, efficiency and welfare, provided that the terms of trade lie within the opportunity cost ratios. However, there is no guarantee that the gains are distributed equally amongst the trading countries. Although restraints on free trade will probably reduce world welfare, individual countries may feel that it is in their self-interest to restrict the freedom of trade. Not all the arguments put forward to justify restrictions on trade are strictly economic: social and political factors are also involved.

Economic arguments

❶ **The protection of infant industries** This argument is quite strong when there is scope for industries to benefit from economies of scale. A newly established industry, in for example a developing country, may be unable to compete with other countries in which established rivals are already benefiting from economies of scale. Protection may be justified during the early growth of an infant industry. This argument is closely related to **strategic trade theory**. Supporters of strategic trade theory argue that not all comparative advantage need be the product of luck and history; governments can use industrial policy, including financial aid to industry and subsidies, to invent or create comparative advantage for selected industries. Nevertheless, governements have to exercise considerable wisdom, choosing the best from a host of potential uses of resources, if they are to end up 'picking winners' or 'national champion' industries, rather than frittering away national resources through the protection and subsidy of 'national losers'.

❷ **To avoid the dangers of overspecialisation** The benefits which result from specialising in accordance with the principle of comparative advantage will not be obtained if the disadvantages of the division of labour outweigh the advantages. **Diseconomies of scale** may be experienced. Agricultural **overspecialisation** can result in monoculture, in which the growing of a single cash crop for export may lead to soil erosion, vulnerability to pests, and falling agricultural yields in the future. Overspecialisation can also cause a country to be particularly **vulnerable to sudden changes in demand** or in the cost and availability of imported raw materials or energy, or to new inventions and changes in technology which eliminate its comparative advantage. The greater the uncertainty about the future, the weaker the case for complete specialisation. If a country is self-sufficient in all important respects, it is effectively neutralised against the danger of importing recession and unemployment from the rest of the world if international demand collapses.

❸ **To cushion home employment** The model of comparative advantage assumes that factors of production are both fully employed and perfectly mobile within countries. If large-scale unemployment exists, there is a case for using factors inefficiently rather than not to employ them at all. Countries may also regard as unacceptable the costs of structural unemployment resulting from complete freedom of trade. Structural unemployment occurs when old industries decline in response to changes in either demand or comparative cost and advantage. There is a **case for selective and temporary import controls** to ease the problems of adjustment to the new conditions, whilst still accepting that in the long run trade should be encouraged and that a country should adapt to produce the goods in which it possesses a comparative advantage. Indeed the neo-Keynesian economists have argued that import controls will boost the economy to such an extent that, although the structure of imports will change, the volume of imports will not actually fall once growth has taken place. This is the **paradox of import controls**, a counter to the free-trade view that 'what keeps imports out, keeps exports in.'

❹ **To prevent dumping** Exports are sometimes sold at a price below their cost of production and below the market price in the country of origin. Dumping may be motivated by the need to obtain foreign currency or a foothold in a foreign market, or by the hope of achieving productive economies of scale.

5 **To avoid unfair competition** It is sometimes claimed that low-wage countries in the developing world exploit local labour in order to produce cheap goods and that such activity is unfair. However, the developing countries are simply specialising in producing goods in which a plentiful supply of labour gives them a comparative advantage. It is essentially a value judgement whether this is fair or unfair.

6 **To raise revenue** Tariffs are sometimes justified as a means of raising revenue for the government, but in modern economies this is a comparatively unimportant source of government revenue.

Political and social arguments

1 **Economic sanctions** Economic sanctions have been used for centuries to buttress political decisions. An **embargo** on trade may weaken a political enemy and it may also encourage cooperation between politically sympathetic countries. Embargoes and other import controls are often imposed on trade in armaments and military goods.

2 Restrictions are also commonly placed on the **trade in harmful goods (demerit goods)** such as narcotic drugs.

3 Restrictions may be imposed for **strategic reasons**, to ensure that a country is relatively self-sufficient in time of war.

ARGUMENTS AGAINST PROTECTIONISM AND RESTRICTIONS ON TRADE

We have already covered the principal arguments involved, in our explanation of the case for trade. We have shown that, subject to some rather strong assumptions about the full employment of resources and the nature of demand, welfare losses will result if countries fail to specialise in accordance with the principle of comparative advantage. Countries may use import controls and other restrictions on trade to gain a short-term advantage at the expense of other countries (the 'beggar my neighbour' principle). However, retaliation by other countries is likely to cause a long-term welfare loss which is experienced by all countries, since protection props up inefficient and monopoly producers and redistributes income in favour of the protected.

THE GENERAL AGREEMENT ON TARIFFS AND TRADE (GATT)

Towards the end of the Second World War, the American and British governments decided to establish new international institutions which would have the general aim of preventing a breakdown of world trade similar to the collapse which had contributed to the interwar depression. The intention was to create an **International Trade Organisation (ITO)** to liberalise trade, and an **International Monetary Fund** (see Chapters 19 and 20) to supervise the postwar system of payments and exchange rates. Because the charter to establish the ITO was never ratified, **GATT**, which was originally a temporary substitute for the ITO, survived as the most important international forum for expanding world trade and seeking the multilateral reduction of tariffs and other barriers to trade.

The General Agreement which came into operation in 1948 was based on four principles:

1 **Non-discrimination** The 'most favoured nation' clause binds countries to extend reductions in tariffs to the imports of all GATT members.

2 **Protection through tariffs** Where protection is justified, it should only be through tariffs and not through import quotas and other quantity controls.

3 **Consultation** between members.

4 **Tariff reduction through negotiation** GATT should provide the framework through which successive rounds of tariff reduction are negotiated.

The history of GATT can be divided into two. During the 1950s and the 1960s the economic climate was such that countries were willing to negotiate tariff reductions, culminating in the Kennedy Round of 1967. In more recent years, until the Uruguay Round of tariff cuts the main achievement of GATT lay in preventing members from reintroducing protectionist measures rather than in achieving any further notable liberalisation of trade. The main advantages of tariff cuts have accrued to the advanced nations. In order to extend the tariff reductions of GATT to developing countries and to help primary producers, the United Nations established the United Nations Conference on Trade and Development (UNCTAD). This started in 1964 and meets every four years. However, because the problems of the developing countries are so diverse, cooperative trade developments have been limited.

The Uruguay Round of tariff reductions

The most recent round of trade talks were launched in Punte del Este, Uruguay, in September 1986, and were originally due to be completed by the end of 1990. However, because of their complex nature they dragged on and on. The **Uruguay Round** of tariff reductions was finally concluded in Switzerland in December 1993, and agreed and later ratified by member countries in 1994.

At Punte del Este the shape of the proposed tariff cuts was clear. Previous rounds of tariff cuts had been restricted to opening up the trade in manufactured goods, leaving primary products and service industries largely unaffected and riddled with protectionism. The Uruguay round proposed to redress this situation by introducing significant tariff cuts on agricultural produce and the trade in services, as well as further reductions in tariffs on manufactured goods. The developed industrial countries of the northern hemisphere would have to cut their farm subsidies, thereby opening up their markets to efficient non-subsidised producers such as Australia and Argentina. In return the industrialised countries would be offered an enlarged global market for the export of services in which they are increasingly specialising. Third World countries were also promised that they could have access to Western markets for their agricultural and other primary products, providing they were prepared to open up their markets to the import of services such as banking, insurance and airlines.

That was the theory of the Uruguay round of talks. In practice it proved extremely difficult for the USA and the EU to agree on tariff cuts for agricultural goods, and for a long time this failure threatened to sabotage the proposed tariff cuts on manufactured goods where there was relatively little disagreement on principle. However, a deal was finally made, and the following substantial tariff cuts for manufactured goods were also agreed:

1 Complete elimination of tariffs and non-tariff measures on pharmaceuticals, construction equipment, medical equipment, steel, beer and, subject to certain exceptions, furniture, farm equipment and spirits.

2 Harmonisation of tariffs at low rates on chemical products.

3 Tariff cuts of up to 50% for high tariff products, i.e. those products which carried tariffs of 15% or above.

4 Tariff cuts of at least one third for other products, including wool, paper and pulp, and scientific equipment.

Some progress was also made in extending GATT rules to services and intellectual property, but considerable protectionism still exists for services, and intellectual property rights are not respected in many countries. However, the agreement which concluded the Uruguay Round included a commitment to set up a **World Trade Organisation (WTO)** to promote the further liberalisation of world trade. The first task of the WTO, which came into being in 1995, is to finish what the Uruguay Round left undone. At the time, negotiations over financial services, telecommunications, shipping and other service businesses needed to be concluded.

18.3 PATTERNS OF TRADE

In the nineteenth century, a **North/South pattern of world trade** emerged in which industrialising countries, such as the United Kingdom, traded manufactured goods for food and raw materials produced in tropical countries and in New World agricultural countries such as Australia and New Zealand. In the twentieth century however, the pattern of world trade has changed, becoming dominated by **North/North exchange** in which the industrialised countries of the First World trade manufactured goods and services with each other. Most of the trade of the developed industrial economies is between themselves and only a relatively small amount of their trade is with the developing world. In 1989, internal trade amongst the developed and industrialised countries of North America and the EC accounted for about 33% of total international trade and less than 15% of trade took place with no involvement by an advanced capitalist country.

THE PATTERN OF UK TRADE

The fact that most world trade takes place on a North/North basis rather than between the developed countries of the the North and the developing countries of the South, is reinforced by the analysis of United Kingdom visible trade shown in Tables 18.1, 18.2 and 18.3.

Major changes have taken place in the structure of Britain's exports and imports over the last thirty years. As Table 18.1 illustrates, in 1955 over one-third of the United Kingdom's trade was with developing countries, while less than a third was with other European countries. This reflected what was still partly a 'traditional' pattern of trade in which the UK exported manufactured goods, largely to Commonwealth countries and other developing countries, in return for imports of food and raw materials. This pattern is now completely out of date, the current pattern of British trade being dominated by the exchange of both exports and imports with other industrial countries, particularly those in the EU.

Table 18.1 *The geographical pattern of Britain's trade*

Visible trade by area	1955		1985		1994	
	Imports %	Exports %	Imports %	Exports %	Imports %	Exports %
EU	12.6	15.0	46.0	46.3	55.9	57.0
Other West Europe	13.1	13.9	17.1	12.0	6.4	4.2
North America	19.5	12.0	13.8	17.0	13.3	14.4
Other developed countries	14.2	21.1	7.5	4.8	7.1	4.0
Total developed countries	59.4	62.0	84.3	80.0	82.7	79.6
East Europe and former USSR	2.7	1.7	2.2	2.0	1.9	2.1
Oil-exporting countries	9.2	5.1	3.3	7.6	2.1	4.4
Other developing countries	28.7	31.2	10.0	10.1	13.3	13.9

The United Kingdom is by no means unusual in its pattern of trade. The largest part of the international trade of all industrialised countries is with other industrial countries. However, what Table 18.1 does not show is a major structural change which has turned the UK from being a net exporter to becoming a net importer of manufactured goods. This change is illustrated in Tables 18.2 and 18.3. From the beginning of the Industrial Revolution until about 1983, the UK benefited from a **balance of trade surplus in manufactured goods**. But in recent years, the balance of trade in manufactured goods has moved severely into deficit, reflecting both the declining competitiveness of British manufacturing in international markets and the absolute decline of manufacturing output which occurred in the years of **deindustrialisation** in the early 1980s. The deficit in manufacturing goods cannot be blamed completely on the poor performance of more traditional industries such as shipbuilding; the UK has a rather serious deficit in the trade of high-tech *sunrise* industries in the field of information technology. Although manufacturing output recovered in the boom of the mid- and late 1980s, it declined again seriously in the recession of the early 1990s and the balance of trade in manufactured goods has remained in deficit, causing a re-emergence of the UK's traditional current deficit problem, despite North Sea oil's continuing contribution to the payments position. Table 18.3 shows how severe the deficit in the visible balance of trade would be without the contribution of North Sea oil, which most commentators believe reached its peak in 1985.

Table 18.2 *The commodity pattern of Britain's trade*

Visible trade by commodity	1955		1985		1994	
	Imports %	Exports %	Imports %	Exports %	Imports %	Exports %
Food, beverages, tobacco	36.2	6.5	10.9	6.3	9.2	8.4
Fuel	10.4	4.6	12.4	21.3	3.9	6.6
Industrial materials and semi-manufacturers	47.9	35.3	31.4	28.4	29.1	30.3
Finished manufacturers	5.2	49.1	43.7	41.3	54.1	54.2
Others	0.3	4.5	1.6	2.7	3.7	0.5

Table 18.3 *Visible balance of trade*

	£m 1975	£m 1985	£m 1989	£m 1994
Food, beverages, tobacco	−2701	−3592	−4875	−3779
Fuel	−3057	+8163	−71	+3113
Industrial materials and semi-manufacturers	−915	−2549	−9540	−2596
Finished manufacturers	+3241	−3102	−15 907	−7810
Others	+99	−1031	+3250	+3643
Total	−3333	−2111	−27 143	−14 715

Trade in oil has, in fact, had several effects on the geographical pattern and commodity composition of Britain's exports and imports. Besides contributing directly to exports via sales of oil to the rest of the world, North Sea oil production has resulted in a considerable saving of oil imports. Less directly, via its effect on the balance of payments and an over-valued exchange rate, North Sea oil production undoubtedly contributed to the uncompetitiveness of British manufacturing industry, particularly in the early 1980s. (This is the so-called Dutch disease effect, which we explain in Chapter 19, though high interest rates, resulting from a tight monetary policy, have probably been mainly to blame for an overvalued exchange rate.) Finally, a further development has been the growth in importance, since about 1970, of the oil-exporting countries, particularly in the Middle East, as a market for UK manufacturing exports.

REGIONAL ECONOMIC GROUPINGS

Free Trade Areas and Customs Unions

GATT allows the continuation of any system of tariffs in operation when GATT was signed. It also allows the creation of either a **free trade area (FTA)** or a **customs union (CU)**, both of which aim to liberalise trade between members, without extending most favoured nation treatment to non-members. Members of a FTA, such as the **Latin American Free Trade Area (LAFTA)**, are free to choose their trading policy with outsiders. Britain was a founder member of the **European Free Trade Area (EFTA)**, but left in 1973 to join the **European Community (EC)**. The European Union, as it is now called, is a customs union, in which a common external tariff restricts members' freedom of action. A customs union usually involves a much closer economic integration between members, who adopt common policies additional to the common external tariff.

With the creation of a **Single European Market** on January 1st 1993, the EU has developed into a proper **common market**, perhaps eventually leading to a full **economic and monetary union** and even a **political union**. Common economic policies have been established which either considerably replace the freedom of separate policy action in member countries (the **CAP** and the **Common Fishery Policy**) or supplement the policies of individual members (**Regional and Competition Policy**). Most members of the EU are or have been members of the **exchange rate mechanism** of the **European Monetary System** (Chapter 20), which has been interpreted as a step towards full monetary union.

The effect on a country of its joining a customs union will depend on the size of the common external tariff, on whether the tariff is applied to all traded goods, and on the pattern of the country's trade. If a growing proportion of the country's trade is with the members of the CU, then there may be a strong case for joining, particularly if the common external tariff is high. However, FTAs are more consistent with the philosophy of GATT than are customs unions. The latter are more likely to encourage trade between members by diverting trade from non-members. The distortive effects of the common external tariff on trade with the rest of the world can depend on the extent to which the CU is inward- or outward-looking. Customs unions can be **trade-diverting** or **trade-reducing** rather than **trade-creating**. They do not take comparative advantage to its logical conclusion, favouring instead internal producers against lower-cost external producers. The members of the EU claim to be outward-looking, citing for example the Lome Convention of 1975 (subsequently renewed) which enables sixty less developed countries to export duty free to the EU, and without reciprocity.

Suppliers' organisations

Occasionally, producing countries cooperate in order to exploit the world market, for example by forming an **international cartel**. Primary producing countries justify the formation of agreements such as that of the **Organisation of Petroleum Exporting Countries (OPEC)** in order to countervail the market power of industrial countries. For most of the 20th century, the terms of trade have moved against primary producers and in favour of industrial countries. Indeed, the adverse effects of the terms of trade on developing countries, together with profit remittances to developed countries, may have far exceeded the benefits of any aid. By creating a monopoly in the supply of a primary product, countries hope to reverse the movement in the terms of trade. International producers' cartels are most effective when governments can control supply, when there is unity of purpose and action amongst members, and when the demand of the industrialised countries is greatest.

Chapter roundup

Although trade gives an international dimension to economics, the theory of trade is essentially based on the concepts of scarcity, production possibilities and opportunity cost, division of labour and economies of scale which we first introduced in Chapters 1 to 6. We now examine some of the complications, distortions and barriers to trade which result from the fact that countries may lack an acceptable means of payment for trade (Chapter 19 on the balance of payments), while in Chapter 20 we see how exchange rates can cause further distortions and uncertainties.

Illustrative questions and answers

1   Essay question

'Britain's trade with the European Union has become more and more important to our national prosperity since the late 1980s.'

(a) What evidence is there to justify the above statement? (5)

(b) How can the "single market" help our national prosperity in the coming years? (8)

(c) The main feature of the UK's trade since 1986 is that it has shown a persistent deficit on current account. Explain what is meant by a deficit on current account and discuss the factors which have caused this trend to persist. (12)   *SEB*

Tutorial note

All the A Level examining boards now require a broad knowledge of how membership of the European Union affects the UK economy and UK economic policy, but unless your syllabus specifies otherwise, a detailed technical knowledge of EU economic policies and institutions is not required. There are two exceptions: the **common agricultural policy (CAP),** and the EU as a **common market** and **customs union**. We shall use these notes to summarise the development of the common market from its origins as the European Economic Community (EEC) in 1957. The EEC later became the European Community (EC), and in the 1990s it was subsumed into the **European Union (EU)**. The name European Community (rather than European Union) is still officially used in a number of specialised areas, most notably European Community law. There is no such thing as European Union law.

In the 1950s, the **Treaty of Rome** set out the general aims of the EEC. These included: the elimination of import controls between member states; the establishment of common commercial policies towards (and a common external tariff against) non-member countries; the adoption of common economic policies in fields such as agriculture; and the *approximation* of the laws of member states to the extent required for the common market to function properly. The Treaty of Rome also made provision for harmonisation for important areas of economic and social policy in member states, for example the harmonisation of indirect tax rates. Member states are required to take all appropriate measures to fulfil the obligations arising out of the Treaty or resulting from action taken by Community institutions such as the European Commission.

When the EEC was founded in 1957, it was hoped that the common market would be fully established within twelve years. In the event this proved optimistic. In an attempt to speed things up, in 1985, the European Commission published a White Paper setting out 282 proposals for new legislation deemed necessary to complete the common market. This was followed a year later by the **Single European Act** which specified the measures to be adopted by member states by the end of 1992 to complete the Community's **internal market**. Many of these came into effect on January 1st, 1993. The Single European Act freed the movement of capital and labour between EC countries. The Act also sought to create a level commercial playing field by preventing countries using artificial devices such as technical standards and administrative controls to exclude imports and to protect their businesses from fair competition from EC countries.

The **Treaty on European Union**, which is the third of the principal EC Treaties or Acts, came into effect in November 1993. This Treaty, which is popularly known as the **Maastricht Treaty**, is particularly significant in extending workers' rights, consumer protection, industry, the environment, and economic and monetary policy. However, so far the UK government has opted out of two important parts of the Treaty on European Union, namely the establishment in the Treaty's Social Chapter of a uniform set of workers' rights throughout the Union, and the third stage of economic and monetary union proposed by the Treaty which involves the creation of a single European currency, possibly by 1999.

Suggested answer plan

(a) Use the data in Table 18.1, which shows how UK trade with other EU countries has grown. Enlargement of the UK to include countries such as Sweden and Austria has boosted the growth of this trade.

(b) (i) Briefly explain the meaning of the single market.
　(ii) Explain how established UK firms can benefit from the larger market.
　(iii) The UK may also benefit by attracting inward investment from outside the EU, e.g. Japanese electronics firms locating transplant factories in Britain.

(c) (i) Define a current account deficit – the money value of total imports exceed the money value of total exports over a period.
　(ii) Using the visible trade figures in Table 18.3, illustrate the trend in the UK current account.
　(iii) State, and then discuss, at least two factors contributing to the deficit, e.g. deindustrialisation or the erosion of the manufacturing base; price and/or quality

uncompetitiveness of British goods; cyclical factors (related to the phase of the business cycle) versus structural factors.

2   Data Question

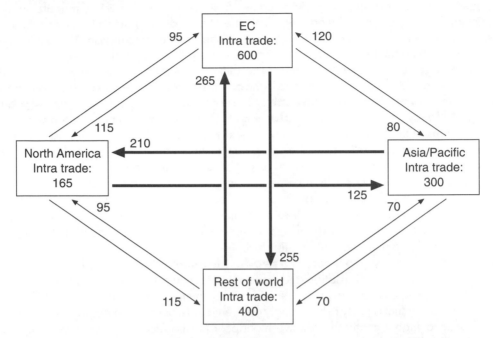

The world economy shows signs of moving towards a system partitioned in three blocks: the Americas, the European Community and the Asia–Pacific region centred on Japan. The United States has signed a free trade agreement with Canada and has started preliminary talks about similar arrangements with Mexico and Chile. There is the possibility of an American free trade zone spanning the continent. The EC is busily engaged in Project 1992, which will create the world's largest single market for goods, services and capital. The economic changes in Eastern Europe, far from slowing the EC's progress down, seem to have speeded it up. If Japan and East Asian economies find more of their goods shut out of Europe and America, an Asia–Pacific block may emerge by default.

(Source: adapted from: 'A Survey of World Trade' in *The Economist*, 22 September 1990)

(a) (i) Calculate and set out clearly the current account position in 1989 for each of:
         the European Community;
         North America;
         Asia/Pacific;
         rest of the world.   (4)
    (ii) Was international trade in equilibrium in 1989?   (2)

(b) The data show that, for the European Community, the value of its internal trade is greater than that of its exports; the reverse is true for the Asia/Pacific region. How might this be explained?   (6)

(c) The article claims that the world economy is 'moving towards a system partitioned into three blocks' (lines 1–2). Examine the economic implications of this for the European Community and for the world economy.   (8)   *ULEAC*

Tutorial note

The data in this question neatly illustrates the modern pattern of world trade. Many students do not realise that during the twentieth century, the pattern of world trade has changed from a North/South to a North/North pattern. Instead of world trade being dominated (as it was in the nineteenth century) by industrialised countries in Europe and North America exporting manufactured goods in exchange for foodstuffs and raw materials produced by tropical countries (which for the most part were their colonies or imperial dependencies), the industrialised economies of the North now trade largely with each other. But at the same time as North/North trade has grown in significance (as illustrated by intra trade data in the question for the EU and North America regions), a large part of world manufacturing, particularly for export, has shifted away from the older industrial areas in western Europe and North America, to the Pacific rim countries of the Asia/Pacific region. These countries include such dynamic Newly Industrialising Countries (NICs) as South Korea, Taiwan and Malaysia, together of course with Japan. The shift of manufacturing industry to the Pacific rim countries and the associated change in the pattern of world trade can both be explained by changes in **comparative advantage**, supplemented by **technology gap** and **product life-cycle** theories. **Technology gap theories** explain the modern pattern of trade in terms of the nature of technical progress. The older, advanced industrial countries have usually been the leaders in developing new technologies and new products and this gives them an advantage, reinforced by economies of scale allowed by long production runs, which the monopoly position of the innovating country creates. However, when the technology matures and becomes available to other countries, comparative advantage may shift to the NICs. Indeed these countries may take the lead in developing later versions of the new technology, and the original leaders may suffer the disadvantage of factories fitted with what has become out-of-date equipment.

Like the technology gap theory, the **product life-cycle theory** explains the pattern of world production, specialisation and trade in manufactured goods in terms of the nature of technical progress. Early in its life-cycle, and immediately following its successful innovation, a product is likely to be strongly differentiated from competing products. Indeed, by creating a highly profitable relative monopoly position for the innovative firm, such product differentiation provides an important motive for technical development. At this stage of the product's life-cycle, manufacture is usually located in the country of origin of the innovative company, where its research and development facilities are concentrated. But at a later stage when the company loses its monopoly over the existing technology, when the product becomes more standardised with agreed international specifications, and when mass production combines economies of scale with the application of routine, relatively unskilled labour, the advanced economies lose their comparative advantage and production shifts to the NICs. Meanwhile, the innovative multinational firms in the advanced industrial countries attempt to maintain their lead by further technical progress and product development, while at the same time owning branch factories or subsidiaries in the NICs in which they manufacture for export back to the developed world the 'older' products well into their life-cycles. As a variant on this theme, North American and European multinationals are increasingly switching out of manufacturing completely by 'contracting out' the manufacture of a finished good or its components to independent producers in the NICs. These goods are then exported back as 'badge-engineered' products, i.e. marketed under the multinational's brand name, but manufactured by and bought in from an independent supplier in an NIC.

A rather different explanation may throw some light on the North/North pattern of intraregional trade within North America and the EU. The **roles of patterns of income, tastes and consumption, or demand conditions** in the world's most important trading countries, may help to explain why so much of international trade involves the exchange of essentially rather similar manufactured goods between already industrialised economies. It can be argued that a country's comparative advantage often lies in producing goods related to its inhabitants' domestic tastes. Close contact with the needs of the domestic market makes a country's firms efficient at meeting domestic demand and very often the inhabitants of other industrial countries with similar incomes, possess similar demand. Trade therefore takes place between countries with similar tastes and incomes. At the same time, high income consumers value choice and product differentiation. A pattern of trade thus develops between industrialised countries in which a very wide range of differentiated manufactured consumer goods is made available to all – for example, automobiles or fashion goods. A single country could seldom provide its consumers with the desired variety, so international trade extends the range of choice.

Suggested answer

(a) (i) Calculate EU export earnings by adding up $115 bn + $80 bn + $255 bn, which equals $450 bn. In a similar way, imports into the EU can be calculated as $475 bn. In 1989 the EU was thus running a current account deficit on its Balance of Payments of $25 bn.

By performing similar calculations, you will find that North America was running a Current Account deficit of $120 bn (since its exports at $315 bn were less than its imports at $440 bn by this amount); whereas the other two world regions both had trade surpluses – $125 bn in the case of the Asia/Pacific region and $20 bn for the 'rest of the world'.

(ii) Since – as yet – the world cannot trade with any other planets in the universe, the current account for the world must exactly balance and be in equilibrium. But note that the countries of the North (North America and the EU) were in deficit to the tune of $145 bn – which was, of course, exactly equal to the size of the combined surplus of the Asia/Pacific countries 'rest of the world'.

(b) The EU is a customs union which was formed precisely to encourage the development of intra-EU trade. As we have explained in the tutorial notes, much of the growth of world trade in recent years has involved already-developed and rich economies trading essentially similar goods and services with each other. By contrast, the Pacific rim countries of the Asia/Pacific region which have provided the engine of growth for manufacturing in recent decades, have been producing largely for export, as their own markets (with the partial exception of Japan) are too small to absorb the high levels of output that they now produce.

(c) As the squabbling amongst GATT members over the signing of the Uruguay round of tariff cuts has shown, there is a danger that countries – the EU and North America in particular – will resort to protectionism, both to reduce trade between each other, but also to fend off cheap imports of manufactured goods from the Pacific rim countries and the other countries of the South. Consider whether arguments for such protectionism (based on unfair competition, dumping, the use of 'slave labour', etc.) are justified, or whether the protectionist stance adopted by the regional groupings will lead to a failure to organise trade in accordance with the principle of comparative advantage, leading ultimately to output and welfare losses for both the EU and the rest of the world.

Question bank

1 (a) Show that a preference for free trade is the logical implication of comparative cost theory. (10)

(b) Why then can barriers to trade ever be justified? (15)   *Oxford & Cambridge*

2 (a) Distinguish between tariff and non-tariff protection. (30)

(b) Japan currently agrees to restrict the quantity of motor vehicles exported to the UK. Analyse the implication of this trade restriction for the economies of both Japan and the UK. (70)   *ULEAC*

Pitfalls

1(a) is a slightly disguised question on the principle of comparative advantage. You need to realise that a country's comparative advantage lies in those goods which it can produce at the lowest comparative cost in terms of other goods foregone. When answering Question 2(b), you must explain that if production does not take place fully in accordance with the principle of comparative advantage, the output and economic welfare of the countries involved may not be maximised. Avoid a xenophobic or petty-nationalistic approach to Question 2.

Key Points

As noted, the principle of comparative advantage is the key theoretical concept both questions are testing. Make sure you explain the concept carefully, preferably using a simple numerical example to illustrate how output gains can result from specialisation in accordance with the principle. You must also display knowledge of different forms of protectionism, e.g. import duties or tariffs and quotas, and show some awareness of the disadvantages and alleged benefits of trade protection.

3 (a) Explain what is meant by the terms of trade and why it is an important statistic. (12)

(b) What are the possible consequences of a deterioration in the terms of trade of a developing country producing primary products? (13) *Cambridge*

Pitfalls

Examination candidates frequently confuse the *terms of trade* with the *balance of trade*. If you made this error in your answer to part (a) of the question, you would score very few marks for part (b), however good your discussion of the balance of trade. You will need more than a single sentence for the second part of part (a).

Key Points

Define the terms of trade as the ratio of average export prices to average import prices. Explain that the terms of trade are measured by the following formula:

$$\text{Terms of trade index} = \frac{\text{Index of average export prices}}{\text{Index of average import prices}} \times 100$$

Briefly state the meaning of favourable and unfavourable movements in the terms of trade, then go on to explain that the terms of trade are an important statistic because a change in country's terms of trade indicate whether the competitiveness of the country's tradeable goods and services is improving or deteriorating. Start your answer to part (b) by stating that the consequences will depend in part on the size of the deterioration, in part upon the causes of the deterioration, and in part upon the elasticities of demand for exports leading to falling export prices, and imports. Develop these points, noting that a fall in demand for exports and a depreciating exchange rate are amongst the most likely causes of a deterioration in the terms of trade of a developing country producing primary products. The immediate consequence is that the country will have to export more in order to purchase the same amount of imports as previously. This may have secondary consequences upon the country's growth prospects and upon the standard of living of its inhabitants.

THE BALANCE OF PAYMENTS

Units in this chapter

Chapter objectives

Chapter 18 explained how the existence of **barriers to trade** such as tariffs and other types of import control can prevent two countries from trading together, even though they would both benefit from international exchange. This chapter investigates how **payment difficulties** may create further barriers to trade. The **structure of a country's balance of payments**, and the various policies the government might use to reduce or eliminate **balance of payments disequilibrium** are examined.

19.1 THE STRUCTURE OF THE BALANCE OF PAYMENTS

THE BALANCE OF PAYMENTS ACCOUNTS

The balance of payments is the part of a country's national accounts which measures all the **currency flows** into and out of the economy within a particular time period, usually a year. Whenever international trade takes place between countries, payment must eventually be made in a currency, or other means of payment, which is acceptable to the country from whom the goods and services have been purchased. Since the balance of payments is an official record collected by a government, the presentation of the currency flows depends on how the government decides to group and classify all the different items of payment. Generalising, the main components of the balance of payments are:

❶ The **current account**.

❷ **Private sector capital flows** (sometimes called the **balance of payments on capital account**).

❸ **Changes in official reserves**.

We shall look at these in turn before focusing on the actual way the balance of payments figures are published in the UK today.

THE BALANCE OF PAYMENTS ON CURRENT ACCOUNT

The balance of payments on current account measures the *flow* of expenditure on goods and services, broadly indicating the country's income gained and lost from trade. The current account is usually regarded as the most important part of the balance of payments because it reflects the economy's international competitiveness and the extent to which it is living within its means. If receipts from exports are less than payments for imports, there is a **current account deficit**; if receipts exceed payments there is a **current account surplus**. The current balance is obtained simply by adding together the **balance of visible trade** and the **balance of invisible trade** which we shall now examine.

The balance of visible trade

Visible trade is perhaps the most important single item in the balance of payments, yet is the simplest to define. The balance of visible trade measures the **value of goods exported minus the value of goods imported**, expressed in the country's own currency. The visible balance is also known as the **balance of trade**. This is a rather misleading term since it implies (falsely) that invisible trade is also included. The balance of trade refers *only* to trade in goods and *not* services.

The balance of invisible trade

The balance of invisible trade is sometimes defined as the **value of services exported minus the value of services imported**. Examples of **service earnings** which contribute to UK invisible exports include: a large part of the earnings of the City of London, e.g. financial services, insurance and brokerage services; and the overseas earnings of British aviation and shipping services.

However, not all invisible exports and imports are strictly services. Amongst other items included in the UK invisible account are: spending in the UK by foreign tourists; gifts of money sent by overseas residents to UK residents; and expenditure by overseas governments on embassies in the UK and by the US government on military bases in the UK. Also in the invisible account are:

- **Net property income from abroad.** British residents owning capital assets which are located in other countries – for example shares in overseas companies – normally receive dividends each year paid on the companies' profits. At the same time profits flow in the opposite direction out of the country to the overseas owners of assets located in the UK, e.g. Japanese or American multi-national companies operating in the UK. Net property income from abroad is the difference between these inward and outward profit flows.

- Since 1973, the UK has been a net contributor to the **European Community budget** within the European Union. Britain's net contribution to the EC budget has become an important invisible import.

- Various types of **aid to developing countries** are also classified in the invisible account.

PRIVATE SECTOR CAPITAL FLOWS

An **outward capital flow** takes place when a country's residents purchase capital assets located in another country. **Inward capital flows** involve residents of other countries purchasing capital assets within the country. **Net capital flows** are the difference between these inward and outward capital movements. A positive net outward capital flow which continues over a period of years means that the country's residents (both individuals and companies) are acquiring overseas capital assets greater in total than the country's own assets being bought by the rest of the world. When the UK abolished foreign exchange controls in 1979, British residents became very large net exporters of capital, presumably because they believed that investment abroad would be more profitable than investment within the UK. This positive net flow of capital out of the UK during the 1980s led to Britain becoming the second largest owner of external capital assets in the world – Japan being the leader. By contrast, the USA became a debtor nation in the 1980s, i.e. assets owned in the US by other countries grew to exceed those owned by America in the rest of the world.

Long-term capital flows

In order to understand properly the importance of capital flows in the balance of payments, we shall distinguish between long-term and short-term capital flows. A long-term capital flow occurs when residents of one country purchase or invest in productive resources located in another country. Such investment can be either **direct investment** or **portfolio investment**. Real or direct investment takes place when United Kingdom owned multinational companies buy or create foreign subsidiaries – an example would be ICI establishing a chemical factory in a developing country. **Portfolio investment** involves the purchase of **financial assets** rather than **physical assets** or directly productive assets. British residents purchasing the shares of overseas companies or the securities issued by foreign governments are examples. The internationalisation or globalisation of world security markets and the abolition of exchange controls between countries, have made it much easier for individuals living in the developed world to purchase shares in any company they wish. These events have led to a great increase in portfolio investment on a truly global scale. Individuals can now buy shares, either directly or through the intermediary of institutions such as insurance companies and unit trusts, in companies whose shares were only previously available on the capital market of the company's country of origin.

Short-term capital flows

The long-term capital flows which we have just described are in large part a response to the **principle of comparative advantage**, reflecting peoples' decisions to invest in economic activities and industries located in countries to which comparative advantage has moved. However, since changes in comparative advantage usually take place quite slowly, long-term capital flows tend to be relatively stable and predictable. The same is not true of short-term capital flows, sometimes known as **hot money flows**. Hot money is the name given to the pool of footloose hard currencies owned privately, usually outside any exchange controls enforced by the currency's country of origin. In contrast to long-term capital movements, hot money flows are largely **speculative**. These flows occur because the owners of funds, who include companies and banks as well as wealthy private individuals, believe that they can make a quick speculative profit or capital gain by moving funds out of one currency and into another. If speculators believe that one currency is going to rise in value while the value of another currency is going to fall (via **movements of the exchange rate**), it makes sense to move funds out of bank deposits or government securities denominated in the currency whose value is expected to fall. The speculator should sell the currency involved, purchasing instead the currency which he expects to rise, prior to placing his funds in a bank deposit or government securities denominated in that currency. A hot money movement may also be triggered by **international differences in interest rates**, as funds flow into countries where interest rates are temporarily high. **International crises**, such as the outbreak of a Middle East war, can also cause funds to be moved into safe havens such as gold and into currencies of countries regarded as politically stable.

CHANGES IN OFFICIAL RESERVES

Visible and invisible trade, together with long-term private sector capital flows, are sometimes known as the **autonomous** or **spontaneous** part of the balance of payments. They are **real flows** in the sense that they result from decisions by individuals and firms to buy goods and services or to invest in productive capital assets. Thus, if imports and capital flows out of the country exceed exports and inward capital flows, there will be a deficit in the autonomous part of the balance of payments. Like any balance sheet, the balance of payments must exactly balance in the sense that all the items included in the balance sheet must sum to zero. It follows therefore, that a deficit in the autonomous part of the balance of payments must be matched by equal **accommodating** flows elsewhere in the balance sheet, which finance the deficit. One way in which the autonomous flows in the balance of payments can be financed is through changes in the reserves of gold and hard currencies owned by the central bank. This is known as **official financing**. The country's central bank can sell or run down official currency reserves to finance the deficit, or undertake official borrowing to supplement its reserves, borrowing for example from foreign central banks or from the International Monetary Fund. A **balance of payments surplus** in the autonomous flows might be financed by accumulating or purchasing official reserves, or by early repayment of debt accumulated by the central bank as a result of past official borrowing. In Chapter 20 we shall relate official financing of a balance of payments deficit of surplus to the exchange rate system, explaining that official financing is significant in **fixed** and **managed exchange rate systems**, but insignificant when the exchange rate is **freely floating**.

THE UK BALANCE OF PAYMENTS

Table 19.1 *The United Kingdom balance of payments 1994*

		£m
Current account		
	Visibles	−10,594
	Invisibles	+8,910
A	Current balance	−1,684
UK External assets and liabilities		
	Transactions in assets	−39,363
	Transaction in liabilities	+35,802
B	Net transactions	−3,561
C	Balancing item	+5245
A + B + C	=	0

Table 19.1 illustrates the method of presentation currently used when the government publishes the UK balance of payments accounts. The current account needs no further explanation, but you will notice that private sector capital flows and official financing are not separately listed in the table. Taken together, they constitute the **transactions** section of the balance of payments, which comprises all private sector and public sector movements of capital funds, including any changes in official reserves. In the table, **transactions in assets** measure the changes in overseas assets which are owned by British companies and residents. The table shows that in 1994, transactions in assets were negative at −£39,363 million. This means that in 1994, the value of the assets which British companies and residents acquired overseas was almost £40 billion greater than the value of any assets they sold. To explain **transactions in liabilities**, we must note that when overseas residents purchase shares in British companies or UK government securities, they acquire a claim against the UK, hence net inward capital flows by overseas residents are recorded as an increase in the United Kingdom's liabilities! When net transactions are negative, as in Table 19.1, the explanation usually lies in the fact that outward investment by British residents and companies acquiring assets in other countries, exceeds inward investment into the UK by foreign multinational companies etc.

THE BALANCING ITEM

As a result of the imperfect nature of data collection, the official estimate of the balance of payments will never be completely accurate. For this reason a **balancing item**, similar to the statistical adjustment or discrepancy in the National Income Accounts, must be added or subtracted as the last item of the balance of payments to make the balance sheet sum to zero. In the years following the first publication of the UK balance of payments, the statistics are continuously revised. A very large balancing item, as in Table 19.1 means that the statistics must be interpreted with caution. Over subsequent years it is usual for the published figures for both the current account and capital flows to change and for the balancing item to become smaller, as it is gradually allocated to a real flow in the balance of payments. Depending on how the balancing item is eventually allocated, it is possible that a current account deficit apparent when the statistics were first published can be transformed into a surplus on later publication, and vice versa.

RECENT CHANGES IN THE UK CURRENT ACCOUNT

As the current account is the most important part of the balance of payments, reflecting the country's trading competitiveness with the rest of the world, we shall examine in some detail changes over the last decade or so in the structure of the major UK trading flows. For most of the 20th century, the UK current account has displayed a **deficit on the balance of visible trade** and a **surplus on the invisible balance**. This can be explained by the emergence of competing industrial countries which have reduced or eliminated the UK's advantage in many manufacturing industries, while Britain has built up a comparative advantage in services, particularly in financial services. Whether the overall current account is in deficit or surplus in any single year has depended on whether the invisible surplus has been sufficient to offset the visible deficit.

Since the mid-1970s, some important structural changes have occurred in the United Kingdom current account, and these are discussed below.

North Sea oil revenues

These have made a significant contribution to the balance of trade, both through **import-saving** and **oil exports**. From the mid-1970s, and reaching a peak in the mid-1980s, North Sea revenues temporarily transformed the current account from deficit to surplus. Oil revenues diminished significantly around 1990 following the Piper Alpha oil rig disaster in the North Sea, but have now recovered somewhat.

The deterioration of the balance of visible trade

The contribution of North Sea oil disguised **the continuing deterioration of the balance of non-oil visible trade**, caused by a growing **propensity to import** and the uncompetitiveness of British manufactured goods. It is thus useful to divide the visible balance into a balance of trade in **manufactured goods** and **non-manufactures**, as well as into the balance of trade in **oil** and the **non-oil** balance. From the 18th century until the 1980s the UK balance of trade in manufactured goods remained in surplus, reflecting the United Kingdom's importance as a manufacturing economy. Around 1982, however, imports of manufactured goods began to exceed exports, moving the balance of trade in manufactures into deficit for the first time since before the Industrial Revolution – apart from in war years. This partly reflects the **deindustrialisation** process, whereby large parts of UK manufacturing industry went into structural decline in the 1970s and early 1980s, and again in the recession of the early 1990s. Although manufacturing output recovered in the boom years of the mid to late 1980s, the deficit in the trade in manufactured goods was not reversed. Some economists argue that the growing deficit in a manufacturing trade can be related to the oil trade surplus of the early 1980s. During the Thatcher years, they allege, North Sea oil revenues were used to finance, not investment in the re-equipment of the UK's manufacturing base, but short-term standards of living through the import of consumer goods. On a more optimistic note, Britain's balance of trade in **automobiles** which, with the influx of car imports in the 1970s and 1980s had been in severe deficit, has recovered. Along with the fall in the exchange rate in 1992 which increased the competitiveness of all Britain's exports, the improved quality of British cars and the coming onstream of Japanese transplant factories in the UK have contributed to this recovery.

Invisible exports

These now account for more than half of the United Kingdom's export credits, rising from 38.5% in 1970 to 52.2% in 1994. Invisible imports have also grown in relative importance, accounting for 43.9% of total imports in 1994. (In 1994, invisibles were slightly less significant as a proportion of the total than they had been a year or two earlier. The growth of trade in goods as the UK and other trading countries recovered from recession explains this.) The growth of invisible exports and imports, in both absolute and relative importance, reflects the changing pattern of world trade in which the world's richest countries increasingly trade specialised services with each other. The rapid growth of the UK's invisible exports also reflects the importance of **dividend income**, or **net property income from abroad**. As we have already noted, UK residents and companies invested large amounts of capital overseas following the abolition of exchange controls in 1979. These investments are now remitting profits which are nearly sufficient to offset the fall in oil revenues in the visible balance, which occurred when the price of crude oil dramatically fell by 50% in 1985 and 1986. After a difficult period in the early 1980s, when it appeared that the invisible earnings of the City of London might decline under the growth of competition from other financial centres such as Tokyo and New York, there was a spectacular recovery in the City's earnings, particularly after the reorganisation of many financial services which followed the 'Big Bang' in 1986. However, the City now faces greater international competition, and previously larger earners such as the Lloyds Insurance Market have been suffering massive losses. At the same time, *outward* interest payments paid to attract the *inward* capital and hot money flows needed to finance Britain's current account deficit have eaten into the positive figure for net property income from abroad.

19.2 THE BALANCE OF PAYMENTS AND ECONOMIC POLICY

BALANCE OF PAYMENTS EQUILIBRIUM AND DISEQUILIBRIUM

Although in an accounting sense the balance of payments must always balance, the country's payments may not be in a state of equilibrium. Balance of payments equilibrium (or external equilibrium) occurs when the current account and private sector capital flows are more or less equal over a number of years. Alternatively, we may define equilibrium in a rather narrower sense, referring only to the current account. The balance of payments is in equilibrium when the current account more or less balances over a period of years. Balance of payments equilibrium is perfectly compatible with occurrence of short-term deficits and surpluses. However, **fundamental disequilibrium** exists when there is a persistent tendency for payments for imports to be greater or less than corresponding payments for exports over a period of years.

THE PROBLEM OF A CURRENT ACCOUNT DEFICIT

While a short-run deficit or surplus on current account does not pose a problem, a persistent imbalance indicates a fundamental disequilibrium. The nature of any resulting problem depends upon the size and cause of the deficit or surplus, and also upon the type of exchange rate regime. The larger the deficit the greater the problem is likely to be. The problem is also likely to be serious if the deficit is caused by the uncompetitiveness of the country's industries. Although in the short run, a deficit allows a country's residents to enjoy living standards boosted by imports and thus higher than would be possible from the consumption of the country's output alone, in the long run the decline of the country's industries in the face of international competition will lower living standards.

A balance of payments deficit is usually considered more of a problem in a **regime of fixed exchange rates** than when the exchange rate is freely floating. The immediate cause of a deficit usually lies in the fact that exports are too expensive in overseas markets, while imports are too cheap at home. There are more deep-seated causes of over-priced exports and under-priced imports, relating for example to domestic wage costs compared to those in other countries. In a **floating exchange rate regime**, the external price of the currency – the exchange rate – simply responds to market forces and falls, thereby restoring export competitiveness and curing the balance of payments disequilibrium. In contrast, when the exchange rate is fixed, **overvaluation** of the exchange rate may occur, which cannot be cured by market forces because, in a fixed system, the exchange rate is not allowed to respond to market forces. In the absence of inward capital flows financing the resulting persistent payments deficit, the country will simply lose official reserves. Official reserves are limited, so a country cannot go on financing a deficit for ever, and eventually it must take action to try to reduce or eliminate a persistent payments deficit.

POLICIES TO REDUCE A BALANCE OF PAYMENTS DEFICIT ON CURRENT ACCOUNT

The three policy measures which a government can use to try to cure a persistent deficit caused by an overvalued exchange rate can be called the **3 Ds**. These are **deflation**, **direct controls** (import controls), and **devaluation of a fixed exchange rate**.

Deflation

Fiscal policy or **monetary policy** can be used to deflate the level of **aggregate demand** in the economy. Deflation is an **expenditure-reducing policy** which cures a deficit by reducing the demand for imports. Because of the unused capacity in domestic industry which it creates (resulting from the fall in demand for domestic output as well as for imports), deflation may also encourage firms to seek export orders so that they make use of their spare capacity. However, many economists argue that this is less likely, because a sound and expanding home market is necessary for a successful export drive, since exports are usually less profitable than domestic sales. In addition to its expenditure-reducing effect, a deflation of demand can also have a subsidiary **expenditure-switching** effect upon the balance of payments. The depression of demand may cause the domestic inflation rate to fall relative to that in competitor countries, thereby increasing the price competitiveness of exports and reducing the competitiveness of imports. Residents of other countries may then switch their demand towards the country's exports, while its own residents switch away from imports, preferring instead to buy domestically produced substitutes.

Deflation can involve **severe domestic costs**, since in modern economies output and employment tend to fall rather than the price level. For this reason, governments may prefer to use the **expenditure-switching policies** of import controls and devaluation, as alternatives to **expenditure-reducing deflation**.

Direct controls (import controls)

Import controls have an immediate expenditure-switching effect upon the balance of payments. **Embargoes** and **quotas** directly prevent or reduce expenditure on imports, while **import duties** or **tariffs** discourage expenditure by raising the price of imports. However, import controls are not aimed at the underlying cause of disequilibrium – the uncompetitiveness of a country's goods and services – and because they seek to gain an advantage at the expense of other countries (the 'beggar-my-neighbour' principle), import controls are likely to cause retaliation, with an undesirable decrease in specialisation and world trade. In any case, import controls may be unavailable to many countries as a policy alternative, because of their membership of a trading body such as GATT which outlaws quotas and discourages the use of tariffs.

Devaluation

The unavailability of import controls has meant that the **real choice** facing countries such as the UK, has been between deflation and devaluation. Devaluation of a fixed exchange rate is mainly expenditure-switching in its effect. Payments disequilibrium is cured in a manner essentially similar to the freely-floating adjustment mechanism already briefly described. By increasing the price of imports relative to the price of exports, a successful devaluation or managed float switches domestic demand away from imports and towards home-produced goods. Similarly, overseas demand for the country's exports increases in response to the fall in their price.

THE MARSHALL-LERNER CONDITION

The effectiveness of a devaluation (and of any expenditure-switching policy) in reducing a payment deficit depends in part upon the **price elasticities of demand for exports and imports**. It is easy to show that when the demands for exports and imports are both highly price elastic, a devaluation can improve the balance of payments. This is illustrated in Fig. 19.1.

Following a devaluation, the domestic price of imports rises from P_1 to P_2, while the overseas price of exports falls from P_3 to P_4. Overseas residents are likely to spend more on the country's exports following a fall in their relative price, while the country's residents will spend less on imports. When demands are elastic – as illustrated in Fig. 19.1 – total domestic expenditure on imports falls by the area (k–h), while overseas expenditure on exports rises by the area (n–m). The balance of payments improves by (k–h) + (n–m).

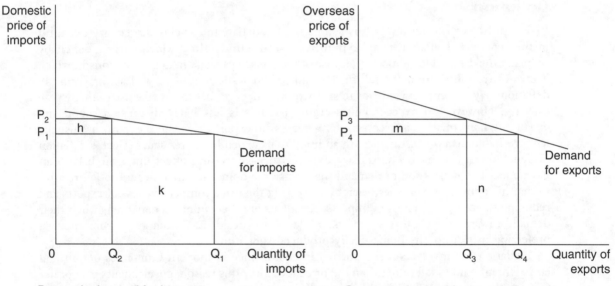

Domestic demand for imports
Overseas demand for exports

Fig. 19.1 The effect of a devaluation or fall in the exchange rate upon the demand for imports and exports when demand for imports and exports are both elastic

It is rather more difficult to see what can happen to the balance of payments if the demands are less elastic. Fortunately, the **Marshall–Lerner condition** provides a simple rule we can use to assess whether a change in the exchange rate can reduce a balance of payments disequilibrium. The Marshall–Lerner condition states that **when the sum of the export and import price elasticities is greater than unity, a fall in the exchange rate can reduce a deficit** (and a rise in the exchange rate can reduce a surplus). If, however, the export and import elasticities are both highly inelastic, summing to less than unity, a fall in the exchange rate might have the perverse effect of worsening a deficit (and a **revaluation** might increase a surplus).

EXPENDITURE-REDUCING VERSUS EXPENDITURE-SWITCHING POLICIES

The Marshall–Lerner condition is a **necessary condition** but not a **sufficient condition** for a fall in the exchange rate to reduce a payments deficit. For a devaluation or downward float to be successful, **domestic supply** of output must be able to respond to meet the surge in demand brought about by the fall in the exchange rate. Spare capacity is needed so that supply may be increased to meet the switching of overseas and domestic demand away from foreign-produced goods and towards the home-produced substitutes. We should regard expenditure-reducing deflation and expenditure-switching devaluation as **complementary** policies rather than as **substitutes** in the task of reducing a payments disequilibrium. Deflation alone may be unnecessarily costly in terms of lost domestic employment and output, yet it may still be necessary to provide the spare capacity and conditions in which a falling exchange rate can successfully cure a payments deficit.

THE J-CURVE

Even if the Marshall–Lerner condition is met and spare capacity exists in the economy, a country's firms may still be unable immediately to increase supply following a fall in the exchange rate. The Marshall–Lerner condition may not in fact be met in the immediate period because elasticities of demand are lower in the short run than in the long run. In these circumstances, the balance of payments may worsen before it improves. This is known as the J-curve effect, which is illustrated in Fig. 19.2.

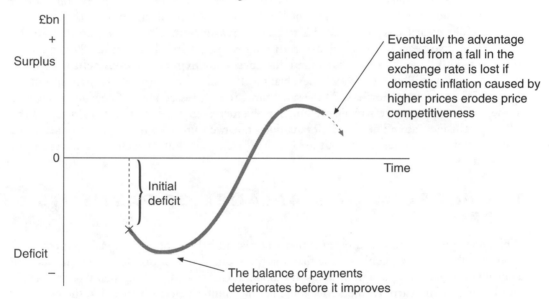

Fig. 19.2 The J-curve effect on the current account following a devaluation or downward float of the exchange rate

The initial worsening in the balance of payments which follows the fall in the exchange rate may reduce confidence in the effectiveness of changing the exchange rate as an appropriate method of tackling a payments imbalance. Falling confidence may in turn cause capital outflows which destabilise both the balance of payments and the exchange rate. The J-curve effect thus reduces the attractiveness of exchange rate adjustment as an instrument to correct payments disequilibrium. Even when the benefits of a falling exchange rate are realised, they may be short-lived. The increased price competitiveness produced by the devaluation is likely to be eroded away as increased import prices raise the country's inflation rate.

THE BALANCE OF PAYMENTS AND AGGREGATE DEMAND

The Marshall–Lerner condition and the J-curve illustrate what is sometimes called the **elasticities approach** to the balance of payments which emphasises the expenditure-switching nature of the adjustment process. However, the need to use an expenditure-reducing deflation of demand to prepare for a fall in the exchange rate reflects the **absorption approach** to the balance of payments. The absorption approach examines the balance of payments from a Keynesian perspective in terms of aggregate demand **absorbing**, or being insufficient to absorb, the economy's domestic output. If spare capacity and unemployed labour exist, an expenditure-switching lowering of the exchange rate can reduce a payments deficit without having to reduce the domestic level of demand, but if all resources are fully employed, national output cannot increase in the short run. In this situation, a devaluation can only improve the balance of payments if the economy is first deflated and domestic demand or absorption reduced.

It is important to realise that even without policy intervention by the government, a current account deficit is deflationary. The payments deficit is a leakage or withdrawal of spending from the circular flow of income, and via a multiplier effect, a fall in the equilibrium level of national income occurs. A current account surplus injects demand into the circular flow of income. This is reflationary or inflationary, depending on whether the economy possesses sufficient spare capacity to meet the switching of demand.

THE DEVALUATION OF THE £ IN SEPTEMBER 1992

Following a massive speculative hot money run on the £ culminating in the events of Black Wednesday, September 16th 1992, the UK Government was forced, much against its will, to take the £ out of the ERM and to allow the exchange rate to be devalued by about 14%. Although at the time it was both unplanned and unintended, the decision to let the exchange rate float downward has been called a **perfect devaluation**. This is because before the devaluation, two years of **expenditure-reducing** recession and deflation in 1990 and 1991 had created the spare capacity required for successful **expenditure-switching**. In the eighteen months following the 1992 devaluation, British firms were able to step up output to meet increased export orders. At the same time, the depressed state of consumer demand in the UK forced importers to absorb much of the increased costs incurred as a result of the falling exchange rate. The 1992 devaluation, however unwelcome to the Conservative Government at the time, turned out to be a significant contributory factor to recovery from recession.

THE PROBLEM OF A BALANCE OF PAYMENTS SURPLUS

While most people could readily agree that a persistent balance of payments deficit can pose serious problems, few people realise that a surplus can also be a problem. Indeed, because a surplus is regarded as a sign of national economic virility and success, many people argue that the bigger the surplus, the better must be the country's performance. To the extent to which the surplus measures the competitiveness of the country's exporting industries, this is obviously true. There are, nevertheless, several reasons why a large payments surplus is undesirable, though a small surplus may be a justifiable objective of government policy. The arguments against a persistently large surplus are discussed below.

One country's surplus is another country's deficit

The balance of payments must balance for the world as a whole, so it is impossible for all countries to run surpluses simultaneously. Unless countries with persistently large surpluses agree to take action to reduce their surpluses, deficit countries will not be able to reduce their deficits. As a consequence and in desperation, deficit countries may then be forced to resort to import controls from which all countries, including the surplus countries, eventually suffer. In the extreme, a world recession could be triggered by a collapse of world trade.

The Dutch disease effect

In the 1950s large quantities of natural gas were discovered in the Netherlands. Much of the gas was exported to neighbouring countries, leading to a large Dutch trade surplus. As a result the exchange rate rose, pricing Dutch manufactured goods out of export markets. When oil was discovered in British North Sea waters in the 1970s, the question was asked: would Britain catch the Dutch disease? Many economists believe that Britain has indeed suffered from the Dutch disease, though North Sea oil has undoubtedly had many good effects as well. Via its effects on confidence and speculation, the oil surplus, which transformed the United

Kingdom's current account from deficit to surplus, attracted a huge hot money inflow. This contributed to an overvalued exchange rate in 1980 and 1981, and to the deindustrialisation and decline of manufacturing industry which the UK experienced in the early 1980s. Arguably, much of the benefit of North Sea oil revenues was lost in financing imports and the upkeep of the unemployed. (An overvalued £ also contributed to the recession at the beginning of the 1990s, though in this case overvaluation resulted from the Government's deliberate decision to enter the ERM at a high instead of a low exchange rate, rather than from any Dutch disease effect.)

A balance of payments surplus as a cause of domestic inflation

Monetarists explain this in the following way. If we assume that the exchange rate is held fixed, a country's domestic money supply is affected by the balance of payments; a surplus tends to increase the money supply while a deficit reduces the money supply. A payments surplus causes the country's currency to be in short supply on foreign exchange markets, which in turn causes the exchange rate to rise. To prevent the exchange rate rising, the authorities must sell their own currency and buy other currencies which are then added to the country's official reserves, but because more of the country's currency is issued, the money supply must increase. Via the quantity theory of money, the price level rises, causing inflation. In the case of a deficit, the authorities sell reserves and buy back and take out of circulation their own currency, causing the money supply to fall. The price level then in turn falls.

POLICIES TO REDUCE A BALANCE OF PAYMENTS SURPLUS

Just as the **3 Ds** (deflation, devaluation and direct controls) can be used to reduce a current account deficit, so their opposite, the **3 Rs** may eliminate a payments surplus. A government can either **reflate demand**, thereby increasing a country's demand for imports; it can liberalise trade by **removing import controls**; or it can **revalue** the country's exchange rate. Reflation, or the expansion of aggregate demand is expenditure-expanding, thereby increasing the demand for all goods, including imports. Revaluation and the removal of import controls, by contrast, are primarily expenditure-switching, switching demand away from domestically produced goods and towards imports.

In recent years there have been frequent calls for Japan and other successful industrialised countries with large payments surpluses, to expand or reflate their domestic economies and to remove any forms of protectionism, including informal limits on imports, so as to help redress the global payments imbalance between the developed and developing worlds. As we have already noted, a large payments surplus either places pressure on a country to revalue a fixed exchange rate, or it will directly cause a floating exchange rate to rise. In either circumstance, an upward movement of the exchange rate will only reduce a surplus providing the Marshall-Lerner condition is met. There may also be a **reverse J-curve effect** immediately following the revaluation, when the payments surplus gets bigger before it begins to get smaller.

Chapter roundup

In this chapter we have investigated the monetary flows into and out of the economy which make up the balance of payments. As Chapter 17 explained, satisfactory balance of payments can be regarded as important objective of macroeconomic policy. A deteriorating balance of payments can constrain or limit the government's freedom of action in pursuing domestic economic objectives, such as full employment and economic growth. The major macroeconomic issues and policies considered in Chapters 14 to 17 all influence, and are often influenced by, the payments position. Similarly, world trade (Chapter 18) and international exchange rates, which we consider in Chapter 20, have a significant impact upon a nation's balance of payments position and performance.

Illustrative questions and answers

1   Essay question

'In the short run a deficit in the United Kingdom balance of payments can be corrected by allowing the exchange rate to float downwards.' (10)

'In the long run a deficit can only be reduced by a fall in United Kingdom real costs of production, relative to its competitors.' (15)

Examine these statements.   *Oxford*

Tutorial note

Devaluation is only really appropriate for curing a current account deficit when the deficit originates from an overvalued exchange rate. For example, capital flows into a currency may raise the exchange rate to a level which makes imports artificially cheap and exports artificially expensive. In this situation a devaluation can be justified. If the causes of the deficit are more deep-seated, stemming from failures to invest, to produce efficiently, or to produce goods of a quality that customers want, devaluation may be a temporary palliative, but not a long-term remedy. Indeed, by shielding a country's firms and workers from the true cause of their uncompetitiveness, a devaluation may prevent the supply-side changes and structural adjustments necessary for a sustainable improvement in the current account. In these circumstances there is also the danger that a devaluation may trigger a vicious spiral of currency depreciation and domestic inflation. The devaluation increases the prices of imported raw materials, energy, food and consumer goods. Rising import costs then feed into domestic cost-push inflation. This destroys the improvement in competitiveness temporarily won by the devaluation, so another devaluation becomes necessary. The cycle of a falling exchange rate and high domestic inflation then continues in an environment unconducive to the changes necessary for proper structural adjustment to take place.

Suggested answer plan

- State that you are interpreting the question in terms of a current account deficit. Define the concept.
- Explain the meaning of devaluation.
- Explain how devaluation can cure a current account deficit.
- Briefly cover the Marshall-Lerner condition and the J-curve effect.
- Explain why a devaluation may not provide a long-term cure if the deficit has causes beyond an overvalued exchange rate.
- Conclude by stating the extent to which you agree or disagree with the statements in the question.

2   Data question

Study the diagram below, then answer the questions which follow.

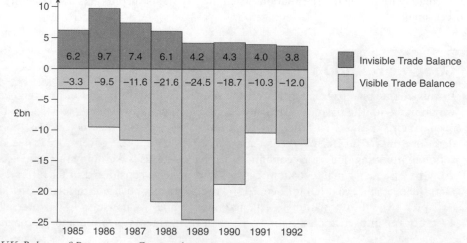

Fig. 19.3 UK Balance of Payments on Current Account

(a) Explain the term 'invisible trade balance' as used in the diagram. (2)

(b) (i) Describe the contribution made by invisible trade to the UK Balance of Payments on Current Account since 1985. (2)

    (ii) Why is the UK balance on invisible trade usually positive? (2)

(c) Describe the trend in the visible trade since 1985. Suggest reasons for this trend. (4)

(d) (i) In what year did the Balance of Payments on Current Account move from a surplus to a deficit? (1)

    (ii) Calculate the size of this deficit. (1)

(e) If this deficit continues, explain the effect on:

    (i) the foreign exchange value of Sterling: (4)

    (ii) employment in the UK. (4)

(f) (i) What measures could the UK Government take to cure a persistent deficit on the Current Account? (5)

    (ii) How might the use of such measures conflict with other economic obejctives the UK Government may wish to pursue? (5) *SEB*

Suggested answer plan

(a) Explain that the invisible trade balance shows the value of invisible exports minus the value of invisible imports. State that invisible trade is trade in services, but there are other invisible items such as net property income from abroad.

(b) (i) Explain that invisibles were in surplus throughout the period, but the surplus fell having peaked at about £10 billion early in the eight year period.

    (ii) You might argue that the UK has a comparative advantage and established position in exporting financial services. Also, as a result of capital outflows in previous years, net property income from abroad was positive.

(c) *Trend* is the key word in the question. You must not confuse cyclical variations (associated with the business cycle) around the trend, with the trend itself. The data seems to indicate a long-term deterioration in the visible balance, with the deficit worsening. To some extent this trend is masked by the cyclical variation around the trend. Higher real income levels sucking imports into the UK and/or growing uncompetitiveness could explain the trend. An overvalued exchange rate might have contributed to the latter – the period covered by the data includes the years when the £'s exchange rate was fixed in the ERM.

(d) Add together the visible and invisible trade balances for each year, and note the first year in which the total is negative. Make sure you show your workings.

(e) (i) In the absence of a net inward capital flow into the UK, a current account deficit creates an excess supply of sterling on foreign exchange markets. Selling of sterling would then depress the exchange rate. This effect might however be negated, either by private sector capital movements, or by official support for the exchange rate, i.e. the Bank of England selling reserves and creating an artificial demand for sterling.

    (ii) A current account deficit is deflationary, taking demand out of the economy. A payments deficit therefore depresses employment, though this may be countered by increased competitiveness brought about by a falling exchange rate.

(f) (i) State the three measures, deflation, devaluation and direct controls, and briefly explain how each might cure a persistent deficit.

    (ii) The key concept for answering this question is the concept of a policy *trade-off*, which is closely related to the fundamental economic principle of opportunity cost. A trade-off exists when two or more desirable policy objectives are mutually exclusive. The more successful a government is in hitting a particular objective, then the worse is its performance with respect to at least one other policy objective! A trade-off exists between the *internal* policy objectives of full employment and growth and the *external* objective of achieving a satisfactory balance of payments (and possibly supporting a particular exchange rate). On many occasions, UK governments have used fiscal and monetary policy to expand demand in order to achieve full employment and economic growth. But as incomes grow, imports are drawn into the economy (via the marginal propensity to import), causing the balance of payments on current account to deteriorate. In order to reduce the payments deficit and/or to relieve speculative pressure on the £'s exchange rate, the government has to reverse policy and introduce tax and/or interest rate increases which deflate or contract the domestic economy. Devaluation has sometimes been seen as offering an escape from this trade-off. However, the attraction of devaluation may be tempered by the fact that a falling exchange rate can trigger inflation and hinder the goal of achieving price stability.

Question bank

1   Explain how, if at all, you would expect the business cycle to affect the UK balance of payments. Discuss whether deficits in the balance of payments on current account should be a matter of concern for the UK government. (25)   *NEAB*

2   (a) Discuss the policies that a Government might use to correct a balance of payments current account deficit. (16)

   (b) How might the problem of current account deficits make it difficult for UK Governments to achieve all of their economic objectives at the same time? (9)
   WJEC

3   (a) Why has the current account of the United Kingdom balance of payments been in deficit in recent years? (13)

   (b) Does the existence of a current account deficit matter? (12)   *AEB*

Pitfalls

There are similarities between all three of these questions, but also subtle differences. You must avoid writing a model answer to a question which has not been set. The wording of Question 1 suggests a possibility that the current account may not be affected by the business cycle. However, this certainly has not been the experience of the UK in recent years. With Questions 2 and 3, possible pitfalls lie in confusing the capital and current accounts, and in not understanding the concept of a trade-off between policy objectives.

Key points

For Question 1 you must explain how and why the current account deteriorates in the upswing and boom phases of the business cycle, and improves during the downswing and recessionary phase. Policies to cure or reduce payments deficits provide the key to Question 2, together with the implications of the trade-off between internal and external policy objectives. Question 3 requires a discussion of the *causes* of current account deficits, followed by some debate on the significance of a deficit. Question 1 also requires this to be discussed. In recent years, the UK government has often seemed to take the view that a current account deficit is simply a private sector matter, and not a concern for the government. According to this line of thinking, a combination of exchange rate depreciation and private sector capital flows will look after the balance of payments.

EXCHANGE RATES

Units in this chapter

Chapter objectives

Chapter 19 examined the structure of a country's balance of payments, emphasising how the mechanism for curing a persistent deficit or surplus depends to a large extent upon the nature of the country's exchange rate regime. This chapter investigates in greater detail the mechanisms through which **freely-floating** and **fixed exchange rates** might restore a balance of payments equilibrium, before describing the various **managed exchange rates** that have existed in the modern world economy. The chapter concludes by examining the roles of the **International Monetary Fund (IMF)** and the **European Monetary System (EMS)**, which have provided the institutional framework within which managed exchange rates have operated.

20.1 FLOATING EXCHANGE RATES

DIFFERENT MEASURES OF THE EXCHANGE RATE

Exchange rates and a **foreign exchange market** exist because different countries use different currencies to pay for internal trade. A currency's exchange rate is simply its **external price**, expressed in terms of another currency such as the US dollar, or gold, or indeed in terms of an artificial unit such as a weighted average of a sample or *basket* of leading trading currencies. In this chapter we shall assume that we are explaining the exchange rate of the pound sterling, expressing the £'s exchange rate in terms of the US dollar. It is worth noting, however, that the convention of quoting exchange rates in terms of the US dollar is of fairly recent origin. Before 1914 most exchange rates were expressed in terms of gold and only after 1945 did the dollar become the near universally accepted standard by which the external values of other currencies were measured. In recent years the dollar has become much less stable, and consequently the US currency has become less useful as a fulcrum or standard against which to measure the value of other currencies. In the UK the **Sterling Index** is now often used to measure the exchange rate. The Sterling Index does not measure the £'s external value against a particular currency. Rather it is a trade-weighted average of the £'s exchange rate against about 16 leading trading currencies, calculated to reflect the importance of each currency in international trade. On 29th. January 1996, the Sterling Index was 83.3 compared to its 1985 index of 100. This means that over the years since 1985, the sterling exchange rate had depreciated or lost nearly 17% of its value when measured against the exchange rates of Britain's most important trading partners.

THE SIMPLE THEORY OF A FREELY FLOATING EXCHANGE RATE

In a regime of **freely** (or **cleanly**) **floating exchange rates**, the currency of a country is regarded as a simple commodity to be traded on foreign exchange markets, its price or exchange rate being determined by the forces of supply and demand. For the time being we shall assume that a currency is demanded on foreign exchanges only for the payment of trade (we are ignoring the **complications caused by capital flows and speculation**), that a country needs another country's currency to purchase imports from that country, and that all countries will immediately sell on the foreign exchange market any holdings of foreign currencies that are surplus to their requirements.

As in any market, the **demand and supply curves for a currency** (in this case the pound sterling) show the amounts of the currency which traders wish to buy and sell at various possible prices or exchange rates. Since we are assuming that people wish to hold foreign currency only for the purpose of financing trade, the slopes of the demand and supply curves for a currency will depend on the levels of exports and imports that are desired at each exchange rate. The lower the exchange rate of the pound, the more competitive are British exports when priced in foreign currencies and the greater the volume of exports. Thus, the lower the exchange rate, the greater the demand for pounds on foreign exchange markets, since foreigners need more pounds to buy a greater volume of British exports at their current sterling price. The result is the downward-sloping demand curve for pounds illustrated in Fig. 20.1.

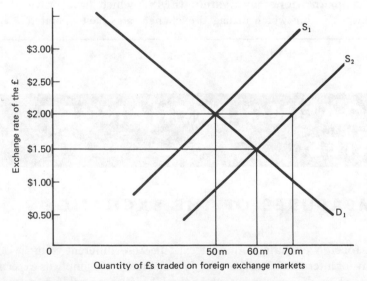

Fig. 20.1 Exchange rate adjustment in a system of freely floating exchange rates

While exports generate a demand for pounds on foreign exchange markets, imports generate the supply of sterling needed to purchase the foreign currencies required to pay for the goods and services demanded. A fall in the exchange rate will reduce the competitiveness of imports when priced in sterling. Provided that the demand for imports is elastic, the quantity of pounds being supplied to pay for imports decreases as the exchange rate falls – and increases as the exchange rate rises – resulting in the upward-sloping supply curve of sterling in Fig. 20.1.

Fig. 20.1 illustrates an initial exchange rate of £1 = $2.00, the demand curve for sterling being D₁ and the supply curve of sterling S₁. Clearly, this is an **equilibrium exchange rate** at which the demand for and the supply of sterling are equal. Since the value of exports (paid for in pounds) equals the value of imports (paid for in foreign currencies), the **balance of payments is also in equilibrium**! This point is well worth stressing: **exchange rate equilibrium** implies **balance of payments equilibrium** and vice versa. Indeed, the two concepts are merely different sides of the same coin, the one an equilibrium stated in terms of an equilibrium price (the exchange rate), and the other an equilibrium of quantities (currency flows). If the balance of payments is in equilibrium there will be no pressure for a change in the exchange rate.

Suppose now that for some reason, such as an increase in the quality competitiveness of foreign goods, the desire to buy imports increases at all existing prices expressed in sterling. More foreign exchange is demanded in order to purchase imports and the supply curve of sterling in Fig. 20.1 shifts rightwards to S₂. $2.00 is no longer an equilibrium exchange rate, since foreigners now accumulate sterling holdings of £70m, whereas they only require £50m to pay for their own purchases of British exports at this exchange rate. The market mechanism now operates to restore simultaneously equilibrium in the balance of payments and an equilibrium exchange rate. The sale by foreigners of the excess supply of pounds depresses or depreciates the exchange rate, thereby increasing the price competitiveness of British exports and reducing that of imports. The process continues until the new equilibrium exchange rate of $1.50 is reached. Conversely, if the initial equilibrium is disturbed by an event such as the production of North Sea oil which moves the balance of payments into surplus, the exchange rate will rise or appreciate until the excess demand for sterling is eliminated and a new equilibrium is achieved.

THE MARSHALL-LERNER CONDITION AND EXCHANGE RATE STABILITY

It is important to stress that the result illustrated in Fig. 20.1 depends critically upon our assumption that the demand for imports is elastic. If demand is inelastic, more pounds will be needed as the exchange rate falls in order to pay for imports. The fall in the quantity of imports at lower exchange rates is insufficient to offset the effects of the higher sterling price of each unit of imports. In these circumstances, a downward-sloping (perverse or backward-bending) supply curve for sterling results. The equilibrium exchange rate is still determined where the demand and supply curves intersect, but the equilibrium may not always be stable. The stability condition is provided by the **Marshall-Lerner criterion** which we introduced and explained in Chapter 19. Provided that the sum of the elasticities of foreigners' demand for British exports and British demand for imports is greater than unity, there will be a tendency to move towards a stable equilibrium exchange rate. Even if the demand for imports is inelastic, provided that the sum of the export and import elasticities is greater than one and that supply is sufficiently elastic, then a floating exchange rate system will correct a disequilibrium in the balance of payments.

THE ADVANTAGES OF FLOATING EXCHANGE RATES

❶ An important advantage of a freely floating (or flexible) exchange rate stems from the nature of the adjustment mechanism just described. According to the simple theory of a freely floating exchange rate, the exchange rate should never be over- or undervalued for very long. In the event of a 'too-high' exchange rate causing export uncompetitiveness and a payments deficit, market forces should quickly adjust towards an equilibrium exchange rate which also achieves equilibrium in the balance of payments – provided of course that the Marshall-Lerner condition holds.

❷ Correctly valued exchange rates are necessary if the world's resources are to be efficiently allocated between competing uses. If efficient resource allocation and use are to be achieved in a constantly changing world, market prices must be free to reflect the shifts in demand and comparative advantage that result from such events as resource discoveries and changes in technology and labour costs. A freely floating exchange rate may automatically adjust to gradual changes in demand and comparative advantage, whereas in a fixed exchange rate system a currency may become gradually over- or undervalued when demand or comparative advantage move either against or in favour of a country's industries.

3 It has been argued (rather naively, as we shall later see) that when the exchange rate is freely floating, the state of the balance of payments ceases to be both a 'policy problem' and a constraint upon the pursuit of domestic economic objectives. Governments can leave market forces to 'look after' the balance of payments while they concentrate on achieving full employment and growth. If the pursuit of domestic objectives causes the inflation rate to rise out of line with other countries, then, according to the **purchasing power parity theory**, the exchange rate will simply fall to compensate exactly for the higher inflation rate. In this way, the competitiveness of the country's exports is always maintained. In a fixed exchange rate system, the country would 'import' unemployment from the rest of the world as a result of its deteriorating competitiveness and because of the need to deflate the domestic economy in order to correct the payments deficit.

4 Equally, a responsible country with a lower-than-average inflation rate benefits from a floating exchange rate which insulates it from 'importing' inflation from the rest of the world. There are two ways of explaining this. If the rest of the world is inflating at a faster rate, a fixed exchange rate causes a country to 'import' inflation through the rising prices of goods it purchases abroad. Alternatively, under fixed exchange rates, excess demand in countries with persistent balance of payments deficits causes inflationary pressure to be 'exported' to surplus countries. The deficit countries escape the full inflationary consequences of the excess demand generated by their economies.

5 When the exchange rate is floating, a country's monetary policy (as well as its fiscal policy) can be completely independent of external influences. This is because the country has no need to keep official reserves to finance a payments deficit or to support the exchange rate. If, for example, the deficit increases, the exchange rate simply corrects the disequilibrium without any loss of reserves. The country's domestic money supply is unaffected by a change in the official reserves, and interest rate policy is not determined by the need to protect the exchange rate.

6 Because a country has no need to hold large official reserves of foreign currencies, resources which would otherwise be tied up in the reserves can be used more productively elsewhere.

THE DISADVANTAGES OF FLOATING EXCHANGE RATES

1 It is often argued that floating exchange rates increase business uncertainty and lead to less specialisation, trade, and investment than would otherwise take place. However, uncertainty is probably not the most serious problem that results from a floating exchange rate. Indeed, **hedging**, which usually involves the purchase or sale of currency three months in advance in the **forward market**, can considerably reduce the business uncertainties caused by floating exchange rates. It is also the case that fixed and managed exchange rates can, on occasion, be just as uncertain as floating rates, particularly when a currency is obviously overvalued, and a devaluation is expected.

2 It is also asserted that a floating exchange rate promotes an increase in currency speculation with all its destabilising effects. There are a number of interesting aspects to this question. While it is undoubtedly true that there was a growth in currency speculation in the years of dirty floating, it may have been less related to floating than to the growth of the pool of footloose hot money – itself a response to the role of the dollar in the Bretton Woods system of managed exchange rates. Secondly, as the events around Black Wednesday in September 1992 illustrate, there is far more scope for speculators to 'win' at the expense of governments in a managed exchange rate system than in a freely floating system. In the former case, a speculator engages in the one-way option of selling currency to the central bank defending the currency, hoping to force a devaluation and to realise a capital gain when the currency is bought back at a lower price. If the pressure fails, the speculator will only make a small loss, since he can buy back the currency at or near the original price. In a freely floating system, however, a speculator wishing to sell must find another wishing to buy – and in the consequent trading the speculator who guesses correctly gains at the expense of the one who guesses wrongly. The successful speculators are those who correctly sell when the exchange rate is too high and buy when it is too low. Their activity speeds the process of adjustment to an exchange rate equilibrium, stabilising rather than destabilising, and smoothing out rather than reinforcing temporary fluctuations.

However, during the regime of dirty floating in the 1970s and 1980s, massive, essentially speculative, short-term capital flows or hot money movements had seriously destabilising effects upon the exchange rates, balance of payments and, indeed, the structure of the domestic economy of a number of countries. At the beginning of the 1980s, hot money flowed into the UK, forcing the exchange rate up to an uncompetitive level at a time when the British inflation rate was above that of her major trading partners. The overvalued exchange rate was a major cause of deindustrialisation and unemployment.

By contrast, in 1985 the exchange rate fell to nearly $1.00 as hot money flowed out of sterling into the US currency causing the American economy to experience the problems of overvaluation. However, by the late 1980s and early 1990s, the pound was once again overvalued, with a major cause being UK monetary policy. Since the early 1980s, UK monetary policy has relied almost exclusively on the use of interest rates to influence the demand for credit and bank lending. High interest rates, aimed at dampening domestic credit, have attracted capital flows into sterling, forcing up the exchange rate. In the early 1990s, many commentators believed that an overvalued exchange rate, locked in to the rate at which the pound joined the **exchange rate mechanism** of the **EMS** in 1990, was once again contributing to renewed deindustrialisation and the growth of unemployment.

3 We have already noted how fixed exchange rates have been blamed for the 'export' of inflation from one country to another. However, other economists believe that floating exchange rates are to blame for inflation and that fixed exchange rates in fact possess a deflationary bias which reduces inflation. In a fixed exchange rate system, such as the ERM, if a country allows its inflation rate to exceed that of its trading competitors, its balance of payments will move into severe deficit. A growing export uncompetitiveness and import penetration will discipline the domestic causes of cost-push inflation through an increase in the level of unemployment and the number of bankruptcies. At the same time the loss of reserves will put pressure on the deficit country to deflate its domestic economy in order to cure the imbalance, but the system is asymmetrical, since no equivalent pressure is put upon the surplus country to cure its surplus.

In a floating exchange rate system, no such discipline exists to make a country reduce its inflation rate. (Indeed, we argued earlier that the lack of such a discipline is regarded by some as one of the virtues of floating exchange rates, allowing a country to pursue domestic objectives unconstrained by the need to support the balance of payments or the exchange rate.) In fact, however, a policy of pursuing domestic objectives irrespective of their effects on the exchange rate contains two serious dangers. In the first place, through the effects of a falling exchange rate upon import prices and hence upon domestic inflation, such a policy may unleash a **vicious circle or cumulative spiral of ever-faster inflation and exchange rate depreciation** which eventually destabilises large parts of the domestic economy and prevents growth and full employment from being attained. Secondly, a simultaneous expansion of demand in a large number of countries untrammelled by the consequences upon the exchange rate can add to excess demand and fuel inflation on a worldwide scale. In an individual country such inflation may be explained in cost-push terms, since it appears to originate in increased import prices, but the true causes probably lie deeper in an international increase in money demand which far exceeds the short-run ability of industries, and particularly primary producers, to increase world supply.

20.2 FIXED EXCHANGE RATES

THE THEORY OF A FIXED EXCHANGE RATE

In the theory of a **freely floating** exchange rate system, the currency's **external** value rises or falls to eliminate a balance of payments surplus or deficit. In contrast, in a regime of **fixed** exchange rates, the currency's external value remains unchanged while the **internal** price level, or possibly the level of domestic economic activity and output, adjust to eliminate balance of payments disequilibrium. We can approach the adjustment process from either a Keynesian or a monetarist perspective.

❶ **The Keynesian approach to balance of payments adjustment under fixed exchange rates** The Keynesian approach to the adjustment process in a system of fixed exchange rates is closely related to the **absorption approach** to the balance of payments described in Chapter 19. Suppose that initially the level of income is in equilibrium so that:

$$Y = C + I + G + (X - M)$$

and that the balance of payments on current account is also in equilibrium with $X = M$. But if exports fall (because for example foreigners believe the quality of UK goods has deteriorated), the current account will move into deficit with $X < M$ and the equilibrium level of income will also be disturbed. From a Keynesian perspective, the **current account deficit represents a leakage or withdrawal from the circular flow of income**. This triggers a negative **multiplier effect**, causing the equilibrium level of income to fall. If we now assume that the level of imports are partly determined by the level of income, via the **marginal propensity to import**, imports will then also fall, partially or completely eliminating the payments deficit caused by the initial fall in exports.

The Keynesian adjustment process we have just described illustrates how a **balance of payments deficit is inherently deflationary**. The leakage of demand represented by the deficit deflates the level of money national income (or nominal national income) within the economy. But nominal income can fall, either because the price level falls, or because the level of real output or income falls. If the domestic price level falls, exports become more price competitive in overseas markets whereas imports become more expensive. Assuming the **Marshall–Lerner condition** holds, the resulting adjustment process which eliminates the payments deficit is essentially **expenditure-switching**. In contrast, if the main effect of the deflation of demand falls not on the domestic price level but on the level of real economic activity within the country, the adjustment process is of a largely **expenditure-reducing** nature. At lower levels of real income, output and employment, fewer imports are demanded.

Conversely, when an increase in exports or a fall in imports moves the balance of payments into surplus, the adjustment mechanism is simply the opposite of the process we have just described. Being an **injection of demand** into the flow of income the **surplus has a reflationary or inflationary effect** upon the level of income and output, depending on whether real activity or prices are stimulated. Either way, nominal income rises. If the real level of economic activity is reflated or stimulated, more imports will be absorbed into the economy to meet the increased real demand being exercised by households and firms. But if the main effect is to inflate the price level, payments adjustment occurs as domestic demand switches to the more price competitive imports, while exports lose their competitiveness in world markets.

2 **The monetarist approach to balance of payments adjustment under fixed exchange rates**

The monetarist explanation of the adjustment mechanism which restores equilibrium in a fixed exchange rate system is similar to the Keynesian approach to the extent that a deficit is eliminated by deflation, and a surplus is reduced by reflation or inflation. However, monetarists emphasise the **linkages between the balance of payments and the domestic money supply** in the adjustment process. This contrasts with the Keynesian emphasis on the role of the linkages between changes in aggregate demand, the national income multiplier and a resulting increased or decreased absorption of imports. As explained in Chapter 19, a balance of payments surplus leads to a shortage of the country's currency on foreign exchange markets. When the exchange rate is fixed, the country's monetary authorities must then supply more of their own currency onto the foreign exchange market and buy other currencies which accumulate as reserves, in order to keep the currency's market price at the fixed exchange rate. This is called **exchange equalisation**. The country's money supply thus expands as new currency is issued to stabilise the exchange rate. According to monetarists, the increased money supply inflates the domestic price level, improving the price competitiveness of imports while reducing the competitiveness of exports. Conversely, a payments deficit leads to a fall in the domestic money supply because the monetary authorities must sell reserves and buy back their own currency to prevent the exchange rate from falling. The resulting monetary contraction as currency is taken out of circulation depresses or deflates the domestic economy, thereby increasing the relative competitiveness of exports.

THE ADVANTAGES AND DISADVANTAGES OF FIXED EXCHANGE RATES

The advantages and disadvantages of fixed exchange rates are closely but oppositely related to the disadvantages and advantages of floating exchange rates which we have already covered in some detail. In summary, we can state that the main advantages usually cited for fixed exchange rates are:

1 certainty and

2 the discipline imposed on a country's domestic economic management and upon the behaviour of workers and firms.

In contrast, the main disadvantages are:

1 in some circumstances uncertainty may actually be increased,

2 a currency may be over- or undervalued, in which case

3 severe costs in terms of unemployment and lost output may be imposed on deficit countries, and

4 in a rigid gold standard system there may not be an adequate adjustment mechanism successfully to cure a payments imbalance.

20.3 | MANAGED EXCHANGE RATES

THE BACKGROUND TO MANAGED EXCHANGE RATES

During the 1920s, world exchange rates were at times fixed (under a system known as the **gold standard**, in which exchange rates were pegged against gold), while, during the 1930s, most exchange rates freely floated. Neither system worked very well. The gold standard was too rigid and the floated freely system was too unstable or volatile. Indeed, both systems were blamed for contributing in part to the **Great Depression** of the 1930s. The rigid gold standard system forced countries with currencies overvalued against gold into domestic policies of deflation which led to high unemployment. Then, following the collapse of the gold standard in 1931, attempts to gain a trading advantage at other countries' expense by floating the exchange rate, together with 'beggar-my-neighbour' protectionism, contributed to the deepening of the Great Depression.

Since the Second World War, exchange rates have never been rigidly fixed and seldom have they freely or cleanly floated. Instead, the exchange rates of the world's principal currencies have to a greater or lesser extent been **managed**. An exchange rate is managed when the country's central bank actively intervenes on foreign exchange markets, buying and selling reserves and its own currency, to influence the movement of the exchange rate in a particular direction. By managing the exchange rate, a country's monetary authorities hope to achieve the stability and certainty associated with fixed exchange rates combined with a floating exchange rate's ability to avoid over- and undervaluation by responding to market forces. But critics of managed exchange rates have argued that, instead of combining the advantages of both fixed and floating exchange rates with the disadvantages of neither, in practice exchange rate management has too often achieved the opposite: the disadvantages of uncertainty and instability combined with the ineffective and wasteful use of official reserves in frequent fruitless attempts by governments to stem speculative 'hot money' flows into or out of currencies.

Since 1945 exchange rates have been managed in a number of different ways, some of which have been closer to a freely floating system, while others have been much more similar to a rigidly fixed regime. The £'s exchange rate has been determined under the following systems:

❶ The **Bretton Woods system** from 1947 to 1972;

❷ **Managed floating** (or **dirty floating**), from 1972 until ERM entry in 1990;

❸ Membership of the **Exchange Rate Mechanism (ERM)** of the **European Monetary System** (EMS), from 1990 until 1992;

❹ Floating once again since 1992.

ADJUSTABLE PEG EXCHANGE RATES

Both the **Bretton Woods** exchange rate system, which lasted from 1947 to 1971/72, and the more recent **Exchange Rate Mechanism (ERM)** of the EMS, were managed exchange rate systems which were closer to rigidly fixed than freely-floating systems. In theory they were both **adjustable peg systems**. Member countries fixed a central parity or peg for their currencies which, in principle, could be devalued or revalued if it turned out to be over- or undervalued. Market forces were free to determine the day-to-day exchange rate of a currency between a **ceiling** and **floor** which bounded the zone of flexibility a few per cent each side of an agreed par value or peg. If the balance of payments moved into surplus, the resulting excess demand for the country's currency would cause market forces to bid the exchange rate up above the peg, moving it towards the ceiling; the exchange rate would be depressed towards the floor in the event of a payments deficit. In an adjustable peg system, member countries intervene in the foreign exchange market to keep their currencies' exchange rates within the prescribed zone of flexibility. As with a rigidly fixed exchange rate system, this is achieved through **exchange equalisation**. When an exchange rate rises and threatens to move through the ceiling, the country's central bank intervenes by artificially increasing the supply of its currency on the foreign exchange market. By selling its own currency and purchasing reserves, the exchange rate can be kept below the ceiling and within the zone of flexibility. Conversely, the central bank sells reserves and buy its own currency to prevent market forces from depressing the exchange rate through the floor.

A persistent payments surplus or deficit will be associated with an equally persistent tendency for the exchange rate to leave the zone of flexibility. This indicates a **fundamental disequilibrium** in the balance of payments and a wrongly valued exchange rate. In an adjustable peg system, deficit and surplus countries are allowed, respectively to **devalue** and **revalue** their exchange rates to achieve a correct alignment.

Both the Bretton Woods system and the ERM were designed to achieve **managed flexibility**, i.e. the advantages of both fixed and floating exchange rates, but with the disadvantages of neither system. In fact, both systems suffered from **managed inflexibility**. Devaluation became effectively ruled out, except as a last resort and sign of weakness, for countries suffering from persistent payments deficits. Pressure was placed on deficit countries to deflate their domestic economies to cure their payments imbalances, but deflation could not be successful without a simultaneous pressure on surplus countries to reflate – and generally this pressure was lacking. In fact, it is always exceedingly difficult to maintain relatively fixed exchange rates if inflation rates differ widely between countries, especially if the inflation rate in deficit countries is markedly higher than in surplus countries. Adjustable peg systems (and rigidly fixed systems) work best when inflation rates converge or are very similar.

DIRTY FLOATING

Whereas the Bretton Woods System of managed exchange rates (and more recently the ERM of the EMS) resembled fixed exchange rates rather than freely floating exchange rates, the reverse is true of dirty floating. **Dirty** or **managed floating** occurs when the exchange rate is officially floating in the sense that a country's monetary authorities announce that market forces are determining the exchange rate, though in fact the authorities intervene unofficially behind the scenes to buy or sell their own currency in order to influence the exchange rate. At one extreme, such intervention can be regarded simply as a smoothing operation in a regime of clean or freely floating exchange rates, but when the intervention is designed to secure an **unofficial exchange rate target** it is better described as dirty floating. After the breakdown of the Bretton Woods System in 1971/72, the currencies of many of the world's trading countries floated in this way, though there were short-lived periods when governments withdrew their intervention and allowed their currencies to float freely.

After 1985, the UK government adopted an unofficial target for sterling which shadowed the currencies of the European Monetary System, particularly the Deutschmark. This was in preparation for an eventual full entry of the pound into the ERM of the EMS. As we explain in the next section, in the late 1980s a high exchange rate was also used by the UK government as perhaps the main instrument in its counter-inflation policy. The Conservative Government hoped that a high exchange rate would act as a discipline against domestic inflationary pressure.

THE RELATIONSHIP BETWEEN EXCHANGE RATE POLICY AND MONETARY POLICY

As we first saw in Chapter 12, in the early 1980s the Conservative Government based its monetary policy on first setting, and then trying to hit, **domestic money supply targets** which it published for measures of money such as M_1 and M_2. We also saw that around 1985 the Conservative Government abandoned targeting the domestic money supply (while the exchange rate floated), as the central strategy in its **counter-inflation policy**. Indeed, while the then prime minister, Margaret Thatcher favoured retaining such a strategy, Nigel Lawson – who was her Chancellor until 1989 – succeeded in switching the thrust of the government's counter-inflation policy towards maintaining the exchange rate at a high parity, a policy which became formalised when the £ entered the Exchange Rate Mechanism of the European Monetary System in 1990.

A **high fixed exchange rate** can reduce inflation in two main ways. Firstly, it reduces the price of imported food and consumer goods (which directly reduces inflation), and also of imported raw materials and energy which has a more indirect effect, via lower manufacturing costs. Secondly, a fixed exchange rate can act as an **external source of discipline** to cost-push pressures within the domestic economy. The theory runs as follows: if workers demand wage rises and firms set prices higher than their overseas competitors, then with a fixed exchange rate, they will lose competitiveness in world markets; the firms are then likely to be punished or disciplined by reduced profits and eventually bankruptcy, while their workers will face the threat of unemployment. However, if firms and workers believe that the government is serious about maintaining a fixed exchange rate and refusing to devalue, then they will quickly realise that it is in their self-interest to moderate price rises and wage claims.

THE EUROPEAN MONETARY SYSTEM

The **European Monetary System (EMS)**, which began operations in 1979, is both a **revival of the adjustable peg exchange rate system**, and a **'joint float'** of the EC currencies against the currencies of the rest of the world. The currencies of the EMS members – or rather those that are members of the system's **Exchange Rate Mechanism (ERM)** – are fixed against each other, but with rather wider zones of flexibility than under the old Bretton Woods System, via a specially created artificial standard or measure, the **European Currency Unit (ECU)**. Inside the 'joint float', currencies can move within the relatively wide and overlapping zones of flexibility. And because the EMS rules supposedly allow for **periodic readjustments or realignments** of the zones of flexibility against the ECU, and require action by both surplus and deficit nations to keep the currencies within the permitted bands, the EMS was (again supposedly) designed to be considerably more flexible or less rigid than the defunct Bretton Woods System.

THE UK AND THE ERM

Initially, the United Kingdom decided to remain outside the EMS, at least as a full member committed to the Exchange Rate Mechanism, but this decision contradicted the spirit if not the rules of EC membership. The members of the EC (now called the European Union, or EU) established the EMS so that the Common Market might function better. With erratically floating exchange rates, the EC would find it difficult to implement its **common economic policies**, such as the **Common Agricultural Policy**. For the United Kingdom therefore, the costs and benefits of joining the EMS ought to be closely associated with the costs and benefits of developing the common economic policies of the EC.

We have already noted that in the late 1980s the sterling exchange rate was managed so as to shadow movements of EC currencies, particularly the Deutschmark. Late in 1990, the UK finally made the decision to become a full member of the exchange rate mechanism of the EMS. At the time the Conservative Government claimed that a major benefit would be the ability to draw on the help of other members to deter destabilising hot money movements into and out of sterling. The more ardent Europhiles both inside and outside the government also claimed that Britain might benefit if the exchange rate arrangements were eventually to develop into full European Monetary Union (EMU), with the ECU becoming a common EC currency and new source of world liquidity.

However, opponents of both fixed exchange rates and of closer UK integration with the EU opposed entry into the ERM, claiming that the system suffers the disadvantages of any system of relatively fixed exchange rates. They argued that the EMS has tended to become a **Deutschmark area** in which the German mark is the key currency. In the joint float of the 1980s (in the period before German reunification), a strong DM tended to pull up the fixed values of the other currencies, leading to their overvaluation against the rest of the world. And although the zones of flexibility had been designed to prevent this happening, great pressure could still be placed on weaker EMS currencies, particularly if member countries experience divergent inflation rates. After 1989, this pressure was exacerbated when the German central bank, the Bundesbank, raised German interest rates in order to dampen domestic inflationary pressures caused by German unification.

By 1992 high German interest rates were forcing the UK authorities to raise sterling interest rates to prevent capital flows out of the pound and to support the high parity at which the £ had entered the ERM. Perhaps more significantly, the combination of a high ERM parity and high interest rates were causing the UK to suffer severely in terms of lost output and high unemployment. Many economists believed that ERM membership had pushed the UK economy into recession and that the deflationary costs could not be justified. And although, at under 4 per cent, the UK inflation rate had converged to near the EU average, there was a growing consensus – outside the Conservative Government – that the £ was overvalued and that its ERM parity could not be maintained. In the earlier years of the ERM, periodic realignments of currencies had taken place which prevented the system from becoming too inflexible. But by the time the £ joined the ERM in 1990, the ERM had evolved – like the Bretton Woods System almost a generation before – into a system of managed inflexibility in which realignments were strongly discouraged. By September 1992 the £'s exchange rate within the ERM became unsupportable, with devaluation becoming a matter of *when* and not *if*. Following a massive speculative hot money flow out of the £, in which the UK authorities used up virtually the whole of the country's foreign exchange reserves in an abortive defence of the ERM parity, the £ was forced to leave the Exchange Rate Mechanism on September 16th. 1992.

Since the devaluation of 1992 and the debacle of exit from the ERM, the £ has once again floated, without much evidence of exchange rate intervention. It is unlikely that the UK Government will attempt to re-enter the ERM in the near future. If the £ does re-enter the ERM, it is likely to be at a significantly lower exchange rate than the parity operating when the £ was originally in the ERM from 1990 to 1992.

THE INTERNATIONAL MONETARY FUND

In earlier chapters we have explained how, in the years following the Second World War, Keynesian economic policies were adopted within countries to pursue the objectives of growth and full employment through an extension of government intervention in the domestic economy. Keynesian economic policies were a response to the Great Depression and to the large-scale unemployment of the interwar years. In part, however, the Great Depression had been caused, and certainly made worse, by the collapse of world trade which followed the breakdown of the gold standard system in 1931. Perhaps it is not surprising therefore, that the 1940s were also the decade in which interventionism was extended to the management of exchange rates, through the creation of the **International Money Fund (IMF)**.

Since its inception at the 1944 Bretton Woods Conference, the principal objective of the IMF has been to promote a growing and freer system of world trade and payments. To achieve this general objective, the original Articles of Agreement of the International Monetary Fund specified that the IMF should:

❶ promote international monetary cooperation;

❷ promote stable exchange rates, maintain orderly exchange arrangements and avoid competitive exchange depreciation;

❸ encourage full convertibility between currencies and an ending of exchange controls;

❹ lend its resources to countries to enable them to correct payments imbalances without resorting to harmful restrictions on trade;

❺ shorten periods of disequilibrium in the balance of payments of member countries.

Certainly, over the near fifty-year period since the establishment of the IMF, the first two objectives have been achieved, at least among the richer members of the IMF, though not for most developing country members. However, the influence of the IMF upon the stability of exchange rates has diminished rather than increased and it is debatable whether the activities of the IMF have had much effect upon the length of periods of payments imbalance or upon the ease with which payments deficits can be cured.

The three main roles adopted by the IMF have been:

❶ An **advisory role** as a consultant giving expert advice to members.

❷ **'Policing' the Bretton Woods System of exchange rates**, until the system broke down in 1971/72. In recent years the IMF has tried, rather ineffectively, to produce orderly conditions in a world of 'dirty' floating. In recent years the IMF's policing role has been directed less at regulating exchange rates, than at limiting the freedom of deficit countries, who wish to borrow from the Fund, to pursue the domestic economic policies of their choice. Although initially established to reflect Keynesian ideas of economic management, in more recent years the IMF has become generally monetarist in both aim and action. As a result, countries are usually required to adopt sound monetarist policies as a condition for the extension of IMF credit. Developing countries in particular, have been severely hit by the deflationary policies forced on them as a condition of IMF loans.

❸ **A banking role**. In 1944 the Bretton Woods Agreement hoped to promote the orderly development of world trade by ensuring an adequate supply of international liquidity to tide deficit countries over temporary payments difficulties. The dollar provided the main source of primary liquidity, but its own weakening eventually contributed to the downfall of the Bretton Woods exchange rates. To supplement the primary liquidity provided by the dollar, specially created **IMF reserves** were intended to supply a source of secondary liquidity. Initially, when the IMF was first set up, each member paid a **quota** (75% in its own currency and 25% in gold) into an IMF 'basket' or **pool of currency reserves** which were then available for member countries to draw upon when experiencing a payment deficit. In the event of a temporary payments deficit, the first part of a country's drawing entitlement is automatic, but beyond a certain limit the IMF can impose conditions upon a further loan. At regular intervals since 1944, the size of quotas and the IMF's overall reserves have been increased.

Chapter roundup

Exchange rates have a great effect on trade and the balance of payments (Chapters 18 and 19). They also influence macroeconomic policy, affecting the level of demand (Chapter 14) and inflation (Chapter 15). We also saw in Chapter 17 how Keynesians advocate a managed exchange rate while monetarists favour either a freely floating or a rigidly fixed regime.

Illustrative questions and answers

1   Essay question

What are the relative merits of fixed and floating exchange rate systems? Discuss the implication of being in or out of the ERM for UK government economic policy. (25)

NEAB

Tutorial note

As the advantages and disadvantages of floating and fixed exchange rates are covered in some depth in the main part of the chapter, we shall not repeat the information here. However as we emphasised there, it is useful to remember that to a large extent, the advantages of floating exchange rates are the disadvantages of fixed exchange rates, and vice versa. It would be a good idea to write a concluding sentence to the first part of your answer indicating whether, on balance, you think floating exchange rates are better than fixed exchange rates.

To answer the second part of the question, you must draw on the UK's experience during and after the period of ERM membership, which lasted from 1990 to 1992. Again most of the material you need is in the main body of the chapter. You must avoid simply writing an historical account. Points to emphasise are: the effect of entering the ERM at a high rather than a low parity; the effect of the exchange rate regime upon monetary policy; and the implications for the £ being a part of the single European currency (the **Euro**), proposed for 1999. With regard to monetary policy, ERM membership restricting the UK monetary authorities' freedom to pursue the monetary policy of their choice. In effect, the rate of interest was unavailable as a policy instrument for reflating the UK economy out of recession in the early 1990s, because high interest rates were needed to support the £'s high parity within the ERM. Refer back also to the explanation in Chapter 19 of why, leaving the ERM in 1992, was a perfect devaluation.

Suggested answer plan

- Define and distinguish between floating and fixed exchange rates.

- Outline briefly how a payments imbalance is corrected in both systems.

- Explain the advantages and disadvantages of both types of exchange rates.

- State that the £ was in the ERM from 1990 to 1992; explain that the ERM was an adjustable peg system which had become extremely rigid by the time the £ entered the system.

- Outline the resulting effects upon the UK economy and economic policy.

- Explain that the devaluation of 1992, though unplanned, turned out to be a *perfect devaluation*, increasing UK competitiveness and stimulating recovery from recession.

- Outline other implications of remaining outside the ERM, e.g. implications for further economic integration within the EU and for European monetary union (EMU).

2 Data Question

The following is an abstract of an article by Professor M. Friedman, published in the Financial Times on December 18 1989.

Study the passage carefully, then answer each of the questions which follow, explaining your reasoning in each case.

THE CASE FOR FLOATING RATES

Discussions of the prospects for a monetary union within the Common Market have generally ignored the difference between two superficially similar but basically very different exchange rate arrangements. One arrangement is a unified currency, the pound sterling in Scotland, England and Wales. Further back in
5   time essentially the same arrangement applied in the late 19th century when pound, dollar, franc, etc., were simply different names for specified fixed amounts of gold. A truly unified European currency would make a great deal of sense.

An alternative arrangement is a system of exchange rates between national currencies pegged at agreed values to be maintained by the separate national
10   central banks by altering domestic monetary policy appropriately. Many proponents of a common European currency regard such a system of pegged exchange rates (the EMS) as a step towards a unified currency. I believe that is a grave mistake. In my opinion, a system of pegged exchange rates among national currencies is worse than either extreme, a truly unified currency, or national
15   currencies linked by freely floating exchange rates. The reason is that national central banks will not, under modern conditions, be permitted to shape their policies with an eye solely to keeping the exchange rates of their currencies at the agreed level. Pressure to use monetary policy for domestic purposes will from time to time be irresistible. And when that occurs the exchange system becomes

20 unstable. That was certainly the experience under Bretton Woods. Even in its
heyday, exchange rate changes were numerous and when they came often
massive.

Experience since then has strengthened my confidence in a system of freely
floating exchange rates, though it has also made me far more sceptical that such
25 a system is politically feasible. Central banks will meddle, always of course with
the best of intentions. None the less, even dirty floating exchange rates seem to
me preferable to pegged rates, though not necessarily to a unified currency.

(a) Why did the author assert that in effect a unified currency arrangement applied
worldwide in the late nineteenth century (lines 4–7)? (5)

(b) What reasons might justify the author's assertion that a truly unified European
currency would 'make a great deal of sense' (line 7)? (5)

(c) Why does maintenance of pegged exchange rates between national currencies
involve separate national central banks 'altering domestic monetary policy
appropriately' (line 10)? (5)

(d) What did the author mean when he argued that 'pressure to use monetary policy for
domestic purposes will from time to time be irresistible' (lines 18–19)? (5)

(e) For what reasons could monetary policy used for domestic purposes cause the
exchange system to become 'unstable' (lines 19–20)? (5)   *WJEC*

Tutorial note

(a) Milton Friedman was referring to the full gold standard exchange rate system in
which a country's currency was exchangeable for a gold at a fixed rate both inside
and outside a country's frontiers. Since much of the currency was gold coin, gold in
effect functioned as the 'unified currency' in all countries which were on the full gold
standard.

(b) Although as a strict or technical monetarist, Professor Friedman has always been a
leading advocate of freely-floating exchange rates, in this article he is arguing that a
truly unified currency, which once established would not allow any exchange rate
adjustments at all between trading countries or regions, would make sense if
countries involved wish to achieve a full economic union. Monetarists often quote the
USA as a model: the United States is a political federation but a full economic union;
any attempt to introduce separate currencies and exchange rates, say between Texas
and Illinois, would harm the development of the continental economy (though
arguably a proliferation of American currencies might benefit some of the poorer
American states which have been suffering from a drift of people and businesses to
the more prosperous states such as California). If the poorer states could devalue a
local currency or allow it to float, they might regain a competitive advantage in the
overall US market.

(c) As Britain's experience in the ERM in the early 1990s has shown, maintaining a fixed
peg exchange rate requires that monetary policy in general, and interest rate policy
in particular, have to be assigned to supporting the exchange rate (for example by
deterring speculative capital flows), which means that monetary policy instruments
may be not available for the pursuit of domestic policy objectives.

(d) But governments may not be prepared continually to sacrifice domestic policy
objectives on the altar of supporting the exchange rate. In the case of an overvalued
exchange rate (for example the sterling exchange rate in 1992), the cost in terms of
deflation, lost output, and unemployment may be extremely high as the economy
suffers both from uncompetitive exports and from the high interest rates which are
needed to support the high parity.

(e) This is simply the opposite side of the argument we have just put forward. If interest
rates are lowered so as to expand or reflate demand in the domestic economy and
encourage economic activity, support of an overvalued exchange rate is immediately
undermined. Speculative capital flows out of the currency are likely to put immediate

pressure on the exchange rate, with the government then facing the choice of a policy U-turn by deflating the domestic economy so as to support the exchange rate, or abandoning the fixed parity and devaluing (or allowing the currency to float).

Question bank

1 'An increase in inflation causes the exchange rate to fall.'

'A fall in the exchange rate increases inflation.'

(a) Carefully explain **both** these statements. (10)

(b) Discuss the implications of these statements for a government's macro-economic policy. (15) *AEB*

Pitfalls

It is impossible to score a high mark for this question unless you identify the two areas of theory which underpin the statements in the stem of the question. Firstly, the **purchasing power parity theory** predicts that if a country's inflation rate is higher than that of the rest of the world, its exchange rate will fall to restore competitiveness. Secondly, a falling exchange rate feeds into **cost-push** inflationary processes within the economy.

Key Points

Explain both statements in terms of the purchasing power parity theory and inflation theory. Then explain the implications of the statements. Both processes may come together, promoting a cumulative vicious downward spiral of exchange rate depreciation and domestic inflation, which ultimately destabilises the economy and harms economic performance.

2 'When a currency is allowed to float freely its exchange rate will be determined by demand and supply.'

(a) Describe those factors which determine the demand for **and** the supply of a currency. (12)

(b) Explain the advantages for an economy of having a freely floating currency. (9)

(c) Explain the reasons why a country may wish to adopt a managed exchange rate system. (9) *SEB*

Pitfalls

The key word in part (a) is *describe*, but to earn all 12 marks some explanation of how the factors you mention affect the demand and supply of a currency is also needed. Part (c) of the question is really a disguised question on the disadvantages of floating exchange rates, though the disadvantages of fixed exchange rates are also relevant.

Key points

Define a floating exchange rate, then list and outline briefly the advantages of floating exchange rates. Explain the meaning of a managed exchange rate. Then explain that a government may wish to manage the exchange rate to try to achieve the advantages of both floating and fixed exchange rates with the disadvantages of neither system.

3 (a) What are the benefits that the United Kingdom has derived from its membership of the European Union (formerly the European Community)? (12)

(b) Discuss the view that the benefits would be greater if all the members of the European Union adopted a single currency. (13) *AEB*

Pitfalls

Part (a) of the question asks for a discussion of *benefits* rather than *costs*. However, you could make the point that, in your view, the benefits are insignificant, or that the costs outweigh the benefits. If you take this view, you must avoid writing a Eurosceptic diatribe against the European Union, however strongly you feel on the subject! Likewise with the single currency.

Key points

Outline at least three benefits of EU membership, e.g. access to a larger market; opportunities for greater economies of scale; inward investment attracted into the UK; EU financial help for particular UK industries and regions. Explain that a single currency (the Euro) would assist the implementation of common economic policies such as the CAP. The adverse effects of sterling crises on the UK economy would become a thing of the past. On the debit side, the UK government would lose much of its freedom of action to pursue the economic policy of its choice. It could no longer pursue an independent monetary policy, and devaluation would no longer be an option to restore UK competitiveness vis a vis other EU member countries.

TEST RUN

In this section:

Test Your Knowledge Quiz

Test Your Knowledge Quiz Answers

Progress Analysis

Mock Exam

Mock Exam Suggested Answers

- This section should be tackled towards the end of your revision programme, when you have covered all your syllabus topics, and attempted the practice questions at the end of the relevant chapters.

- The Test Your Knowledge Quiz contains short-answer questions on a wide range of syllabus topics. You should attempt it without reference to the text.

- Check your answers against the Test Your Knowledge Quiz Answers. If you are not sure why you got an answer wrong, go back to the relevant chapter in the text: you will find the reference next to our answer.

- Enter your marks in the Progress Analysis chart. The notes below will suggest a further revision strategy, based on your performance in the quiz. Only when you have done the extra work suggested should you go on to the final test.

- The Mock Exam is set out like a real exam paper. It contains a wide spread of question styles and topics, drawn from various examination boards. You should attempt this paper under examination conditions. Read the instructions on the front sheet carefully. Attempt the paper in the time allowed, and without reference to the text.

- Compare your answers to our Mock Exam Suggested Answers. We have provided tutorial notes to each, showing why we answered the question as we did and indicating where your answer may have differed from ours.

TEST YOUR KNOWLEDGE QUIZ

1   What is the central economic problem?

2   What are the three economic functions of prices in a market economy?

3   Distinguish between the goods market and the factor market.

4   Distinguish between individual demand and market demand.

5   Define planned demand and realised demand.

6   Explain the equilibrium equation: planned demand = planned supply.

7   Why may a demand curve shift?

8   Distinguish between the market period, the short run and the long run.

9   What are the conditions of supply?

10   What is a buffer-stock policy?

11   Distinguish between a 'bad', a 'good' an 'economic good' and a 'free good'.

12   Define opportunity cost. What is the opportunity cost of this exercise you are currently attempting?

13   Who is economic man or economic woman?

14   Define utility.

15   State the consumer's objective in both maximising and minimising terms.

16   What are the constraints facing a consumer in the market?

17   Explain the condition of equi-marginal utility.

18   Distinguish between an income effect and a substitution effect.

19   Distinguish between a normal good, an inferior good and a Giffen good.

20   List reasons why a demand curve may sometimes slope upwards.

21   What is consumer surplus?

22   Explain the shape of the average fixed-cost curve.

23   Explain the principle or law of diminishing returns.

24   What is the relationship between marginal and average returns?

25   How do marginal returns affect marginal costs?

26   Why is a short-run ATC curve U-shaped?

27   Explain the short-run supply curve of a competitive firm.

28   Distinguish between decreasing returns to scale and the 'law' of diminishing returns.

29   Must the long-run AC curve be U-shaped?

30   Distinguish between technical efficiency and productive efficiency.

31   What are external economies of scale?

32   Write out the formulas for income elasticity of demand and price elasticity of supply.

33   What is meant by elastic demand?

34   What elasticity does a rectangular hyperbola display?

35   What is the most important determinant of price elasticity of demand?

36   Contrast the income elasticity of demand of normal and inferior goods.

37   What can be inferred about the demand relationship between two goods with a cross-elasticity of (+)0.3?

38   Why is perfect competition an unreal market structure?

39   Why is a perfectly competitive firm's average-revenue curve horizontal?

40   Distinguish between normal and abnormal profit.

41   Explain the relationship between average revenue and marginal revenue in monopoly.

42   How does elasticity of demand affect monopoly?

43 Is perfect competition efficient?

44 How do economies of scale affect productive efficiency?

45 In what way is monopolistic competition similar to (a) perfect competition and (b) monopoly?

46 Define an oligopoly.

47 Why is there no general theory of oligopoly?

48 Why may oligopolists collude together and what forms might the collusion take?

49 Define price discrimination and what are the necessary conditions for successful price discrimination?

50 Distinguish between a public good and a private good.

51 Define an externality.

52 How do externalities affect allocative efficiency?

53 What is a merit good?

54 Why may the distribution of income and wealth be regarded as a market failure?

55 How may a mixed economy be defined?

56 What is meant by regulatory capture?

57 What is a natural monopoly?

58 List alternative possible approaches to the problem of monopoly.

59 What is the theory of contestable markets?

60 Distinguish between collective and non-collective restrictive trading practices.

61 Distinguish between privatisation, contractualisation, marketisation and deregulation.

62 What is an internal market?

63 What is competitive tendering?

64 Why may a worker's supply curve of labour bend backwards?

65 What is marginal revenue product (MRP)?

66 Distinguish between economic rent and transfer earnings.

67 What is collective bargaining?

68 What are the objectives of macroeconomic policy?

69 Distinguish between a progressive and a regressive tax.

70 Relate the PSBR to the budget deficit and to the National Debt.

71 Define fiscal policy.

72 What is fiscal drag?

73 List the four functions of money.

74 What is the money multiplier?

75 List the three main motives for demanding money.

76 What is liquidity preference?

77 List four ways in which the Bank of England might use monetary policy to reduce bank lending and the money supply.

78 What is meant by fully-funding the PSBR?

79 How may interest rates affect total bank deposits?

80 What are the three ways of measuring national income?

81 Derive a savings function from $C = a + cY$.

82 What is the equilibrium level of national income?

83 What are injections and leakages of demand in a four-sector economy?

84 Distinguish between nominal and real national income.

85 What is a deflationary gap?

86 What is meant by demand management?

87 Explain the national income multiplier and state its formula.

88 What is crowding out?

89 What is an automatic stabiliser?

90 Explain the role of business confidence and expectations in the marginal efficiency of capital theory.

91 Express the accelerator theory as an equation.

92 List four types or causes of unemployment.

93 State the quantity theory of money.

94 Distinguish between demand-pull and cost-push inflation.

95 What is the Phillips curve relationship?

96 Briefly explain the terms: Keynesianism; monetarism; supply-side economics.

97 Distinguish between absolute advantage and comparative advantage.

98 List the policies that might reduce a balance of payments deficit on current account.

99 Distinguish between flexible, fixed and managed exchange rates.

100 What are the following: IMF; IBRD; EC; EMS; ERM; EMU; CAP; GATT?

TEST YOUR KNOWLEDGE QUIZ ANSWERS

The chapter number in which the answer can be found is given in brackets at the end of the answer.

Award yourself one mark for each correct answer. Do not give yourself a mark if only part of the answer is correct.

1 Resource allocation, involving the allocation of scarce resources between competing uses. (1)

2 Signalling, the creation of incentives, and the rationing function. (2)

3 The goods market is the market for outputs, i.e. finished goods and services, whereas the factor market is the market for inputs or factors of production, such as labour. (2)

4 Individual demand is the planned demand for a good exercised by a single individual, whereas market demand is the sum of the planned demands of all the individuals or prospective buyers in the market. (2, 3)

5 Planned demand is the *ex ante*, desired or intended demand of prospective buyers, whereas realised demand measures the quantities of the good which the buyers actually purchase (also known as *ex post*, actual or fulfilled demand). (2, 3)

6 Only when planned demand = planned supply can both buyers and sellers fulfil their market plans. When this condition holds, there is no excess demand or excess supply in the market, and hence no reason for the price to change – the market is thus in a state of rest or equilibrium. (2)

7 A demand curve will shift if any of the conditions of demand, such as income and tastes, change. (2, 3)

8 All the factors of production are fixed and none are variable in the market period; in the short run at least one of the factors of production is fixed and one is variable; in the long run all the factors of production are variable and none are fixed. (4, 5)

9 A supply curve will shift if any of the conditions of supply change. The conditions of supply include costs of production or the prices of the inputs into the production process, the state of technical progress, and any taxes imposed upon (or subsidies given to) firms which vary with the firm's output. (4)

10 A buffer stock is used to stabilise agricultural prices, based on the principle of buying the agricultural product and accumulating a stockpile when there is a glut, and then releasing supply onto the market from the stock in the event of a bad harvest. Exchange equalisation or the use of the country's foreign exchange reserves to stabilise or manage the exchange rate (Chapter 20) works on a similar principle. (6)

11 When consumed, a 'good' yields utility, whereas a 'bad' yields disutility or displeasure. Note that a 'good' becomes a 'bad' if consumed beyond the point of satiation. The supply of an economic good is limited relative to demand, so the problem of scarcity arises, requiring rationing through prices, or some other mechanism. By contrast, a free good is available in unlimited quantities and with no costs of production at zero price.

(2, 3, 9)

12 The opportunity cost of any action, choice or decision is the next best alternative foregone. For example, the opportunity cost of attempting this test could be the sacrificed opportunity to watch a football match or play on a computer games machine.   (2, 7)

13 Economic man or woman always acts rationally in the sense of trying to maximise his or her self-interest or private benefit. He or she never makes a decision which is known in advance to be against his or her self-interest.   (2, 3, 7)

14 Utility means usefulness and fulfilment of need encompassing pleasure and satisfaction.

(3)

15 The consumer's (assumed) objective is to maximise the utility that can be achieved from spending his limited income on the goods or services that are available to buy. This objective can also be defined in terms of the minimisation of the outlay or expenditure needed to purchase a desired bundle of goods.   (3)

16 The budget constraint, i.e. limited income and a given set of prices at which goods are available; given tastes and preferences; given availability of goods and a time constraint.

(3)

17 The 'condition of equi-marginal utility' holds when the ratio of the marginal utility to the price is equal for all goods. When the condition holds, a consumer maximises utility (subject to the constraints faced) and has no incentive to change the bundle of goods purchased.   (3)

18 The substitution effect of a price change relates to the fact that following a price change, to maximise utility a consumer must substitute more of the good which has become relatively cheaper in place of other goods previously demanded which are now relatively more expensive. But a price fall also affects the consumer's real income or purchasing power, enabling the consumer to buy more of all goods because he is better off. This is the income effect of the price change.   (3)

19 Demand for a normal good increases with income, whereas demand for an inferior good declines as income increases. A Giffen good is so inferior that the perverse income effect following a price fall (causing less to be demanded as the consumer feels better off) outweighs the substitution effect. The result is an upward-sloping demand curve.   (3)

20 The Giffen good effect; Veblen goods or goods of ostentatious consumption or status; goods for which price is taken as an indicator of quality; and asset demand or speculative demand for goods.   (3)

21 Consumer surplus is the utility a consumer gains from the consumption of a good over and above the price paid.   (3)

22 The AFC curve falls towards zero as output increases; this is explained by the spreading of overheads.   (4)

23 The law of diminishing returns states that as a firm increases output in the short run by adding more of a variable factor of production such as labour to its fixed factors such as capital, eventually an extra worker will add less to total output than the previous worker who joined the labour force, i.e. the marginal product or returns of labour will begin to fall.   (4)

24 (i) When marginal returns > average returns, average returns rise;
(ii) When marginal returns < average returns, average returns fall;
(iii) When marginal returns = average returns, average returns are constant.

(4)

25 Diminishing marginal returns to the variable factors of production cause the firm's short-run marginal costs to rise. (4)

26 The spreading of fixed costs and increasing marginal returns to the variable factors of production combine to cause ATC to fall as output is increased at low levels of output. But eventually the law of diminishing returns sets in, causing marginal costs to rise. When MC rises above ATC, the ATC curve will be 'pulled up' at higher levels of output.   (4)

27 The firm's short-run supply curve is its short-run MC curve, above AVC. (4)

28 Decreasing returns to scale occur in the long run if a change in the scale or ALL the firm's inputs, including capital, leads to a less than proportionate increase in output. By contrast the 'law' of diminishing returns relates to the short run when at least one of the firm's inputs or factors of production is held fixed. (4)

29 No; it will only be U-shaped if increasing returns to scale at low levels of output are followed by decreasing returns to scale at higher levels of output and scales of operation. It would be quite possible, for example, for there to be increasing returns to scale at all possible scales of operation, in which case the LRAC curve would be downward-sloping throughout its range. (4)

30 Production is technically efficient if output is maximised from a given set of inputs or factors of production. This will also be productively efficient if the cost of producing the output is minimised. Productive efficiency can be thought of as the translation into money costs of production of the concept of technical efficiency. The most productively efficient of all the firm's possible levels of output is located at the bottom of the firm's LRAC curve. (7)

31 External economies of scale are reductions in a firm's long-run production costs which result from the growth of the whole industry or market of which the firm is a member. (10)

32 Income elasticity of demand = $\dfrac{\text{Proportionate change in quantity demanded}}{\text{Proportionate change in income}}$

Price elasticity of supply = $\dfrac{\text{Proportionate change in quantity supplied}}{\text{Proportionate change in price}}$

(5)

33 Unless otherwise qualified, elastic demand refers to price elasticity of demand; it means that a change in price results in a more than proportionate change in demand. (5)

34 Unit elasticity of demand, i.e. neither elastic nor inelastic. (5)

35 The availability of substitutes. (5)

36 The income elasticity of demand is positive for normal goods and negative for inferior goods. (5)

37 The two goods are substitutes and a 10% rise in the price of one good causes a 3% increase in demand for the other good. (5)

38 Because it is impossible in real life for all the conditions of perfect competition to hold at the same time, e.g. a completely uniform good and a very large number of buyers and sellers, each with perfect market information. (7)

39 Provided the firm sells its output at the ruling market price for the whole industry, it can sell any amount it wishes. Price or average revenue is therefore the same, whatever the level of output the firm chooses to produce and sell. (7)

40 Normal profit is defined as the minimum profit an established firm must make to stay in the market, while being insufficient to attract outside or new firms into the market. Since normal profits are treated as a cost of production which must be covered for a firm to remain in the market, they are included in a firm's cost curves. Abnormal profits (also known as above-normal and super-normal profits) are any profits over and above normal profits. (7)

41 Since the monopolist faces a downward-sloping AR curve, indicating that to sell more the price must be reduced, the MR curve must be below the AR curve. If the AR curve is linear (a straight line), the MR curve will also be linear and twice as steep as the AR curve. (7)

42 The profit-maximising level of output will always be located under the elastic section of the monopolist's AR or demand curve. (7)

43 Provided there are no economies of scale, externalities and that every firm in the economy is perfectly competitive and in long-run equilibrium, it can be shown that each firm would be productively efficient (producing at the lowest point on its ATC curve) and allocatively efficient (P=MC). For the economy as a whole this would mean that all resources would be fully-employed and it would be impossible to increase production of one good without

reducing production of at least one other good, or to make one individual better-off without making at least one other individual worse off. (7)

44 A firm must expand to benefit from full economies of scale if it is to be productively efficient. (7)

45 Monopolistic competition is similar to perfect competition in that there is a large number of firms and there is freedom to enter or leave the market in the long run; it is similar to monopoly in that each firm faces a downward-sloping demand curve for its product (since the products are differentiated and partial substitutes for each other). (8)

46 Oligopoly is best defined as an industry containing a small number of firms, with each firm needing to take account of the likely reactions of the other firms when deciding its own best market strategy. (8)

47 Because a different theory would be appropriate for each set of assumptions about how the rivals would react to an oligopolists price and output decisions. (8)

48 To reduce uncertainty and give themselves an easier life. Also, the theory of joint-profit maximisation shows that by acting as a single monopolist, the oligopolists can make larger joint profits than if they act separately and competitively. The oligopolists may enter into restrictive collective trading agreements, or a cartel agreement in which they restrict output, carve up the market and hike up the price. (8)

49 Price discrimination occurs when a firm charges different prices to different customers for the same good with the same costs of supply, the different prices being based on the fact that some customers are prepared to pay a higher price than others. The firm must first identify the different customers with different demands, and then keep the markets separate so as to prevent seepage. (8)

50 A pure public good is defined by the properties of non-excludability and non-diminishability (or non-rivalry), whereas a pure private good displays the opposite properties of excludability and diminishability. (9)

51 An externality is a spin-off effect, delivered and received as a benefit or a cost outside the market, i.e. a price cannot be charged for it. (9)

52 Allocative efficiency occurs when P=MSC. A competitive market system may ensure that P= MPC, but if negative externalities or external costs such as pollution are generated in the course of production (with MSC = MPC + MEC), it follows that P < MSC. In this situation, the price of good is too low since it does not reflect the true marginal cost of production which includes the cost of the negative externality which is being dumped on third parties. Being too low, the price encourages too much production and too much consumption of the good whose production generates the negative externality. (9)

53 Merit goods have two properties. Firstly, the social benefits to the whole community resulting from their consumption are greater than the private benefits to the individual consumers; hence there is a case for the state to encourage their consumption. Secondly, the long-term private benefits to the individual resulting from consuming a merit good such as education or health care may exceed the short-term private benefits. Left to themselves, individuals may be guilty of short-termism by deciding to consume less than is in their long-term interest. This reinforces the case for the state to encourage consumption. (9)

54 A highly unequal distribution of income and wealth is often regarded as a market failure on the grounds of inequity (unfairness) rather than inefficiency. (9)

55 A mixed economy is usually defined as containing a mix of private sector and public sector economic activity, though this definition can be extended to containing a mix of market and non-market economic activity. (1)

56 Regulatory capture refers to the situation when the regulator of an industry or market acts in the interests of the companies he is supposed to regulate and against the interests of the consumers he is supposed to protect. (10)

57 Strictly speaking, a natural monopoly occurs when a particular part of the world has a monopoly over the supply of a mineral or raw material which cannot be produced elsewhere. Usually, however, the term natural monopoly is used rather differently to describe an industry where economies of scale combine with limited market size so that there is only room in the market for one firm benefiting from full scale economies. The

utility industries, such as water supply, provide another example, as there is a case for just one water or gas main, etc. serving each street. (6, 10)

58 (i) Monopoly busting or breaking the monopoly up into smaller firms;
(ii) allowing the monopoly to exist but exposing it to severe regulation;
(iii) deregulation and removal of barriers to entry
(iv) taking a private monopoly into public ownership;
(v) privatising a nationalised monopoly;
(vi) taxing excessive monopoly profits. (10)

59 The theory of contestable markets is a part of the new (free-market) industrial economics which argues that it is not necessary to break up or severely regulate an established monopoly if the market can be made potentially contestable by removing barriers to market entry. (10)

60 Collective restrictive practices are undertaken jointly by two or more firms via a restrictive agreement such as a cartel agreement. A non-collective restrictive practice is unilaterally undertaken by a firm, e.g. a refusal to supply a particular customer or retail outlet.
(6, 10)

61 Privatisation involves the transfer, usually through sale, of assets such as nationalised industries from the public sector to the private sector. Contractualisation is a related policy of putting out services to contract supply or tender, e.g. some police services are likely to be contracted out to private security firms. Marketisation (or commercialisation) involves shifting the provision of services from the non-market sector (where they are financed by taxation) into the market sector, where the services are commercially provided and sold at a market price. Lastly, deregulation means the abolition of previously imposed regulations, to remove unnecessary red tape and barriers to market entry. (10)

62 An internal market is a market **within** an organisation such as the National Health Service, in which one part of the organisation, e.g. GPs or **purchasers**, trade with hospitals or **providers**. (10)

63 Competitive tendering involves public sector organisations, such as the Civil Service, inviting private sector businesses to tender to undertake part of their work. The work is 'contracted out' to the private sector business which offers the best value for money.
(10)

64 A backward-bending supply curve of labour results when the income effect of a wage-rate change becomes stronger than the substitution effect. (11)

65 A worker's marginal revenue product measures the extent to which a firm's sales revenue rises as a result of employing one more worker. The MRP is calculated by multiplying the worker's marginal physical product (the output produced by an extra worker) by the firm's marginal sales revenue: (MRP = MPP x MR). (11)

66 A worker's transfer earnings is the minimum wage he must be paid to prevent him transferring out of the labour market, either by moving to another job or through choosing unemployment in preference to working; by contrast, economic rent is the wage a worker is paid over and above his transfer earnings. (11)

67 Collective bargaining occurs when a trade union bargains collectively on behalf of its members with an employer or employers over conditions of work, including pay. (11)

68 Full employment, economic growth, price stability or control of inflation and a satisfactory balance of payments are usually listed as the four main objectives of macroeconomic policy, though not necessarily ranked in the order given here. A satisfactory or fair distribution of income and wealth might be included as another objective, though some might classify this as a microeconomic objective. (17)

69 A tax is progressive if the amount of tax paid rises at a faster rate than income; it is regressive if the tax paid rises at a slower rate than income. (13)

70 When the public sector's finances are in deficit with public spending exceeding revenue, the deficit has to financed by borrowing. The public sector financial deficit and the PSBR are approximately equal. But both are flows, whereas the National Debt is a stock: the National Debt is the accumulated stock of outstanding central government debt. (13)

71 Fiscal policy can be defined quite generally as that part of the government's overall economic policy in which the government tries to achieve its policy objectives using the fiscal instruments of taxation and public spending. (13, 17)

72 Fiscal drag occurs when the government fails to revise income tax thresholds upwards at the same rate as inflation. This means that, in real terms, the tax threshold shifts lower down the income pyramid, dragging the low-paid into the tax net.   (13)

73 (i)   Medium of exchange or means of payment;
    (ii) store of value or wealth;
    (iii) unit of account; and
    (iv) standard of deferred payment.   (12)

74 The money multiplier (also known as the credit multiplier, the deposit multiplier and the bank multiplier) measures the relationship between a change in the reserve assets (including cash) in the banking system, and the resulting change in total bank deposits.   (12)

75 The transactions motive, the precautionary motive and the speculative motive. Taken together, the transactions and precautionary motives make up the demand to hold active money balances as a medium of exchange, whereas the speculative motive relates to holding passive or idle money balances as a wealth asset or store of value.   (12)

76 Liquidity preference relates to the speculative motive for holding or demanding money balances, which Keynes identified. As the rate of interest falls, people will prefer liquidity in the sense of wishing to hold money as a wealth asset in preference to interest-earning bonds, though expectations of future interest rates and bond prices also influence the decision about which form of wealth asset to hold.   (12)

77 (i)   Contractionary open market operations;
    (ii) 'over-funding' the PSBR or funding the National Debt;
    (iii) imposing direct controls on bank lending; and
    (iv) raising the Bank of England lending rate.   (12)

78 Fully-funding the PSBR is generally taken to mean that the government finances the PSBR by borrowing outside the banking system by gilt sales, etc., so that government spending and borrowing have an overall neutral effect on the money supply. However, in the March 1993 budget, the Chancellor slightly relaxed the official definition of full-funding.   (12)

79 If interest rates rise on non-money financial assets such as bonds, total bank deposits should fall as people make decisions to hold these assets rather than bank deposits. But these days the banks themselves make interest payments to attract deposits. A rise in the rate of interest offered on time deposits relative to the rate of interest available on non-money financial assets would cause bank deposits to grow – and also cause broad money aggregates such as M4 to grow at the expense of narrow money measures, such as M2.   (12)

80 (i)   By adding the values added of all the productive industries in the economy;
    (ii) by measuring expenditure upon output; and
    (iii) by aggregating the incomes received by all the factors of production.   (14)

81 Substituting $(Y - S)$ for C in the equation for the consumption function:
    $C = a + cY$ and rearranging, we arrive at : $S = -a + (1 - c)Y$
    or: $S = -a + sY$.   (14)

82 It is the level of national income at which planned expenditure equals the level of output produced in the economy.   (14)

83 The injections of demand into the circular flow of income are investment, government spending and export demand. The leakages from the flow are saving, taxation and imports.   (14)

84 Nominal income is the money income which people receive, whereas real income is the purchasing power of money or nominal income, i.e its command over goods and services.   (14)

85 A deflationary gap is a measure of the extent to which the level of aggregate demand in the economy is insufficient to bring about full employment at the equilibrium level of income, associated with the level of aggregate demand.   (14)

86 Demand management is the name given to government fiscal and/or monetary policy which aims to influence and control the level of aggregate demand in the economy, for example to stabilise the business cycle or to trade-off between policy objectives such as reducing unemployment and controlling inflation.   (13, 14, 17)

87 The national income multiplier (which is also known as the Keynesian multiplier) measures the relationship between a change in any of the components of aggregate demand (such as investment or government spending) and the resulting change in the equilibrium level of national income. The formula for the multiplier is: $\dfrac{1}{s + t + m}$

when the leakages of demand, s, t and m all vary with the level of income.   (14)

88 Crowding out is the name given to the neoclassical or anti-Keynesian view that an increase in government spending has little or no effect on the overall level of output in the long run because it largely or completely displaces private sector spending and output.

(13, 16, 17)

89 Progressive taxation and demand-led public spending on unemployment pay and welfare benefits are automatic stabilisers, tending to dampen, reduce and stabilise the fluctuations in the business cycle. (14)

90 According to Keynes's 'marginal efficiency of capital' theory, investment is a function of the expected rate of return and profitability of the various capital projects in which businesses are considering investing. The state of business confidence, and businessmen's expectations of the future, colour perceptions of expected future profitability; an increase in business confidence will cause an uprating of each investment project's expected future rate of return, causing the MEC function to shift rightwards.   (14)

91 $I_t = v(Y_t - Y_{t-1})$, where v is the accelerator.   (14)

92 (i) Classical or real wage unemployment;
(ii) frictional or transitional unemployment;
(iii) structural unemployment; and
(iv) Keynesian or demand deficient unemployment.   (15)

93 The quantity theory of money is a theory of inflation which argues that the underlying cause of inflation or a rising price level is a prior increase in the money supply or stock of money in the economy, created or condoned by the government.   (15)

94 In the demand-pull theory of inflation, the price level is pulled up by excess demand for goods and services and/or the wage level is pulled up by an excess demand for labour. In the cost-push theory, increased production costs (wage costs, imported raw material costs, etc.) push up the price level, as monopolistic firms mark up prices in order to maintain profit margins. (15)

95 The Phillips curve relationship is an inverse statistical relationship between the rate of wage inflation and the level of unemployment, which apparently existed – according to the research of A W Phillips – in the UK economy from the 1860s to the 1950s.   (15)

96 (i) Keynesianism is the name given to the body of economic theory and policy associated with John Maynard Keynes (1883–1946) and his followers, the Keynesians. Keynesianism is the economics of government interventionism in a market economy and the use of fiscal policy to manage the level of aggregate demand in the economy.
(ii) In its narrow meaning, monetarism centres on the view that the amount of money in the economy is largely responsible for both the level of money national income and the price level, and that if the money supply increases at a faster rate than real output, it will cause inflation. In its broader meaning, monetarism is associated with anti-Keynesianism, the promotion of the free market and distrust and dislike of government interventionism.
(iii) Supply-side economics is another and more recent manifestation of free-market and anti-Keynesian economics. It centres on the proposition that fiscal policy should be used, not to manage demand Keynesian-style, but to create incentives to workers and entrepreneurs to increase the supply of labour, entrepreneurship and output in the economy. (16, 17)

97 Absolute advantage is an application of the concept of technical efficiency. A country possesses an absolute advantage over other countries if it can produce a larger absolute output from the same inputs (or produce the same output with fewer inputs).

Comparative advantage is measured in terms of opportunity cost. A country possesses a comparative advantage (even though it may still suffer an absolute disadvantage) if, by increasing output of a particular product, compared to other countries it sacrifices less of the alternative products that it might have produced.   (18)

98 Expenditure-reducing deflation (i.e. contractionary fiscal and/or monetary policy to reduce the level of aggregate demand in the economy) and expenditure-switching devaluation and import controls.   (19)

99 (i) Flexible (or floating) exchange rates are determined by market forces, or the supply of and demand for currencies.
   (ii) By contrast, an exchange rate is fixed if the country's monetary authorities buy and sell their own currency and reserves of other currencies, to prevent market forces taking the exchange rate away from an officially declared par value or parity.
   (iii) Managed exchange rates, which include dirty floating and fixed peg systems, lie between these extremes.   (20)

100 (i)   The International Monetary Fund;
    (ii)   the International Bank for Reconstruction and Development (the 'World Bank');
    (iii) the European Community;
    (iv)   the European Monetary System;
    (v)   the Exchange Rate Mechanism (of the EMS);
    (vi)   European Monetary Union;
    (vii) the Common Agricultural Policy (of the EU);
    (viii) the General Agreement on Tariffs and Trade.   (6, 20)

PROGRESS ANALYSIS

Place a tick next to those questions you got right.

Question	Answer	Question	Answer	Question	Answer	Question	Answer
1		26		51		76	
2		27		52		77	
3		28		53		78	
4		29		54		79	
5		30		55		80	
6		31		56		81	
7		32		57		82	
8		33		58		83	
9		34		59		84	
10		35		60		85	
11		36		61		86	
12		37		62		87	
13		38		63		88	
14		39		64		89	
15		40		65		90	
16		41		66		91	
17		42		67		92	
18		43		68		93	
19		44		69		94	
20		45		70		95	
21		46		71		96	
22		47		72		97	
23		48		73		98	
24		49		74		99	
25		50		75		100	

My total mark is: out of 100

ANALYSIS
If you scored 1–25

You need to do some more work. You are not yet ready to take the Mock Exam because you do not have sufficient knowledge or understanding of the syllabus content. Look at the list of chapters at the beginning of this book and revise those chapters on which you scored poorly in the test. When you consider you have completed your revision, get a friend to ask you questions (not necessarily those in the Test) and if you are still weak on some chapters, look at them again. You should then attempt the Test Your Knowledge Quiz again.

If you scored 26–50

You are getting there, but you must do some more work. Go through the list of chapters on the contents page and mark those which you could not answer questions about correctly in the Test. In addition, look through the Practice Questions at the end of each chapter and the notes which accompany them. Go over some of your weak topics with a friend and then attempt the Test Your Knowledge Quiz again.

If you scored 51–75

You are nearly ready to attempt the Mock Exam, but to get the best out of it, brush up on those chapters which the Test shows you have not fully understood. Also look at the Practice Questions at the end of each chapter and check those questions which relate to the subject areas you do not feel confident about. You should then be ready to go on to the Mock Exam.

If you scored 76–100

Well done! You can tackle the Mock Exam with confidence although you will first need to revise some of the chapters which let you down in the Test Your Knowledge Quiz. Reassure yourself that there are no gaps in your knowledge and then set aside a time to do the Mock Exam.

General Certificate of Education Examination

ADVANCED LEVEL
ECONOMICS

Paper 1

Time allowed: 3 hours

THURSDAY 2 JUNE, AFTERNOON

Answer FOUR questions. TWO from Section A and TWO from Section B.
All questions are weighted equally.

Candidates are strongly recommended to read through the paper before attempting the questions.

Candidates are reminded of the need for good English and orderly presentation.
Credit will be given for the relevant use of diagrams.

SECTION A: DATA QUESTIONS

Answer 2 of the 3 questions

1 The data below was taken from the leader article in the *Daily Telegraph* of 29th March, 1989. It looks at two aspects of the market for petroleum, the change in the number of petroleum outlets and variations in its price in the European Community (EC).

Petroleum Outlets in the UK

	1978		1988	
	Total Supplied	Company Owned	Total Supplied	Company Owned
Esso	5 931	1 094	2 685	1 496
Shell	5 440	1 191	2 886	1 586
BP	5 101	889	2 119	1 257
Others	11 823	n.a.	12 326	n.a.
Total	28 295		20 016	
Visibles	−10 290			

Average Retail Prices of Petroleum per Gallon (£), March 1989

Italy	2.61	Belgium	1.83
Ireland	2.16	Spain	1.81
France	2.14	UK	1.80
Netherlands	2.01	West Germany	1.69
Portugal	2.00		

(Note: n.a. – not available)

(a) (i) How has the number and distribution of petroleum outlets changed between 1978 and 1988? (3)

    (ii) Account for the above changes. (5)

(b) (i) From the data, what is the most likely market structure of petroleum retailing in the UK? Explain your answer. (3)

    (ii) What other information would you require in order to make a fuller assessment?

(3)

(c) (i) Given that the UK and Italy produce competing products, if the retail price of petrol is 31% higher in Italy, can we assume that transport costs for Italy are 31% higher than those for the UK? Explain your reasoning. (6)

    (ii) Over the last 15 years, all EC countries have experienced increased petroleum prices.
Suggest what effects this increase may have had on:
      a road freight transport operator;
      a chocolate manufacturer. (5)

Oxford & Cambridge

2

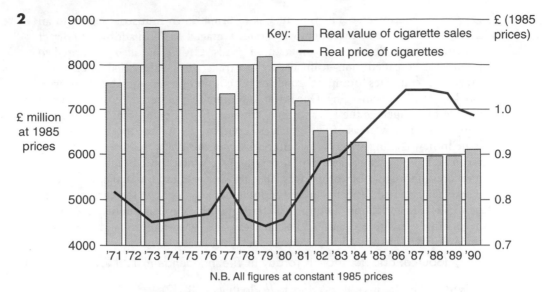

N.B. All figures at constant 1985 prices

FILTERING OUT THE PROPAGANDA

The tobacco industry shows a touching concern for the poor. A majority of Britain's 17 million smokers are in the lowest income groups, the industry's lobby group, the Tobacco Advisory Council, has told the Chancellor as he ponders his options for the 1991 Budget.

5   Hence 'tobacco taxation is the most regressive of all central Government taxes', according to the industry's submission to Mr Lamont. And so (surprise, surprise) he is being urged not to repeat last year's imposition of a 10 pence increase in the price of a packet of 20 cigarettes.

    Mr Lamont also finds himself being urged by the anti-smoking pressure
10 group, Action on Smoking and Health (ASH), to put an extra 32 pence on a packet. This would bring the real price back up to its 1987 level and consumption would fall by between 6.8 and 8.4 per cent.

    The tobacco industry says that any steep rise would add 0.57 per cent to the Retail Prices Index, damage export performance and employment prospects.

15   Despite the industry's apparent worries about its health, analysts County Natwest Woodmac point out that between 1980 and 1988 the UK industry's average profit margins grew from 8.3 to 11.9 per cent.

Source: © *The Guardian*, 2 March 1991

Answer **each** of the following questions, explaining your reasoning in **each** case.

(a) Explain, using diagrams, why cigarette producers are able to shift a large proportion of the specific tobacco tax on to consumers. (7)

(b) What does the data suggest about the relationship between cigarette prices and sales? (4)

(c) What economic arguments could be made for a steep increase in tobacco taxes ? (7)

(d) Explain the tobacco industry's arguments for not increasing tobacco tax. (7)

WJEC

3   **THE ACHILLES HEEL IN GATT**

The General Agreement on Tariffs and Trade was founded in 1948 under the auspices of the United Nations as 23 countries began to revive free trade after World War II. GATT's aims were to liberalise trade in industrial goods and so improve the prospects for growth in world trade. At the time, direct tariffs on
5 industrial goods averaged some 40%, partly a legacy of the war, but also a reflection of the 1930s, one of the most protectionist periods this century. Today, some 96 countries are members and a further 28 countries apply GATT rules on an informal basis.

GATT's crowning achievement was to bring down industrial tariffs to an
10 average 4.7% since its inception, when rates averaged 40%. In addition to direct
cuts in customs charges in manufactured goods, GATT has also attempted to
reduce the so-called 'non-tariff' barriers to trade. It has also tried to curb the
practice of countries 'dumping' goods below cost in overseas markets. However,
two key trends are emerging. One is the shift in trading patterns towards regional
15 trading blocs such as the EC and the Caribbean Free Trade Area. The other is
the growth in new areas of trade such as services. Perhaps the most contentious
issue in new trading areas is agriculture. During the 1980s there was increasing
recourse to subsidising farm exports by the EC, which the US countered with
measures of its own. As world prices fell, subsidies rose and the struggle for other
20 markets intensified. This has caused acrimonious discussion in the current round
of GATT negotiations. In practical terms, if the current round of GATT
negotiations fails there is a fear that, in areas such as agriculture and services, a
trade war will ensue and protectionist laws proliferate.

(Source: adapted from P Torday in *The Independent*, 13 November 1990)

(a) What is meant by 'non-tariff' barriers to trade (line 12)? (2)

(b) Examine the economic reasoning behind GATT's attempt 'to revive free trade after World War II' and 'liberalise trade in industrial goods' (lines 2–3). (6)

(c) Examine the consequences of a trade war and protectionist measures in areas such as agriculture and services (lines 22–23). (6)

(d) Examine the implications of 'the shift in trading patterns towards regional trading blocs' (lines 14–15). (6)   *ULEAC*

SECTION B: ESSAY QUESTIONS

4 'Prices are the most effective means of allocating resources.' In the light of this statement, discuss the case for and against the introduction of meters in place of the current system of water rates (flat-rate charges) as a method of pricing water. (25)
AEB

5 (a) Discuss the factors which give rise to a firm being dominant in a market. (50)

(b) Explain how such a firm might be expected to behave if it wishes to preserve its market domination. (50)   *ULEAC*

6   'Privatisation has created private monopolies.'

'Privatised monopolies never benefit consumers.'

Critically evaluate these statements. (100)   *ULEAC*

7 Explain what you understand by the term 'externalities' and how they might arise in production and consumption. To what extent might 'global warming' be considered an externality and, as such, be solved by economic measures? (25)   *NEAB*

8 (a) Which factors influence the supply of labour? (12)

(b) Which factors influence the demand for labour? (12)

(c) If the Government imposed a minimum wage rate for a particular group of workers, how would this affect the market for their labour? (6)   *SEB*

9 (a) Distinguish between the PSBR and the PSDR. (20)

    (b) In the financial year 1988–1989 the PSDR was £7bn. In the financial year 1992–93 the PSBR was £35bn.
       (i) Examine the circumstances which could account for these contrasting situations in the state of the government's finances.
       (ii) Analyse the economic consequences which might be expected to follow from such a marked change in the government's finances. (80)   *ULEAC*

10 What are the potential advantages and disadvantages to the UK economy of international agreements such as the Single European Market and the General Agreement on Tariffs and Trade? (25)   *WJEC*

MOCK EXAM SUGGESTED ANSWERS

1 Tutorial note

(a) (i) The total number of petrol stations fell by over a third during the decade. Each of the three big oil companies reduced the outlets they supplied by approximately half, but they actually increased the number they owned as well as supplied.

    (ii) Some of the independent outlets previously supplied by the 'majors' probably went out of business over the decade, or they may have been bought up by one of the three big companies, with the remainder being either bought up or supplied by an oil company that would be covered by the label 'others' in the table. If you want to give greater depth to your answer, you could explain the changes in terms of the competitive advantages of larger petrol stations on prime sites which enjoy high daily sales, and the disadvantages suffered by smaller, usually independently owned petrol outlets. However, since only five marks are available, avoid the temptation to overwrite.

(b) (i) You must resist the temptation to stray away from the actual information in the data when answering this part of the question. You can glean from the data that petrol **wholesaling** is oligopolistic, since three firms supply over half the retail outlets. Petrol **retailing** is rather less oligopolistic – in 1988 only a fifth of petrol stations were actually owned by the big three suppliers. However, this figure represents a significant increase on a decade earlier, so there appears to be a trend towards greater concentration of ownership on petrol retailing.

    (ii) It is well known that there are seven large oil companies worldwide, nicknamed the 'seven sisters'. These include firms such as Texaco. Indeed in the UK there are 69 recognised petrol suppliers. A greater breakdown of the 'others' category would therefore be useful to ascertain the importance of the other large and medium-sized oil companies and the number of forecourts they own and supply. Petrol sales by supermarket chains such as Sainsbury's and Tesco have also grown rapidly in recent years, but this is not shown by the data. Information about the amount of petrol sold by 'Big-Three owned' petrol stations in comparison to independently owned outlets would also be useful.

(c) (i) The answer is no, if only because fuel costs are only one part of total transport costs. But you can also argue that prices create incentives for people to alter their economic behaviour, and in particular high prices create the incentive to economise. Thus the higher price of petrol probably leads to Italian road transport prices being higher than in the UK, but not necessarily by as much as 31%. Over the years, higher petrol prices have encouraged Italians to drive smaller, more fuel-efficient cars; company cars, which are notorious for encouraging wasteful use of fuel, are less common in Italy; and there may be more miles of motorway which promote more economical use of fuel. Larger, more fuel-efficient lorries may also be more common in Italy, and higher fuel prices may discourage unnecessary journeys. Elasticity of demand is also relevant to your answer: demand would have to be completely inelastic for expenditure on petrol to rise by a full 31%, following a price increase of 31%.

(ii) Assuming that the price of diesel fuel rises by in a similar way to petrol prices, road freight transport operators have seen significant increases in their operating costs. However, we must be careful to distinguish between **nominal** and **real** increases in the price of petroleum. Although nominal prices have risen, petrol's real price is not significantly higher than it was before the first 'oil crisis' in 1973/4. The general price level has risen more or less in line with petrol prices. Thus road freight transport operators have generally raised their own prices to pass on the increased fuel prices they have to pay. As we have already noted, higher fuel prices also encourage operators to search for greater fuel efficiency, e.g. by purchasing larger lorries. And in so far that real fuel prices have risen, they will have contributed to lower profits and possible bankruptcies amongst the less efficient hauliers. Chocolate manufacturers may have experienced similar effects, but probably on a lesser scale because fuel costs are less significant than for transport companies. Chocolate manufacturers may have enjoyed greater scope for switching between alternative energy sources – for manufacturing, if not for transport – though other fuels such as gas and electricity may also have seen similar price changes.

2 Tutorial note

With part (a), it is important to obey the instruction to use diagrams (note the plural!) even though it is difficult to see why more than one diagram should be necessary to answer this part of the question. You should draw one diagram in which the demand curve is price inelastic, followed by a second diagram in which demand is relatively elastic. A comparison of the diagrams will then show that, following an upward shift of the supply curve resulting from the imposition of the tobacco tax, the cigarette producers can raise prices and pass on most of the tax to consumers when demand is inelastic, as shown in your first diagram.

As you write your answer to part (b), you should note that the data does not support the assumption that the demand for cigarettes is inelastic! Having identified the negative or inverse relationship between tobacco prices and the value of sales (i.e. a rise in price leads to a fall in total expenditure on cigarettes), you should be reminded of the simple rule to indicate elasticity of demand. The rule states: if total consumer expenditure rises following a fall in price, then demand is elastic. You could actually calculate the elasticity from the numerical data included in the passage and the graph. The passage states that a rise in the real price of cigarettes from about 98 pence to their 1987 level of approximately 105 pence (or about 7%), is expected to reduce demand by between 6.8% and 8.4%. This calculation indicates that the price elasticity of demand for cigarettes is more or less unity. The fact that demand for cigarettes is possibly slightly elastic (according to the data) does not mean that the cigarette producers won't raise prices by more or less the full amount of the tax. Rather, it means that if they do raise prices significantly, they will suffer a more than proportionate drop in sales.

Note that the data shows changes in real prices and the real value of sales, rather than nominal prices and the nominal value of sales, unadjusted for the effects of inflation. While it is not necessary to explain this difference in your answer, it is important that you understand the difference between real and nominal data in economics. Also, with this type of question, don't fall into the trap of simply copying out the data. The examiner is testing your ability to separate the key changes or relationships identifiable from the data from the 'background noise'.

If the demand for tobacco products were highly inelastic (an assumption which as we have just noted the data does not actually support!), an increase in tobacco tax would prove to be a very good revenue raiser for the government. However, this is probably not the main point the chief examiner was looking for when he set part (c) of the question. Because tobacco is a demerit good, the main reason for a tax increase on cigarettes is to reduce their consumption, and this is the main point you must make in your answer.

With regard to part (c), the passage contains brief statements of a number of arguments used by the tobacco industry as a part of a campaign against increased taxation of tobacco products. Three of the arguments are probably correct, namely that tobacco taxation is regressive, adds to inflation and may cause unemployment, but the fourth argument, that taxation of tobacco harms the country's trading position, is dubious to say the least. The question asks you to explain the arguments, so you must resist the temptation to drift into a discussion of their strengths and weaknesses.

Suggested answer

(a) Cigarette producers can only shift a large proportion of a specific tax on tobacco onto consumers if the demand for tobacco is inelastic with respect to price changes. This situation is illustrated in the left-hand panel of the diagram below. In this diagram, the demand curve D_1 and a supply curve S_1 represent demand and supply conditions before a specific tax is imposed upon cigarettes. Equilibrium price and quantity are P_1 and Q_1, with the area OQ_1AP_1 showing both total consumer expenditure and the total income or revenue received by all the firms in the market. When a specific tax is imposed, conditions of supply change and the supply curve shifts upwards to S_2. The vertical distance between S_1 and S_2 represents the tax per unit levied by the government. Unlike a percentage (or ad valorem tax) such as VAT, a specific tax (or unit tax) is independent of the price charged for a good. It is levied on the physical quantity of tobacco in a packet of cigarettes, and not upon price.

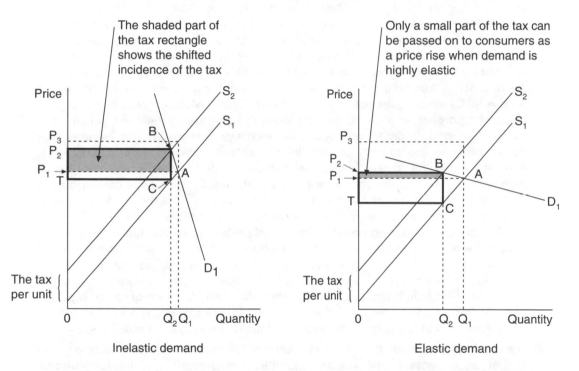

Inelastic demand

Elastic demand

The tobacco firms will of course try to pass on to the consumers as much of the tax as possible by raising the price of cigarettes. However, their ability to raise price by the full amount of the tax is limited by elasticity of demand. When demand is inelastic, the firms can pass on most but not all of the tax. If they firms raise the price by the full amount of the tax to P_3, an excess supply will result because at P_3 consumers are unwilling to purchase as much as the firms are prepared to supply. Market forces would reduce the price to P_2 to clear the excess supply. At the new equilibrium price of P_2, the government's total tax revenue is shown by the rectangular area $TCBP_2$. This rectangle can be divided into two parts, which show respectively the shifted incidence and the unshifted incidence of the tax. The shaded rectangle above the original pre-tax equilibrium price P_1 represents the shifted incidence of the tax. This is the part of the tax which the firms successfully pass on to the consumers via a price rise. However, the firms fail to shift all the incidence of the tax; the part of the tax rectangle below P_1 measures the unshifted incidence of the tax which the firms are unable to pass on. The more inelastic the demand curve (as in the left-hand panel of the diagram), the greater is the firm's ability to shift the incidence of a tax so that consumers indirectly pay it via a price rise. However, when demand is elastic (as in the right-hand panel of the diagram) most of the tax must be borne by the firms and that in the limiting case – when demand is perfectly elastic – none of the tax can be passed on to consumers as a price rise.

(b) The data provides information about real prices and the real value of cigarette sales. This means that the data has been adjusted to get rid of the distorting effects of inflation – the adjusted data is measured at 1987 prices. The data shows that the real price of cigarettes and the real value of expenditure on cigarettes are inversely related; when the real price falls (as between 1977 and 1979), expenditure on cigarettes rises, and vice versa. According to the data therefore, the demand for tobacco products is price elastic, which conflicts with the assumption underlying the question in Part (a)! Total consumer expenditure would have to fall following a reduction in the real price of cigarettes for demand to be inelastic.

(c) Economists classify cigarettes as a demerit good. They argue that if cigarettes are made available at market prices in the absence of taxation, the price is too cheap and overconsumption of tobacco products takes place. Two slightly different arguments both lead to this conclusion. In the first place, smokers discharge negative externalities into the air which are received as a utility loss by other people. These external costs include the deterioration in health experienced by passive smokers as well as the general unpleasantness non-smokers suffer from breathing in tobacco smoke. The whole community may also have to pick up the cost of medical care when smokers suffering from tobacco-related diseases such as lung cancer and heart trouble are looked after in NHS hospitals. As a result, the social costs of consumption suffered by the whole community exceed the private costs to the individual smokers. In the absence of taxation, the privately optimal level of cigarette consumption (where MPB = MPC) exceeds the socially optimal level (where MSB = MSC). By raising the price of cigarettes, a tobacco tax can close this divergency between private and social cost and benefit and create an incentive for smokers to reduce their consumption to the socially optimal level. Secondly, the long-term private costs experienced by the smokers themselves (which include the costs of eventual health deterioration) exceed the short-term private costs (mostly the money cost of buying cigarettes). There is a case for taxing tobacco products to raise the short-term cost of smoking so as to save smokers from their own shortsightedness.

A completely unrelated economic argument centres on the fact that when inflation occurs, the real value of the specific tax on tobacco falls – unless the nominal value of the tax is raised each year in line with inflation. The passage implies that the fall in the real value of the tax (which had not been adjusted upwards sufficiently each year) was the cause of the falling real price of cigarettes. An extra 32 pence of tax on a packet of cigarettes was therefore needed to bring the real price of cigarettes back up to its 1987 level and to 'claw back' the erosion of the real value of the specific tax.

(d) The first argument made by the representative of the tobacco industry pressure group is that an increase in the tax on cigarettes, being regressive, has undesirable distributional consequences between rich and poor. A regressive tax falls more heavily upon the poor than on the rich, taking a larger proportion of their income. Tobacco taxation is indeed regressive, for the simple reason that a larger proportion of higher income groups have given up smoking in response not to taxation, but to the effectiveness of health education about the harmful effects of smoking. Health education has been much less effective for lower income groups, leading therefore to the situation in which taxes on cigarettes fall more heavily on the poor.

Three other arguments are also mentioned. It is alleged that increasing the tax on tobacco is inflationary. In so far that the price rise will raise the Retail Price Index which measures inflation, this is true. An increase in the tax on cigarettes could also be inflationary if it caused workers to push for higher wages in order to restore their real wages eroded by the price rises. However, if the tax rise enabled the government to reduce its deficit and to take demand out of the economy, demand-pull inflationary pressures would in fact be alleviated.

The tobacco industry also argues that unemployment will grow. Obviously, if the tax is effective in reducing demand for tobacco, then cigarette factories will close or scale down, and workers will be made redundant. However, jobs could well be created elsewhere in the economy when ex-smokers spend their income on other goods.

The last argument quoted in the passage is that increased taxation of tobacco products will damage UK export performance. It is difficult to see the logic of this argument. The tax on cigarettes sold in this country is not imposed on cigarette exports, and since all tobacco (the raw material in cigarettes) is imported, a reduction in smoking ought to improve rather than deteriorate the balance of trade. There are perhaps two ways in which the tax might weaken export performance. Firstly, the higher inflation rate resulting from the tax may adversely affect the country's export competitiveness. Secondly, the decline of the domestic market for cigarettes may lead to a loss of economies of scale, which raises manufacturing costs and makes it more difficult to export cigarettes profitably.

3 Tutorial notes

(a) Non-tariff barriers include quotas and other quantity restrictions, administrative restrictions and 'red tape', and export subsidies.

(b) At the end of the Second World War in 1945, it was generally agreed that the Great Depression had certainly been made worse, even if it had not been caused by, the wave of protectionism that had swept the world in the 1930s. The USA and the UK were the prime movers in the creation of GATT (though the US senate refused to ratify legislation which would have established a much stronger World Trade Organisation) in the belief that the growth of prosperity and the world economy in the postwar era depended on the liberalisation of world trade. Use the principle of comparative advantage to explain how, in theory at least, total world output can increase if countries specialise and trade their surpluses.

(c) This is really the opposite of the previous part of the question: protectionism might mean that the benefits of specialisation in accordance with the principle of comparative advantage will be lost, output and welfare will decline and unemployment grow. On the other hand, countries which might lose out or suffer from a completely liberalised world economy may gain from protectionism, though possibly only in the short term, and at the expense of other countries.

(d) Draw on the section in Chapter 18 on customs unions and free-trade areas. The results will depend on whether regional trading blocks are 'inward' or 'outward' looking, 'trade promoting' or 'trade restricting', and upon whether the really strong and effective trading blocks, such as the EU, end up as 'rich men's clubs', lining their own nests at the expense of the poorer countries in the developing world.

4 Tutorial note

You must avoid the temptation to ignore the statement that provides the lead into the question. Start your answer by explaining briefly the **signalling**, **incentive** and **rationing** functions of prices, and then go on to state that – in the absence of various forms of **market failure** – prices certainly do provide an effective way of allocating resources between competing uses. In competitive markets, prices can succeed in equating supply with demand in an economically efficient way, and ensuring consumer sovereignty and choice.

Another feature of efficient competitive pricing (which promotes **allocative efficiency**), is that the consumer should pay a price which equals the marginal cost of supplying the good or service consumed (P = MC). When water is in plentiful supply and in the absence of drought, the short-run marginal cost of supplying water is very close to zero. Hence the case for paying for water through a flat-rate charge (the water rate) which is independent of the amount of water consumed. In this situation water is a **quasi-free good** which is consumed by households up to the point of satiation where marginal utility is nil. The flat-rate charging system can also be supported on two further grounds: administrative convenience, and because clean drinking and washing water is a form of **merit good**. The argument here is that if water is metered and people are charged according to the amount they consume, there might be a harmful deterioration in public health as the poor react to the new pricing system by washing less and flushing the toilet less often. And under the water-rating system, small (usually better-off) households generally cross-subsidise larger (and usually poorer) families. Some economists justify this on social policy grounds.

What, then, is the case for introducing water metering? Firstly, the abolition of the household rating system when the poll tax was introduced in the late 1980s, means that the basis for administering the water rate no longer exists. A new method of pricing water therefore has to be introduced, though of course it could be a modified flat-rate charge based on property values and the new council tax. The government has instructed the water companies to introduce a new pricing system by the year 2000. More significantly, the greater use of 'water-guzzling' household appliances such as dishwashers and garden sprinklers has shifted the demand curve for water to the right (compared to the 1960s, demand has increased by 70%), while a decline in rainfall (in the South East of England) has moved the supply curve leftwards. With zero prices encouraging people to consume up to the point of satiation, this has led to a shortage of supply and excess demand. Economic theory suggests that the price mechanism should therefore be used to ration demand and to provide a source of finance for increasing long-run supply through reservoir construction or a grid system to transport water from the wetter north west of Britain to the drier south east. Metering is a perfectly acceptable method of pricing for the other 'utilities', gas and electricity, so why not water? Virtually every other country in the world uses a metering system to charge for water, apparently without any significant problems. It can also be argued that any problems affecting the poor which might result from the introduction of metering are better dealt with through the social security system than by requiring some water consumers to cross-subsidise others. The poor could be given special payments or vouchers to help pay their water bills.

But the water companies are **regional monopolies**, and here economic theory suggests that if left to themselves, monopolies will exploit the consumer by charging a price in excess of the marginal cost of supply, in pursuit of monopoly profit (see Chapter 7). Hence, there is a case for strong and effective external regulation of water prices through the **Office of Water Supply (OFWAT)**, whichever system of pricing is eventually introduced. And where household water metering has already been introduced, the flat-rate charge has not been abolished completely. Instead, a two-tier pricing system is used. The metered price reflects the short-run marginal cost of supply, while the flat-rate charge helps to finance long-run supply improvement, including improvements to meet EC environmental regulations.

Suggested answer plan

1 Explain briefly how prices allocate resources.
2 Explain why economists generally belief that, in the absence of market failure, prices are the most effective way of allocating resources.
3 Outline the case for the flat rate charge, and the case against metering.
4 Then argue the case for metering.
5 Introduce the elements of market failure in the water industry (water as a merit good, and the supply companies as privatised monopolies) and suggest that whichever method of pricing is used, some intervention by the government or by an external regulator such as OFWAT will be necessary to ensure the 'socially optimal' level of consumption.

5 Tutorial note

Having based your answer to the first part of the question on the causes of monopoly, you might organise your answer to the second part around a distinction between 'virtuous' and 'less-virtuous' strategies for maintaining monopoly power and market domination. The 'virtuous' method of market domination is, of course, to produce products or brands which consumers perceive to be the best. New product development, the research and development of more efficient methods of producing existing products, keen pricing, aided and abetted by patenting, market research and advertising and marketing can all be regarded as part of a 'virtuous' market domination strategy. At the other extreme, a 'less-virtuous' strategy might centre on the unfair and even criminal use of barriers to market entry, trading-restrictive practices and the corrupt obtaining of favours from other businesses or government officials. In real life of course, it may sometimes be difficult to draw the line between legitimate and illegitimate business strategies to promote market domination. For example, when a dominant firm sharply reduces prices in the face of increased competition from a new market entrant, does this represent simply the (virtuous) cut and thrust of the market place, or is it something more sinister, such as the temporary reduction of price below cost to see the newcomer off, to be followed by a hike to the old price level once the firm's dominant position has been restored?

Suggested answer plan

1 Explain briefly that 'dominant in a market' means monopoly or a high degree of monopoly power.

2 List and briefly describe each of the causes of monopoly power, e.g. natural monopoly; legal monopoly; economies of scale, etc.

3 Explain that if market domination has resulted from the firm being more innovative, efficient and competitive than its rivals, with its eventual monopoly position being the result of successful competition, it may well try to maintain its position by 'more of the same', i.e. continued R&D, investment, market research and marketing, and keen pricing.

4 However, firms often use anti-competitive methods to maintain market domination, e.g. artificial barriers to market entry and unfair trading restrictive practices. Give examples, and explain that, although these are often illegal, firms may break the law and try to get away with it.

5 Another strategy is to take over or merge with rival firms, though again the law may make this difficult.

6 Tutorial note

To answer this question properly, you must first explain both of the quoted statements. Then you must get on with the critical evaluation. This means you must indicate the extent to which you think each statement is true, and if completely or partially true, whether the two statements taken together are consistent with each other or whether one statement overrides the other.

Suggested answer

The industries which have been privatised were previously nationalised industries. As nationalised industries they were monopolies, and Conservative governments believe that nationalised industries are inefficient. Before the beginning of the privatisation programme in the early 1980s, Conservative politicians frequently argued that a major reason for privatisation was to promote competition through the break-up of the state monopolies. However, at the time of their privatisation many of the nationalised industries were natural monopolies which are difficult to break up into competitive smaller companies without a significant loss of economies of scale and productive efficiency. The Conservative Government also faced a practical conflict between the aims of promoting competition and raising revenue. To maximise revenue from the sale of a nationalised industry such as BT or British Gas, the government chose to sell the industry whole, without breaking up the monopoly. At the time of privatisation therefore, the change of ownership tended merely to switch industries from public to private monopoly, with little evidence that either competition or efficiency was being promoted – despite the introduction of some market discipline via the capital market.

The second statement in the question is more contentious. It is undoubtedly true that monopolies *can*, and indeed may, more often than not, exploit their position so that the consumer does not benefit to the extent that that they would if there was more competition, but this is not inevitably true, and in some circumstances monopoly can benefit consumers. The standard case against monopoly is that compared to a competitive firm, a monopoly restricts both consumer choice and output artificially, and hikes up the price, so as to make monopoly profit at the consumers' expense. However, the consumer can benefit if the monopoly innovates (and achieves gains in dynamic efficiency) and/or achieves economies of scale. The consumer may benefit from new products or improved quality of existing products in the former case, or from reductions in costs being passed on as lower prices in the latter case.

Most of the privatised industries such as British Gas and BT were not only monopolies at the time they were privatised; as utility industries, they were natural monopolies. A natural monopoly is said to exist when economies of scale and total market size combine to make it impossible for more than one firm to benefit from full economies of scale. Utility industries such as gas, water and electricity supply, sewage disposal, telecommunications and postal services, are usually cited as the most obvious examples of such natural monopoly. These utility industries have a particular production and marketing problem; they must deliver their service into millions of separate homes and places of work, usually through distribution grid of cables or pipelines. High fixed costs of investment in these distribution networks, together with ongoing maintenance costs, mean that there is an obvious case for only one gas pipeline or electricity cable per street, so as to avoid unnecessary duplication. In the past, the strength of this argument led to general agreement that utility industries should be organised as monopolies. Economists argued that, for utility industries and other natural monopolies, the main policy choice should not be between competition and monopoly, but between two different systems of ownership: public versus private monopoly. The key question was: 'Should natural monopolies be organised as nationalised industries, or should they be left in private hands, but subject to strong and effective public regulation?'

At the time of privatisation, the Conservative Government chose the latter course. The Government took the view that because the industries were natural monopolies, they should remain monopolies in order for the consumer to receive the benefits resulting from economies of scale. However, the Government also believed that regulation was necessary in order to prevent the privatised monopolies from exploiting the consumer.

In fact, many economists now believe that it is wrong to restrict choice on the best way of organising the utility industries to what they see as the narrow choice between public and private monopoly, important though that choice still is. They argue that technical progress now makes it possible to introduce competition into industries such as electricity and gas and that therefore, the monopoly position of these industries has become increasingly less natural. Barriers to entry which previously it was thought impossible to break down, can now be removed. As a result, new telecommunication, electricity and gas supply companies can enter the market to contest the position of the dominant utility companies, the previously nationalised businesses. Where it is still commercially not feasible to build new distribution networks, the regulators can ensure that the new market entrants can use at a fair rent those owned by BT, British Gas or the National Grid. I have already argued that the second statement in the question is not always true. Because of recent developments, the first statement that 'privatisation has created private monopolies', though true at the time of privatisation, has, with the passage of time, become less true. Nevertheless, privatised utility companies such as BT and British Gas still enjoy a dominant position in the market, and there is a long way to go before their monopoly position and power completely disappears. With the water companies, the process hasn't even begun; they remain privatised monopolies, though whether OFWAT, the regulator can ensure that they benefit the consumer, is a moot point.

7 Tutorial note

The first part of the question is straightforward and has been explained, with examples, in Chapter 9. Start the second part by arguing that **global warming** can have a natural explanation, relating to periodic changes in the world's climate that take place over thousands of years. If global warming occurs naturally, then it should not be regarded as an externality, i.e. a spin-off or side-effect of mankind's activities discharged and consumed outside the market. However, in so far that current evidence links global warming to the greenhouse effect, caused by mankind's emissions of carbon gases and other pollutants, then the phenomenon is indeed an externality. Explain that most people regard global warming as a **negative externality**, fearing that much of the world's population will eventually suffer from rising sea levels and the spread of desert climates. But indicate that for some peoples and countries, the benefits of global warming may exceed the costs, for example in regions where warmer and longer summers will allow new crops to be grown.

Like any negative externality, global warming might in principle be reduced or eliminated by economic measures such as pollution taxes, regulation and devices such as the sale of 'licences to pollute'. But because global warming is literally an externality dumped on the whole world community by the action of individual economic agents, action on a world scale is needed to slow the process down. Effective action by a single country – even as large as the USA – or by a handful of countries to reduce the pollutants that they emit, will be insufficient to deal with the problem because pollution is likely to grow as Third World nations develop their economies. Arguably, the action on a world scale that will be necessary to reduce global warming will also significantly reduce economic growth and living standards. This will be unacceptable to many governments, particularly in developing countries. They may argue that existing global warming is a First World problem in that it has been caused by pollutants overwhelmingly emitted by already industrialised countries, but that the First World countries are demanding a Third World solution, i.e. a slowing down of the growth process necessary to transform the developing countries into modern competitive economies. As the 1992 Rio de Janiero Conference on environmental issues clearly shows, it is almost impossible to get countries to agree to take concrete action which, arguably, is in their long-term interest, if the results of such action are likely to be against their short-term interest. And even if action could be agreed to impose carbon taxes or firmly regulate pollution, there would then be all sorts of problems in effectively enforcing and policing the action on a world scale.

Suggested answer plan

1   Precisely define an externality as a 'good' or 'bad' generated and received outside the market.

2   Distinguish between pure production, pure consumption and mixed externalities, giving examples (see the table in Chapter 9).

3   Briefly indicate why externalities are a market failure, i.e. there is no incentive for the correct quantity of an externality to be produced and consumed, where MSB = MSC.

4   If global warming is a natural phenomenon, i.e. not caused by man, then it is not an externality.

5   But if it results from pollution emissions, global warming is a negative externality, perhaps on a cataclysmic scale.

6   However, for some people global warming may produce more external benefits than costs. Give examples.

7   Explain that, in principle, pollution taxes, regulation, etc. might reduce global warming, but there seem to be overwhelming obstacles preventing the effective introduction of such measures on a world scale.

8 Tutorial note

In part (a), it is important that you go beyond a mere list of the various factors influencing supply. Distinguish between an individual worker's supply of labour and the market supply exercised by all the workers in the labour market. Make sure you relate your answer to one of the basic principles of microeconomics, namely that every economic agent is assumed to have an objective it wishes to maximise, in this case utility.

The advice given for part (a) is also relevant for part (b), though in this case the nature of a firm's demand for labour is ultimately dependent on its assumed business objective, usually taken to be profit maximisation. Avoid turning your answers to both these questions into an explanation of the factors influencing the elasticity of demand for (and supply of) labour, though there is some scope for bringing these factors into your answer.

Take care not to rewrite part (c) of the question as 'Discuss the effects of a national minimum wage upon the UK economy'. It is important to focus your answer on 'a particular group of workers' as specified in the question. A good answer must apply theory, but there is some scope also for using evidence from examples of minimum wages in different countries.

Suggested answer

(a) Underlying the theory of the supply of labour is the assumption that households supply more labour only if by so doing, they increase total household utility. An individual's supply curve of labour derives from exactly the same utility maximising assumption which underlies the theory of consumer demand in the goods market. The utility which a worker derives from the supply of his labour can be divided into two parts, which taken together are called net advantage. Net advantage includes firstly, the utility of the wage (or strictly the utility of the goods and services bought with the money wage) and secondly, the utility of work (popularly known as job satisfaction or dissatisfaction). Different types of work yield different degrees of job satisfaction and dissatisfaction. When a worker enjoys his job, the net advantage of work is greater than the mere utility of the wage. In this situation, a worker will be prepared to work for a money wage lower than the wage he would accept if no pleasure were to be gained from the work itself. However, many types of work, including much routine assembly line work in factories and heavy manual labour, are unpleasant, yielding only job dissatisfaction. In these circumstances, the supply curve of labour reflects the fact that the hourly wage rate must provide some compensation for the unpleasantness of the work involved.

Ignoring job satisfaction or dissatisfaction, then a worker's net advantage equals the utility of the wage. Because time is limited (there being only 24 hours in a day), the decision to supply one more hour of labour time must also mean that the worker has chosen one hour less of leisure time. Labour time and leisure time are substitutes for each other. The money wage (or strictly the goods the wage buys) and leisure respond to the law of diminishing marginal utility. When more labour is supplied at a particular hourly wage rate, the extra income yields less and less extra utility. At the same time, each extra hour of leisure sacrificed results in an increasing utility loss. To maximise utility, the worker must supply labour up to the point at which: MU of the wage = MU of leisure. When the MU of the wage = MU of leisure, a worker is in equilibrium in the sense that he has no incentive to supply more hours of labour time at the going hourly wage rate, providing his utility functions for goods and leisure are unchanged. A higher wage would be needed to encourage the worker to supply more labour beyond this point. This is the substitution effect of a wage rise – more labour is supplied as a worker responds to a wage rise by substituting labour time for leisure time.

An income effect also influences the supply of labour. The income effect of a wage rate increase results from the fact that for most people 'leisure time' is a normal good and not an inferior good. A rise in the hourly wage rate increases the worker's real income, and as real income rises, so does the demand for the 'normal' good, leisure. Under some circumstances the income effect of a wage rise is more powerful than the substitution effect; as a result workers respond to wage increases by supplying less labour.

There are a number of factors besides the wage and the utility of work which influence the supply of labour. These include: the abilities or skills required; the length of the training period, the influence of any restrictive practices and government legislation; relative wage rates in other occupations and the level at which unemployment pay is set; and for the market supply of labour, factors such as the existence of a pool of unemployment and the overall size of the economy's labour force.

(b) The market demand for labour is simply the sum of the demand for each of the firms which comprise the labour market. A firm's demand for labour is a derived demand, in that the services of labour are demanded not for any utility directly yielded to the firm, but only because they are necessary as inputs to produce outputs of goods and services for sale at a profit in the goods market. Assuming a profit-maximising objective on the part of firms, there can be no demand for factor services in the long run unless the firms sell the outputs produced for at least a normal profit in the goods market.

Providing that we assume that firms have profit-maximising objectives and that labour markets are competitive, a firm's demand for labour is determined by the marginal revenue product (MRP) of labour. To explain this, it is necessary to examine the factors that a profit-maximising firm must take into account when considering whether it is worthwhile to demand the services of one more worker. The firm needs to know by how much: total output will rise; total sales revenue will rise when the extra output is sold in the goods market; and total costs of production will rise as a result of paying the worker his wage. The amount by which total output rises is known as the marginal physical product (MPP) of labour, for example the additional automobiles or loaves of bread produced by an extra worker. To convert this into a money value or MRP, we must multiply the worker's MPP by marginal revenue, or the addition to the firm's total sales revenue resulting from the sale of the extra output.

Because the law of diminishing returns operates as a firm takes on more labour, MPP and MRP both fall as employment increases. As a result in a competitive labour market, the firm's overall demand for labour becomes determined at the level of employment where the MRP of labour equals the wage. For the firm to demand more labour beyond this point, the wage rate would have to fall.

A growth in labour productivity, resulting perhaps from technical progress, or from increased demand for the good the workers are producing, can increase the MRP of labour. In either case, the demand curve for labour is likely to shift rightwards. However, some forms of technical progress, such as automation, may reduce rather than increase the overall demand for labour even though they increase the productivity of the workers still retained. The relative prices of capital and labour, and the ease with which capital can be substituted for labour, are further factors influencing the demand for labour.

(c) The following diagram shows the possible effect of imposing a minimum legal wage for a particular group of workers. The first and most obvious point to make is that for the minimum wage to have any effect, it would have to be imposed *above* the equilibrium or market clearing wage W*. Thus, if a national minimum hourly wage rate of around £4 were to be introduced in the UK, it would have no effect in most labour markets as wage rates are already considerably higher than this suggested minimum rate.

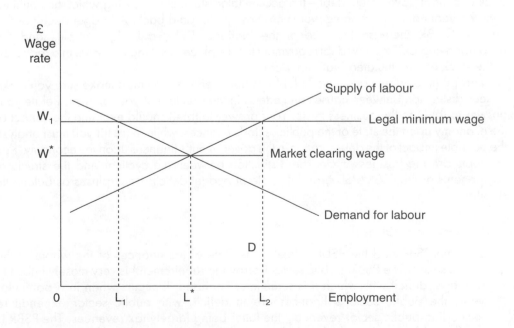

Assuming that a minimum age is imposed above the current wage rate of W*, the effects will depend in part on *how far* above W* the minimum wage is set at. Suppose for example, the minimum wage rate is set at W_1. At this wage rate L_1 workers are willing to work, but employers reduce their demand for labour to L_2. According to the diagram, employment falls from L* to L_1, but unemployment (those willing to work at the minimum wage, but without jobs) would actually be rather greater, equal to L_2 minus L_1.

This analysis assumes that employers' demand for labour is elastic. If demand were inelastic and workers could not be replaced, the fall in employment would be considerably less. Also if the demand curve for labour shifts rightwards (perhaps because demand for the good or service being produced is increasing), an overall increase in employment may result. Also, by boosting consumption and aggregate demand, a minimum wage might increase the overall demand for labour, though this effect would not be significant if only a few groups of workers benefited from the minimum wage.

A number of other factors could also have an influence. Economic theory suggests that in a monopsony labour markets (i.e. one employer only) the effect of wage increase can actually be to increase the level of employment. Some employers may be able to shift employment to low-wage countries in a process known as social dumping. Also, if the minimum wage is not enforced, employers may simply ignore the law, or hire self-employed people on short contracts to get round the law.

Providing a minimum wage is not significantly higher than the wage previously paid in the free market, the evidence seems to support the view that there will be little or no reduction in employment. A recent study of wages in fast food restaurants in the USA, shows that the minimum wage introduced in a number of states has had no effect on employment. In the UK, there is little or no evidence that the abolition of minimum wages in low-wage occupations previously protected by Wages Councils has increased the levels of employment.

9 Tutorial note

The most common error which candidates make when writing about the PSBR is to define it in terms of central government alone (i.e. to confuse the PSBR with the central government borrowing requirement, the CGBR). The central government borrowing requirement is by far the main component in the PSBR, so if you make this error it will not be heavily penalised. A much more serious error would be to confuse the PSBR with the National Debt. The budget deficit and the borrowing requirement are examples of economic **flows** (which are the difference betweeen the two much larger flows of government or public sector expenditure and revenue), whereas the National Debt is a **stock**. The National Debt is simply the total stock of central government debt – the accumulated stock of borrowing which has built up over the years and which the government has not yet paid back. A budget deficit and a positive CGBR increase the size of the National Debt, a budget surplus and the accompanying CGBR allow debt repayment to take place, resulting therefore in a reduction in the stock of accumulated National Debt.

Part (b) (i) is about *causes* while (b) (ii) is about *effects*. You must make sure you make a clear distinction between causes and effects in the structure of your answer. Relate your answer to (b) (i) to the business cycle. Your answer to (b) (i) should examine the impact of the economy upon the state of the public sector's finances, while in (b) (ii) you must analyse the possible impact of the deterioration in the government's finances upon the economy. Key concepts are the business cycle, the distinction between the cyclical and the structural components of the PSBR/PSDR, and the role of budget deficits or surpluses as automatic stabilisers.

Suggested answer

(a) Both the PSBR and the PSDR relate to the state of the finances of the whole of the public sector. The PSBR (public sector borrowing requirement) is very closely linked to a budget deficit with which it is sometimes confused. It occurs when in a particular year, the public sector's finances are in deficit, with public sector expenditure exceeding public sector revenue – the latter being largely tax revenues. The PSBR is the *flow* of borrowing which must be undertaken to finance the public sector deficit.

The PSBR can be broken down into three components: the CGBR, the LABR and the PCBR, each relating to a particular part of the overall public sector, namely central government, local authorities and public corporations.

A PSDR (public sector debt repayment) occurs when there is a budget surplus and a negative PSBR. In this situation, public sector revenues exceed expenditure, and the government can use the surplus revenues to buy back previously issued debt, thereby reducing the size of the public sector debt (and the National Debt or stock of central government debt, which is the main part of the public sector debt).

(b) The first part of part (b) relates to the distinction between the cyclical and the structural components of the public sector deficit and borrowing requirement. The cyclical component varies at different stages of the business cycle, being greatest in the downswing and the recession, conversely reducing and even disappearing in the recovery and boom phases of the cycle. The structural component of the deficit and PSBR is that part which is independent of the business cycle, being determined by the underlying structure of the economy, and increasing (or declining) in response to longer-term structural changes taking place in the economy.

The financial year 1988/89 occurred in the 'Lawson boom', right at the end of a long cyclical upswing in the UK economy which started in 1981 and ended when the economy once again entered recession in 1989/90. During the upswing of the business cycle, the public sector's finances improved for two main reasons. On the one hand, economic growth, higher real incomes and boosted consumer confidence meant that receipts from personal income tax, corporation tax on company profits and expenditure taxes such as VAT were buoyant. Meanwhile, on the expenditure side of the government's finances, boom conditions meant that unemployment fell rapidly, which in turn led to a fall in the demand-led or cyclical component of public expenditure – unemployment benefits and poverty-related welfare payments. In response to mainly cyclical factors, public sector receipts exceeded expenditure, leading to the PSDR of £7 billion. Two non-cyclical factors also contributed significantly to the improvement in the public sector finances in the 1980s, namely the boost to the government's coffers from North Sea oil revenues and the receipts from a succession of privatisations of previously nationalised industries.

The explanation for the PSBR of £35 billion in 1992/93 is simply the obverse of that for the boom years of the late 1980. The financial year 1992/93 occurred just after the end of a long and deep recession, and before recovery could once again improve the public sector's finances. The decline in output, incomes and expenditure caused tax revenues to fall, while growing unemployment increased public spending on welfare benefits. While the main cause of the large PSBR lies in cyclical factors related to the recession, a number of structural factors were also serving to worsen the government's finances. These included a fall in the North Sea oil revenues as oil extraction began to decline, fewer privatisation proceeds, and increased public spending on the elderly as the number of old people in the British population increased.

In so far that the deterioration of £42 billion in the public sector finances between 1988/89 and 1992/93 was cyclical rather than structural, its main effect might simply have been to ameliorate the fluctuations in the business cycle. This is because a cyclical deficit or surplus in the government's finances functions as an automatic stabiliser, dampening, reducing or stabilising the downswings and upswings of the economy. The recession had been cuased largely by a collapse of demand in the economy. However, as the cyclical component of the deficit increased between 1988/89 and 1992/93, demand was injected back into the economy, partially offsetting the initial reduction in aggregate demand. This rendered the recession less severe than if there had been no automatic stabilisers (progressive taxation and welfare payments). And if the deterioration in the public sector finances was 100% cyclical, there would be no further effect of any significance. In future years, the deficit will simply wither away as the economy recovers from recession and the public sector finances moves towards surplus once again.

By contrast, if a significant part of the PSBR of £35 billion were structural, if it were allowed to persist, the effects might be severe and harmful. It is possible that the borrowing required to finance the PSBR might crowd-out private sector investment. To explain this, we assume that the government fully-funds the PSBR by selling gilt-edged securities and National Savings securities to the general public. Monetarists argue that this leads to crowding out of private sector investment. In order to persuade the general public to buy the extra debt the government is selling, the guaranteed annual interest rate offered on new issues of gilts must be raised. This in turn raises interest rates generally and crowds out or displaces the private sector investment by making it more expensive for firms to borrow or raise funds on the capital market through new issues of corporate bonds and shares.

In this situation, the government might decide to take steps to eliminate the structural component of the deficit. In the short-term, this would have to mean tax increases and/ or public spending cuts. Here there is the danger that the recovery would be nipped in the bud, leading to a return to recession and the growth once again of the cyclical PSBR, but the government might believe that this is a risk worth taking in order to get the structural deficit down. The government might also believe that the structural component of the PSBR will reduce in the long-run anyway as the supply-side reforms it has introduced over the years succeed in changing the structure of the UK economy for the better.

10 Tutorial note

This question asks for a discussion of the costs and benefits for a single country (the UK) resulting from signing multilateral trading agreements with other countries. The words *potential* and *such as* are significant. You can discuss advantages and disadvantages which might not materialise until some point in the future. The wording of the question does not require a discussion of either or both of the examples of multilateral agreements mentioned in the question, though most candidates would probably base their answers on these. Both of these agreements relate to trade, so take care not to drift into other forms of multilateral agreement such as membership of the International Monetary Fund which deals with means of payment rather than trade. Finally, while the wording of the question does not require an assessment of whether the advantages exceed the disadvantages, you should develop your answer beyond a mere list of advantages and disadvantages.

Suggested answer

The General Agreement on Tariffs and Trade (GATT) and the Single European Market are both examples of multilateral trading agreements which the UK has signed – though strictly the Single European Market is not itself an agreement but the result of an agreement, the European Community's Single European Act which was implemented in the UK with the passing of the European Communities (Amendment) Act 1986. This legislation specified the measures to be adopted by member states by the end of 1992 to complete the Community's internal market. The EC was already a customs union (with a common external tariff but tariff-free internal trade) long before 1993. The Single European Act was concerned with removing non-tariff barriers to trade and specialisation within the Community; it sought to create a level commercial playing field by preventing countries using artificial devices such as technical standards and administrative controls to exclude imports and to protect their businesses from fair competition from EC countries.

In assessing the potential advantages and disadvantages to the UK economy of the Single European Market, it is necessary to consider both the likely costs and benefits of the Market for all member countries of the European Community (now usually called the European Union or EU), and any special factors which relate to the UK. The main advantage of the Single Market lies in the fact that individual countries can gain access to a high-income market of over 200 million people, allowing their firms and industries to benefits from long production runs and economies of scale. The Single Market may be expected to promote trade and specialisation amongst members in accordance with the principle of comparative advantage. As a result, the European Union's production possibility frontier may move outwards, resulting in individual countries enjoying faster growth rates and higher living standards than would have been the case had the Market not been created.

While the Single Market may promote free trade between members, it certainly distorts and perhaps reduces trade between EU countries and the rest of the world. The gains to EU members may be offset by losses elsewhere in the world economy. Such losses experienced by the rest of the world may impact on the advantages and disadvantages of the Single Market for a member country like Britain, which enjoyed substantial trade with the rest of the world before joining the EC in 1973. Opponents of UK membership of the EU argue that for Britain the disadvantages of membership have exceeded the advantages. In particular they argue that Britain has lost access to imports of food at cheaper world prices; that British manufacturing firms have been unable to compete with their continental rivals which has exacerbated the deindustrialisation problem; and that the UK's contribution to the Community budget and the non-trade EU policies which the British government has had to adopt, have added to the costs of British business and made the economy less competitive. Exactly how much weight should be given to arguments such as these is a matter of dispute, but there is no doubt that by the time the Single Market was completed in 1993, well over 50% of UK trade was with other EU countries and that much of the inward investment, for example in Japanese-owned *transplant* factories, from which the UK is benefiting, would not have taken place had Britain remained outside the Single Market. On balance, the evidence indicates that the advantages of membership of the Single Market for the UK exceed the disadvantages.

With regard to GATT, it is possible to be even more confident that the advantages of signing the agreement for the UK exceed the disadvantages. Since its formation in 1948, GATT, has been the most important international forum for expanding world trade and seeking the multilateral reduction of tariffs and other barriers to trade. Under the auspices of GATT there have been eight 'rounds' of negotiations to reduce tariffs and other trade barriers since the Second World War, culminating in the recent Uruguay round. During this period the average tariff on manufactured goods has been reduced from 40% to under 5%. Since most of the tariff reductions negotiated through GATT had affected manufactured goods rather than primary products, manufacturing countries such as the UK have been the main beneficiaries. However, it is worth noting that nowadays manufacturing accounts for less than 20% of United Kingdom GDP, while services have risen to over 60%, though a significant proportion of services cannot be traded internationally. As yet, the tariff reductions negotiated by GATT hardly affect trade in services (though within the EU, the Single European Market has addressed this issue), so given the changing structure of the UK economy, any future benefits for the UK economy of further GATT negotiations will depend to a significant extent on whether the removal of trade barriers is extended to trade in services.

INDEX